A History of Canadian Economic Thought

Routledge History of Economic Thought Series

HB121.A2 N45 1991
0134106549451
Neill, Robin.

A history of Canadian
economic thought /
1991.

2004 03 09

A History of Australian Economic Thought
Peter Groenewegen and Bruce McFarlane

A History of Japanese Economic Thought
Tessa Morris-Suzuki

The History of Swedish Economic Thought
Edited by Bo Sandelin

A History of Canadian Economic Thought

Robin Neill

London and New York

First published in 1991
by Routledge
11 New Fetter Lane, London EC4P 4EE

Simultaneously published in the USA and Canada
by Routledge
a division of Routledge, Chapman and Hall Inc.
29 West 35th Street, New York, NY 10001

Reprinted 2001

Routledge is an imprint of the Taylor & Francis Group

© 1991 Robin Neill

Typeset by Michael Mepham, Frome, Somerset
Printed and bound in Great Britain
by Intype London Ltd

All rights reserved. No part of this book may be reprinted or reproduced or utilized in any form or by any electronic, mechanical, or other means, now known or hereafter invented, including photocopying and recording, or in any information storage or retrieval system, without permission in writing from the publishers.

British Library Cataloguing in Publication Data
Neill, Robin *1931–*
   A history of Canadian economic thought. – (Routledge
history of economic thought series).
   1. Canada. Economics. Theories, history
   I. Title
   330.1
   ISBN 0–415–05412–5

Library of Congress Cataloging in Publication Data
Neill, Robin.
   A history of Canadian economic thought / Robin Neill.
     p. cm. — (Routledge history of economic thought series)
   Includes bibliographical references and index.
   1. Economics—Ontario—History. 2. Economics—Québec
(Province)—History. 3. Economics—Canada—History.
   I. Title. II. Series.
   HB121.A2N45 1991
   330'.0971—dc20   90-9147
                                                                         CIP

ISBN 0–415–05412–5

To Sharon and Natalie

Contents

Preface ix
1 The economics of settlement 1
2 The economics of the Maritimes 21
3 Pensée économique, dix-neuvième siècle 39
4 The economics of John Rae, 1822–34 57
5 The Nationalist School, 1830–90 72
6 Monetary theory and policy, 1812–1914 92
7 Some intrusions of history, 1890–1930 109
8 The staple thesis, 1920–40 129
9 Pensée économique, vingtième siècle 149
10 Keynes in a small open economy 172
11 The economics of the West 191
12 A North American discourse 204
13 Conclusion 226
Notes 228
Bibliography 263
Index 290

Preface

If there must be a conclusion to this account of the history of economic thought in Canada, I offer the following.

It is possible to discern a distinctive Canadian economics prior to 1900, indeed, a separate, distinctive economics in each of English and French Canada. After 1900, by using and defending themselves against a common Euro-American discourse in economics, the separate economics of English and French Canada expressed themselves in the schools associated with H. A. Innis and F.- A. Angers. After 1950, beginning with the acceptance of Keynesian theory, Canadian economics, as a whole, integrated itself into a broader, positivist, Euro-American discourse.

Major contributions in Canadian economics have come in the field of economic development, particularly in the works of John Rae and H. A. Innis; and we may conclude that the staple theory is an adequate explanation of Canadian economic development only in one period, though it is an adequate explanation of Atlantic Canadian and western Canadian development in all periods. Canadian monetary theory and policy have been anchored in nineteenth-century British Banking School theory and policy.

But such a summary is a gross oversimplification. An understanding of Canadian economics requires familiarity with all the details and nuances of the full account.

There are outstanding economists dealing with the history of economic thought and with economic methodology who teach and write in Canada: Sam Hollander, *The Economics of David Ricardo*[1] (I give only examples); and Larry Boland, *The Foundations of Economic Method*.[2] They have no place in this history of economic thought in Canada, because this history is about economics as a product of the Canadian experience. There are members of my own Department at Carleton who have continental if not international reputations: Richard Carson, *Comparative Economic Systems*,[3] and three more recent texts; Soo-Bin Park, 'Some Sampling Properties of Minimum Expected Loss (Melo) Estimates of Structural Coefficients';[4] and Richard

Brecher, Editor of the *Journal of International Economics*. They do what they do as well as anyone in the world, but they fight on another battlefield and they will win their citations elsewhere. Their economics does not grow uniquely out of the Canadian experience. It belongs to the broader Euro-American economic discourse into which Canadian economics has integrated itself in the second half of the twentieth century.

There have been others who have written about the history of economic thought in Canada. I cannot fail to mention Craufurd Goodwin, Irving Brecher, R. Warren James, François-Albert Angers, and Gilles Paquet. To these, and to the many others who wrote shorter pieces, my debt is deep. The present work does not sum up and replace what they have done, but I have attempted to consult and cite every preceding contribution to the history of economic thought in Canada, so that, if I have not built well, I will have eased the way for someone else to build better.

I would be remiss not to express gratitude to those who agreed to review the manuscript prior to publication. They must remain anonymous, because their own contributions to Canadian economics are part of the subject under consideration. Their comments and ominous silences have been the basis of substantial improvements in the text. I wish to thank Christina Thiele for making it possible for me to produce readable text; and Lynn Franklin, who was the agent of Carleton University's generosity with computer time. Jill Vickers, Director of the Institute of Canadian Studies at Carleton, provided an office, a kind of safe house, in which I worked during the sabbatical year in which the writing took place. Members of the Department of Economics at Carleton were dependably forthcoming when asked about their areas of special knowledge. Sharon Neill graciously agreed to proofread the text, and upgrade the bibliography.

Robin Neill

1 The economics of settlement

All five of the easternmost political divisions of what is now Canada came into existence with a problematic reliance on primary product exports. In Newfoundland the fishing interests opposed permanent settlement of the Island, but, in the end, they were the instrument by which settlement occurred. France encouraged settlement in New France, using a grant of monopoly in the fur trade as a reward, but, in the end, settlement occurred and succeeded despite the fur trade. Nova Scotia became a British possession as a result of military and naval advances up the east coast of North America. Settlers in the new colony tried to repeat the pattern of balanced growth that had characterized the colonies to the south, but with very limited success.

In each case the situation of the colony elicited written comment, an assessment, and some kind of remedial proposal; which, invariably, was not put into effect. These constructions or commentaries, as the most eminent of historians of economic thought, Joseph Schumpeter, would have put it, were 'pre-analytic' and 'pre-scientific'. They were not theories, but only the elements of a definition of the problems around which theories would eventually cluster. From a certain point of view, however, in the Canadian case, definition of problems is all that there is to economic thought. Well-articulated theories, classical, neoclassical, neo-Keynesian, and others, eventually came to have currency; and, on occasion, the debate in Canada generated significant contributions to their elaboration. From the beginning, Canada has been a full participant in western civilization in this respect; but, perhaps because of that, or as a result of the country's special characteristics, its economic thought, Canadian economics, generally speaking, has not lifted itself above the level of debate to the level of consensus.

Frank Underhill, an acknowledged Canadian historian, once said that Canadians are 'incapable of tragedy'. He meant that they have no common ideal, no sense of common destiny. They have no perceived historic mission that they might betray. He was partially right. What they have is a competition of ideals and perceived identities. So it is with economics in Canada, much of which is a debate about national development in which the participants take regional points of view.

NEW FRANCE

When Richard Caves elaborated a 'vent for surplus' theory in 1965,[1] with the intention of describing the economic development of Canada, he posited an uninhabited geographical frontier from which a surplus of primary products could be exported. The northern half of North America was inhabited, however, and the skills and equipment of the indigenous peoples were important for the survival of the first Europeans, and especially for the exploitation of the fur trade that Caves was describing (see chapter 11). In agricultural technique the Europeans had little to learn from the natives, except remedies for scurvy and black flies, of course. So, ironically, with respect to the non-export sector of the colonial economy, Caves was correct. For agricultural purposes the land was treated as uninhabited, the native population being pressed into reservations as cultivation spread. In a double irony, in the early years, the institutional arrangement within which agriculture was carried on prohibited exploitation of primary products under conditions typical of 'an empty land'. In an attempt to expose and remedy the weaknesses of that particular form of settlement Pierre Boucher produced the first work in economics in Canada.[2]

The seigneurial system of land settlement was not an unconscious transfer of French feudalism to North America.[3] The seigneurs were, in fact, private entrepreneurs who were granted lands on the condition that they settle and administer them according to regulations laid down in France. Much of the value of the lands, the oaks used in ship building, the minerals, was reserved for the state; making it clear that the land was granted for agriculture, not for commercial exploitation. Further, to prevent speculation, there was a 20 per cent tax on the value of land at the time of sale. To prevent absentee ownership the seigneur was required to establish a residence and administer his grant on the spot. The entire scheme, including similar regulations to ensure the stability of the *habitants*, strongly militated against aggressive profit taking by the grantee. Regulations preventing the erection of a building on a property of less than one and a half acres protected the *habitants* against crowding and consequent high rents. Concentrations of population did take place at Quebec and Ville Marie (Montreal), but no villages were authorized among the seigneuries until 1753, just a decade before the British conquered the colony. Denial of commercial profit to the seigneurs, and to others, was intended to encourage settlement by ensuring a higher standard of living for the *habitants*. Which it did, though only in the short run, if Boucher was right.

Pierre Boucher, a former Governor at Trois Rivières and a seigneur by virtue of his success in subduing the Iroquois, was well acquainted with the problems of settlement in New France. He listed them: the climate, the Indians and the scarcity of settlers. Nothing could be done about the climate, but solving the problem of numbers would also solve the problem of Indian raids. Accordingly, Boucher focused on the density of settlement in any given area as the target variable for policy. Under the seigneurial system the settlers spread themselves along the one great means of communication, the St. Lawrence River. The result was a population too scattered for economic or military co-operation. Concentration of settlers in smaller areas, with consequent higher land-to-labour ratios, would have produced a surplus product, a 'social dividend', arising from mutually beneficial exchange. Success in settlement, then, required not only a large immigration, but some means to fix the settlers to the soil about the larger centres. The necessary concentration of labour could be maintained, Boucher added, only if the settlers were denied property of their own and excluded from the quicker returns and more exciting life of the fur trade.

Boucher was the first in a series of writers, ending with Edward Gibbon Wakefield, to understand the function of a division of labour and its relationship to property rights and costs of transportation in settlement policy. He was the first, without a formal, explicit statement, in an even longer series of economists who selected internal and external economies of scale as the operative element in the development of the Canadian economy, rather than the availability of natural resources. In short, he began the debate into which would be built the analytic advances of economic science and, eventually, the vast resources at the disposal of the modern economics profession. He had no appreciable influence on policy in France or New France.

In comparison with New England, settlement proceeded slowly. The seigneurial system was enforced, and, in its own way, was a success. The *habitants* enjoyed a simple, secure life, better, on the whole, than that of their class in France. They produced enough for themselves and the fur trade. In some years there was a surplus for export. It was never very large, and never reliable. In the main, they existed for themselves, centring their lives about the residence of the seigneur, his mill, and the Church. When France's commercial and political influence came to an end, and, eventually, when the fur trade passed off to Hudson Bay, the *habitants* remained.

Early writings about settlement and economic conditions in Canada tended to be descriptive geographies containing very little that approached economic analysis. Nova Scotia, in particular, seems to have produced these accounts in abundance, beginning with that of the Acadian, L.- A. Denys.

French settlement in Acadia (the Maritimes) was most successful in its eastward advance from Port Royal along the Annapolis Valley. The colony began its existence under something like the seigneurial system, but lack of interest on the part of France and periods of isolation from the mother country resulted in the emergence of freehold. There was no immigration, no pressure to advance rapidly, and no great amount of arable land to expand into in any case. If it had not been for their persistent connivance with the French forces at Louisburg, after the English had taken Port Royal and established Halifax, the Acadians might have continued their apparently idyllic existence. As it was, many of them were expelled from their lands when they interfered with the advance of British control.

On the rocky Atlantic coast the Acadians lived in scattered fishing communities with no significant agriculture. The fortress at Louisburg was completely dependent on outside sources for food. Some provisions came from the Bay of Fundy, and an effort was made to settle Isle St. Jean (Prince Edward Island) in the Gulf of St. Lawrence. Even so, and with supplies coming from France, a lively trade sprang up with the New England colonies. New Englanders, however, were quite prepared to trade with the fortress one week and attack it the next. In general, the southeast coast was unsuited to farming. With the exception of the speculator, L.- A. Denys, whose interests were at stake, no one seriously considered agricultural development on the Atlantic coast, except the 'Dutch' who settled at Lunenburg in 1853.

Having received a large tract of land from the French government, Denys tried to make his fortune by directing French policy towards its development. Despite his efforts, including the publication of his book in 1672,[4] no action was taken. Eventually he lost his rights to someone who stayed closer to power in France. Denys was over-optimistic, but his arguments form the beginning of an explanation of what French settlement there was, or soon would be, on Cape Breton, the Gaspé and Newfoundland, where similar conditions prevailed.

According to Denys, settlement on the southeast Acadian coast would have improved the cost structure of French off-shore fishing operations. Most French fishing vessels came directly from France with supplies of salt for on-board curing. They returned to their home markets having made contact with the American coast only to purchase or gather food, water, and wood for fuel. Denys's contention was that the cost of supplies to the fishery, in terms of storage space, time and/or barter price, was higher than necessary. If the home government's desire to establish settlers was made effective in Acadia, the settlers would find a ready market for their supplies in the demands of the fisheries. The outbound vessels would have a paying cargo of settlers and settlers' effects. Mutual exchange of surplus would make both operations profitable.

The theoretical soundness of this primitive plan for balanced growth, in which economies of scale were implicitly assumed to characterize the interaction of primary product exports and internal development, established the other side of the debate over economic development in Canada; that is, the debate over the importance, in empirical fact and as a policy goal, of staple-related dependent growth; but it brought no benefit to Denys. Still, even while he was writing, small French settlements were growing in Newfoundland and along the Gaspé, where resident fisheries and dry-curing were combined with some agriculture and tied in with wet-cure operations on the Banks. The strength of the arrangement was enough to keep the Gaspé and Newfoundland from involvement with settlement centred in Quebec.

ATLANTIC CANADA

From the seventeenth to the nineteenth century, literature on Newfoundland contained very little in the way of economic analysis, but something in the way of political economy, of both the critical Marxian and the more conservative variety associated with 'the new industrial economics'[5] of the 1980s. Both approaches to economic behaviour centre attention on the efficiency generating characteristics of the structure of property rights, though Marxists would not use these terms to describe their interest.

Problems in the Newfoundland fishery, according to John Reeves,[6] were associated with connivance by the 'Adventurers' of West Country England to keep the enforcement of property rights in line with their short-run interests:

> When they wheedled a poor planter into debt, they took his fish by force from him, and would even break open his house to get it. ... [The] Adventurers claims to a free fishery seem to be these; namely, to be free of all inspection from government; no justices, no courts, no custom-house.[7]

Reeves may not have fully understood the nature of what he described,[8] but the sorry state of Newfoundland depicted in his account was confirmed by Arron Thomas,[9] who described the island as

> a continual scene of Rapine and Robberys. No law was to be met with, and although a court was established in St. John's it was regarded no more then [sic] a Thief does a Pound for confining strayed cattle.[10]

There was another side to the simple story, however. Harold Innis depicted the ascendancy of the West Country Adventurers as a victory for 'commercialism' over state-supported, monopoly-control of British external trade, somehow foreshadowing the eventual political separation of America from Europe and 'the appearance in 1776 of Adam Smith's *Wealth of Nations*'.[11]

Newfoundland was not alone in its eighteenth-century disorder. The relative calm associated with separate political jurisdictions in seventeenth-century North America was blown away by the wars that would establish national boundaries at the close of colonial land seizures. Until the nineteenth century what came to be Atlantic and central Canada was little more than a military border zone between rival imperial powers. So it was that, during the eighteenth century, military and naval concerns dictated the location of urban centres, and influenced the growth of economic activity. There were no contributions to economic thought until political order was once again established. In central Canada, that is in Upper and Lower Canada, economics arrived with the settlers who came from Britain to join the influx from the former New England colonies. In the Maritimes it appeared among the Loyalist immigrants themselves.

The Maritimes have a separate and unique history with respect to economic development, and so they have a separate and unique economic thought and policy. The question of economically appropriate forms of land settlement that had exercised Boucher in seventeenth-century New France, and that would preoccupy Upper Canadians after 1800, could not retain a central position in the concerns of Maritimers. Attempts at agricultural settlement in Newfoundland failed. Whether the settlers were legislated off the Island because it failed, or to ensure that it would fail, want of arable land relegated agriculture to a very small place in the Newfoundland economy. In the rest of Atlantic Canada, taken as a whole, agriculture was never a dominant, leading sector, despite efforts to make it so. In consequence, the economics of land settlement remained latent in the agricultural possibilities of central and western Canada during the years without economic thought in which the fur trade extended the geographic frontier of what would be Canada.

THE CANADAS: 1763–1840

For eighty years between the Conquest and the union of Upper and Lower Canada in 1840, settlement increased slowly but steadily. The fur trade was not a factor in this. The timber trade was. These years were also the years between Adam Smith and David Ricardo. So, when Upper Canadians began to discuss and write about land settlement, they did so with a theoretical assist from the mother country. Before the period ended the combination of old world theory and new world circumstances produced the fundamentals of capital theory.

Upper Canadian settlement was not a backward linkage from the fur trade. No one has ever suggested that it was, but keeping the obvious things in mind is necessary for understanding the economics of Canada, and so, for understanding economics in Canada.

Cut off from markets and sources of capital in France, the fur trade came under the control of Scottish provisioners and other merchants who had arrived with the British forces coming north from New England. Within twenty years, the United States War of Independence reduced British North America to the northern half of the continent, forcing Montreal-based fur traders to move their operations north and west. Supply lines lengthened, overheads increased, and the number of agents exploiting the trade declined as companies amalgamated. Eventually there was only the North West Trading Company, reorganized annually in two groups, the Montreal partners and the wintering partners in the west. By 1811 this organization had penetrated to the Pacific coast. In 1821, crumbling under the difficulty of maintaining co-operation over such a vast territory with only the canoe for communication, it passed into the hands of the Hudson's Bay Company. Loss of the fur trade was not a serious blow to the economy of Montreal. To the *habitants* in Lower Canada, and to the British settlers in Upper Canada, it was of no consequence.

There were both backward and by-product linkages between settlement and the timber trade. Where agriculture was a backward linked activity, that is, where settlement occurred to meet the demands of the timber trade for food supplies, it tended to be weak. It was located in areas best suited to lumbering, rather than agriculture, and the settlers divided their time between farming and lumbering. Where settlement was a by-product linked activity, that is, in those areas settled by immigrants availing themselves of cheap transportation across the Atlantic on otherwise empty timber ships, in Upper Canada along the St. Lawrence River and the Lower Great Lakes, agriculture was strong.

The timber trade itself, in the beginning, was not a commercially viable operation. It was an outgrowth of the Napoleonic blockade of Europe, a trade that became viable only with preferential treatment in the British market. It began in the Maritimes in 1793. By 1806 it was centred in Quebec City, the first raft from the Ottawa region reaching the city in that year. The trade virtually by-passed Montreal. When it finally penetrated Upper Canada in the area east of Lake Huron it was operating with saw mills to produce lumber for markets in the United States. The trade was not a crucial market for the settled areas of Upper Canada (Canada West) located to the south. It was more important in the Ottawa Valley and along the line of trade from Arnprior through Perth to the United States. When the preferences were removed, and, with the demise of the sailing ship, the square timber and mast trade to Britain ended, agriculture in Quebec and Ontario was not substantially affected. Again, no one has questioned any of these things, but for that reason it is important to keep them in mind.

Between 1763 and 1840 most Upper and Lower Canadians were engaged in agriculture. Settlement from France ended with the Conquest, and thereafter the French in Canada grew by natural increase, achieving, during the period in question, one of the highest birth rates ever recorded anywhere. Following the American War of Independence, dissenting Loyalists migrated into the Eastern Townships in Quebec, where the seigneurial system was not in force, and into Upper Canada. By 1785, there were 5,000 Loyalists between Montreal and Detroit. When Upper Canada was constituted a separate colony in 1791, it had 25,000 residents. After 1812 the flow of immigration came from Britain, rather than from the United States. By 1825 Upper Canada had a population of 158,000, compared to Lower Canada's 479,000. By 1840 it had 432,000, compared to Lower Canada's 717,000. By 1870 the population of Ontario (Upper Canada) had surpassed that of Quebec (Lower Canada).

Settlement after the Conquest was not entirely, perhaps not even largely, organized from within the Canadas. Prior to the War of 1812, Governor Simcoe actively promoted immigration from the United States, and there continued to be government agencies for receiving, advising and even transporting immigrants after the Loyalists and other Americans stopped coming. Most settlers came on their own, however, with their own capital, or they made arrangements through settlement companies and other agencies established with British capital. The Canada Land Company aided and supervised settlement on lands owned by the Company in the Huron Tract north and west of York (Toronto). The British American Land Company settled the Eastern Townships south of Montreal.

Relationships between colonial governments and the land companies, and between the governments and the settlers were less than satisfactory. The governing Council attempted to arrange settlement for its own benefit, as the settlers saw it, and not for the general good of the colony. In Upper Canada, payments to the government coming from the land companies made it possible for the established powers to govern without recourse to taxation, and so without recourse to the elected assembly. John Galt, Secretary and Resident Manager of the Canada Land Company, was dismissed from his position when the Lieutenant Governor of Upper Canada reported him to the directors for alleged connivance with a party of 'radical' settlers. The radicals complained that the unelected Council of land holders and members of the established Church were a positive hindrance to the economic advance of the colony. This was the root problem dealt with in the next phase of Canadian economic thought.

THE ENVIRONMENT IN ECONOMIC THOUGHT

Advancing settlement in Canada was a counterpart on the frontier of the Empire to Britain's advance through the industrial revolution. During the eighty years from 1763 to 1840 Britain changed her attitude towards the Empire, moving from mercantilist control to liberal decontrol. In consequence, the structure of colonial government became obsolescent, its office holders pressured by their own subjects and by liberal-minded representatives of the Imperial government to conform to an order that had no apparent place for them.

Economic theory was not a critical factor in the liberalization of the British Empire. Economic science and the liberalization of the Empire were two products of the advance of industrialization, and of the information environment contributing to and flowing from industrialization.

By 1759 Quesnay had elaborated a macroeconomic model of an economy, his *tableau économique*; and, more to the point with respect to settlement, he had built into his model assumptions that justified a single tax on the return to land. By 1752 Hume, having elaborated his specie flow mechanism and the quantity of money theory of prices, had developed a justification for abandonment of the mercantilist policies of the old British Empire. In 1776 Adam Smith, in his simple system of liberty, expounded the principle of exchange based on a division of labour. These principles, conceptions and theories underpinned a new, radical, Whig doctrine, laissez-faire. It emerged from the enclosures, from industrialization, from reaction to change, and from demands for a new economic order. It gave economics a place of importance as the concept of rent, independently formulated by West, Torrens, Malthus and Ricardo,[12] proved to be a telling instrument in rationalizing the deconstruction of Mercantilism.

GOURLAY IN UPPER CANADA

In Upper Canada the concept of rent became the chosen instrument of a bombastic, radical reformer.[13] Robert Gourlay was an egotistical, abrasive and inflammatory pamphleteer who agreed with no one but himself and, perhaps, William Cobbet. He was, nonetheless, the first of a number of Scots who brought economics to English-speaking, central Canada, and gave it its characteristic form.

Gourlay was born into a prosperous landed family. He studied law under Hume at Edinburgh University. He was aware of the twenty-one volume *Statistical Account of Scotland*, published in 1793, because its author, Sir John Sinclair, had been a frequent visitor in his home during the period in which the *Account* was prepared. In fact, he had, himself, become an author of some importance before he emigrated to Canada. His article, 'An Inquiry into the State of the Cottagers in the Counties of Lincoln and Rutland',[14] was cited with approval in the second edition of Malthus's *Essay on the Principle of Population*. His major work, *The Village System; being a scheme for the gradual abolition of pauperism, and immediate employment and provisioning of the people*,[15] was an earlier publication of ideas presented by Robert Owen.

While still in England, in response to an unsolicited request, Gourlay sent a dozen copies of one of his pamphlets to a certain Edward Wakefield, who wanted to distribute them to his associates. After Gourlay had exhausted himself, fruitlessly expounding his ideas in Upper Canada, Wakefield, through Governor-General Lord Sydenham, had them formulated into Canadian law.

Gourlay's theory of land settlement[16] was rooted in the complementarity of industrialization in Britain and agricultural frontier development in Canada. The key policy instrument in his proposal was a tax on rent accruing to land.

Unconsciously following Boucher, Gourlay began his proposal with the proposition that the value of land depended on the density with which it was settled. The greater the density of settlement, the greater the benefit from a division of labour and exchange of the product. Ricardo, according to Gourlay, had attributed the value of land to variations in its fertility. His own observation of Upper Canada led him to the conclusion that, from the point of view of the natural qualities of the soil, all land was of a similar productivity. Given homogeneity in this matter, the economic return to land depended on the density of the population residing on it, and on the availability of transportation to centres of dense population. Supported by data gathered for his *Statistical Account of Upper Canada*,[17] Gourlay formulated a simple, linear relationship between land values and inhabitants per acre: $Y = 240 X$ where Y was value in pounds sterling, and X was inhabitants per acre.

The policy consequences of this conclusion were not inherently radical. Settlement should proceed evenly, leaving no empty patches, unless the quality of the land was poor. Roads and canals should be built to raise the availability of transportation, and so to increase the extent of the division of labour and the value of the lands. The state should take up the task of building the roads and canals, financing this with a tax on land rents. The tax on rents, being a tax on real economic rent, would not affect the margin of cultivation, and so would not affect the rate of settlement.[18]

Gourlay's Scottish Enlightenment view on the role of public debt in the development process was not vintage laissez-faire. Before leaving England he had written the following:

> So far as taxation stimulates to industry and so far as national debt affords a safe deposit for its surplus gains, both are desirable. The desideratum is to make safe the place of deposit by keeping taxation within bounds, while

industry is stimulated to the utmost. Our national debt is national capital, and could its interest be paid out of the surplus earnings of skill and industry it should not be reduced a farthing ... it indicates increasing powers of production ... if taxes overburden the wheels of industry, then its time to reduce them, or make rents and interest bear a greater share of the burden. Rent and interest are the overflowings of production; and with power to regulate these overflowings national debt cannot be too extravagant in amount.[19]

His immediate goal was elimination of the British tariff on incoming grains. That would reduce land rents, which, in turn, would reduce the price of the wage good, food. The end result would be lower wages and higher profits in manufacturing. His expectation was that the increased supply of grain would come from Canada, produced there by the emigrated surplus population of Britain. His conclusion was that

'breeding itself will pay. I say it in full consideration of all the reasoning of Mr. Malthus.'[20]

Conditions in Upper Canada with respect to the ownership of land were substantially different from those of Britain. In the colony land was so plentiful that few, if any, rented land from non-resident owners. There was no rentier class whose income could be taxed. There were absentee owners, however, who held land in speculation against an increase in its value. Because these lands constituted patches of non-settlement they reduced the extent to which the division of labour could take place, and so reduced the return to land in general. Gourlay proposed that all such lands be taxed into use or auctioned off to private owners who would subject them to cultivation. The scheme was theoretically sound, but it worked against the interest of the owners, who included the colonial civil elite, their friends and the established Church. When these opposed his proposals, Gourlay attacked them publicly and without mercy.

The forces of conservatism and anti-revolution that lost in the United States, won in Canada.... Some gaw, silly Canadians lent aid to despotism. ... I wish to see you throw aside all taxes but one, upon land, by which you might correct the wicked state of property now existing; which smothers you up among reserves and the unoccupied lands of drones and absentees. I wish to see you obtain a loan from England for the execution of great works on security of such a tax. I wish to see 50,000 immigrants annually settled on waste lands of the Crown.[21]

In substance it was a simple idea: borrow to pay for an increased immigration and settlement, then pay off the loan by taxing back the increased land values consequent upon the increased settlement. It was an idea that haunted the economics of land settlement in Canada for over a century.

When the quantity of currency became an issue in the colony, Gourlay adjusted and reapplied the substance of his proposal. At the termination of the War of 1812 Britain stopped paying for military needs in the Canadas. Military bills on England ceased to circulate with the reduced demand for supplies, and a not-unusual post-war depression set in. Gourlay conjectured that the reason for the depression was inadequate demand and an inability to hold goods off the market to force prices up. If more money were available both demand and the ability to withhold supply would be strengthened.

> Paper money has not caused the present distress; but the cessation of that activity which kept it afloat.... Let profitable employment be found for all that are willing to work: let Government again issue its paper in every direction, where it can yield a certain return and mankind may flourish in peace as in war.[22]

He did not take this line of thinking to the point at which banking and the issue of currency became yet another instrument for generating growth and development. Within his lifetime others would (see chapter 4).

For his contribution to analysis of the economic situation of the colonies, and to policy, and for his vituperative attacks on the establishment, Gourlay was burned in effigy, lashed, imprisoned and driven into exile. His legacy was a radical party of Gourlayites who were the historical roots of William Mackenzie's rebellion in 1837, and of the Reform Party that won responsible government in 1848.

JOSEPH BOUCHETTE: ANOTHER STYLE

The importance of Gourlay's position was reinforced by the calmer, more ordered presentation of Joseph Bouchette, Surveyor-General of Lower Canada.[23] Bouchette expressed himself in his reflections on a British Parliamentary bill to provide for the emigration of unemployed workers.

> It [the bill] ensures, in some degree, the respectability of the immigration. It restricts it, at least as far as the aid is concerned, to able bodied labourers and their families. It guarantees the province against the pauperism of the individuals who emigrate under its provisions by providing them with the means of substance for a time, and its contemplating the scheme of their employment upon public works, promises also to contribute vastly to the improvement of that part of His Majesty's dominion abroad.... But the opening of roads, the excavation of canals, the erection of mills, are all the labours of milder seasons....[24]

Bouchette pointed out that with seasonal work it would be impossible to earn enough to purchase land, or even enough to purchase the means to settle on free land. It would be better, he suggested, to provide the immigrant with a two-year grant of land near a public works project from which he could earn a wage. At the end of the two-year period, when, presumably, the project would be complete, the land could be sold to the worker at a price that would include the increment in land value in consequence of the project's completion.

The advantages likely to flow from this immediate allotment of land, are, that it will prevent separation of families, remove the immigrant bodily from the cities, lay the groundwork of a settlement directly, and throw the settlers much sooner upon the produce of the soil for subsistence. Much of the realization of these benefits, however, would depend upon the plan that might be adopted in distributing the land and locating the settlers. Any system that would disjoint a settlement should be studiously avoided and every possible means studied of concentrating the labour and energies of an infant colony.[25]

POLICY AND IMPLEMENTATION: TO 1867

In general, the goal in these early writings was economic development. The question was, how could a surplus be generated? How could the capital necessary for growth be secured by pledging the consequences of the growth it would generate?

Prior to 1840, development policy was tied to the idea of uniting Upper and Lower Canada.[26] There were two reasons for this. It would provide a broader base of revenue on which to borrow; and it would help to get around the uncooperative attitude of the Lower Canadian Assembly, which had little interest in the ambitions of Montreal's anglophone merchants or of Upper Canada's speculators. The Upper Canadians, on their side, were aware that they would be outnumbered in a united legislature, and had to be induced into union by an Imperial guarantee on the interest on a loan of £1,500,000. The money was used to complete the St. Lawrence and Welland Canals.

So union was achieved, and, with union, following the advice of Edward Gibbon Wakefield, a scheme for rational alienation of lands was adopted.

Wakefield wrote *Appendix B* to the 1839 *Durham Report*,[27] acknowledging his debt to Gourlay. He returned to Canada in 1841 to act as confidential adviser to Governor-General Sir Charles Metcalfe until 1844. Because he was influential in his own time, and because his work foreshadowed an important theme in subsequent Canadian economic thought, Wakefield deserves some attention.

14 *A history of Canadian economic thought*

WAKEFIELD IN CANADA

At the core of Wakefield's 'Art of Colonization'[28] lay an alternative to the wages fund doctrine.

> Bentham's *Manual of Political Economy* [states that]... no kind of productive labour of any importance can be carried on without capital... [but] it does not follow that because labour is employed by capital, capital always finds a field in which to employ labour. This is the *non sequitur* always taken for granted by Bentham, Ricardo, Mill, McCulloch and others. Adam Smith, on the contrary, saw that there were limits to the employment of capital, to the employment of labour; the limits namely of the field of production and of the market in which to dispose of surplus product.[29]

Wakefield's point was that capital will employ labour if labour in employment will generate even more capital, and that this would be true of the colonies where 'the field of production' was growing.

> By pouring labour only into England, you would not increase the capital of that country, because the increase of labour would not find employment, but as labour creates capital *before* capital employs labour, and as, in America there is capital enough for the employment of more labour, and room for the employment of more capital, therefore, by pouring labour only into America, you would provide more capital for the employment of still more labour.[30]

This, if it is true, opens a fatal wound in any theory based on the proposition that growth is separate from development, that is, that growth is a consequence of an increase in physical capital. It was not that the quantity of the factor combined with labour was unimportant, however, and here Wakefield drew on the insight that Gourlay shared, unconsciously, with Pierre Boucher; but labour was productive of capital only when sufficiently concentrated to ensure a division between tasks, and exchange. If the institution of private property in land encouraged land grabbing and the dispersal of labour, then private property was, in that particular, an inefficient institution. The size of a grant of land, he wrote, 'should never be so large as to encourage hurtful dispersions; as to promote [the] cutting up of capital and labour into small fractions.'[31]

Wakefield's particular solution for Canada was to require settlers to pay for their land. That would ensure that they would stay in concentrations, in the cities, for instance, where they would be productive, before dispersing themselves in agricultural pursuits. The proceeds from land sales were to be used to fund the immigration of more settlers.[32] He was so intent on ensuring this that, contrary to his laissez-faire compatriots, Wakefield was ready to accept tariff protection[33] if it would ensure concentration of labour and a division of tasks.

When Wakefield's suggestions moved from the Earl of Durham's report to Sydenham's Land Act of 1841, nine-tenths of all the alienated lands of Upper Canada were still unoccupied, and nineteen-twentieths of all the surveyed land in Lower Canada was unsettled.[34] There was still good land, but it was locked up in the hands of 'land poor' speculators. So, by the time his proposals were adopted, there was little land left on which they could have had an effect.

Wakefield had recommended that further alienation of Crown lands cease, and that policies be adopted to hasten the development of lands already granted. A tax on wild lands would have encouraged their settlement and provided the revenues to improve roads and canals and to assist and regulate immigration. For the sake of uniformity and co-ordination of roads and canals, the tax was to be imposed evenly on the Canadas, and the work was to be centrally controlled. Contrary to regulations dating from the War of 1812, United States citizens with frontier experience were to be encouraged to move north. When the sale of Crown lands was again permitted, the price was to be set in such a way that it would secure an ample and constant supply of labour for hire, insofar as that could be done without forcing the settlers into the United States where land was cheap. If both the higher prices and the tax were adopted, and if the proposed public works were carried out, according to Wakefield,

> the proprietors of the wild lands [would be] induced and enabled to settle their grants, and... labouring immigrants [would] be enabled to obtain employment for wages [and]... out of their savings, to purchase land at the proposed price....[35]

The benefits of the scheme would not have been realized immediately, of course, so Wakefield proposed a loan of 150,000 to get the works underway. The loan would be repaid from the taxes on wild lands, land sales and from the sale of timber licences.

THE ROLE OF STAPLE EXPORTS

Too late to make a significant difference, indifferently enforced, and constrained by land alienation policies in the United States, Gourlay's theory, grounded by Wakefield in controversy surrounding the wages fund doctrine, became the official basis of development policy in united Canada between 1840 and 1871. The theory made no explicit reference to primary product exports as an instrument of growth, but that notion was not incompatible with it, and, if agricultural produce could be categorized as a primary product, a staple export base theory (see chapters 8 and 12) could have been the heavy implicit burden of a supporting account of the general condition and situation of the colony.

In Joseph Bouchette's account,[36] the role of the colonies was to provide a vent for British surplus population, the colonies receiving the reciprocal advantage of an increasing number of settlers. Similarly, the colonies were to provide a vent for the surplus manufactures of Britain, and Britain was to provide a market for the raw produce of the colonies: fish, timber and agricultural produce, the exchange being to their mutual benefit. The colonies were to provide military benefits to the Empire, insofar as they were in a commanding position *vis-à-vis* the United States, and insofar as they were an alternative to the Baltic as a source of timber and wheat. In return for this, Canada was to receive protection against military expansion in the United States. Loyalty to the Empire would mean lower taxes and a preferred position in Imperial markets, particularly, according to Bouchette, in that former preserve of the New England colonies, the British West Indies.

The staple theory, in one form or another (and Bouchette presented it in one form) has a long lineage in Canada, but is it normative or descriptive? Is it an account of what should have happened, but did not; or of what did happen, but should not have happened; or what combination of fact and prescription is correct? The French had little success in linking the agriculture of New France with their West Indies colonies. There was no agricultural staple export for the seigneuries. Had the British succeeded where the French had failed? Not in Lower Canada, according to Henry Taylor.

Henry Taylor was an itinerant writer and book pedlar, and a supporter of the mercantile interests of Montreal, whose hopes Bouchette had articulated. Taylor was aware of the realities of the situation.[37] If Canada was to be exclusive supplier of grain to the West Indies, it would have to produce a lot more grain than it did. In his view, the traditional methods of cultivation in the seigneuries involved soil exhaustion and low yields. He proposed that one farm in every fifth parish be made a government demonstration farm. It would be rented from the owner, modernized and returned to the owner when he had mastered the new methods, and when his neighbours had seen what could be done. Another farm would then be rented, and so it would go until, largely through the demonstration effect, all farms would be modernized.

Taylor's scheme was ignored. Instead of becoming a major supplier of foodstuffs for export, Lower Canada experienced what was perceived to be a *crise d'agriculture*.[38] Not highly commercialized in the first place, agriculture in Lower Canada went through a period of natural disasters and apparent stagnation in the first third of the nineteenth century. It did not supply a staple for export, nor was it linked to any other staple export.[39]

Upper Canada fared better, but not in a way that satisfied Montreal's ambition to be an emporium for the whole interior of the continent, nor in a way that satisfied the requirements of a staple theory of growth. Montreal undertook a series of torturous efforts to build canals and arrange tariffs to get the midwest United States, for purposes of trade, included in the British Empire. This brought it into conflict with the interests of Upper Canada where agriculture, in a different way from that of Lower Canada, was developing without fundamental reliance on exports.[40]

THE ECONOMICS OF SETTLEMENT, 1871-1931

The next time Canada turned its attention to land alienation it reverted to a policy of free land. The Dominion of Canada, a federation of the old colonies, copied the United States homestead system, first in an Order-in-Council of March 1, 1871, and definitively in the Dominion Lands Act of 1879. In their machinations against the slave states, the northern states of the United States had selected a policy of free land. Following the experience of Oregon it seemed that the policy of pre-emption directed against the South would work also against British North America; and that the interior of the continent would belong to whoever could seize it. The law of capture held. Having had alienation policy settled in this way, the Dominion had to meet the economic costs of development by some means other than land sales.

In the case of western Canada, agricultural development was synonymous with the development of an export industry. It was Canada's post-1867 experience in nation building that generated the staple theory and the conflicting reinterpretations and negations of that theory during the forty years of debate that followed the Second World War.

When Clive Southey considered the connection between the staple thesis and the policy of free land[41] he set out a theoretical basis for concluding that the wheat staple generated no rent, and may have reduced the standard of living in Canada. His argument (which I follow only in a general way) started by positing a primary product export linked to a cluster of industries producing goods that could not be imported as cheaply as they could be produced domestically. Growth and development were the result of improvements in industrial processes in the staple exporting country, increased demand from the external market, or a combination of these factors. If growth had occurred as a result of expanding external demand, it should have left a residue of high land values, the capitalized rent accruing to prairie farm land. In the presence of free land, however, settlement proceeded, unimpeded by the cost of land, to the point at which settlers earned only what they could earn elsewhere, so there was no rent.

Had the owner of the land, the Dominion government, sold the land, settlement would have been limited to those willing to pay the price, and the return from farming would have had to be higher to cover this extra cost. Fewer farms, or only the better farms, or the better farmers, would have been involved. Further, though Southey did not press his argument this far, the price paid would have gone to the government, and could have been used to defray those costs of settlement that, for greater efficiency, fell to it.

In the absence of land sales, there are a number of ways in which a government might finance its part in the settlement process. In the absence of sales, and consequently of rents capitalized in the value of land, there is still a return to land, though not to a landowner. As in the case of any open access resource, such as the fisheries, the return to the resource is 'dissipated' in an increase in the amount of equipment used to exploit the resource. In a case of open access agriculture, the return to land shows up in larger numbers of settlers and increased equipment sales. The government could extract its revenue through a tax on the profits of equipment producers, or through a tariff on imported equipment, either of which would raise the cost of farming, just as would a price on the land, and reduce the number of settlers. Of course, the total return to the resource would then be smaller, and there would be no land rent.

Three broad questions can be asked about the economics of settlement in nineteenth-century Canada. Why was the system of land sales, suggested by Gourlay and Wakefield, and formally put in place under Sydenham in 1841, replaced with a system of free grants in 1871? With what did the government replace the revenue from land sales as a source of revenue to defray its share of the cost of settlement? And finally, does the change in policy indicate anything about the source of growth and development in the Canadian economy, whether it was external demand or internal industrial advance?

Answers to the first two questions have been provided by Chester Martin.[42] In the early part of the nineteenth century the United States had supported its public debt with tariff revenues. For some time, during the rise of the frontier interests and their alliance with the south, revenues from land sales removed that justification of the tariff, though the tariff was not removed. When free land became a device for containing the expansion of slave states, the earlier justification for the tariff was put back into place. When the United States, dominated by the north, decided to fill up the continent by the law of capture, the purposes of the Dominion, which were to hold and settle the Canadian west, had to be achieved by the same means. Raising the necessary revenue to finance settlement fell to the tariff in Canada because of the competition of free land in the United States. According to Martin:

> The Dominion could well afford to give the land away for nothing: it was quickly discovered that customs and excise revenues from rapid

immigration attracted by free homesteads could be much more profitable than land sales. The Dominion, as the Hon. Frank Oliver once observed, could 'make millions out of the lands of the Northwest and never sell an acre'. The increase in customs and excise revenues netted the federal government 'a greater profit than it could conceivably have made through the use of the lands for revenue purposes'.[43]

The situation was much more complicated than a simple choice between land sales and tariff revenues would suggest, but the fact that that choice was there to be made became an important element in the life of the tariff in Canada. When Innis summed up the policy he put it in the following way.

> How can we guarantee that we shall get a reasonable share of the abnormal profits which accompany the exploitation of natural resources so that we can at least pay the interest on the capital we have borrowed to construct our railways and perhaps pay off some of the mortgage.... Excess profits taxes or corporation taxes are notoriously unsuccessful.... The alternative is of course the tariff on machinery and equipment used for exploitation. A carefully adjusted tariff may make it possible to skim off a substantial portion of the cream by taxing equipment, raising costs of production and thereby reducing profits which would otherwise flow off into the hands of foreign investors.[44]

The immensity of the task, the unpredictability of its results and the bargaining power of private enterprise were factors which necessitated extensive government support. Such support proved impossible without reliance on the tariff. Revenue from land proved unsatisfactory and the tariff guaranteed east-west traffic by restricting imports from the south, building up industries in the east and providing revenue for construction.[45]

THE PLACE OF THE STAPLE THEORY

The final question to be answered is whether the selection of a mode of alienation had any significance with respect to whether growth was a consequence of increasing external demand for the primary product, or of improvements in domestic industry? Despite *prima facie* evidence to the contrary, the answer seems to be no. In a general way for the Maritimes, and more specifically for the Canadas, the period 1840 to 1871 was exceptional with respect to land policy. Prior to 1840 and after 1871 (until 1930) the rule was free land. During the period, the rule was land sales.[46] The 1840-71 period has been designated as the time when a capitalistic labour market became evident, and manufacturing as a separate activity became important.

These developments were more successful in Canada than in the Maritimes, but that can be related to the weaker base of the Maritimes in agriculture, depriving it of market size, and to the development of agriculture in Canada in relative independence of any primary product export, even in the agricultural sector itself. In this period the Nationalist School of protectionism flourished (see chapter 5). This was the period in which the monetary schemes of the Birmingham School were linked to the tariff in explicit proposals for independent, balanced growth (see chapter 6). The policy of land sales seems to belong to the regions and times in which reliance on primary product exports was least. There is, however, no logical connection between free land and reliance on external demand for a primary product. Assuming reasonably efficient capital markets, in the absence of the rule of capture forced on Canada by the sectional dispute in the United States, western agriculture, resting on a wheat staple export, could have been financed by land sales.

Debate over the sources of growth and development in the Canadian case has not turned on the economics of land settlement.

2 The economics of the Maritimes

Economic thought in Atlantic Canada can be described as economics in the context of action. That could mean the economics of planning for independent or, at least, self-paced growth, or the economics of planning for adjustment to external economic developments; that is, planning for maximization in a position of dependency. For over two and a half centuries in the Maritimes there has been some of both, with a great deal of the descriptive groundwork that is the pre-requisite of planning. After the failure of agricultural settlement in Newfoundland in the seventeenth century there were no further attempts at independent economic growth there. When Newfoundland joined Confederation in 1949, the Maritimes were about to enter their second period of planning for relatively independent self-paced growth. At some point in the 1970s the Maritimes reverted to planning for maximization in a position of dependency, so the economics of all of Atlantic Canada again became of one kind.

The designation 'economics in the context of action' deserves some explicit definition. The phrase 'independent or, at least, self-paced growth' will be defined in recounting the history of economic thought in the region.

Abraham Gesner's work will serve as an example of 'economics in the context of action'. His mid-nineteenth-century analysis of the New Brunswick economy represented the highest fashion in continental North American and European economic thought. In the course of his analysis Gesner outlined the benefits of tariff protection. It is unlikely, despite his stingy references, that he was unaware of the work of more widely read protectionists, such as H. C. Carey in the United States, Frederick List in Germany or even Isaac Buchanan in Canada. Gesner was not alone. The protectionist doctrine carried the day in the economics of continental development throughout the late-nineteenth-century Euro-American world. By the end of the century even Britain was slipping back into explicitly protectionist policies.

However fashionable, and however much his doctrines may have influenced policy, Gesner made no contribution to economic analysis. Indeed, it would seem that none of the protectionists made contributions to economic analysis. In his *Economic Theory in Perspective*, which is intended to be a history of economic analysis, Mark Blaug makes no mention of List or of John Rae, and he accords Carey only three footnote references, one of which is just a mention that Carey's theory of rent was refuted by Wicksteed. Blaug's omissions point to a distinction between economic analysis and economic thought.

François-Albert Angers (see chapter 3) captured the distinction in his dictum, 'There was economics before there were economists'. Blaug, himself, points to the distinction from another direction when he rejects the context of discovery in favour of the analysis discovered. This same distinction provides the basis for a history of economic thought focusing on the context of action.

In the context of action, economic thought has two aspects. The first is a positive description of some particular market, industry or economy. This is a description of the *economics* of some institution, a statement of how its component parts, with all constraints and goals in view, fit together and work. When the term economics is understood in this way, there is an economics of Canada, a Canadian economics, as Harold Innis presumed there was when he produced the periodical *Contributions to Canadian Economics* (see chapter 8). And there is an economics of the Maritime Provinces. The second aspect of economic thought in the context of action is a policy prescription, an action directive, intended to exploit or improve the economics of some institution.

Policy prescriptions in the economics of an institution are normative. The norm may or may not be the objective efficiency criterion of economic analysis. If it is, then economics in the context of action and economic analysis are identical. Economic analysis *per se*, however, is unattached to any particular time or place. It grows out of an abstract concern with the structure of markets, and not out of a practical concern with what should be produced and traded in a particular market, as seen by agents in the market. Those who make decisions for firms or small open economies are unconcerned with market-wide, objective efficiency. Their concern is with their own position and with the survival and economic welfare of the institutions they control. They are concerned with Canadian economics, or with the economics of Enterprise Inc., or with Maritimes economics. They maximize with subjective efficiency in mind. Austrian Economics, as that term is normally understood, is not Austrian economics in the context of action.

A history of economic thought in the Maritime Provinces of Canada may not throw light on the history of economic analysis; but the economics of the Maritimes does not turn on that. If there were no contributions to economic analysis in the Maritimes there is still a large body of literature dealing with the economics of a unique time and place, and that is a contribution to positive economics. In fact, some economic thought in the Maritimes has been a contribution to the economics of Canada; some, a contribution to economic analysis. Here, however, attention is turned to the economics of the Maritimes, and, by extention to Newfoundland, to the economics of Atlantic Canada.

THE FUNDAMENTAL DILEMMA

The economics of Atlantic Canada has been rooted in long-run dependence on fishing, forestry, mining and maritime transport. This dependence has been the occasion of recurring economic recessions. In consequence, there have been recurring attempts to expand activities, agriculture and manufacturing, that, presumably, would not be subject to recessions. Of course, periodic recessions in primary product and commercial activities imply periodic expansions. During expansions the policy thrust towards a more independent, industrialized economy has lapsed. In Newfoundland, where economic independence seems out of the question, recessions are characterized by resentment of those who are presumed to have made great fortunes during the expansion periods of the Island's resource industries.

In these matters Atlantic Canada is not entirely outside the experience of Canada as a whole, but there is a difference. Maritimes economics is marked by a distinctive recurring theme. The region's major metropolitan centre, Halifax, so runs this theme, is somehow economically disconnected from the hinterland economic activity of its region. If the Maritimes is not to be a hinterland to some external metropolitan foreland, if Halifax is not itself to be a hinterland, but a foreland urban centre, then Halifax must become the exclusive metropolitan centre for the hinterland activites of the region. The two must get together. Halifax must become the 'growth pole' of the region, but it has not.

THE BOSTON CONNECTION

The literature of Maritimes economics begins with the opening general comments of Otis Little's report, *The State of Trade in the Northern Colonies Considered with an Account of their Produce and a Particular Description of Nova Scotia.*[1]

> The riches of a country consist in the number of its inhabitants if they are properly employed.... Workers in Nova Scotia, with relation to home, in consideration of the West Indies Trade, are of value in ratio of 5 to 1.

Hence the recent loss of 10,000 men as a result of war there is the same as 50,000 at home. Much is to be gained by replacing these men.[2]

Otis Little elaborated. The short supply of labour in Nova Scotia kept wages high, and this, in turn, raised the cost of agricultural produce. An increase in the number of farmers would lower the cost of food, and, incidently, increase the market for British manufactured goods. Further, an outflow of emigrants and manufactures from Britain would reduce freight rates by spreading overheads in transportation. Workers were needed for the fisheries as well. If Cape Sable shore were settled it would support a winter cod fishery. The basic need, however, was to improve agriculture. Settlers would have to be supported for at least a year, but while clearing the land they could produce ship timber, planks, masts, deal boards, shingles, loops and staves; all of which might be carried from their settlements by ships supplying them with horses, cattle, swine and other materials to begin farming. Boston would take what provisions they produced in surplus.

Little made his report just before that brief span of years in which New England and Nova Scotia were both governed from England. It was delivered two years before the founding of Halifax, and seven years before the expulsion of the Acadian neutrals, when British control had yet to be extended to Cape Breton and Isle St. Jean (Prince Edward Island). Halifax was founded in 1749 as a military and naval base to offset French fortifications at Louisburg on Cape Breton Island. Both Halifax and Louisburg, having been built on the rocky, southeast coast, were completely dependent upon distant sources of food. The expulsion of the neutrals followed upon their supplying the fort at Louisburg, and attacking an English settlement at Dartmouth across the Narrows from Halifax. After the expulsion and the conquest of New France, settlers moved north from New England; and the whole east coast of North America, under English rule, was centred on Boston.

Within twenty years the American War of Independence severed the Boston connection.

Separation of the United States from the British Empire created new possibilities for the Nova Scotian economy, if it could restructure itself. Insofar as Nova Scotia had been a hinterland to Boston, the Revolution forced upon it a degree of independence. Insofar as there was a need to replace New England in the triangle of trade between Britain, North America and the West Indies, further settlement and development in Nova Scotia became likely, but the character of development would be important.

According to one account, Nova Scotia would have to avoid the mistake of the French in Canada, which was their willingness to pour energies into

a temporary branch of commerce, which yielded, indeed, a temporary flow of wealth and revenue, but was utterly destitute of that foundation for its continuance which alone can constitute the real worth of any trade or make it useful to a colony ... this was the fur trade, which, unhappily, engrossing all their attention limited them from giving due encouragement to agriculture, which, in a new country, is the only sure defence against present and future evils.[3]

The account was incorrect with respect to the activities of the French in New France and Acadia, but it captured the dilemma of Maritimes economics. It could have been argued that want of arable land, and other factors, gave the region a comparative advantage in non-agricultural, primary product exports, but the case was not clear then, and it has remained unclear.

THE DILEMMA AND THE FIRST AWAKENING

There were obstacles to agricultural development other than want of arable land. The Scottish crofters who settled on the eastern peninsula had only a primitive knowlege of farming. The quasi-military purposes served in the location of settlers, and a land grant system that played into the hands of speculators ensured that, even where the soil was suitable, agricultural development was given the worst possible start.[4] The situation was most evident on Prince Edward Island where the soil was quite good. Until 1806, when steps were taken to reduce the oppressive effects of a system of absentee ownership, settlers abandoned their lands to pursue fishing and lumbering. Thereafter agriculture expanded at the expense of the fisheries.[5]

Evidently there was room for improvement. With continued hostility between Britain and the United States, the possibility of the Maritimes replacing New England in the British Empire led to a policy of internal developments that formed the basis of the first industrial and 'intellectual awakening of Nova Scotia'.[6] Under the circumstances, commercial and agricultural/industrial development complemented one another, and support for agriculture came from the mercantile elite of Halifax. The settlers, through their agricultural associations, did much for themselves; and there were some outstanding leaders of opinion. Thomas McCulloch, following the Scottish tradition in education, established Pictou Academy in 1816 to train students in practical as well as academic matters. In 1821 McCulloch published a series of fictional letters in the *Acadian Recorder* in which he used satire to contrast the quick but fleeting gains from timber and ship building activities, and the slow but lasting gains from agriculture.[7] In another set of letters in the *Acadian Recorder*[8] John Young provided information on farming techniques and encouraged the formation of agricultural associations.

Young was familiar with the writings of the Physiocrats and Adam Smith, and he was able to use their theories, necessarily modified, to express the economics of the Maritimes. What he saw was an economic system in which agriculture was underdeveloped. That is, that sector of the economy which, for both Smith and the Physiocrats, was supposed to be the basis for natural development, was so weak that the laissez-faire policies of Smith and the Physiocrats seemed inappropriate. Young thought the Physiocrats to have made a correct beginning. The proper sequence of economic development was agriculture first, and manufacturing second. Nova Scotia, of course, began with military activity, commerce and fishing, and then came to agriculture. Smith had correctly amended Physiocratic doctrine by assigning as much importance to manufacturing as to agriculture, though Young did not accept Smith's reasons for so doing. Smith had stated that manufacturing was productive simply because 'its receipts were sufficient to pay wages and to replace worn out capital'.[9] It was Young's opinion that

> The mechanic powers in manufactures are as productive of wealth and as free and unbought as vegetation; and the capital employed yields a rate of interest not less than that payable to the landlord on account of rent.[10]

Young thought that the best use of capital in any country lay in the development of agriculture and manufacturing, and like the Physiocrats and Smith, he deplored any mercantilist policies that might inhibit such use of capital. His reasons for agreement were decidedly practical. Without balanced growth the province would be caught in 'the dealings of a shrewd and opulent trader with a poor and dependent customer [in which] the balance of profit leans too strongly on one side.'[11]

His opposition to the use of tariffs to encourage manufactures had a similar practical twist. Agriculture had not progressed far enough in the Martimes to provide the cheap wage goods that would make labour inexpensive. 'We must wait half a century before we can prudently and successfully engage in them.'[12]

Economic thought in the Maritimes has always been a search for an industrial strategy. Like francophone *Québécois* of the early twentieth century (see chapter 9), Maritimers looked for *la politique qu'il nous faut*. And like the writers of the *Ecole des Hautes Etudes* they indulged in economic geography, taking inventory of the stock they would have to deploy when the policy was found.[13]

With the exception of Haliburton's classic *Account*,[14] there was no theory and little policy in any of these compendious descriptions. Like the industrial strategists of the mid-twentieth century (see chapter 12) Haliburton deplored external ownership of provincial debt, because it entailed the export of capital generated in the colony, and he regretted the presence of a transient military and commercial class, because its members retired to other parts of the

Empire, taking the wealth of the colony with them. In a series of letters published in *The Nova Scotian* in 1835[15] he challenged Haligonians to emulate the industry and initiative of their Yankee cousins, and suggested that if they did not take steps to develop their hinterland in the Annapolis Valley, they would lose out to their rivals in St. John, New Brunswick.

In the 1820s and 1830s, with the support of the mercantile interests of Halifax, Nova Scotia's legislature enacted bounties and subsidies in aid of agriculture and manufacturing. Nothing draconian, but enough to indicate the direction of policy.[16] When support from mercantile interests fell off, these policy initiatives came to an end. In the 1830s and 1840s Britain's dismantling of her mercantilist system entailed expansion of free ports in the West Indies and in the Maritimes. The carrying trade between Canada and, especially, New England and the West Indies promised good returns. So Maritimers turned from the prospect of replacing New England in the Empire to being the intermediary between New England and the Empire. The general direction in which the economics of the Maritimes was moving at the end of the 1840s was recorded by Lieutenant Governor Harvey.

> Nova Scotians are becoming to a large extent the carriers to Canada of tropical and foreign productions.... Nature has designed Nova Scotia for a commerical country.... The farmer's sons in the midland counties where shipbuilding is also carried on, become shipwrights, mariners, masters of coasters and plaistermen.... Farther east the coal trade, the supply of West India produce to Canada or of agricultural products to Newfoundland offer the enterprising their attractions. The west has its grindstones, cordwood and other articles to carry to the United States.[17]

The dilemma of Maritimes economics had not been solved. Enthusiasm for free trade contributed to the failure of free trade. When Nova Scotia acquired the right to declare free ports at its own discretion, pressure to do so in particular cases became irresistible. The result was over-investment in view of the amount of trade to be shared around. In the 1850s trade between Canada and the West Indies began to bypass the Nova Scotian ports. Whether as a last move in the way of freeing trade, or as a first move to counteract the imminent loss of markets, Nova Scotians agitated for intercolonial free trade, and for reciprocal free trade with the United States. Both of these, by different paths, would be preliminaries to Confederation of the British North American colonies, an outcome that too late was seen to be not in the interests of mercantile Nova Scotia.

Emerging iron and coal interests of the Maritimes interior saw Confederation in a different light. After 1850 the pendulum of success in the debate over independent or dependent development began its backward swing towards protectionism.

THE DILEMMA'S OTHER HORN

The most articulate protectionist the Maritimes ever produced was Abraham Gesner. He wrote at least four reports for the New Brunswick government, parts of a geological survey that mapped the colony between 1839 and 1842. In 1846 he reported to the province on the Londonderry iron and coal deposits. He wrote two books: *New Brunswick, with Notes for Immigrants*,[18] and, his major work, *The Industrial Resources of Nova Scotia*.[19]

Gesner's principle line of attack singled out what he alleged to be the economically corroding effects of the staple trades.[20] They had no long-run benefits, and they permeated the population with a lack of energy and a desire for ease and extravagance.

> The Americans effectively prevent the importation into their country of manufactured or calcinated and ground gypsum by levying a high duty on the article. The labour of the Nova Scotian is therefore confined to shipping the crude material.[21]

> It is vain to suppose a free trade system will be beneficial to a new and struggling colony which has nothing to export but raw materials; it is rather calculated to enrich an old commonwealth, whose people by their skill and labour make such raw materials valuable and return them for consumption. The result of the system alluded to has been that the suppliers of raw materials at last become the hewers of wood and drawers of water to the manufacturers.[22]

In 1849, just prior to the burst of North American railroad construction that preceded the Civil War in the United States, the whole of the North Atlantic economy experienced depression. In the Maritimes the carrying trade 'failed', the Annapolis Iron Company folded, and the General Mining Company of Nova Scotia ceased smelting operations. Gesner saw the long-run implications. A policy of autarchic development presumed a market of some sufficiently large size. The British North American colonies would have to become one economy. A railroad would have to be built to connect the markets of the Maritimes with those of Canada. Gesner thought their strengths were complementary. The Maritimes had fish, coal and iron. Canada had agriculture. Building the larger economic union would require capital. Gesner suggested a system of land grants to finance the railroads, an Imperial loan guarantee and an issue of paper money.

There had been a protectionist faction in the Maritimes all through the period in which the opening of free ports and the upswing in commerce was achieving free trade in North America. Free trade was an Imperial policy, supported only by those whose interests coincided with the Empire's. In Nova Scotia, in 1847, 1848 and 1849, the press carried a debate over tariff protection in which a local, industrial development policy was elaborated. In 1852 protectionist legislation was proposed but defeated in the Assembly. Having suffered a second defeat in the New Brunswick Legislature, very shortly after, The Society for the Encouragement of Agriculture, Home Manufactures and Commerce turned to the possibility of protectionist policies in a united British North America. The hopes underlying this policy peaked immediately after Confederation in an advocacy of railroad extension and tariffs as instruments of economic expansion.[23] 'Standing on one leg is so uncomfortable a position that the only animals in nature that seem to adopt such an unstable position are a goose and a one-sided free trader.'[24]

There were, then, two elements in the Maritimes working towards Confederation: the mercantile interests who wanted free intercolonial trade, and the iron, coal and railroad interests who wanted a market big enough to justify protection and independent development. The merchants, perceiving that they would be absorbed or diminished by the agents of Montreal and Toronto, withdrew their support immediately before union. The iron and coal interests had no cause to repent until after the 1914–18 war. These two factions, and the ambivalence and the dilemma that they represented, were personified in Nova Scotia's pre-eminent nineteenth-century leaders, Joseph Howe and Charles Tupper.

THE DILEMMA PERSONIFIED

Joseph Howe was heavily influenced by the early nationalist and protectionist literature of the German Historical School.[25] His attempts to generate policies based on such considerations led him into conflict with a privileged colonial Council dominated by Halifax mercantile interests. He challenged their control over the banking system of the province,[26] and he challenged Halifax to stir itself over internal developments in the form of canals and, eventually, railways.[27] In the late 1840s Howe was elected at the head of a reform government on a platform of economic development that was to link Halifax with the other centres of Nova Scotia for the sake of mutually beneficial exchange.

> Indeed, so closely identified would Halifax become with the business and improvement of those five townships that every acre brought into cultivation, every child born within their limits, would become a hostage for its growth and prosperity.[28]

Like a contemporary developer in Montreal, John Young (see chapter 7), Howe wanted free trade and government development strategies at the same time. When the cost of canals and railways became clear to him he consulted the works of E. G. Wakefield and R. Carmichael Smythe (see chapters 1 and

5),[29] and began a campaign for a publicly owned intercolonial railway to be built with the aid of Imperial loans. Government interference and ownership were one thing, however, and the tariff was another. In this Howe distanced himself from the policies of Charles Tupper. Howe was not a protectionist or a nation builder. He was primarily interested in the Maritimes, and he took the side of those Halifax interests that opposed Confederation.

Charles Tupper represented the iron and coal interests of Cumberland County. He was an explicit protectionist, and, in his own view, he was the one who coined the term 'the National Policy' used to describe the platform adopted by the federal Conservatives during the long period in which they were in power between 1877 and 1896 (see chapter 6). His reasons for favouring this policy were those of his day. Protection would prevent the exodus of the young to the United States by creating a domestic market for farmers, and full employment among labourers. He wanted a 'distinctively national policy of protection and internal improvements to gather in foreign capital'.[30]

Following a brief period of industrial expansion, the pendulum of Maritimes policy began its backward swing. In the 1880s continentalization of economic activity in Canada drained the Maritimes of ownership and head offices. Whether for political reasons or economic reasons, and which is correct is still a topic for economic historians in the region, the Maritimes failed to keep pace with the industrial heartland of Canada.

FROM BETTER TERMS TO MARITIMES RIGHTS

Until the First World War, reaction took the somewhat truncated form of a search for some redress within the established framework. Joseph Howe eventually acquiesced in Confederation, and joined the federal Cabinet to work for 'better terms'. His successor as leader of the Maritimes separation movement was Premier William Fielding of Nova Scotia. When Fielding appeared at the Inter-Provincial Conference at Quebec City in 1887, he denied that his presence in any way indicated that he would take Nova Scotia out of Confederation. As he saw it, the tariff and railway policies that were supposed to have generated an iron and steel industry in the Maritimes had worked entirely to the benefit of Ontario and Quebec. But Fielding, too, capitulated, joining the seemingly free trade Liberal Cabinet of Wilfrid Laurier to fight for 'better terms'. In return for these capitulations, the Maritimes eventually acquired the Sydney steel works and a freight rate structure that generated some traffic to central Canada.

During the 1896–1913 wheat boom, which was also a railroad expansion boom, the steel mills, the coal mines and the railways of Nova Scotia were busy, even though grain exported from the west largely bypassed St. John and Halifax. With the end of the wheat boom and bankuptcy of two of the three transcontinental railways by 1914, demand for steel rails from the Sydney mills fell off. In fact, the advent of the internal combustion engine was closing the era of iron, coal and steam. What little the Maritimes had to offer the rest of Canada was losing its appeal. Following the First World War, persistent stagnation revived the search for a Maritimes development policy.

THE ECONOMIC HISTORY OF THE MARITIMES

The rise of the Maritimes Rights Movement was contemporary with the birth of the Toronto School of History, and the formation of the staple export paradigm centreing on the figure of Harold Innis (see chapter 8). One aspect of the staple export paradigm was an economic interpretation of Confederation and the National Policy. That is to say, with acceptance of the staple thesis it became part of the generally accepted economics of Canada that political union of the Maritimes and the Canadas was justified on grounds of economic efficiency. The claim of the Maritimes Rights Movement was that inequities in the arrangement removed the efficiency argument in the case of Nova Scotia, at least.[31]

Sides were clearly drawn from the beginning. For those in the Movement, the relative decline of the Maritimes was a direct consequence of Confederation and the National Policy. In 1867 the British North America Act had denied the Maritimes the instruments it needed to conduct economic policy. Trade and commerce, elements of the power to tax, and jurisdiction over the fisheries had been transferred to the Dominion government. Expansion into the west with railroads and settlement conferred no benefits on the east coast. Ontario and Quebec benefited from the acquisition of new territories. Montreal benefited as a transcontinental railway terminal. The Maritimes had contributed to an expansion that had drained its resources and exposed it to competition from central Canadian manufactures expanding behind a tariff wall that the Maritimes did not want. On the other side of the debate there was an assertion that the Maritimes was relatively backward because it had a weak resource base, a poor location with respect to major continental markets, and because it lacked initiative.

Academics approached the economics of the Maritimes from the positive and descriptive point of view of the last generation of English-speaking members of the German Historical School.[32] Where the Maritimes Rights proponents, like the 'better terms' proponents before them, argued from Confederation and the National Policy as a cause, to the economic decline of the Maritimes as an effect, the economic historians argued from the changing constraints of technology and geography as a cause, to Confederation, the National Policy, and the relative decline of the Maritimes as concurrent, joint effects.

Prior to Confederation the Maritimes had experienced relative prosperity because of its favourable resource base and location in relation to a North Atlantic economy built on a 'wood, wind and water' technology. Those were the years of the intellectual and industrial awakening of Nova Scotia, when 'Bluenose' schooners dominated a carrying trade to the ports of the Atlantic east coast and beyond. By the time of Confederation, steam transportation, on land and sea, had shifted the frontier of economic development to continental land masses, and had reorganized ocean transportation. The new possibilities and the high overhead costs associated with the age of 'iron, coal and steam' demanded new financial and market arrangements that left the Maritimes in a peripheral position. Indeed, the search for efficient arrangements in the Maritimes, itself, had been a factor in the continentalization of the economy.

It had been a condition of the Maritimes participation in the advances of the late nineteenth century, so the economic historians said, that it accept the position of a marginalized region. Economic independence would have left it technologically and economically obsolescent. As it was, it was left with an advanced sector in the northeast, relying on the new technology and continental markets, and a declining maritime-commercial sector, the head offices of which moved to Toronto, Montreal and New York. The transition had been difficult, but there was the Canadian connection, the Intercolonial Railway, and increasing inter-governmental transfers to ease the way. The Maritimes, in this view, were better off in Confederation than out.

The arguments of the historians made sense of the period before 1914, but they were not to the point of contemporary Maritimes problems. The age of 'iron, coal and steam', in its turn, was passing, and the tenuous link of the Maritimes to continental Canada was becoming even more tenuous. Even the coal and steel sector ceased expansion. The economics of the Maritimes, it seemed, had to become independent development, or there would be no development at all. C. R. Fay put the matter clearly.

> The channels by which the wheat crops of the west are marketed should be decided primarily in the interests of the west ... The true interest of the Maritimes lies in the development of their own hinterland ... the plea should be for natural self development.[33]

THE SEEDS OF A SECOND AWAKENING

From the beginning there were three elements in the revived search: a suggestion that the Maritimes should separate and take control of its own destiny; a suggestion that the Dominion government should 'compensate' for the injustices of Confederation and the National Policy by accepting 'the economic rehabilitation and expansion of the Maritimes as a national enterprise'; and a grass-roots, self-help, social uplift programme, the Antigonish Movement.

The Antigonish Movement is best understood as an attempt to rationalize existing economic activities.[34] Contemporary production and marketing technique had left the scattered primary producers of the Maritimes with a sense of being exposed to the economic power of giant, continental corporations. In response, the Movement organized consumer and producer co-operatives to generate a sense of countervailing power and self determination, and to introduce improved techniques and organization. The Movement accepted the marginalization of its constituency, and undertook to rationalize, rather than to augment and develop, its economic activity, an approach that has persisted among Maritimers.[35]

Academic economists, mostly historians, developed a solution that started from assertions about the role of the Dominion government in the opening of the West. They wanted the regional development activities of the central government to be generalized to include all the regions of the country. And it was development, not rationalization that was suggested.[36] The Rowell-Sirois Commission[37] recommended equalization grants to bring social services up to a national standard, but that was not development. 'Doles and subsidies may be necessary but they should be replaced, whenever possible, by expenditures devoted to helping the less fortunate communities to stand on their own.'[38]

The Jones Commission of 1934 had recommended an Economic Council for Nova Scotia, to carry out economic investigations, to co-ordinate industrial and scientific research, to disseminate knowledge and to furnish advice on the best methods of utilizing the natural resources of the province, and of promoting and developing its industry and trade.

Born just before the Second World War, the Economic Council had a difficult childhood. With the onset of war it fell off the policy priority list altogether, and when the idea was revived after the war, circumstances had changed. The federal government had assumed responsibility for the unemployed, and the possibilities of compensatory fiscal and monetary policies as instruments for stabilizing the general level of economic activity were being recognized. Burton Kierstead suggested that, given the regional structure of the national economy, the greatest multiplier effect could be achieved by government spending in regions providing markets for the products of other parts of Canada.[39] Yet another Royal Commission,[40] the 1944 Dawson Commission, recommended replacing the Nova Scotia Economic Council with a Research and Development Board. In 1954 a quasi-private, Atlantic

Provinces Economic Council was established. In 1958, with federal help, the Atlantic Provinces Research Board came into operation.

In the late 1950s regional development became a way of life in the Maritimes. By 1965, the Economic Council had produced *A Development Program for the Atlantic Provinces*.[41] Not to be outdone, the federal government formed the Atlantic Development Board in the early 1960s, and endowed it with one hundred million dollars. As T. N. Brewis pointed out, there was an inevitable logical progression from income transfers to economic rationalization, and from rationalization to development.[42] The Nova Scotia Voluntary Planning Board, established in 1963, produced its first plan for economic development in the region. It called for the highest possible rate of growth. By 1969, when a whole complex of federal economic initiatives was absorbed into a new Department of Regional Economic Expansion, professional economists had already produced several sub-regional development plans.

Much of the literature produced in the context of these research, planning and development initiatives was sophisticated, quantitative description, but a small portion of it was theoretical, making the exercise something of a repeat of the early-nineteenth-century Intellectual Awakening. L. J. Walinsky divided the quantitative material into two schools of thought.[43] The first school attributed slow growth in the Maritimes to a poor resource endowment and location. The second attributed it to out-migration of human capital, particularly entrepreneurial talent. Given these explanations of slow growth, Walinsky listed the proposed remedies: 'capital grants and loans, public provision of industrial estates, tax incentives, industrial housing, vocational training ... labour mobility programs, provision of essential infrastructure, and so on.'[44] The studies were a latter-day repeat of the spate of statistical descriptions that characterized the 1830s and 1840s. The attributions were new. Walinsky gave no analytic explanation of the connection between the causes to which problems were attributed and the remedies proposed.

A core of non-neoclassical development theory was articulated into the particular conditions of the Maritimes. The Maritime region, having a well-defined middle class, operational financial institutions and stable and expanding industries, could not be considered underdeveloped, or even depressed, except in a relative sense. Further, the relative depression could be attributed to special, though sizeable, elements in the agriculture and fisheries sectors. From this it was deduced that general improvement could be achieved by encouraging migration from depressed to prosperous sectors within the region. Not only would this raise the standard of living of the migrants, without the more difficult move to other regions of Canada, but the consequent concentration of demand in urban centres, and the retention of population, skilled and unskilled, would raise standards in the progressive regions as well. In part, new employment could be found by expanding prosperous staple export activities, and by attracting 'foot loose' industry; but, in the main, improved productivity and new enterprise would follow from 'agglomeration effects', and 'dynamic imbalance effects' in the centres of growth. Growth and development would be achieved, not so much by federal government support, as by stuctural changes leading to metropolitan–hinterland interaction within the region.[45]

The economics of the Maritimes as understood at the time of the (Deutsch) Royal Commission on Maritime Union (1970) was a conscious application of François Perroux's theory of growth poles (*pôles de croissance*), of Gunnar Myrdal's analysis of polarization and spread effects, and of A. O. Hirschman's concept of progressive inter-sectoral adjustments.

THE NEW ECONOMICS AND THE OLD ECONOMICS

By 1980, within a decade of the Deutsch Commission, the pendulum of Maritimes economics had reversed one full swing. An energy crisis, potential offshore oil, and extension of the exclusive economic development zone to two hundred miles off the coast, had changed the orientation of development programmes, the philosophy of development, and the structure and importance of the Department of Regional Economic Expansion. New approaches – a conservative philosophy, emphasizing neoclassically defined efficiency, and western Marxist, New Canadian Political Economy – changed the style of writing, but not the fundamental dilemma of the economics of Atlantic Canada.

Literature accumulated along three lines: economic history, written by historians, Marxist political economy, and, more or less neoclassical analysis. The discourse focused on acceptance of, explanation of, rationalization in the face of, and complaints about the effects of Atlantic Canada's reliance on primary product exports.

In the 1970s and 1980s regional economics developed a stronger neoclassical component everywhere in Canada (see chapter 12). The change was part of a new and rising fashion of 'down-sizing' and 'privatization' in government. The energy crisis, coupled with these alternative public passions, first restructured, then devastated the federal bureaucracy charged with regional development.

FROM DREE TO MSERD AND BEYOND

The federal Departments of Regional Economic Expansion and of Industry, Trade and Commerce had been set up in the 1960s when Canada's reliance on primary product exports was questioned, both as to fact and desirability (see chapters 11 and 12).[46] Regional disparities in income were associated with the heavy reliance of some regions on primary production for international markets. So, originally, the Department of Regional Economic Expansion was mandated to generate sufficient alternative economic activity to make them economically independent; that is, free from the need for income transfers from the rest of Canada. Analysis underlying the economic development aspects of the *Report* of the Deutsch Commission provided the beginnings of a theoretical underpinning for such programmes, and, in the informational environment of the high period of the neo-Keynesian paradigm (see chapters 9 and 11), it seemed that appropriate credit conditions and fiscal assistance might spread manufacturing and income evenly across the nation. The Department of Industry, Trade and Commerce had a similar mandate. IT&C had grown out of the post-war manufacturing boom in Canada, when it was thought that devastation in Europe and the Orient had created a Canadian niche, or the opportunity for a niche, in international markets. IT&C was national and international in scope. DREE was national and regional. There was no thought of joining the two.

By the mid-1970s Europe had recovered, North America had a trade deficit, and newly developed countries on the west Pacific rim were out-producing the United States in some significant lines of manufacturing. 'Deindustrialization' seemed to be the inevitable future. Stagflation gripped the economy as oil prices soared to ten times their value in just under a decade. In fact, for the first half of the 1970s, resource prices outpaced inflation. As if to make sure that Atlantic Canada would get caught up in the new circumstances, the federal government declared exclusive economic development rights over an additional 187 miles off the Atlantic coast, encouraged easy credit for expansion of the fisheries, and began promotion of offshore oil exploration.

The idea of national and regional independence based on manufacturing simply evaporated. The Department of Regional Economic Expansion, in particular, withdrew support from promising infant industries and weakening obsolescent industries (when it could) in order to 'back winners' in the open market.[47] In the Maritimes this meant support for resource export industries. Industry, Trade and Commerce moved in the same direction to come into line with new energy-related 'mega-projects'. Together they reasserted the staple theory idea of forward and backward linkages from primary product exports (see chapter 12). Perceptions of regional independence were submerged in projections of inter-regional and international dependence. The two departments were merged in a New Ministry of State for Regional Economic Development, and then subjected to a long process of downsizing. Before the offshore produced any oil, the energy resource bubble burst. Over-expansion in the fisheries ended in bankruptcy during the financial crisis of the early 1980s.

Atlantic Canada's reversion to, rationalization of, and complaints about, dependent growth were inevitable.

THE 'NEW' ECONOMICS OF THE MARITIMES

The output of academic economists in the region was evident in the published papers of the annual meeting of the Atlantic Canada Economics Association. In 1971, under the guidance of Joe O'Connell, then a member of the Atlantic Provinces Economic Council and Chairman of the Department of Economics at the University of Prince Edward Island, the academic economists of the four Atlantic provinces formed an association to serve as a forum for discussion, and as an instrument to tie them into planning initiatives being taken at that time. The Association's publication, *A. C. E. A. Papers*, has featured material relevant to regional concerns.[48] Local interest notwithstanding, *A. C. E. A. Papers* revealed a high level of competence in the latest model-building and econometric techniques.[49] Evidently, some of Canada's most provincial of provincial universities encouraged original work on some of the most profound questions in economic theory and history.[50]

More than in any other region of Canada, economic history, rejecting the positivistic restraints of Cleometrics (see chapters 10–12), migrated into Departments of History in Faculties of Arts. The quality of the results, evident in the pages of *Acadiensis*, was further proof that there is more than one way to skin a cat. Most of the work was a search for long-run factors shaping the regional economy. What happened after Confederation? Was relative decline immediate? Was it invariant over industries and regions? The questions were answered, but in more than one way, and debate over the causes of backwardness continued. Were they political consequences of Confederation, structural consequences of capitalistic development, or inevitable effects of efficient advance in both the continental and Maritimes economies? Nonetheless, historians of the Maritimes economy painted a very clear picture of a peripheral, dependent, and industrially 'underdeveloped' North American region.[51]

The third area of Atlantic Canadian economic thought did not properly fall into the domain of economics, but into that of the New Canadian Political Economy (see chapter 12). Comments on it would be beyond the scope of this survey if it were not laced with some interesting economic history. A brief citation will serve to capture the tone of the many works in this genre.

In this book, I argue that the Canadian state through its planning function speaks in the name of liberal capitalism (equality of opportunity, free market competition) but acts in the name of corporate capitalism (privileged access to markets, concentration of capital). The state granting program through the Department of Regional Economic Expansion (DREE) negates its own target goals (re-instating market valuation) through its actions. The more the state intervenes in the economy, the more it produces non-market forms (bigger state bureaucracies, increased corporate power).... The history of Newfoundland is the history of dependency. From the mercantile system's strangle-hold on the cod fishery of the nineteenth century to Alcan and Asarco's iron fist in the mining industry of the twentieth century.[52]

The point seems to have been that all the arguments about a poor resource base, poor location, technological obsolesence, and so on, were the fabrications of the allied bureaucracies of corporate capitalism and the modern state. The real cause of regional poverty was the creation of a class of partially employed workers that could be exploited in the form of cheap labour, and the exploitation of monopoly power by fish-processing companies that reduced the fishermen to debt and kept them there by paying low prices.

Some of the works in the genre were excellent histories of industrial organization.[53] The work of Richard Apostle, Gene Barrett and Tony Davis, associated with the Gorsebrook Research Institute at St. Mary's University, was a good source of economic data on the smaller fishing communities, fishermen's organizations and the interface of the fishermen with both small and large processor-buyers.[54] There were few, if any, Atlantic Canada industrial organization studies in the New Institutionalist paradigm that played an important role during the 1970's neoclassical revival.

Whatever its manifestation, in the 1980s economic thought in the Atlantic region was characterized by an acceptance of the region's dependence on primary product exports. Its major thrusts were to elaborate historical or institutional explanations of this constraint and to prescribe appropriate maximizing behaviour. Indeed, the whole history of economic thought in Atlantic Canada is an account of the region's attempts to escape or minimize the consequences of reliance on a particular set of primary product exports.

3 Pensée économique, dix-neuvième siècle

In the case of Quebec, as in the case of the Maritimes, economic thought was economics in the context of action, even though the intent, better, the connotation, of action in Quebec was radically different. However incongruous it may seem now, because Quebec is one of the two provinces that have democratically chosen membership in the Canadian federation, francophone *Québécois* are, technically, a conquered people. In consequence, for the French in Canada there is a reality that can be called *notre peuple*. There is a *collectivité* that does not sit well with the liberal assumption underlying neoclassical economics, the assumption that nothing counts but the value judgements of individuals in a decentralized power structure. So, when we speak of economics in the context of action being the concerns of those who, in speaking or writing of the state of the economy, made social action conscious of itself, we must remember that history had made francophone Quebec conscious of itself before any consideration of economics. In certain matters, whether efficiency is served or not, the operative welfare function is not that which sums up the wants of disconnected individuals. In Quebec 'the optimal amount of coercion is not zero'.[1]

Focusing on the way in which the politics of francophone Canadians has biased their economic thought may be a mistake, because there is much that is not distinctive in economic thought in Quebec. The fanaticism with which the French have resisted cultural absorption is a measure of the extent to which they have not succeeded. They are part of North America. The economics profession plays the role in public and private institutions in Quebec that it plays in the rest of Canada. Its members process market information, and do consulting studies on the costs and benefits of economic ventures. They fill shelf after shelf with local, regional, provincial and national development projects and Royal Commission studies. Quebec academic economists grind out doctorates. They publish in refereed journals. Still, all of this has occurred long after the birth of *la pensée économique au*

Québec, in fact, much of it has occurred after the demise of *la pensée économique*.

La pensée économique preceded in time the emergence of an economics profession in Quebec: 'la pensée économique. En fait celle-ci et, comme la vie économique, elle n'attend pas les économistes pour exister. En ce sens, il y a toujours une pensée économique.'[2]

We will begin with the unself-conscious roots of what will develop into a distinctive economic thought in Quebec, but we must first find some definition of economics, some point of view on economics, that will give us an entrée into what was, until the Second World War, a totally unfamiliar information environment to an anglophone. This can only be done by accepting, uncritically, the definitions proposed by those among economists in Quebec who developed what was unique to the subject there, and by immersing ourselves, however briefly, in the history of the Quebec economy as seen by someone important enough to influence its informational environment.

The following definition was developed by François-Albert Angers to permit him to include Esdras Minville in the corps of those whom he considered francophone economists.

Le milieu de la pensée

It is an economics that has little room for what are called 'scientific' expositions, that is, general and abstract presentations based on observations or existing theories. Its principal and intense preoccupation is to put economics in the service of a particular goal, that is, 'the economic independence of French Canadians'. Given the special situation of the French in North America, any other preoccupation would seem unconscionable. Nonetheless, it is not less scientific, in another sense, than the economics of others who are less explicit about their practical preoccupations.

It is no secret, for example, that Adam Smith wrote the *Wealth of Nations* in the light of England's situation in the eighteenth century, and that he concluded that laissez-faire was the best policy in that situation. Other countries did not adopt that policy because it was not in their interests. The Marxists opposed it because it was not in the interest of the class of people they represented. Keynes, too, for all his abstract reasoning, adjusted theory to the problems of England in the 1930s, and rationalized a particular kind of government intervention. And Frederick List opposed liberalism and liberal economics because it was contrary to the interests of Germany in the nineteenth century. Economists in Quebec, after the fashion of Adam Smith and J. M. Keynes, have turned to economics with the problems of Quebec in mind.

The policy conclusions of 'scientific' economics were not to the point in the problematic relations of Quebec with the rest of Canada and with foreign interests. Traditional economics had been developed in 'old countries' looking for some new equilibrium following the changes of the industrial revolution. Quebec, on the other hand, was and is a country in which everything was, and still is, to be done. It is a developing country. Besides, Quebec lived in a political system that threatened its national character, something that was not true of those countries in which economics developed with the values of culture spontaneously rising through the theory. Economic thought which is distinctive to Quebec has always referred economic questions to their cultural and social consequences in the broadest sense.[3]

La naissance de la pensée économique

At the very beginning of economic thought in Quebec, in 1840, when Lord Durham recommended responsible democratic government and the absorption and assimilation of the French, François-Albert Angers found Etienne Parent.[4]

As editor of the weekly publication, *Le Canadien*, Parent had repeatedly and consistently approved of the British political institutions that the *Canadiens* had had imposed on them as a result of the Conquest. So, it was a personal blow to him when Durham's proposed political and cultural absorption of the French was embodied in the Act of Union. His consequent verbal abuse of British authority earned him four months in prison. He opposed the use of violence, even and especially during the Rebellion of 1837, but that did not prevent him from devoting the rest of his life to the tasks of a patriot.

Union of the two Canadas did not accomplish the assimilation of the French. It provided a focus for the articulation of Quebec nationalism, one element of which was Parent's contribution in economics.

There was no treason or rebellion, if those are the words in this case, in the writings of Etienne Parent, and why should there have been? The promise of responsible govenment was made good in 1848 when the francophone population of Canada was only slightly less than a majority. From a certain perspective, the French had been given the country, and Parent chose to look at it that way. So, to redraw the picture of the position of the French in Canada, and to work deeper into the sense of *la pensée économique* we turn to Esdras Minville's reconstruction of the circumstances of Quebec in the nineteenth and early twentieth centuries.

After the Conquest the *Canadiens* withdrew to the communal life of their relatively independent, that is non-commercialized, agriculture, counting on their natural increase to regain for them in economic and social life what they had lost politically. Unfortunately, the expansion of their community and its characteristic activities was blocked by large land holdings, forest reserves, and the setting aside of lands for 'freehold' tenants. The anglophone government did not help, and, in fact, showed no interest in agriculture in the seigneuries. The merchants who came to control the government treated the colony as a source of raw materials for England, and a market for its manufactured goods. Following the brief prosperity of the War of 1812, agriculture fell into depression, and then into crisis, exacerbating the political situation, and leading to the Rebellion of 1837. The official response to the rebellion was the subjection of the colonial executive to the wishes of a largely francophone Assembly in a united Canada.[5]

As a consequence of its War of Independence, the United States had extracted itself from British colonialism. This put it in a position to begin its long climb to industrial supremacy, according to Minville, at a time when the economy of Lower Canada was stagnating and its seigneuries were becoming over-populated. The resulting exodus to the United States began in the 1830s, peaked in the 1860s, and continued until the 1920s.

With the achievement of responsible government, Canada should have undertaken a programme to expropriate the large land holdings, plan and support settlement, and encourage commercial activities that would lift the economy from its narrow dependence on agriculture. In those years, however, the popular policy was laissez-faire. In the period immediately after the achievement of responsible government, especially in the years of the Reciprocity Treaty with the United States, those who held that what was good for Britain was good for the colonies had the upper hand. So, according to Minville, it was not until the National Policy of 1878 that Canada extracted itself from British colonialism.

Under the National Policy railroads were built and settlement undertaken, but most of the initiatives were taken in Western Canada. Railroad construction and settlement in Quebec were given very little support. Industrialization in Quebec came in the form of alien, liberal, individualistic institutions. Though it looked like progress, and some *Canadiens*, despite their agricultural background and their want of capital, did well for a time, the working class suffered, and in the great merger movement of the 1890s many of the successful *Canadiens* were bankrupted, bought out, or subsumed under larger American or Anglo-Canadian corporations. Even at that, the basic problems growing out of these developments did not become fully evident until the depression of the 1930s, so Minville said.

Having accepted Angers's definition of *la pensée économique*, and Minville's perspective on the economy in which it developed, we may be in a position to understand what it was.

ETIENNE PARENT

Etienne Parent's over-riding goal was to inflame the entrepreneurial spirit of his people. With responsible government assured, he assumed that the political struggle of the *Canadiens* was over, and that their survival as a people would depend on their commercial and industrial competence. It was imperative, then, that they correct the prejudice that he perceived them to have against careers in business. He thought they preferred to 'vegetate' in the 'mediocre professions', that is the legal and clerical professions that were peripheral to great economic undertakings; and that, in consequence, they were being economically exploited. He conceded the importance of agriculture, but not of the traditional, routinized agriculture that he observed in Canada East. The time had come for the *Canadiens* to develop a progressive outlook.[6]

Although he made few explicit references to the economics of his contemporaries in England or in France, Parent wrote as though he had extensively read their works. He had much to say in favour of the study of political economy, and much, in general, to say in favour the policy of laissez-faire that had great support among British economists. Still, his acceptance of political economy had a certain ambivalence. On the one hand, he seemed to think that the study of political economy, which was the product of scholarly contemplation of economic activity and policy, would produce business acumen. On the other hand, he was not ready to trust the future of his people to political economy's policy prescriptions.

The distinctive character of Parent's economics was a consequence of his compulsion to bring the special interests of the French in British North America into the domain of the fledgeling science. Consider his address on the role and importance of commerce in modern (mid-nineteenth-century) civilization.[7] After a brief introduction, in which he expanded on the origins of market exchange and the separation of manufacturing from commerce, Parent proceeded to a panegyric on commerce as a stimulant to progress, and of free trade as a means to the efficient allocation and full employment of resources. As he moved on to consider the immediate economic problems of Canada, however, the tone of his address changed. The commercial and manufacturing interests of a young country had an obligation to retain control over, and to develop the resources at their disposal.

> Un pays pas plus qu'un particulier, ne doit tirer du dehors ce qu'il peut faire lui-même.[8]

> En ma qualité de libre échangiste, je suis en principe opposé aux primes d'encouragement tout comme aux droits protecteurs. Mais je ne suis pas de ceux qui disent: Périsse la Patrie plutôt qu'un principe; mais je dis: vive la Patrie avec les principes intacts, si ça se peut, mais avec les principes modifiés, s'il le faut. Les principes de l'économie politique ne sont pas absolus comme ceux de la morale. ... Je suis bien prêt à admettre que dans un jeune pays où les capitaux et l'expérience manquent, il est bien à propos de protéger dans les commencements les industries évidemment viables.[9]

Protection and subvention were not the *sine qua non* of economic development and growth in the classical economics Parent would have read. Capital, a surplus of productive power, would have to come from somewhere: from savings, according to Nassau Senior, from expropriation, according to Karl Marx.

> Qu'on ne dis pas non plus que les capitaux nous manquent: car s'il n'y a pas partout accumulation de capitaux en peu de mains, partout il y a l'association. Ce qu'un homme ne peut pas faire, deux, quatre, dix cent le peuvent, sans gêner leurs opérations ordinaires.[10]

Of course, he was quite right. Capital could, and would be centralized and allocated to more efficient uses than those to which it could be put in the hands of its scattered, original owners, but he did not specify the source of capital or the institutional intermediaries through which it would be centralized. These things were being specified by someone else who had lived in Montreal in the 1820s (see chapter 4).

Sometimes Parent was a nineteenth-century liberal, and sometimes he was not. It depended on whether liberalism ran contrary to the values and aspirations of his people. Nowhere is this more evident than in his 1852 address, *Considérations sur le sort des classes ouvrières*. Elements of the address were consonant with an extremely hard-headed liberalism, but they were rooted in Parent's fear of atheism and of the emigration of his fellow citizens to the anglophone, racial melting pot to the south. Thus he advised the workers to refrain from breaking the laws of economics as established by God and set out by Adam Smith. They should adhere to their Catholicism, because, in the last analysis, they would be unable to raise wages by striking. If their situation became too desperate, they could return to the land. The answer to the labourer's problems was government support for new agricultural settlements, and the frugality of the workers themselves. They ought to avoid luxury. They ought to establish savings banks. They ought not to go to the United States, and they ought not to become communists. And, the final appeal, 'Notre nationalité avant tout'.

A great and recurring theme in economic thought in Quebec has been the loss, the absence, and the re-establishment of a francophone bourgeoisie. It has been restated in at least four major revisions up to the work of Jean-Luc Migué (see chapters 9 and 12). In yet another address given in 1852, *De l'intelligence dans ses rapports avec la société*, Parent gave the theme its classic form.

THE MISSING BOURGEOISIE

The root proposition, in Parent's version of the story, was an assertion that men are naturally unequal, and that, in consequence there is a role for authority in society. It was, in fact, a dictate of natural law that society have a ruling elite made up of its most intelligent members. The problem in Canada was an unfortunate, historically determined bias in the elements constituting the francophone elite. At the time of the Conquest, so his statement ran, noble French families abandoned the colony to the English. This opened the way for the establishment of an anglophone business and governmental elite, and for the ascendency of an ecclesiastical and legal elite in francophone society. Dominance of the clergy in social matters had serious consequences once responsible government was achieved, both for the inter-relationship between the Church and the state, and for the general direction of French Canadian energies in politics. In Parent's view, the steps necessary for the survival of the French could not be taken unless a counterbalancing, non-clerical, francophone economic elite was established.

Parent's ruling elite was to be truly superior, its members somehow deserving of their position, the most meritorious in a meritocracy. The way to produce an elite of this sort was to train the best, and have the best of the best rise to the top. The way to a non-clerical elite was through a reconstituted school system. Other solutions to the social problems of Canada were being suggested, socialist solutions rooted in emotion and the tumultuous opinions of the common people. In a system ruled by reason, the solution would be based on reason. Parent wanted the school system reformed.

All the reforms suggested by Parent were eventually carried out. His suggestions with respect to the accumulation of capital, the formation of an economic elite, the reformation of the school system, and the displacement of the ecclesiatical authorities, were achieved in Quebec long after his death, though not in a way that he could have foreseen. His major suggestion with respect to agriculture was achieved, in substance, in 1854. With evident stagnation in the seigneuries, and a visible drain of emigrants to the United States, on the one hand, and a concurring French caucus in the Assembly, on the other, it was possible to upgrade agriculture by disestablishing the seigneurial system, without having it appear that the English-speaking were suppressing an element in francophone culture.

AGRICULTURE AND ABOLITION OF THE SEIGNEURIAL SYSTEM

A number of francophones, including some of the clerical elite, wanted the seigneurial system abolished. Its original purpose had been achieved. New France, Quebec, was settled to the point that there was out-migration. As a device for attaching people to the soil by reducing the level of exploitation of the settlers, it had been a success. As an instrument for generating a surplus, or facilitating adaptation to new techniques and circumstances, it seemed wanting. Clement Dumesnil began his campaign to have the system abolished during the agricultural crisis of the early 1830s,[11] only a year before Amury Girod published a handbook of improvements in agricultural technique, challenging traditional seigneurial practices.[12] Dumesnil accused the seigneurs of doing nothing to improve farming technique, and of taxing the improvements made by others, especially improvements in transportation.[13]

In time, criticism produced proposals for alternative arrangements. In 1851, twelve missionaries in the Eastern Townships, apprehensive about the decimation of their parishes, raised the alarm about emigration to the United States. They wanted government action on a new settlement policy. '(1) Imposer une taxe de douze sous par acre sur tous les terres incultes de la couronne, du clergé et sourtout des grands propriétaires. (2) Etablir un bon système de voirie plus en rapport avec ses localités.'[14]

This complaint, clearly, was not unique to the seigneurial system. It was the complaint laid against the land system of Upper Canada by Robert Gourlay in the 1820s and 1830s. The problem was related to the rent on land. How could the surplus produced in agriculture be organized so that it would be put at the service of those improving and expanding the industry? This was the question addressed by M. A. Kierzkowski, Directeur de la Société d'Agriculture.

From his considerable experience with agricultural improvement schemes in Europe, prior to his arrival in Canada in 1842, Kierzkowski had concluded that the distinctive characteristics of property in the form of land necessitated special credit arrangements to ensure that agriculture would be as economically progressive as commerce or manufacturing.[15] Among the *Canadiens*, in particular, he saw a need to clarify land titles and the conditions of their transfer, and a need to set up *une rente consolidée* as a basis for agricultural credit. The first use of this *crédit foncier* would be the buying out of the seigneurs.

By the time of Montreal's Grand Anti-Seigneurial Convention of 1854, it was generally conceded that the seigneurial system was an important factor in the difficulties of agriculture in Canada East. With some compensation from the public treasury, it was abolished. This put agriculture in Quebec on a more favourable footing to benefit from the improvements in transportation flowing from the sixty years of railway expansion that characterized the Canadian economy from 1854 to 1914.

THE TARIFF AND INDUSTRIALIZATION

For all the complaints about backward agriculture and assertions of distinctiveness by francophones, they seem to have kept up reasonably well with the rest of the country. When the 1850s turned the thoughts of Maritimers and English-speaking Canadians to tariff protection for industrialization, railway expansion, and new settlement, francophone Quebec agreed. Perhaps this common response was a consequence of stronger lines of communication between the components of British North America as technological and political factors moved them towards confederation and continental expansion. More likely, since they were all enveloped in the informational environment of expanding western industrialism, their responses, rooted in their distinctive circumstances, were made similar by a common stimulus. Canada West's more agressive response with respect to the reformation of monetary institutions was an exception (see chapter 6).

Though not unchallenged, protectionist sentiment was popular among francophone Canadians in the middle of the nineteenth century.[16] Louis-Joseph Papineau, leader of the Rouge in the Rebellion of 1837, had included a high protective tariff in his proposed programme, and at least a portion of his party continued to support protection through the 1840s. When the economic downturn of 1849 directed policy towards free trade with the United States, government support for railway expansion became the principal form of development policy advocated by francophones. Most realized expansion occurred on the frontier in Canada West, Joseph Cochon's efforts on behalf of the Montreal to Quebec City railway, notwithstanding.

Confederation was an act of separation for the Canadas. Ontario and Quebec emerged with separate governments, and Ontario, in particular, bent every effort to establish and widen its political autonomy. It was not joined by Quebec in this activity until the Interprovincial Conference of 1887. Nova Scotia threatened to withdraw from the union from the beginning.

With the partial separation of Quebec as a result of Confederation it becomes more difficult to determine when French Canadians were concerned with Canadian development and when with Quebec development. To some extent economic nationalism in Quebec was integrated into the protectionist movement that carried the whole of Canada in 1878. In some instances arguments for protection in Quebec were as pan-Canadian as those put forward by Isaac Buchanan in Ontario (see chapter 5).[17] In others this was not the case. J.-A. Mousseau promoted economic nationalism as a device for the support of French culture. Confederation was necessary as the only means of defending francophones against the consequences of the overall anglophone presence in North America. Protectionism was the economic instrument necessary for the federation's survival. The Conquest had eliminated the francophone economic elite and brought about deindustrialization of the French population. Protectionism was the corrective needed. 'C'est notre devoir, spécialement le devoir de ceux d'entre nous qui sont Canadiens-français, de créer une industrie nationale....'[18]

Cléopas Beausoleil, editor of *Nouveau-Monde*, repeated assertions that tariff protection would correct an unfavourable balance of trade, reverse economic slumps, and lead to industrialization. So widely accepted was this sort of thinking that the Quebec Legislature formally endorsed protection. Even Wilfrid Laurier, who would subsequently lead the federal Liberals on a platform of free trade with the United States, gave the policy formal, public support. The movement reached its peak shortly before the election of 1878, with Beausoleil pressing arguments drawn from Frederick List and the American protectionist, Henry Carey.

> Voila pourquoi la valeur de la propriété baisse, l'agriculture dépérit, l'argent se concentre dans les villes pour de là passer à l'étranger et se trouve remplacé par le papier-monnaie, la population demeure stationnaire ou diminue même à cause de l'émigration. Cet état de chose ne peut qu'empirer de jour en jour... parce que nous consommons plus que nous produisons... et que la balance du commerce est contre nous.[19]

If the French in Canada had expected that westward expansion was going to mean an expansion of the existing linguistic structure of the Dominion, what actually happened must have been a disappointment. The French were outnumbered. Louis Riel, who attempted to lead the mixed French and native Métis in the establishment of a separate nation on the Prairies, was hanged. The residents of Manitoba, the first Prairie province, in one more act that enhanced the jurisdiction of the provincial governments, refused publicly to fund French Catholic schools. The money that was expended on railways and settlement under the National Policy was expended largely in the West, where the French were outnumbered, rather than in Quebec. Even Northern Ontario, which had the same dubious agricultural prospects as the Laurentide in Quebec, received considerably larger benefits.

In truth, protectionists in both English- and French-speaking Canada were disappointed. The National Policy of balanced growth that emerged from the situation of Southern Ontario and Southern Quebec in the middle years of the nineteenth century, was carried away by the forces of history (see chapters

4, 5 and 7) to become a policy of continental expansion based on the export of a primary product. Without betraying the complexities of history, it can be said that these disappointments led to the election of a Liberal government in Quebec first, and then to the election of a formally free-trade Liberal government under Laurier at the federal level in 1896. When Laurier issued his Reciprocity Manifesto prior to the election of 1891, and Beausoleil responded,[20] they were not debating the principal forces shaping the Dominion.

Late-nineteenth-century free trade arguments were not unprecedented in Quebec, but, apart from the ambivalent Parent, the preceding literature was thin. There were always some free trade supporters among the Rouge faction. Arthur Dansereau supported the position,[21] and there was at least one annexationist[22] who, like Goldwin Smith, despaired of the economic and political viability of Canada and suggested union with the United States.

RAILWAYS AND AGRICULTURAL EXPANSION

Deflection of the National Policy by the exigencies of the new transcontinental economy meant that railway expansion came to be associated with the geographical extension of agriculture, rather than the improvement of transportation in industrializing regions. For francophones, railroads, forestry and agricultural expansion within Quebec became the inseparable trinity in promotional literature.[23]

Pushed from behind by evident overcrowding in the older areas of settlement, and by emigration to the United States, and led on by the buoyant overconfidence of Canada's greatest railroad boom, the government of Quebec moved into the colonization railway business. Its target was the sparse farm lands of the Laurentide. Its instrument was le Chemin de Fer du Nord. Like so many other Canadian railways of the time, this chosen instrument proved itself a commercial failure, and fell into long-term dependence on government support. The Premier explained to the people the possibility of financial support from France to cover the debt of the Montreal–Quebec line that the Canadian Pacific Railway had refused to absorb.[24] Eventually the C. P. R. agreed to take the route at a reduced price, and the Premier apologized that governments with political priorities ought not to run railways in any case.[25]

Internal settlement in Quebec was not an unalloyed success. It had hardly run its course when it was reversed by a massive movement of the agrarian population into urban centres. There is an element of tragedy in the hope that many had for the future of the French founded on agricultural settlement. The literature speaks for itself, but it is well to remember that if heads were counted it might turn out that the French in Quebec fared no worse than the

English- or Ukrainian-speaking in the West, or the French- and English-speaking in northern Ontario. On the Prairies

> More than 41 per cent of original homestead entries from 1870 to 1927 were cancelled: more than forty-one out of every hundred Canadian homesteaders fell by the wayside before acquiring patent to their original homesteads. How many after acquiring patent turned their homesteads over to speculators and land companies it would perhaps be impossible to estimate.[26]

We can begin the review of the literature with the work of Stanislaus Drapeau, a civil servant and journalist, whose approach was as typical as anyone's could be.

Drapeau's first work, *Etudes sur les developments de la colonisation du Bas-Canada depuis dix ans: 1851–1861*,[27] was a history of agricultural settlement, but it concluded with suggestions for settlement policy: more public funds for an accelerated road building programme, publicly supported settlement agencies, land grants, the establishment of a special department of settlement, and public support for settlers' associations. Really, an all out effort to finally establish the French fact in Canada. 'Colonisez ... c'est assurer la conservation de notre nationalité.'

His second work, *Coup d'oeil sur les ressources productives*,[28] was a general treatment of the resources and economic institutions of Canada. Its conclusion was a general condemnation of any stinting in settlement programmes. No country, he asserted, with resources and useful works would be impoverished. Why, then, he asked, had there been stinting with respect to settlement in Quebec? The money was going to the West, where massive immigration was reducing the francophone population of Canada to a minority position. Drapeau suggested a separate immigration and settlement division for Quebec. Later he wrote *Le guide du colon français, belge, suisse, etc.* for the Dominion Government. In these works there was no reference to the technicalities of farming new lands, or the economic prospects of so doing. Only will and effort were seen to be necessary for success.[29]

François A. H. LaRue, a graduate of Louvain and a Professor of Medicine at Laval University in Quebec City, was more comprehensive in his approach to settlement, but less 'typical' in more than one way. He promoted scientific agriculture as an academic subject. He wrote a three-volume economic geography of Quebec[30] based on data published by La Société d'encouragement de l'industrie locale. His general assessment of the role of settlement in the economic future of Quebec appeared in a final, two-volume work, *Mélanges historiques littéraires, et économie politique*.[31] LaRue's advocacy of agricultural expansion in Quebec was predicated on the failure of the National Policy and of Confederation itself. Canada could not survive and industrialize without United States capital and markets, and LaRue saw North American free trade and annexation as the inevitable consequence. For this reason it was necessary for Quebec to develop a prosperous agricultural base. It would provide a natural foundation on which manufacturing could develop. Given industrialization, he speculated, annexation could be negotiated with assurances that the moral and material base of the French nationality would be preserved in North America.

Some of the works on settlement, perhaps the most important, were outside of the normal limits of economics, but we are being guided by F.- A. Angers and Esdras Minville, and we are doing what we can to capture the economic aspect of the informational environment of nineteenth-century Quebec. There were descriptive works, and books giving practical advice to settlers, such as one would find anywhere in Canada.[32] Some of Joseph Tassé's works belong in this category,[33] but much of his work was of a romantically aspirational genre, the most important contribution in which was the work of Antoin Gérin-Lajoie.

JEAN RIVARD L'ECONOMISTE

Who could have had better connections in francophone Canada than Antoine Gérin-Lajoie? Coming from a prominent family himself, he married the daughter of Etienne Parent. From 1845 to 1852 he edited the influential *La Minerve*. His son, Léon Gérin, became the most important sociologist of the next generation, and of several generations after, in Quebec. Gérin-Lajoie's two major works, *Jean Rivard le défricheur*[34] and *Jean Rivard l'économiste*,[35] bridged the gap between the *politique économique* of Parent in the nineteenth century and the *sociologie économique* of Gérin in the twentieth.

Gérin-Lajoie's work was more in the tradition of sociology than of economics. His general goal and chosen form of expression were drawn from the writings of the French sociologist, P. G. F. Le Play, who used the literary form of the novel to promote a reform-oriented social science. He had read the foremost English economists of his time without adopting their Whig proclivities. If he favoured any economic position it was that of the old school of Physiocracy, according to which all surplus product came from agriculture, all other forms of economic activity being 'sterile'.

Gérin-Lajoie romanticized agricultural settlement and its associated small industries in order to draw his francophone contemporaries away from the liberal professions and from the market for industrial workers. He echoed the message of his father-in-law, Etienne Parent, without mentioning commercial and industrial careers in the larger urban centres. His exemplar, Jean Rivard, was an idealized pioneer, first clearing the land, then establishing village co-operative industries. Rivard embodied a call to individuals and to the state to co-operate in a rather well defined policy of economic development.

To the francophone writer, the last era of Euro-American extensive agricultural expansion was a phenomenon in Quebec and for francophone Quebec. In reality, the Quebec experience was a small part of the final filling up of the arable lands of North America. Everywhere the same stages were traversed. Farmers' organizations were formed and exercised political power. Agricultural colleges were established and farming became an applied science. Everywhere a new term eventually came to describe the settlement movement: in English, 'back to the land'; in French, *'repeuplement'*.[36] The rural–urban shift accompanying industrialization swamped the agrarian development schemes of late-nineteenth-century America.

In Quebec the new circumstances were registered first in a small way in a small book written by a Montreal journalist, Henry-Gaston Testard de Montigny.[37] Francophone survival through agricultural expansion was still acceptable as a positive programme, but it was no longer sufficient to the desired end. There was a new threat. United States trusts, exploiting the resources of the Canadian economy, were exhausting the basis of future wealth. In a writing style that reflected the 'muck-raking' era of United States journalism, De Montigny linked the effort to 'seize the land' to a more generalized programme of domestic ownership, exploitation and conservation of all natural resources.

There can be no doubt about the success of the colonization programme for francophone Québécois. Their numbers expanded rapidly. They would survive. As with the seigneurial system, the per capita growth rate was not as high as they would have liked, but the extensive growth rate was impressive. In 1918 Edouard Montpetit wrote *La veillée des berceaux*[38] in which he exposed the problems entailed in the rapid growth of Quebec's population and its associated rural–urban shift. Perhaps there was something unique, or uniquely severe, in Quebec's problems in this regard: urban overcrowding, large families with low incomes, inadequate housing and a growing need for social workers. It was an unexpected side effect of *la revanche des berceaux*, which had been a motivation for extensive agricultural settlement in Quebec.

The last of the settlement literature came with the depression of the 1930s, and was, perhaps, largely a product of those years. L'abbé Georges-Marie Bilodeau[39] preached a 'back to the land' gospel with strong emphasis on the survival of French culture in the face of the onslaught of *Américanisme et matérialisme*. His arguments were a confusion of naive Physiocracy, natural law and religion.

The settlement movement was spent. In any case, after Errol Bouchette's early-twentieth-century call, *emparons nous de l'industrie* (see chapter 9), economic thought in Quebec found itself on a very different part of the path described by François-Albert Angers in the passage cited at the beginning of our treatment of *la pensée économique au Québec*.

MONETARY INSTITUTIONS: THE QUEBEC VIEW

Apart from the effects of the nationalist bias, lionized by Angers, there is one other element of economic thought in nineteenth-century Quebec that seems to have been quite distinctive when compared with the literature of English-speaking Canada, that dealing with money, and financial institutions. Much of Quebec's concern in this matter was related to the settlement movement, in particular, to the role of credit in agriculture; but, of course, the role of credit in industrial and commercial pursuits was also in question.

Concern with agricultural credit was a natural outcome of the abolition of the seigneurial system. Reorganization consequent upon abolition came amid propitious circumstances. Trade expansion in primary products, associated with the Canadian–American Reciprocity Treaty, was in full swing as the United States built up to its Civil War. Markets for Canadian natural products were good, making the forest cleared by settlers a viable cash crop. It was a period of general expansion, but it was marred by recurring financial crises. Francophone Quebec responded within its own tradition.

In 1862 a convention was held at Ste. Hyacinthe to inaugurate a system of land banks. Anglophone Quebec, as represented by its press, was opposed. A certain George Henry Macaulay drew up a brochure in English to meet the situation.[40] It explained itself in its title: *The System of Landed Credit, or La Banque de Crédit Fonçier: the working of that institution in Europe with regard to its principles and advantages and... the introduction of the system into Lower Canada briefly considered.*[41] The general idea was to establish banks that would lend to farmers on the security of their land. The credit of the banks, themselves, was to be based on public subscription, and guaranteed by the credit of the province.

The crédit fonçier idea was slow to catch on in nineteenth-century Quebec, and the resulting institutions did not become major players in the financial system. Perhaps for that reason the scribbling set gave it scant attention. In a notable exception, in 1875, *La Revue Canadienne* carried a series of six articles, in which the character and advantages of the scheme were spelled out in considerable detail.

Quebecers, anglophone and francophone, have always been conservative in their approach to money and banking. Rural francophone Quebec did not need a sophisticated money system for most of its transactions, and anglophone Montreal was the established banking centre of Canada throughout the nineteenth century. Neither group had any time for the heretical monetary ideas that characterized economic thought on the frontier in Canada West. In Quebec, even the innovations were conservative, the outstanding example being the savings banks of François Vezina.

François Vezina was a prominent businessman and financier who was intent on easing the credit problems of the less fortunate, without having the government interfere in the banking system. According to his biographer, J. C. Langelier,[42] Vezina controlled a two-tier banking enterprise, a savings bank operation for low-income groups, and a commercial bank for entrepreneurs. The savings bank operation came first.

> Les Caisses d'Epames ne sont pas, à proprement parler, des institutions de crédit, elles n'ont pas pour mission de fournier un capital a ceux qui en sont momentairément privés, mais de faciliter l'accumulation du travail, d'encourager l'économie, de réunir les plus petites épargnes pour les transformer en un capital productif[43]

In 1848, with the help of the St. Vincent de Paul Society, Vezina started his first savings bank, la Caisse d'Economie Notre-Dame du Québec. His banks multiplied rapidly. In 1860 he established la Banque Nationale, an association of the principle merchants of the French-speaking community, to meet the needs of commerce and industry.

Vezina undertook a wide-ranging study of political economy, and produced several books, including *Les Banques* and *Le Département de la Trésorerie provinciale*.[44] *Les Banques* was a criticism of an 1868 plan of the Solicitor General, John Rose, to establish the United States system of national banking in Canada. Vezina preferred the 'Scottish System' of private banking. In his 1860 work on the Treasury he had attacked a similar proposal made by the then Minister of Finance, A. T. Galt. Vezina feared that a government bank would monopolize the issue of currency and then suspend conversion, to the detriment of the country and of the private banks.

The initiatives criticized by Vezina were two of the important moves in the general evolution of banking in nineteenth-century Canada. Wide-ranging discussion of money and banking, and the institutional innovations that occurred in the United States in the first seventy years of the nineteenth century spilled over into Canada, and affected, particularly, the western frontier. In the long run, British monetary thought informed opinion in Canada, but in 1868, the national banking system of the United States was the centre of attention (see chapter 6). Sides in the debate were well formed. Isaac Buchanan, an Upper Canadian businessman and politician, wanted an irredeemable paper currency. A. T. Galt, a Lower Canadian businessman and politician, favoured a government bank and a redeemable currency. Buchanan opposed the idea of a government-owned bank because he saw it as an instrument of financial stringency. Vezina opposed the government bank because he saw it as an instrument of inflation. Buchanan's notion that capital could be generated and industrialization supported by fiddling with the monetary system made no sense to Vezina for whom 'le seul moyen d'augmenter le capital est l'éparne'. Together, for opposite reasons, Vezina and Buchanan defeated the government bank proposal in the 1860s. Other forces defeated it definitively in 1881.

In the 1890s the Caisse Populaire movement of Alphonse Desjardins became the rising innovation among financial institutions in francophone Canada. Its essential idea was that of the co-operative movement, but in banking. In a certain sense it was for Quebec what Social Credit became for Western Canada. Of course the two movements were not at all alike in their approaches to the problem of credit, but that is the point. The difference points up the difference in the economic thought component of the information environments in the two societies. The West was willing to embrace the Dionesian forces of frontier development. Quebec, francophone Quebec, moved more cautiously in pace with its distinctive growth path.

The Caisse Populaire was modelled on European attempts to provide consumers and farmers with credit. It was an end-product of the earlier crédit foncier movement. In part it was a move against usury. In part it was simply a means to keep farmers in business. According to Desjardins, it succeeded by using the local parish as a social unit that could generate the goodwill necessary to operate a mutual confidence society. It was, in fact, a social uplift movement, with financial aspects taking second place.[45] Still, it took deposits and advanced credit. It was part of the social uplift idea that the funds accumulated would be used for economic development in Quebec.

The first Caisse Populaire was established at Lévis in 1895 with the help of the social action group, le Cercle Pie X de la Jeunesse Catholique. The second appeared in Montreal in 1909. Between 1909 and 1912 the movement caught on all over Quebec. It has since become as much an established business as the wheat pools of the Prairies.

To mention parallel development in Quebec and English-speaking Canada is, of course, not in the spirit of F.- A. Angers or Esdras Minville, and we have now strayed too far from the path towards which they pointed for us to pretend to be under their guidance. Much that happened in Quebec was part of what happened to the rest of Canada. The Rebellion of 1837 occurred in both Upper and Lower Canada. The internal railway expansion and agricultural development scheme in Quebec had a mirror image in Ontario. If Quebec looked on Confederation as a move in the direction of autonomy, it did so less than Ontario, which sighed with relief at getting out from under the weight of the French and of Montreal. Still, from the point of view of francophone Quebec there was a difference that showed up in that economic thought 'qui n'attend pas les économistes pour exister'.

56 A history of Canadian economic thought

With respect to our more general goal, which is to see the Canadian economy as reflected in its distinctive contributions to economic thought, and to see its contributions to economic thought insofar as they are a product of the distinctive aspects of its economy; in particular, to do this with respect to the economic activities of the francophone population of Quebec, the conclusion seems clear. In the nineteenth century there was no discussion of staple exports, or external markets, nor, indeed, was there much discussion of markets at all. There was interest in the development of manfacturing within Quebec, behind a protective tariff. Etienne Parent's protestations notwithstanding, few favoured free trade. The major interest was agriculture, and railway development and financial development in relation to agriculture, and industrial development in relation to agriculture (I am referring to Gérin-Lajoie). We have the economic thought of an economy growing slowly, even painfully, but substantially, on an independent agricultural base. If there was little in its economic thought that drew on the emerging science of political economy in the greater world of Euro-American civilization, it was, as Angers said, because political economy seemed irrelevant to the circumstances and the goals of francophone Quebec.

The anglophone population saw things differently (see chapters 1, 5, 7 and 11), but in Quebec City they were a nineteenth-century enclave that moved away when the timber trade that interested them came to an end. The eastward movement of wheat and the railways, and the development of some new staple exports, would keep the anglophone enclave in Montreal until well into the second half of the twentieth century.

4 The economics of John Rae, 1822–34

Note: This chapter has not been written for the general reader. Although it deals with matters of fundamental importance for the history of economic thought in Canada, it can and should be passed over by anyone not interested in economics for its own sake.

In vision and originality, Rae far surpassed economists who were successful.... The *Statement of Some New Principles*... with ten additional years of work, graced by an adequate income, could have grown into another, and more profound *Wealth of Nations*.[1]

The fundamental importance of Rae's work for formal economic theory is beyond question. Both Bohm-Bawerk and Irving Fisher conceded that the substance of their principal insights into capital theory were first expounded by Rae. J. S. Mill's infant industry argument for protection was a weak paraphrase of sections of Rae's *New Principles*. Thorstein Veblen drew the concept and the term 'conspicuous consumption', and probably his concept of the dichotomy between the engineer and the price system from Rae; but, all of this has been better stated in R. Warren James's, *John Rae Political Economist: an Account of His Life and a Compilation of His Main Writings*.[2] The present work has its own purposes, and does not repeat or replace James's work in this regard.

We are not here dealing with economics in the context of action. We are not recounting pre-scientific accounts of how the economy of some region worked, or how, in someone's opinion, it should have worked. We will be able, nonetheless, to draw conclusions about the nature of the Upper Canadian economy. John Rae came to Canada when he was a mature scholar, and he left it long before his contribution to science was complete. The principal insight of his theory may have been fully developed before he left Scotland, or before he left continental Europe. That makes no difference, because he was able to elaborate his theory with the experience of the Canadian frontier in full view. His book is thick with examples drawn from the life-styles and activities of a number of countries and peoples, but the native peoples of the St. Lawrence lowlands, and the frontier communities of the European settlers in Upper Canada are among those most frequently mentioned. There is no need to overdo the extent to which he used the Upper Canadian experience as an example. It was a source of examples, as good as any other, as he elaborated a theory of independent growth, independent, that is, of primary product exports and imported capital (see chapter 11). Rae's work reflected the nature of the economic activity to which it so frequently referred.

This should not be surprising. Upper Canada was not fundamentally dependent on an exportable cash crop; and no one said it was, until Vernon Fowke, looking at Upper Canada from Saskatchewan one hundred years later, saw what looked like a straight path to where he was standing (see chapter 11).[3] The economy of Upper Canada developed and grew by means of those processes that could be called, alternatively, neoclassical or Smithian, if it were not for the fact that the debate over development and growth in Canada has hinged on a distinction drawn between the two, a distinction on which Rae's theory of development and growth was built. Upper Canada's development and growth were primarily independent. Its economy was the experiential foundation of a nationalist school of economics and economic policy, the efforts of which terminated in the 1876 National Policy of the Conservative Party of Canada (see chapter 5).

Rae's influence on the formation of the National Policy was both direct and indirect. John Stuart Mill's infant industry argument, drawn from Rae's *New Principles*, was the centrepiece of Macdonald's speech when he announced the National Policy in the House of Commons. Other protectionists, whose works influenced the informational environment in which the National Policy was accepted, and Macdonald, himself, in another place, cited Rae directly.[4]

The point is that the character of the economy, the analysis growing out of it, and the policy growing out of the analysis, were all of one piece in mid-nineteenth-century Canada. After the political fractionation and geographical expansion that constituted and followed Confederation in 1867, the character of economic development and growth was biased by the addition of regions relying on primary product exports, and by the informational environment of what H. A. Innis has called 'imperfect regional competition'.[5] The dependent development and growth that characterized that later period in Canadian history produced the staple theory that has been attributed to Innis.

Innis and Rae were very different characters and their economics were fundamentally different. Still, there were important similarities in their concepts of scientific social science, and neither thought that the sources of economic development and growth had been captured in contemporary economic theory. For both of them the inventive faculty of mankind, the most important element, had been overlooked. Apart from that, however, they were each archetypical of very different worlds. Their works embody or have inspired the substantial differences that underlie debate over the economics of Canada; but that is what has to be demonstrated if a principal hypothesis of the present work is to be substantiated.

The immediate task is to explain the economics of John Rae. We begin with some remarks on the general nature of capital theory, the questions it has sought to answer, and the difficulties encountered, for difficulties there have been.

The Nature and Limitations of Capital Theory

Capital theory is a war zone, a 'no man's land', in the world of economics. It is a place where giants have done battle. Adam Smith, Karl Marx, Eugene Bohm-Bawerk, Irving Fisher, Joan Robinson and Kenneth Arrow have striven mightily, without a victor emerging. So we must not expect too much of a chapter in a history of economic thought in Canada. If it states the desideratum of the theory, and the extent to which it has been achieved, insofar as they are relevant to economic thought in Canada, it will be enough. The difficulty of the chapter will be, however, that what is relevant to the work of John Rae is the core of the theory.

The desideratum in capital theory is an explanation of how the quantity of goods and services in an economy increases, whether it increases absolutely (extensively), or in per capita terms (intensively). The explanation is that goods and services are produced with instruments of production, called capital goods, or, simply, capital; so the quantity of goods and services increases when the quantity capital employed increases. But, what, then, is the explanation of an increase in the quantity of capital employed? That could depend on the form that capital might take, and it has been seen to be, alternatively, simply instruments, money, stored-up labour in the form of wage goods, stored-up labour in more time-consuming or roundabout ways of production, or the totality of an economy's productive power. These forms of capital may simply be alternative definitions of much the same thing, about which all capital theorists have written. Karl Marx used these ideas, distinguishing himself by suggesting that the quantity of capital depended on some form of expropriation, that is, theft. Adam Smith and other classical economists thought that capital increased as a result of abstinence, that is, saving.[6] John Rae attributed the increase in capital to the invention of more productive ways of doing things.

In the formative period of neoclassical theory, a century after the appearance of Rae's *New Principles*, the idea of invention as the source of capital was lost, and capital was given a particular, limited definition. Rae had distinguished capital from money and from stored-up past labour. Marshall and J. B. Clark distinguished only between capital and money. By the 1930s, capital was generally taken to be an unspecified, undifferentiated, homogeneous aggregate of productive power, measured as a sum of monetary values. In this form it seemed to be distinguishable from other factors, but in fact, it was not.

The principal difficulty of modern capital theory flows from this definition of capital. To measure capital as a monetary value, and to derive that value from the interest that the monetary value earns, is to talk in a circle. It is to fail to see Stephen Leacock's point about circular reasoning: capital is worth what it earns, and it earns what it is worth.[7] The question seems to have been, whether to measure capital in some absolute way, as in the case of the classical economist's unconsumed surplus, or in a relative way, that is by the relative value it would have in exchange. If the latter, then there has to be some physical thing, distinguished from money, to which the money value can be attached. Labour is worth so much money per hour. Land is worth so much money per hectare. Capital is worth so much money per what? The statement, capital is worth a dollar per dollar of capital, says nothing at all.

The difficulty can be shown to exist in another way. It was generally thought, at least until the end of the nineteenth century, that capital accumulation proceeded by lengthening the time over which labour was applied in production before output appeared. (John Rae's idea of the length of time over which an instrument is exhausted is similar, but not identical to this.) As this form of accumulation occurred, meaning as the production period lengthened, the marginal benefit from lengthening the period fell. So lengthening of the period would proceed until its marginal benefit fell to equality with the interest that would have to be paid on the money borrowed to keep productive factors in operation with no product yet appearing. So accumulation takes place until the return to capital falls to equality with the return to money. But, if capital is measured in money, then it is accumulated until its return falls to equality with the return to itself; which seems absurd. So there is no theory here that explains the increase of goods and services in an economy, extensively or intensively.

Let us come at this one more time, but this time we begin to elaborate Rae's theory. Irving Fisher took a piece of Bohm-Bawerk's late-nineteenth-century theory, disassociated it from the idea of capital as an instrument of production, and developed the modern theory of interest (the return to money) using the idea of time preference. (John Rae's effective desire to accumulate was the source of this idea. The two are not identical, or, at least, Rae did not use the idea in the same way as Fisher.) Given a range of time preferences among consumers, some preferring to consume immediately and others having a weaker preference for present consumption, those with a weaker preference for present consumption could lend to those with a stronger preference in return for a larger repayment in the future, that is, they would receive principle and interest. (The analysis is much more complex than this because it requires assumptions about incomes per period, and assumptions about the pattern of changes in time preference over different agents and different periods.) This, of course, says nothing about where the interest comes from other than that it is a consequence of redistribution of something over agents and time; but let us drop this line of questioning.

Suppose all agents in an economy had a strong and equal preference for present consumption. There would be no lending and no interest, no investment and no growth. It was something like this pattern of time preference that Rae thought to be the major block to capital accumulation. He referred to it as a selfish, or, present-minded form of behaviour that frequently could be observed in different societies; in that of the native North Americans, for example, because their nomadic life left them so exposed to uncontrollable loss of possessions that any other behaviour would not have been appropriate.[8] Under other circumstances, however, the 'social and benevolent affections'[9] lead men to procure goods for others and to provide for the future, and this leads to both 'augmentation' and 'accumulation' of instruments;[10] that is, to development and growth, by which 'the increase of stock or capital' is brought about.

SMITH, RAE AND THE SCOTTISH ENLIGHTENMENT

Reference to the 'social and benevolent affections' marks Rae as a product of the Scottish enlightenment. As any one who has read Lionel Robbins's *Essay on the Significance of Economic Science*[11] knows, this does not put Rae into irreconcilable opposition to every element in neoclassical theory.

Adam Smith had identified accumulation with saving (in Rae's version of Smith),[12] and had treated it as a phenomenon arising in the context of self-seeking exchange. Self-seeking economic activity led to a division of, that is, a specialization in, economic functions. Specialization, in turn, led to the use of capital in production, the supply of which came from saving. The use of capital facilitated a further specialization in functions with a consequent increase in production and saving. In this way industry was augmented by accumulation up to the limit of the market,[13] or so Smith said.

Rae disagreed. Invention augmented capital. Invention led to a greater variety of commodities and instruments (commodities being easily transported instruments)[14] which, in turn, led to specialization in the tasks of labour, and to exchange.[15] That is to say, augmentation of capital through invention was the occasion of the specialization of tasks and of exchange, and not the other way around, as Smith had it. The role of saving was not to augment capital, but to facilitate the division of tasks and the exchanges that follow from the augmentation of capital. Indeed, the specialization of tasks that accompanies increasing exchanges would, in itself, stifle augmentation through invention, if the 'effective desire for accumulation'[16] did not overwhelm its effects.

Rae truly did intend to stand Smith upon his head.

THE DEFINITION OF CAPITAL

Throughout, Rae had a consistent view of capital as an agent in a growth process that was quite other than the processes of allocation and exchange. Capital was not one of the factors of production. It was all of them considered as instruments.

> a field is an instrument.... Flour is an instrument.... all tools and machines are instruments ... houses, ships, cattle, gardens, household furniture, factories, manufactured goods and stores of all sorts are, in this sense, instruments.[17]
>
> In general then, all those changes which man makes, in the form or arrangement of the parts of material objects, for the purpose of supplying his future wants, and which derive their power of doing this from his knowledge of the cause of events, and changes which his labour, guided by his reason, is hence enabled to make in the issue of these events, may be termed instruments.[18]

In this way, then, Rae defined capital. To escape the principal difficulty of modern capital theory, he had to have it measured by something other than its money value, something other than its value in exchange. He was aware of this need.

All instruments were directly or indirectly formed by labour guided by intelligence. They all had a capacity to satisfy wants, and in time their capacity to do so was exhausted, that is, consumed.[19] Still, the measure of their capacity was *not* their relative ability to bring about certain results in satisfying wants.[20]

Instruments had a capacity to bring about events that would take a certain amount of unaided labour to produce. Instruments were formed by labour, however, so there was a numeric relation between the amount of labour taken to produce them and the amount of labour they replaced. Now, a length of time intervened between the formation of an instrument and its exhaustion, that is the termination of its ability to replace labour. Suppose all instruments lasted forever. Unless they replaced no labour at all, there would be some time at which they would have replaced double the labour used in producing them. The sooner this time arrived, the greater the capacity of the instrument; that is, the more 'quickly returning' instruments would have the greater capacity. So, by setting the amount of labour replacement at some proportion of the labour used in making an instrument, ten years for two to one, or three years for two to one, (or twenty to one in ten years or thirty to one in ten years) an *index* of the capacity of instruments could be estimated.

But was this measure of capacity not based on a relative measure, the value of labour in exchange?

According to Rae, all instruments were valued in exchange in proportion to the amount of labour used to produce them.[21] By comparing instruments with one another according to the rate which they exchanged for one another, and choosing one of them as numeraire, an estimate of the value of all instruments could be made. This would be a measure of 'relative capital'.[22] The measure of 'absolute stock, and absolute capital' was the *index* 'expressing in present days' labour the whole capacity of the instruments owned by a society'.[23] A day's labour is a day of labour, not its relative value.

Under certain circumstances the relative and absolute value of capital would change independently of one another. To understand this it was necessary to understand that capital increased in two ways, by 'augmentation' and by 'accumulation'.

Depending on the strength of its desire to provide for the future, its effective desire to accumulate, a society would form and use instruments with a certain capacity, as measured in absolute value. If the desire was strong, it would form instruments even of the more slowly returning types. If it was weak, only those of the more quickly returning types.[24] The process of forming the instruments was accumulation.

Capital also increased by invention, the application of intelligence in rearranging instruments to permit them to exhaust their capacity in a shorter period of time, that is, to replace (say) ten days' labour in a year, rather than in three years.[25] Capital increasing in this way increased by augmentation.

Now, suppose the relative measure of capital was the same as its absolute measure, and suppose further that invention doubled the capacity of stock; then the absolute value of the stock would be double its relative value.[26] Rae states that when a society had formed all those instruments that return in a period consonant with its effective desire to accumulate, 'the absolute and relative stock must, it is obvious, agree'.[27] Whether Rae was correct in this particular or not, what he had shown was that the absolute value of capital could change while its relative value remained unchanged, at least in the short run; and that, therefore, the absolute value of capital was distinct from its relative value.

Rae measured capital in a way that was distinct from its relative value, that is, its value in exchange, and so he avoided the principal difficulty of modern capital theory.

THE RELATIVE MONEY MEASURE OF CAPITAL

In Rae's definition capital is distinct from money, but he was aware of the basis of confusion in this matter. He explained it in the following way.

Instruments are exchanged for one another according to their relative value. In a money economy their relative value was expressed in units of money, and this was a convenient way for this to be done. Further, when exchanges were made on credit, and instruments borrowed through the medium of money, an instrument with a certain future return would not be lent unless the borrower paid the future return. Further still, when someone borrowed money to undertake an enterprise, he would want to make more from the enterprise than he would return to the lender, to compensate himself for his own labour in the matter; and someone lending out an instrument would look to what he could earn with it himself, before he let it out. Accordingly there would be a general correspondence between the speed of return of instruments based on the effective desire of accumulation, the rate of interest, and the rate of profits in a society, taking these things on average.[28]

All this being recognized, Rae then cautioned, while the system of calculation associated with exchange was convenient for practical purposes, it was not substantially correct, because

> According to it, stock is regarded altogether, as measured by money, and an amount of stock is considered, simply, as an amount of money, or something that will bring money. The stocks, therefore, of different countries, are viewed as differing merely in amount, and every increase or diminution of the stock, of the same country, as a simple addition or subtraction, of an homogeneous quantity.[29]

A change in the amount of stock was not so simple as a change in 'the rows of digits employed to mark the amount of money by which they are estimated'; but this was not always recognized, and a number of fallacies had been the consequence.[30]

A FALLACY OF CLASSICAL CAPITAL THEORY

The rate of profit generally 'corresponded' to (which is not 'was the same as') the extent to which instruments had been formed up to the more slowly returning types. If the effective desire of accumulation was strong, and, in general, society had worked up instruments to satisfy it, the rates of interest and profit would be low. If the effective desire of accumulation was weak and, in consequence, society relatively poor, instruments would be of the quickly returning types, and profits and interest would be high. If, however, a wealthy country experienced a general augmentation of capital through invention, so that instruments, in general, were of the quickly returning type, profits and interest would also be high there. Eventually, when the preference for future goods, the effective desire of accumulation, had worked itself out, profits and interest would fall in the wealthy country, which would have become even wealthier. So it was that high profits and interest could indicate either poverty and a stagnant country with little capital, or wealth and a progressive country with much capital; and the level of profits and the interest on money could not be taken as an indication of the amount of capital, contrary to the pronouncements of Adam Smith, Sir Joshua Child and some other writers.[31]

This, then, was John Rae's theory of capital. It is important, not only as economic theory, but as economic theory in Canada. It corresponded to the economy in which it was expounded. It was repeated by later writers in Canada. It was the intellectual foundation of the National Policy of economic development in the immediate post-Confederation period. Whether the theory is correct in any absolute or ultimate sense is irrelevant to the purposes of a history of economic thought, but it did address and resolve the principle difficulties to be dealt with. It allowed of both a relative and an absolute measure of capital. It allowed that capital could be considered as a homogeneous aggregate, a sum of monetary values, for some important practical purposes, thus permitting comparison between the quantity of capital, the profits on capital, and the rate of interest. It stated, however, that relative value in exchange was not the same as absolute value, that, in fact, capital was a heterogeneous collection of instruments embodying human intelligence. On the basis of these distinctions, the theory separated capital accumulation and augmentation from relative prices, and the level of profit and the rate of interest from the wealth and progressiveness of a country. Further, on the basis of this separation, the theory provided the groundwork for a critique of the policy of laissez-faire, especially in a new and developing country such as Canada.

RAE AND THE ECONOMICS OF UPPER CANADA

As we begin to consider the policy implications of Rae's theory, and, therefore, its implications for the economics of Canada, a caution of our own is in order. We may speak as though Canadian policy was drawn reasonably from a reasonable base in knowledge, but we must remember that, in fact, the historical circumstances of policy formation are a much more murky business. We may say that Prime Minister Macdonald cited Mill, who cited Rae, but the historian, Keith Johnson, will say that Macdonald was in a drunken stupor most of the time and never knew what he was saying. Our argument has to be, not that policy was drawn reasonably from a reasonable basis, but that the persisting, underlying historical conditions of the country produced 'corresponding' observations, theories, and policies, despite the non-rationalities of the policy-making process. In early-nineteenth-century Upper Canada, as in late-nineteenth-century Canada (see chapter 7), it was the forces of history, including the rationalities and non-rationalities of people, that carried events to their conclusion.

Rae's identification of invention, as distinct from saving, as a sufficient condition for an increase in capital opened the door to some different policy conclusions; because it exposed the possibility that capital, measured in money, might be consumed in order to increase capital measured in absolute terms. Indeed, capital consumption might be directly related to an increase in capital through invention, and arguments found in *The Wealth of Nations*, to the effect that any reduction in capital in the form of a reduction of savings reduces growth, would no longer bear scrutiny.[32] The argument, also found in *The Wealth of Nations*, that taxes always reduce capital and so reduce wealth, could not apply when consequent invention reduced stock to quicker returning forms than the effective desire to accumulate would dictate; for then the return would be sufficiently high to provide for both the accumulation and the tax. 'Taxation [would] be paid out of revenue, not out of capital.'[33] Further, Rae concluded, any tax that went to foster invention would increase capital and wealth more than it would reduce it. In fact, in general, any change in the relative valuation of instruments that was associated with an augmentation or accumulation of capital would lead to an increase in wealth. In other words, any interference with relative prices, for example, by way of a tariff on imported goods, if it was associated with augmentation or accumulation of instruments, would lead to an increase in wealth.

By arguments such as these, John Rae sought to show the basic flaw in the system of Adam Smith, and to point out the conditions in which the policies associated with it were wrong-headed; but his attack was on a much broader base, and better organized than simply this. Smith was not only wrong in the specification of capital, a detail in his system, he was also wrong in basing all motivation in selfishness, with no allowance for social and benevolent affections, and, more seriously, his approach to his subject was unscientific, according to John Rae.

ON THE FALLACY OF SMITH'S SYSTEM

Consider the question of motivation, which Rae approached by showing a dichotomy between the acquisition of wealth by individuals and the accumulation of wealth by a nation. An individual might become wealthy by acquisitive redistribution of wealth among the people of a nation, but the nation itself would not thereby become wealthy. Even pages in *The Wealth of Nations*, according to Rae, admitted the advantage of the transfer of manufactures from one country to another in which they had not up to that time been pursued,[34] transfers that were not accomplished by the efforts of individuals acting alone. The start-up problems were too large to be motivated by individual acquisitiveness. Not unusually the transfers were made by migrating manufacturers who had been forced to leave their countries of origin for political reasons. Accordingly, any expenditure by the state which would spread the costs of importation of manufacturing over a larger number of agents and over a longer period of time, and which would provide security against the risks leading to failure, would lead to an increase of capital and wealth. Similarly, in cases in which the benefit would accrue to all of society and in some measure only[35] to individuals bearing the cost of importing the manufacturing, that is, when there were externalities, unless steps were taken by the legislator to have all of society bear the cost through taxation, the possible increase in wealth would not occur. Further, Rae continued, it is not unusual for the costs of those producing the first few items of a new manufacture to be high, but when the task is well learned and many items are easily produced, costs fall. Accordingly, protection for infant industries can lead to cheaper products and greater wealth.[36] In short, there was no necessary connection between the undisturbed self-seeking of individuals in the market and an increase in the wealth of nations; and the burden that Smith placed on the individual's selfishness as a source of development and growth was more than it could bear.

Rae was fully aware of the benefits of trade. His statement of the gains from trade in the presence of comparative advantages, elaborated without reference to David Ricardo, or anyone else, is clearer and more persuasive than similar statements found in most modern classroom texts.[37] Rae's point was not that Smith was all wrong, but that there were clear exceptions to his *system*; so, as a *system*, that is, as a general explanation of the economics of society, and as a basis for policy, it failed. Free trade was good in general, but not in every case. Where natural endowments were the basis of comparative advantage, free international exchange was the best policy.[38] Where advantages were not natural, but learned, they could be transferred;[39] and the transfer of technique from one country to another would not only increase wealth directly, but would stimulate further invention as the need to accommodate the production process to new circumstances was met.[40] Finally, the importation of luxuries, that is commodities which do not contribute to further wealth, would reduce the extent to which expenditures were made on instruments that do; so, any interference with trade that would inhibit the former and encourage the latter, again according to Rae, would lead to an increase in wealth.[41]

Rae's broad policy conclusions are succinctly put in the concluding sections of his book.

According to the view of the nature of stock, and of the causes generating, and adding to it, which has been given in this book, it would seem that its increase is advanced:

I. By whatever promotes the general intelligence and morality of society; and that consequently, the moral and intellectual education of the people makes an important element in its progress.

II. By whatever promotes invention 1. By advancing the progress of art and science within the community 2. By the transfer from other communities of the sciences and arts therein generated.

III. By whatever prevents the dissipation in luxury, of any portion of the funds of the community.[42]

The fundamental error on this subject of Adam Smith, and the present prevailing school of political economists in England, lies in their assuming, that what is true concerning an individual, is true also, concerning a community, and maintaining consequently, that every impost is so much absolute loss to the society, and every diminution of it, so much gain. Before this assumption can be made good, with regard to any particular impost, it is necessary that the three following questions concerning it should be determined.

1st Will the duty so levied, by directly or indirectly effecting an improvement in the arts, increase the absolute capital of the society?

2nd Will it prevent future waste, by the transfer of an art producing useful commodities, the supply of which is liable to sudden interruption?

3rd Does it fall partly or altogether on luxuries, and is its real effect, consequently, not to diminish, by so much, the annual revenue of society, but only to apply a part of it, which would otherwise have been dissipated in vanity, to supply funds for the necessary expenditure of the legislature.[43]

THE BACONIAN BASE OF THE SCOTTISH ENLIGHTENMENT

The basis of Rae's critique of Adam Smith's scientific method was drawn from the inductivist procedures Rae had found in Francis Bacon's *Novum Organum*. Smith, according to Rae, had a few hypotheses, about which he had gathered likely ancillary hypotheses and facts. The resulting system was logically consistent and did offer an explanation of much, but it was not based on the root causes of things, which could be discovered only slowly and by induction. Smith's system was about *relations*, not *causes*. It seemed to offer explanations on surface consideration, but, on further consideration, it became a means for explaining away inconsistent facts.[44] An hypothesis that something is so can be negated by a single counter-example. In the case of Smith's system there were many counter-examples; so, his system was fallacious, to use Rae's term, and, when applied in situations involving the counter-examples, it produced erroneous policies.

Rae, himself, did not have a system like Smith's 'system of natural liberty'. Rae had a theory of the augmentation and accumulation of capital on the basis of which he gave a new and, he thought, more scientific explanation to the important truths found in Smith.

The theory of exchange, in Rae, is firmly rooted in capital theory, and, in consequence, is an emendation of Smith's theory. For Rae, the extension of exchanges follows from an increase in the variety of instruments produced through invention. With specialization in the production of each of the variety of instruments, which is possible only if there is a concomitant increase in exchanges, a more intense use is made of instruments of production. This moves the instruments of production into more quickly returning orders, that is, they return what they are going to return sooner. Given a fixed effective desire to accumulate, this, in turn, leads to greater accumulation. For Smith it had been otherwise. The propensity to 'truck and barter', leading to exchanges, generated specialization, and specialization led to the invention of instruments of production.

THE ROLE OF BANKING IN ACCUMULATION

Rae's explanatory comments on money and banking grew directly out of his theory of exchange. These comments, which draw heavily on his observation of the Upper Canadian frontier, provided a firm, rational foundation for the idea of *national credit* or *social credit* that was the characteristic concept of a long and persistent line of monetary 'heretics' over a century of frontier settlement in Canada. The heretics forgot, if they ever knew, the foundation that Rae had given to their 'soft money' schemes (see chapter 6). Still, they knew there was something to the idea of monetary expansion, even though they could not rediscover it, or looked for it in the wrong place. That something, we know from reading Rae, was not just a desire to have the interest lowered on their, admittedly, often excessive debt.

The frontier of development, not yet having worked up instruments to the desired order, found more profitable use for its specie by investing it in instruments to be imported from developed areas; leaving it with a shortage of specie for the exchanges that would facilitate the use of the imported instruments. The first recourse was barter. The second recourse was credit at the general store. That allowed a time lapse between purchase and payment, and it permitted the settlement of debts between the customers of the store by an accounting book transfer of credit or debt. The third recourse was banks. This reduced the transaction costs of the storekeepers, who were not specialized in ascertaining the creditworthiness of potential customers and, consequently, were exposed to the moral hazard of default. By becoming 'the general lenders and receivers of society' the banks became specialists and did the job at a lower transaction cost. Further, with banks taking deposits, enormous economies were made in the use of specie, because payment could then be made by cheque. The increase in the 'celerity' of circulation consequent upon the introduction of banks, and the increase in the money supply with the use of fractional reserve paper money, made it possible to carry out more exchanges. This, in turn, made it possible to augment and accumulate more capital. In frontier circumstances it was altogether likely that an increase in the velocity of circulation, and an increase in the quantity of money, would be more than matched by an increase in production and exchange, so that the value of money would not decline, and indeed would probably increase.[45]

THEORY FROM THE POINT OF VIEW OF CAPITAL

Rae's book was about development and growth. Everything in the book is consistently rooted in capital theory.

> Adam Smith sets out from exchange, and makes it, and the division of labour consequent on it, the source of stock, whereas I have endeavored to show that exchange is the result of the increase of stock, and subsequent division of employment, that the necessity for its existence is a circumstance retarding the increase of stock, and that the benefits of the art of banking spring from the facility which that art gives to the process.[46]

What Rae would have said on other topics we do not know. According to Warren James, whose work includes a number of Rae's essays and articles, Rae's major work, a 'statistical account of Canada', was lost.[47]

Before we leave Rae there is one more passage from his *New Principles* to which we must attend. It adds nothing to what has already been said about the economics of John Rae. Its purpose is to accentuate a point that Rae made with respect to Adam Smith, a point to which we shall return in greater detail, citing other sources, when it is time to draw conclusions about the economics of Canada and economics in Canada.

> The celebrated author [Rae is talking about Smith] admits, that a manufacture may be introduced by operations of the legislator, sooner than it could otherwise be, and thus come to be made at home as cheap or cheaper, than abroad. But then, he says, in spite of these apparent advantages of

such a proceeding on his part, it must be wrong, because it is contrary to my system. And before you can prove that it is justifiable, you must prove that the benefits resulting from it could not possibly have happened some other way. [Then Rae cites Smith directly] 'Though for want of such regulations, the society should never acquire the proposed manufacture, it would not upon that account necessarily be poorer in any one period of its duration. In every period of its duration, its whole capital and industry might still have been employed, though upon different objects, in the manner that was most advantageous at the time. In every period its revenue might have been the greatest which its capital could afford, and both capital and revenue might have been augmented with the greatest possible rapidity'.[48]

Here we have Rae citing a passage from *The Wealth of Nations*, in which Smith makes the point at which Rae takes most offence. Smith is saying that the quantity of wealth is tied to the quantity of capital pre-existing the production of wealth, whatever else happens, and that there is no way to increase the quantity of capital except by saving, and that the possibility of underemployment of capital is not to be considered.

In the late 1950s, Hlya Myint[49] criticized J. S. Mill for criticizing Adam Smith for not, at one point, taking the line of argument that, in fact, Smith did take in the passage cited above. (We have Rae criticizing Smith for taking a certain position, and Mill criticizing Smith for not taking it, and Myint criticizing Mill for criticizing Smith. This puts Rae and Myint on the same side.) Myint did this in his elaboration of Smith's 'vent for surplus' argument with respect to primary product exports as an engine of growth. Myint's point was later picked up by Richard Caves, and misconstrued, and, later still, Caves's point was taken up by Urquhart. At about this same time (the 1960s) Harry Johnson and Ted Chambers took up John Rae's position with respect to the process of development and growth. (Neither made reference to Rae.) Chambers then entered into a debate, at some academic distance, with Caves and Urquhart over the matter in so far as it related to the historical experience of Canada. Johnson did not enter the debate on this level.

These matters, having to do with an underlying hypothesis of the present work, will be dealt with more thoroughly in the two concluding chapters, 10 and 11, but especially in chapter 11.

5 The Nationalist School, 1830–90

In the middle years of the nineteenth century there was a degree of independent growth in Canada. It was stronger, perhaps much stronger, in the Canadas than in Atlantic Canada; and its characteristics were different in each of the regions that eventually became Ontario and Quebec. What the precise balance was between dependent and independent development and growth in any of these regions, or in British North America as a whole, at one subperiod or another in the nineteenth century, is a question that has been pointedly asked, but not answered (see chapter 11). The political fractionation and geographical expansion that constituted Confederation eventually tipped the balance, for Canada as a whole, in favour of growth dependent on primary product exports; but that did not happen immediately in 1867. Between 1866 and 1896 there was a quasi-closure of the staple export producing frontier.[1] In those years the central Canadian economy grew at a steady pace, unaided by any significant expansion of staple exports.[2]

It is consistent with our understanding of economic thought as an account of the economics of Canada, that the middle years of the nineteenth century were characterized by theories and policies of independent development and growth, culminating in the National Policy of 1876. Even Craufurd Goodwin, who clearly thought protectionism was wrong for Canada, a 'rebellious policy', and a 'jump on a popular band wagon', admitted that most Canadians favoured protection in this period. His chapter on commercial policy, if we judge by counting pages and references to books written in Canada, is dominated by protectionist literature.[3]

We must emphasize, of course, that we refer to the National Policy of 1876. There was still a National Policy twenty years later in 1896. The National Policy of 1896, made famous by historians in the *inter bellum* period of the twentieth century,[4] was a policy of dependent growth, supported by the oft-mentioned three pillars: the tariff, the railways and western settlement, with the tariff being largely a revenue tariff to underwrite the building of the railways. The National Policy of 1876, in contrast, was a policy of independent development and growth, with manufacturing the targeted leading sector. When Macdonald introduced it in the House of Commons, it contained not even a hint of railway and agricultural expansion in the Northwest Territories.[5]

There were, in fact, two aspects to national development policy in the minds of economic opinion makers in the middle years of the nineteenth century: a fiscal aspect and a monetary aspect.[6] Only the fiscal aspect became law, as might have been predicted from the way Macdonald ignored the monetary aspect in his announcement. (His speech is quoted at length at the end of this chapter.) Why the policy of development by means of a national fiat currency was rejected is a separable story (see chapter 6). How the National Policy of independent development and growth was subverted, and became a clumsy and half-hearted attempt at free trade linked with vigorous agricultural expansion, is also a separable story (see chapter 7). We are here concerned only with the economic thought underlying the 1876 policy of tariff-generated independent development and growth.

The story of the National Policy of 1876 that we are about to recall relates only to that element of Canadian economic thought arising from the conditions of Upper Canada, subsequently Canada West and Ontario. To avoid misconception, we have to qualify the importance of that region in originating and implementing the policy. There was definite support for protection in the Maritimes and strong support for it in Quebec. Even British Columbia, in a moment of weakness in the late 1860s supported protection. Canadian policy was not made in Ontario alone. Indeed, it may not have been made in Canada. The United States was born with a protectionist bias rooted in the aspirations of Hamilton and Madison. Even in its most decentralized period, 1820 to 1860, the United States national government enacted 'The Tariff of Abominations' in 1828 and the 'Compromise Tariff' of 1833. During the Civil War, protection became an entrenched element in American fiscal and commercial policy, lasting without abatement until 1935. Given the importance of the United States informational environment for Upper Canadians, and the frequent reference made by Upper Canadian writers to United States literature, it seems a fair statement that Upper Canadian protectionism was part of a North American phenomenon. Our point here cannot be that Canadian policy was made in Ontario, but only that there was a deep consistency between the conditions of economic life in Upper Canada, the economic thought that grew out of those conditions, and the National Policy of 1876.

UPPER CANADIAN ECONOMICS: A CONJECTURE

Before reviewing the literature of economic thought in nineteenth-century

Ontario we must make reference to a certain conjecture about the character of the Upper Canadian mentality that has received considerable attention in the fields of history and political science.[7] While the general nature and implications of the conjecture are beyond our present concerns, the implied conjecture that grows out of it with respect to Upper Canadian economic thought is not. That conjecture is that there was, in the nineteenth century, an Upper Canadian Economics, in the same sense that there was, in the late nineteenth century, an Austrian Economics.

We have defined the economics of Canada to be what people thought was happening, or should have been happening in the economic activities of the country. It is made up of description, analysis and policy proposals. It is distinctive because of the specific environment of economic activity with which it deals. It is what I think Innis meant when he called his journal *Contributions to Canadian Economics*, though I have to admit that the conjecture that we are about to state haunts my judgement in that matter. Austrian Economics is not distinctive because it is about Austria. It is distinctive because it is rooted in a certain method of analysis and in a particular concept of value.[8] If we could establish that Upper Canadian economic thought was rooted in a certain method of analysis and a particular concept of value, then we would have established that there was an Upper Canadian Economics, in the same sense that there was an Austrian Economics. The conjecture is that there was.

The conjecture is an historical conjecture, so we turn to historical events to establish it. The account begins in England with the defeat of the Tories in the Glorious Revolution of 1688.

Having acceded to power in 1688, the victorious Whigs promptly divided into two factions; Court Whigs, typified by those involved in, or close to, government, and Country Whigs, typified by the conservative, landholding gentry. The former were less interested in democratic restraints on government, and more interested in promoting commerce and the Empire. They saw government as a progressive force in the economy, actively promoting industry and manipulatively restraining the factious democratic forces that would disrupt peace and security. Country Whigs were opposed to centralization and to any favouritism shown to commercial interests. They deplored the use of patronage as an instrument of state.

This division of British opinion, it is conjectured, carried over to America, where the Country Whig ideology inspired (or rationalized) the Revolution (the War of Independence) and became momentarily dominant in the Union during the early-nineteenth-century Jacksonian era. In England, itself, during the same period, the Court Whig ideology and policy was swamped by liberalism and laissez-faire, and had to stand aside, protesting, as the Empire was dismantled. In Canada, the defeated and dispossessed Court Whigs of the former New England colonies, took possesion of Upper Canada; and, even after British liberal policy had established democratic, responsible government, and after bouts of annexationism and free trade, the Tory party that represented them remained the dominant political force in the province. In Canada the Court Whigs came close to achieving what they had advocated for the American colonies for over a century, a federation within the Empire. As Adam Smith had pointed out,[9] federation, with colonial representation in an Imperial Parliament, would have been a device to permit the more ambitious in the smaller, distant communities to find a higher outlet for their energies, and to rescue the main task of government, the promotion of commerce, from the passion and tumult of the democratic spirit that characterized local politics.

What needs to be shown, if our conjecture with respect to the existence of an Upper Canadian Economics is to be credible, is that within the Court Whig ideology there was a distinctive analytic method and a distinctive concept of value upon which a distinctive economics was built. That there was a distinctive analytic method is beyond doubt. In the eighteenth century, Court Whig ideology had been formed by the outpourings of the Scottish Enlightenment, the analytic methods of which were those of the empiricists, Francis Bacon and Isaac Newton. That there was a distinctive concept of value, distinct, for example, from the subjective value of Austrian Economics's selfish economic man, is equally beyond doubt; for the Enlightenment's concept of man, rooted in the natural histories of David Hume, was that of a naturally sociable animal, moved by benevolence to seek the common good.

The economics built on this dual foundation can be found in the writings of Adam Smith, whose work, apart from his own theoretical innovations, which were derived from French Physiocracy with its policy of laissez-faire, and from a new and partially digested concept of individual liberty, was rooted in the informational environment of the Enlightenment. The Enlightenment's underlying concept of economic development was inseparable from Smith's four stages of growth. Except for his rejection of protection, which was justified on the basis of a theory of capital[10] that John Rae corrected, Smith's policy preferences were those of the Court Whigs. He suggested that domestic trade was to be preferred to foreign trade, because it generated more wealth.[11] The sovereign was to be assigned a supportive role with respect to education.[12] Both of these policy stances were characteristic of nineteenth-century Upper Canadian economists. Smith assigned to the sovereign a supportive role in the development of commerce, for example, when he suggested that a tax used to support improvements in transportation might reduce costs more that it raised them,[13] an argument used by A. T. Galt to justify the Canadian tariff of 1858.

There were two parts to Adam Smith. The earlier, theoretical, part of *The Wealth of Nations*, the part on exchange, the division of labour, selfishness and the natural system of liberty, was taken into the hypothetical abstractions of classical political economy. With those instruments nineteenth-century British Country Whigs decried the role of government in economic matters and, basing their arguments on abstract assumptions about a technologically static society, they proposed laissez-faire. The later, historical and empirical, part of *The Wealth of Nations*, the part that fitted more comfortably into the traditions of the Enlightenment, was taken into the economics that appears in the works of Robert Gourlay, John Rae and Isaac Buchanan, all of whom migrated to Upper Canada from Scotland during the period of the Enlightenment.

The conjecture is the following. In a supportive informational environment, generated by a remnant of Court Whigs in the United States, a more committed remnant of Court Whigs, reinforced by fresh infusions from the traditions of the Scottish Enlightenment, was able to hold a dominant position in Upper Canada. This fragment of eighteenth-century British society supported its policies with an economics that was empirical and historical, rather than theoretical and abstract, and with a notion of man as a benevolent, public-minded citizen, rather than individualistic and selfish. From its point of view, classical political economy was a fallacious concoction of hypothetical abstractions based on the presumption of mathematical regularity in a technologically and culturally static society. Its view of man as basically selfish and irremediably corruptible led to the pessimistic and hopeless conclusion that man could do nothing, socially, to advance civilization. 'The common feeling of the free traders is that everything should be left alone.... On the contrary, everything is improved by art.'[14]

The conjecture is not that the Canadian nation was formed and directed on the rational basis of a Court Whig ideology and economics. The conjecture is that there was an Upper Canadian Economics. The most that can be said with respect to the founding and directing of the Canadian economy is that it was, in its institutions and aspirations, consistent with an Upper Canadian Economics; because other forces were at work, forces that subsequently carried the nation in another direction altogether. The Canadian economic historian, Tom Easterbrook liked to repeat a statement referring to the Fathers of Confederation, 'They builded better than they knew'; which is another way of saying, 'They builded other than they knew'.

If there was an Upper Canadian Economics, it did not survive the arrival of the professional economists in early twentieth-century Canada (see chapters 7 and 8). Adam Shortt, yet another Scot trained in Edinburgh, rejected British, liberal banking theory in the case of Canada, because it was unsuited to the early stages of economic development; but Shortt's historical empiricism was informed by the German Historical School.[15] Harold Innis reconstructed the stages of growth, and theorized about the Canadian tariff in a way that was reminiscent of Smith, but, again, the inspiration was, ultimately, the German Historical School. The conjecture here is about nineteenth-century Upper Canada.

Having stated the conjecture, we will leave it. Even elevating it to the status of an hypothesis, without attempting to verify it, would not further our task, which is to outline Canadian economics in another sense. Still, to raise the issue of a *pensée économique au Québec*, or of a possible Upper Canadian Economics, is not inappropriate in a history of economic thought in Canada. We will leave the conjecture as it is to haunt our review of the economic thought of Canada West in the middle years of the nineteenth century.

THE DOMINANT PROTECTIONIST BENT

Protectionist sentiment in Upper Canada first appeared in the agricultural sector, and came to be associated with manufacturing only when a certain level of development had already been achieved. Craufurd Goodwin began his account of the literature on protection by pointing out that the first request for protection, voiced in the Upper Canada Assembly in 1821, was directed against agricultural produce coming in from the United States.[16] Probably it was direct evidence of the antagonism between Upper Canadian settlers and Montreal merchants. The latter wanted free trade with the United States in order to expand Montreal's hinterland. The settlers did not want competition from the American Midwest. Goodwin reports no theorizing on that occasion. In 1835 a protectionist bill passed the Legislative Assembly only to be rejected by the Council. The bill was a follow-up to a committee report to which there was appended a lengthy discussion of the arguments for protection and free trade.[17] We pick up the thread of analysis there.

Both sides of the question of protection were given consideration. The argument for free trade was common sense on the benefits of exchange. The argument for protection, stated with a positive tone, was given more space, and carried the day. Most of the presentation was drawn from United States sources. It featured the economic success of the Union. The United States, so the *Report* ran, had prospered under protection. Wages had risen above Canadian levels. The Friends of Domestic Industry in New York reported that the tariff had created a secure and stable market in which investment and invention had been free to generate growth. There may have been no burden placed on domestic consumers, because, when the protected country of import was a major market and the product was a joint product in the country of export, the burden of the tariff fell on the producing exporter. Sometimes protection was a good thing for an individual country. Britain may not have favoured protection, but Britain had already developed its industrial capacity. In America, the *Report* concluded, that was not yet the case.

The apparent complete reliance of the *Report* on the United States case and United States sources may be misleading. The case made is reminiscent of John Rae's more sophisticated position, and just a year earlier a group of Bostonian protectionists had had Rae's *New Principles* published to give support to their position. Goodwin remarks that it is likely that Rae's views had been published in Upper Canada even before that.[18]

ISAAC BUCHANAN: COMMERCIAL POLICY

John Rae had not finished writing his *New Principles* when, in 1830, Isaac Buchanan arrived from Scotland to represent a large mercantile organization. He became a merchant and railway promoter in his own right, and an active member of Macdonald's Liberal-Conservative Party. His biographer, H. J. Morgan,[19] credited him with a crucial role in the elimination of the Clergy Reserves, and in the establishment of the public school system. He was the leading figure in the founding of the Association for the Promotion of Canadian Industry in 1858, and he was still active and involved at the founding of the National Currency League in 1876. He was a Member of Parliament, and a pamphleteer.[20]

Buchanan's major work, *The Relations of the Industry of Canada with the Mother Country and the United States*, runs for 525 pages. The first 115 contain an introduction by Morgan. The last 125 contain some additional papers, an article by a United States protectionist, Horace Greeley, and an account of the founding of the Association for the Promotion of Canadian Industry. It is all edited by Morgan. The introduction is a scramble of lengthy citations from Buchanan's speeches, articles and pamphlets. The main body of the book is also a scramble of citations, but its content focuses on Buchanan's position with respect to reciprocal free trade between Canada and the United States. Morgan was not fastidious with respect to sources.

First and foremost, Buchanan was an advocate of Imperial monetary reform. Secondarily he was a protectionist, and not a doctrinaire protectionist. His principle objection to the advocates of free trade among the classical economists was a derivative of his objections to the gold standard and the way in which he perceived that system to affect domestic money supplies in specific international trade situations. He was in favour of free trade, if it was reciprocal, as in the case of the Reciprocity Treaty between Canada and the United States (1854–66), because if it was reciprocal it would not disturb domestic monetary conditions. There would not be an outflow of gold in exchange for an inflow of commodities. Buchanan would have extended the Reciprocity Treaty to form a North American common market.

Following the doctrines of H. C. Carey, E. Peshine Smith, and Horace Greeley in the United States, insofar as he chose, Buchanan objected to the advocates of free trade because of their unbending fanaticism. It was really the doctrinaire tendency of their style of reasoning that was unacceptable. He opposed the 'sophisms' and 'fallacies' of the 'Cosmopolitan' 'Political Economists' of Britain, especially of J. R. McCulloch. Trade policy should depend on circumstance, not on unsubstantiated hypotheses. Buchanan could see no problem of inconsistency in his suggesting that the Empire's manufacturing sector be decentralized by freeing up North American trade behind a common North American tariff.

It is very easy for those of us who are on the after side of Marshall and the marginalist revolution to miss the point of the mid-nineteenth-century protectionists. They were not opposed to trade. They did not think that Canada should grow bananas. But neither did they think exclusively in terms of relative scarcity and allocation. Low prices were not automatically associated with wellbeing. A low general level of prices was associated with depressed economic conditions. And, in any case, money prices were nominal. The real price of a commodity was the amount of labour required to produce it. Whether relative prices were related to relative amounts of labour required in production was an issue discussed by the political economists. The protectionists were concerned with the general level of the labour price of all commodities. That was, for them, the only indication of the prosperity of a people, and there was no necessary connection between that and exchange based on relative prices. If interference with relative prices would reduce, by whatever sequence of events, the general or absolute scarcity of goods, then that interference was warranted. Beyond that, the protectionists said what is now stated in any introductory text about exceptions to the doctrine of comparative advantage.

The case that Buchanan makes for protection begins with a glance at what had happened in some historical cases, an account of which countries were protected, and which were flourishing. The cause-and-effect relationship is asserted to run from protection to industrialization and prosperity. Case after case is cited: Germany, Russia, Belgium, the United States.[21]

His analysis begins with an assertion that no one consumes who does not first have an income from producing something.[22] The case of rentiers is not considered. It follows that a portion of the work-force not producing anything does not consume anything. So, if the importation of foreign-made commodities reduces a portion of the work-force to unemployment, consumption will fall by the ratio of their incomes, that is, the value of their erstwhile productions, to total consumption. The unemployed lose all their incomes. Hence statements such as the following. 'You are going to take off a customs duty of 5 per cent, but you are going to lay on a confiscatory property tax of 100 per cent.'[23]

The free trade response to this is, of course, that those who lose their jobs find alternative employment in an industry in which their country has a comparative advantage, in which their labour is more efficiently employed, and in which their incomes are higher than they would have been in a protected economy. For Buchanan, that is all hypothetical, and he produces historical examples: India, Portugal, Turkey, Ireland.[24] In those countries the unemployed in consequence of free trade remained unemployed, or found less remunerative employment.

If a country abandons free trade to take up protection it experiences the logical opposite to what happens if it moves the other way. 'If you develop your producing power so as to produce at home (although at one per cent dearer) what you used to produce abroad, consumers lose one where producers gain 100. The nation at large gains 99.'[25] Assuming, of course, for complete symmetry, that the country adopting protection has an unemployed body of workers to start with.

In this theory, attention is on increasing the general level of production, and on the level of employment. It is macroeconomic theory in which relative prices are immediately irrelevant. Hence statements such as the following. 'Reflect and you will find that the wise policy is not that which prematurely grasps anyhow at *cheapness*, but that which develops the producing power of the country.'[26]

Buchanan made a further case for protection on the grounds that the 'home multiplier is greater than the foreign multiplier'. He cited Adam Smith on this, and J. B. Say. Domestic trade was more advantageous because what was spent for domestic goods 'replaces another capital', which, for Buchanan, seems to mean that everything spent on domestic goods stayed in the country in the form of wages, interest, rent and profit.[27] This further case was not crucial to Buchanan. The argument from employment effects was crucial.

McCulloch received particular vilification as a fallacious political economist, because it was in McCulloch that Buchanan found a refutation of his theory of the employment effects of free trade. McCulloch stated that a shift to foreign sources would not cause unemployment, because the workers would shift to producing something for export to the foreign source. Buchanan responded. Not only was McCulloch's conjecture contrary to historical experience, but the conjecture was unfounded in theory. The foreign buyer would be supplied by the home producers who formally supplied the domestic producers who, in consequence of free trade, were unemployed and neither supplied nor purchased anything. To prevent unemployment 'a new double foreign market' was necessary.[28]

The Nationalist School, 1830–90 81

This convoluted explanation is not without merit, and it is worth unravelling in order to see the kind of economics with which Buchanan was working. Buchanan, himself, thought the point important enough to expand on by way of a 'numerical' example and a diagram.

Assume two countries, A and B; and two goods, X and Y. In autarchy, X and Y are produced and traded within both A and B. Now introduce trade on the basis of comparative advantage in which B produces X, and A produces Y. The first thing that happens, necessarily, in regard to production, is the cessation of production of X in A, and of Y in B. Market forces naturally bring this about. Once unemployed, through the cessation of production in the two countries, the workers purchase nothing, and the number of exchanges in the two countries, taken together, falls by half.[29] Buchanan cites Ricardo, *Principles of Political Economy*, chapter 26, on this, from a passage in which Ricardo stumbles into the admission while trying to refute Smith on the point of the home trade 'replacing another capital'.[30] 'The result is, whenever you import instead of producing, you are a loser by the change till your additional exports double the value of the new imports.'[31]

The argument was over the dynamics of the shift from autarchy to trade, and over the efficiency of capital and labour markets. If everything worked perfectly, there would be no unemployment, and with specialization on the basis of comparative advantage the workers in both A and B would be better off as a result of trade. Buchanan's point was that the static, mechanical world of McCulloch's model, in which this would happen, was a fantasy. Things never worked perfectly, but with the application of intelligence they might work better.

An argument that appears elsewhere in protectionist literature, that transportation costs can be eliminated by production within the domestic market, shows up in Buchanan as well. This would not be a sufficient cause for decentralized production if decentralization entailed a loss of economies of scale. Besides, if there were no economies of scale involved, market forces could be relied upon to move the locus of production, without protection, unless the vested interests of the carrying trade could prevent it. But, why should they? In a perfect informational environment they, too, would see the profitability of an arrangement based on decentralized production. They would undertake it themselves. The protectionist's point had to be that, in historical cases, the informational environment was not perfect.

Buchanan closed his case with a citation from H. C. Carey and an idea drawn, probably, at whatever remove, from John Rae. From Carey, reliance on primary product exports leads to resource exhaustion, whereas the source of manufactures is renewable. From Rae, it cannot be said that a country does not have sufficient capital to undertake manufacturing because it is 'manufactures that cause the growth of capital – facilitating as they do the development of the powers of man.'[32] It is not quite Rae. In fact it is a misapplication of Rae, but it is Rae's point that is being misapplied.

John Rae and Isaac Buchanan are an interesting pair. Both were nationalists. That is to say, both were protectionists, which means they did not think an international connection to be essential to development, growth, or full employment. Indeed, both held that there were circumstances in which tariff barriers would improve economic conditions. Both had monetary and banking theories leading to the conclusion that monetary expansion could be consistent with real economic prosperity. There the similarity ends. Rae elaborated a methodologically well-founded, formal theory of capital, a theory of long-term development and growth. His comments on money and banking belong to microeconomic analysis. Buchanan's approach was a tumble through aspects of short-run macroeconomic fiscal and monetary theory. Other members of the Nationalist School, John Maclean and J. B. Hurlbert, in particular, were narrow, standard protectionists in comparison with Buchanan and Rae, having little or nothing to say about monetary policy.

JOHN MACLEAN AND J. B. HURLBERT

John Maclean, born in Glasgow in 1825, was yet another Scot who migrated to Canada. He was a noted journalist. In 1869 he established *The People's Journal*. He became editor of *The Canadian Manufacturer* in 1881, and editor of the Toronto *World* in 1884. He was active in the Conservative Party. He wrote three books and several articles on economic questions.[33]

Jesse Beaufort Hurlbert, was a native-born Canadian of United Empire Loyalist parents. He acquired a degree in the United States, became Principal of Upper Canada Academy in Coburg in 1839, and Professor of Natural Science at Victoria College in Toronto in 1841. In 1891 he entered the Dominion civil service. Hurlbert stands at the beginning of the professionalization of economics in Canada. He wrote several books.[34]

Protectionist economics in the last half of the nineteenth century in Upper Canada (Ontario, after 1867) was less theoretically sophisticated than Rae's, and more formal and organized than the pamphlets produced in the tumult of Buchanan's career. The presentations were almost ritualized. First a critique of the then-fashionable political economy, its preconceptions, its allegedly scientific method, its specific arguments with respect to protection and free trade, and its policy conclusions. Then a repetition of standard arguments for protection, nothing beyond what Rae and Buchanan had said, but with more attention to immediate administrative considerations, and some new details. Hurlbert appears to have lifted entire passages from Buchanan.[35]

Considering the popular character of their publications, Maclean and Hurlbert allocate a remarkable amount of space to the methodology of the opposing view. The Baconian assertion that the hypothetical deductive method of the classical economists, that is, the ahistorical and abstract theorizing of Ricardo and McCulloch[36] is not scientific, is repeated again and again. Its allegedly true status, a rationalization of policy favouring a special class of citizen, is given more emphasis. For example, Hurlbert makes references to the 'tyrant traders of the earth', and to how England, having 'run mad with trade', had gone into relative decline in the last half of the century.[37] The problem with the deductive method of the Political Economists lay in its unverifiable assumption that there is a mathematical stability in the reaction of human agents.[38] Without warrant in empirical evidence, they presumed that economic activity tended to a state of equilibrium with the frictionless ubiquity of an electric circuit.[39] They asserted that value in exchange and the ratio of international trade to national income were the criteria of increasing wealth, when it was logically possible for wealth to increase without an increase in the ratio of trade to income, and relative scarcity was irrelevant to the general level of wealth. Accordingly, the Canadian protectionists claimed, the assertions of the Political Economists were both theoretically and empirically unwarranted. 'Cheapness' in terms of labour expended was the true criterion of wealth.[40]

For their own part the Canadian protectionists relied on empirical, that is historical, evidence,[41] and on Adam Smith's four stages of development. Prosperity and protection were shown to be historically concurrent, and theoretical explanation was provided by an assertion that different commercial policies were justified in different circumstances as defined by the four stages.[42] If a country was in the early stage of development, and was incapable of further development, then it should trade for the products that development produces. If it was capable of development, then it should seek development to avoid the inevitable exhaustion of the resources used to produce the commodities it had to export.[43] Canada was capable of development, so it should adopt a policy of industrialization, that is, a protective tariff.

In addition to the general agruments taken from Buchanan, John Rae, and Henry Carey, Hurlbert and Maclean had a number of detailed debating points to make. For example, given the difficulty of assessing income levels for direct taxation, the tariff was the most administratively feasible tax, and some tax would have to be levied to pay the necessary expenses of government.[44] If desirable, the tariff could be made progressive by being biased against luxuries.[45] Part of the tax would be paid by citizens of the countries from which the protected goods were imported.[46] And, finally, J. S. Mill had protested that a revenue tariff was incompatible with protection, but what he had pointed out, in fact, was that there was a trade-off between the tariff's revenue and protective functions. Both would be achieved to some extent.[47]

The picture of international trade presented in the works of Maclean and

84 A history of Canadian economic thought

Hurlbert, is one of open economic warfare in which the power of nation states to protect, subsidize, assist by way of conferred monopoly and by facilitating dumping was everywhere evident.[48] In the turbulence and uncertainty of such conditions protection would establish secure and stable domestic markets, in reponse to which, for example, agriculture could develop more efficient production techniques.[49] The problem was uncertainty in a number of ways. For example, while free trade on the basis of comparative advantage was the best policy in theory,[50] the existence of the comparative advantage could not be known until production of various commodities had been tried. Besides, not all comparative advantage was natural. Some advantages were acquirable.[51] The plea was not for protection in principle, but for common sense. The tariff was not to be applied in such a way as to prevent 'natural selection' among domestic firms, and not in cases in which there was clearly a natural comparative disadvantage.[52] In general the arguments for protection were rooted in considerations of technological progress, uncertainty and the dynamics of the system. On historical and practical grounds it was suggested that tariff protection could be appropriate in a developing country such as Canada.

FROM THEORY TO POLICY

The remaining members of the Nationalist School, the politicians who carried the policy into practice, were all Fathers of Confederation: D'Arcy McGee, A. T. Galt, and Sir John A. Madonald, himself. These are only the English-speaking Canadians, of course. Support for tariff-generated development among French-speaking Canadians and from the Maritimes, in the person of Charles Tupper, has already been mentioned.

McGee elaborated his programme of political and economic expansion in the 1857 issues of his tri-weekly, *New Era*. His goal was political union of the British North American colonies, their economic integration, and their political and economic separation from the United States. He wanted a new northern nationality, and for that to survive and flourish there would have to be an integrated and separate national economy. He proposed an intercolonial railway to facilitate specialization and trade between the Maritimes and Canada, and a tariff to ensure that the main lines of trade were internal, and not north and south between the components of the federation and the United States.[53] McGee, the spokesman for the Irish Catholic faction in Montreal, could hardly be called a Court Whig. He was a visionary. During the dealing and manipulation between factions at the Quebec Conference, McGee was silent. He approved the end result, not the means.

Alexander Tilloch Galt, whose motivation was doubtfully altruistic, but whose importance in the process of nation building cannot be denied,[54] was a typical Court Whig. His contribution to the literature on protection was an extended explanation of the Tariff of 1858, in which he alleged that Adam Smith's argument for tax-based public improvement of transportation facilities was, in fact, the explanation of his Government's fiscal policy.[55] The costs of transportation would fall more than the tax would raise the price of goods transported. In the end, the cost of the goods to consumers would be less than before the tax. So, Galt argued, British manufacturers would have a better market in Canada for having had a tariff put on their wares.

Macdonald was the quintessential Court Whig, managing the factions and manipulating the forces of democracy with patronage and programmes of development to realize the good of the Empire.[56] His contribution to the literature on protection was a remarkable speech in the House of Commons in which he announced his party's National Policy. It was the National Policy of 1876. Its desideratum was tariff-generated development, with manufacturing as the leading sector. Railways received no explicit mention, only a passing implicit remark, and the expectation projected was that population would move out of agriculture. This is not the agriculture staple, export-based expansion of the National Policy of 1896. Perhaps Macdonald was in a drunken stupor and unaware of what he was saying, but his speech makes quite evident what it was that he was unaware he was saying.

> When the opportunity offers, during the course of the present Session, I shall move 'That it be resolved, that this House regrets that His Excellency the Governor General has not been advised to recommend to Parliament a measure for the re-adjustment of the tariff, which will not only tend to alleviate the stagnation of business, deplored in the speech from the Throne, but also afford encouragement and protection to the struggling manufacturers, and industries as well as the agricultural productions of the country.'... I do not intend to enter into any long series of remarks on the great theories of free trade and protection; but one thing is very remarkable – that in all this discussion, and in all the various discussions which have taken place since the beginning of the Session, hon. members, or some of them, think that free-trade is political economy. Political economy in [sic] a great science, as yet experimental – a science which embraces in connection with the political system, in the widest terms, all that concerns the material progress and prosperity of a nation and of all nations. Free-trade is a very subordinate branch of it, but it is a branch; it has been elevated, and it was raised in the time of Cobden, owing to the great success of free trade in bread, almost to be a religion, and since his death it almost seems that it has been degraded into a superstition; but, Sir, free trade, as has been said again and again *ad nauseam*, must be reciprocal. Free trade, free intercourse between nations, means what the

word expresses; it does not signify that one nation must bind the other to that phrase, without regard to disturbing causes, or the situation of the nation itself, or of foreign nations, or the difference of tariff. Free trade does not mean that a country, under all circumstances, must open its doors to all nations, no matter what their customs may be, no matter what their financial system may be, and without exercising any judgement, or using any guard, or employing any protection with regard to the country itself; this is not the opinion of any really great Political Economist. This view is perhaps held by the minor lights of the Manchester School; but the great Political Economists have always admitted the existence of disturbing causes, and have always held that there are other things as important, and more important to a nation, than the mere aggregation of wealth, and the supremacy of free trade or protection. The collective interests of a nation must be considered. They are various, and a nation must stand on its own ground. Theorists, with regard to free trade, have laboured under a misapprehension, and have advocated a false science, opposed to the protection of the industries of a country under any circumstances. Now that is not the opinion of John Stuart Mill. His celebrated passage, in his book, which has been so often quoted, I will quote again. It has been repeated by him in the last edition of his book in the same words that it was in the first. His position has been attacked; I myself have heard it assailed by political economists in the Political Economy Club, in England; but this man, superior, as we have been informed by the hon. member for Welland, to Adam Smith, lays down in this work, which he leaves as his legacy, the principle that there are circumstances connected with the manufacturing interests of a nation which not only excuse, but justify protection.... This is the passage:-

'The only case in which, on mere principles of political economy, protecting duties can be defensible, is when they are imposed temporarily (especially in a young and rising nation) in hope of naturalizing a foreign industry in itself, perfectly suitable to the circumstances of the country. The superiority of one country over another in a branch of production often arises only from having begun it sooner. There may be no inherent advantage on one part, or disadvantage on the other, but only a present superiority of acquired skill and experience. A country which has this skill and experience yet to acquire, may in other respects be better adapted to the production than those which were earlier in the field, and besides, it is a just remark of Mr. Rae, that nothing has a greater tendency to promote improvements in any branch of production than its trial under a new set of conditions. But it cannot be expected that individuals should at their own risk, or rather to their certain loss, introduce a new manufacture and bear the burthen of carrying it on until the producers have been educated up to the level of those with whom the processes are traditional. A protecting duty, continued for a reasonable time, will sometimes be the least inconvenient mode in which the nation can tax itself for the support of such an experiment. But the protection should be confined to cases in which there is good ground of assurance that the industry which it fosters will after a time be able to dispense with it; nor should the domestic producers ever be allowed to expect that it will be continued to them beyond the time necessary for a fair trial of what they are capable of accomplishing.'

This is the principle laid down by Mill, the leader of the modern school of political economy in England, a Free-Trader in the best sense of the word. I say this extract I have now read applies to the circumstances of Canada. We are a young country, just emerging from the first struggles with the forest. We have but little realized capital as yet; the manufactures of the country, with a few small exceptions, having scarcely taken root. They are lying alongside of a country which has had the advantage pointed out by Mr. Mill, of having commenced first. The manufactures of the United States have been going on for a long period of time, and large amounts of capital have been realized: all these things we have to fight, in addition to the fact of our industries being in their infancy, and the other disturbing influences not alluded to by Mr. Mill, which add to the reasons why our manufactures have the same right to be encouraged that the child has to look to the parent for guidance until able to walk alone. Mr. Mills [sic], the Free-Trader, goes much further than many gentlemen in this House who will vote against the resolution. He does not speak of a revenue tariff which would afford incidental protection to our manufacturers as being justifiable, but he lays down the broad principle to encourge native industries; if they are fitted for the circumstances of the climate, soil and people of a country, protection ought to be given, and is justified on the true principles of political economy.

But we hear hon. gentlemen say it is not for the interest of the manufacturers themselves to have protection. It would create monopolies, and monopolies bring on apathy and lethargy. If Mr. Mills [sic] thought it was not in the interest of the manufacturers to protect them, he would not have said so in the passage I have read. He holds it out for the purpose of encouraging infant manufacturers in their struggling state, and lays it down that it is not only excusable and defensible, but justifiable. He thought reasonable protection would be for the benefit of the manufacturers themselves; but in this country we are not called upon to break our heads upon theories.

We know perfectly well in the circumstances of this Dominion, a young country extending from sea to sea, almost without bounds, that the development and improvement of our resources, the great works that will be undertaken by the country, will, for long after we who are here will be no more, call for a large revenue. If this be true, as a matter of course in the adjustment of the tariff, taxation should be so imposed as to do the least harm and the most good. We cannot have in a young and comparatively poor country like this, direct taxation. We have handed that source of revenue over to the Local Legislatures and municipalities. When you take our local rates and the certainty that in the not distant future the Local Legislatures must resort to direct taxation, you will see that source of revenue will not afford hopes of our being able to resort to it. We must trust our customs, therefore, as the principal source of our future revenue. Now, what can be more reasonable than to so adjust the tariff for revenue purposes that it will enable us to meet our engagements, and to develop our resources, the duties falling upon the articles we ourselves are capable of producing.

The Government of which I was a member since 1854 pursued the same course. They laid down this principle, that the taxation should be adjusted in such a way as to be as little burdensome as possible upon the people, and be placed on those articles which we can profitably produce ourselves. That policy was laid down strongly by my colleague at that time, the present Hon. Sir Alex. Galt. He laid down for us the principle of a national policy, that we should consider our own interests only, and that in an adjustment of the tariff we should endeavor to foster all these various industries of which I have spoken. We steadily adhered in practice to that principle. Sometimes when the principle of free trade or a cry for a reduction of the pressure of taxation arose we had to yield. We were overborne occasionally, and had to make some steps backward, but on the whole, we held steadily to the principle and carried it out as strongly and uniformly as we could. We were forced at one time to reduce the tariff to a considerable extent; at another time, not very long ago, we took up the national policy, which has been made a matter of ridicule, and carried it, certainly not by a large vote. With a very short sighted policy on the part of the manufacturers of Canada that national policy was opposed by them. If they had known their interest they would not have joined in the attack made upon it, and if they have, to a certain degree, had it recoil on their heads, it is because they opposed it so blindly.

I believed then, and I believe now, that the two must go hand in hand – that you cannot sever them. I believe it is the interest of the agriculturist to have a certain market at his own door. I believe it is not in the interest of the great agricultural community to be forced to look to a foreign market altogether for the sources of their prosperity and for their purchases. I believe no nation has ever heretofore, or will ever hereafter, rise to any eminence in civilization, the arts and sciences, or prosperity of any kind, unless it honours agriculture and encourages manufactures. To be sure, we hear from the Finance Minister – a gentleman whose parliamentary courtesy is only exceeded by his financial ability – that it would have the effect of driving people from the country into the town. It is not every man can be or likes to be a farmer, and the man who is unwillingly made one will always be a failure. There is no life in the world in my estimation more happy and enviable than a farmer's under the circumstances in which he is placed in Canada. It is a pleasant independent life, bringing domestic happiness and all that the expression implies, but still, all men are not to be farmers. There is the man of constructive genius, who feels that his function in life is to become an artisan or mechanic, to enter into a trade, or some of the other various pursuits. These aspirations of the young men of the country are not to be checked or discouraged. On the contrary, that country is the best and will be most prosperous where every man has the utmost freedom to choose that mode of life, and exercise the abilities God has given him freely and without limit.

It would be almost pedantic to refer to the those of antiquity, [sic] but looking at all those which have been civilized in the earliest history, sacred or profane, you will find that wherever a nation has emerged from barbarism they have built up great cities. So it is in modern times; look at the Hansiatic towns, the commercial cities of Italy and the Low Countries. But it is said, as a reason why we should not encourage manufactures, that it has a tendency to induce young men to leave the country and go into the towns. Why, the policy of the Government will not keep the young men chained as serfs of the soil in our land. Their policy will not send them into our towns, but into the towns of the United States, where they encourage all kinds of mechanical pursuits.

We have heard a great deal about this 'Chinese wall'. As I said a little while ago, the principle of protection, to a moderate extent is justifiable, and the true principle of political economy. If you build this wall it will be like a dam which backs up the water of a stream until it overflows the country and does a great deal of mischief, but if the dam is raised so as to allow a moderate part of the water to go over, that water can be used for fertilizing, manufacturing, and for other good purposes. Therefore, the proposition I would hold up is simply that the dam should be raised high enough not to retain the water altogether, for that would ravage the country instead of doing it a service, but that we allow a certain amount of the stream to percolate over....

But I tell the Hon. Finance Minister that he admitted there was such a thing as a slaughter market, and he had too much reason to believe our market was occasionally used for that purpose. Now, our manufacturers may be interfered with by this slaughter process from other sources, as has been argued. When there is a depression of trade in the neighbouring country, goods must be sold; that happens also in our own country. We see frequently in times of great depression, similar to the present, when merchants are becoming insolvent, every kind of goods thrown upon the market, and slaughtered, so to speak, to the great injury of solvent traders. That cannot be avoided, and it is right that it has the compensatory advantage of giving cheap goods to the purchasers. But it gives no real compensating advantage for the permanent real injury that is done to the trade of the country by the ruin of those merchants, and by the want of confidence thus induced by the spread of ruin, for the actual insolvent whose goods are slaughtered will make other insolvents. But while we cannot avoid that, and it is greatly to be regretted that we cannot do so, we can, to a great extent, regulate our trade so as to protect our dealers against the depression which exists in the neighbouring country. When it happens that there is a forced sale of stocks in that country, in consequence of which the honest trader is compelled either to shut up his shop, or enter into competition with insolvent estates, it is possible so to regulate the tariff as to protect our own people.

But besides the evil of making this country a slaughter market, there is another very serious one of sending goods into this country for the purpose of bringing down prices here, injuring our manufacturers, and driving them out of the market and afterwards getting control of the market. It is said that such a thing never happened. Why, do we not see it happening in our own country? Have we not seen, for instance, one steamboat line trying to drive off another steamboat line for the sake of getting a monopoly? Did we not see the Syracuse salt manufacturers sending in their salt some years ago for the avowed purpose of destroying our infant salt works? Do we not see at this moment the ruinous competition of two cables from Europe to Canada? Do we not see the Anglo-American Company trying to sweep out the Direct? Do we not know that in England railways are run against each other at ruinous rates for the purpose of getting control of trade? And then there are combinations of workmen all over the world together with associations of employers of labour. We have also the Iron Masters Association of England, and the Iron Masters Association at Pittsburgh in the United States, both of which are as one man: and therefore it is not strange that persons in the United States think it to their interest to crowd our market with their goods for the purposes of destroying our infant manufactures. If this is permitted to go on, the confidence of our manufacturers is destroyed, and their capital lost, it may be years and years before that confidence can be restored and that capital replaced. In the mean time, we shall have come to take the goods of the foreign manufacturers at their prices....[57]

Neither the economics of the Canadian economy, nor the economic analysis growing out of the economics of the Canadian economy, nor the policy growing out of that analysis, in the middle years of the nineteenth century, was substantially dependent upon, explanatory of, or directed towards agricultural staple-based dependent growth.

6 Monetary theory and policy, 1812–1914

In Canada, as in Britain and the United States, nineteenth-century monetary theory evolved 'hand in glove' with the evolution of financial institutions. Much of the theory turned on the question of the role of government in relation to changing forms of the payments system. Events, theory and policy interacted with one another in a tangle of influences and effects. The Canadian case was very convoluted. It was a product of its own distinctive circumstances, principally of the highly regionalized nature of its economic and political organization. It was also a product of ideas and market forces arising in the United States and Britain. In the United States political theories relating to the degree of centralization in the Union and the role of government in assisting economic enterprise had as much to do with monetary theory and institutions as did purely economic consideration of exchange and capital formation. There was an echo of this in Canada where Jeffersonian and Jacksonian attacks on the monied plutocracy had a familiar ring to reformers objecting to the privileged position of the colonial elite in the banking system of British North America. The geographic and economic proximity of the United States was matched by powerful influences carried to Canada by immigrants from Britain and by Imperial officials.

This short chapter cannot recount the richness of events and opinions relating to monetary theory and policy in nineteenth-century Canada West. Fortunately, there are other sources. Once again the account here can build on Craufurd Goodwin's book which refers to all the main works in question.[1] In addition there is Adam Shortt's awesome account of institutional and legislative developments,[2] E. P. Neufeld's masterful *Financial System of Canada*,[3] and R. C. McIvor's *Canadian Monetary, Banking and Fiscal Development*.[4] These supports notwithstanding, there are special difficulties in recounting the economics of Canada in the nineteenth century with reference to money and banking. Harold Innis, who dominated Canadian economic history in what must be considered its most flourishing years, dismissed Adam Shortt's work on monetary policy in order to tell his own story entirely in terms of fiscal policy. In consequence the financial and real aspects of Canadian economic development have never been pulled together. Little can be done here to remove this debilitating lacuna from Canadian economic history.

It is well to re-establish, as in the last chapter, that our subject is the economics of Canada West, that is, Ontario. In other matters it is not correct to think of *Canadian* economic thought as flowing from this one source. In the case of monetary theory, if we include English-speaking Quebec, it may be possible so to do. After all, the advance of monetary institutions was fairly even across the British North American colonies. Enos Collins's bank appeared in Halifax about the same time that banks appeared in the Canadas, that is, about 1820. The political reform movement in Nova Scotia under Joseph Howe was as much an attack on close colonial elite control over banking as were the reform movements of Mackenzie and Papineau in the Canadas. Everywhere the banks were associated with the cities that acted as centres to the multi-modal Canadian economy: Halifax, Quebec City, Montreal, Kingston, Toronto. This was the historical root of the oligopolistic character of Canadian banking. We may assume similarities in the informational environments in which these events took place. There were also regional dissimilarities, radicalism in Ontario, conservatism in Quebec, and a more rational responsiveness to the needs of trade in the Maritimes. But banking came under federal jurisdiction in 1867, so the system was homogenized. Gradually the functioning head offices migrated to Montreal and Toronto, and finally Toronto. The now centralized, homogenized, yet oligopolistic system has been a product largely of what happened in Ontario, and English-speaking Quebec, in the middle years of the nineteenth century. Rural Quebec had a distinctive monetary system. Our assumption must be that that system was subsumed into the commerical banking system of the cities, leaving no traces of itself, except, perhaps, in the role of savings banks in francophone Quebec.

External influences on the formation of Canadian banking are clearly perceptible. Domestic influences have been crucial. R. M. Breckenridge stressed the influence of Scottish branch banking, coming with the migration of personnel.[5] Adam Shortt stressed the importance of United States institutions as models, particularly the Bank of the United States, their influence coming by way of market contacts between Boston and New York, on the one hand, and Halifax and Montreal, on the other; and it is impossible to read Shortt's account without been impressed by the powerful position of at least one Imperial official who was awash in the theories of the English Currency School. In the end, however, it was the demands of a young and developing, and seriously fractionated, economy that gave the system its essential characteristics.

94 A history of Canadian economic thought

Nineteenth-century monetary theory in Canada turned on the nature and the development of the banking system. The banking system, in turn, developed in tandem with the economy. But causation worked both ways, and certain assessments of the nature of the Canadian economy in the twentieth century have hinged on the nature and functioning of the banks in the nineteenth. We must begin our account of nineteenth-century monetary thought with a review and extension of the development of the Canadian economy in those years.

THE HISTORY

The process by which Canada slowly achieved monetary, fiscal, and finally commerical independence within the Empire was accompanied by a gradual assertion of its natural internal fractionation. At the time of the rebellions of 1837 Canada was six separate colonies. The union of Upper and Lower Canada following the Durham Report was as complete as union would be in Canada. It was unworkable. Thereafter a process of disintegration set in. When Confederation and trans-continental expansion occurred between 1867 and 1873, four additional colonies and the Northwest Territories were tied into this process of disintegration. In the meantime responsible government in internal matters was achieved first in Nova Scotia, then in Canada in 1848. Autonomy in monetary matters was achieved in 1853 when the British North American currency system was unified by a universal, official adoption of the dollar as the unit of measurement.[6] Fiscal autonomy was achieved with the adoption of the tariff of 1858.[7] Dominion status came with Confederation in 1867. Full autonomy came with the Statute of Westminster in 1931. Between 1867 and 1931 the disintegrating trend towards provincial autonomy clearly established itself.

These political events were related to a number of technological and economic factors. At the beginning of the period the principal means of transportation were the natural waterways and some less than satisfactory roads. Between 1810 and 1850, the St. Lawrence River was supplemented with canals. Between 1850 and 1866, the system of canals was paralleled by a system of railways running from Quebec City to Windsor and Sarnia on the United States border. By 1876 the railway system had reached Halifax on the Atlantic coast, by 1882, Vancouver on the Pacific coast. During this period Canada may have emerged from primitive reliance on agriculture and primary product exports; but that is what is in question. Manufacturing, as a significant separate activity with an entailed labour market, appeared in Canada between 1850 and 1880.[8] As late as 1850, perhaps as late as 1870, there were hopes in Nova Scotia that deposits of coal and the proximity of iron ore would make the Maritimes the industrial core of Canada. The pull of continental markets and the availability of United States coal and ore frustrated these hopes. An industrial corridor grew up along the lower St. Lawrence Drainage Basin from Montreal to Hamilton.

The central question in all of this is whether or not the emergence of manufacturing delivered Canada, as a whole, including its far-flung western appendages, from substantial dependence on primary product exports. Was there a point in time, or a period, when a 'take-off' into self-sustaining growth occurred? Ken Buckley has suggested that the end of substantial reliance on primary product exports came with the termination of the fur trade out of Montreal in 1821.[9] Walter Rostow suggested that the 'take-off' occurred about 1896, but even this later date has not been generally accepted.[10] If 'take-off' did not occur, then, that it did not occur is a matter of considerable consequence in our understanding the debate over monetary theory and institutions in the middle years of the nineteenth century.

The question may be reformulated. To what extent was industrial development in Canada simply part of industrial development in the Atlantic basin, and so an entirely dependent phenomenon? According to Watkins, Levitt and Naylor it was, or it became, an essentially dependent phenomenon.[11] If Naylor's view is the correct view, the critical moment came with the failure of the National Currency League in its move to have a national fiat currency included with the tariff in the National Policy of 1876.[12] At that moment, according to Naylor, Canada succumbed to the reactionary tendencies of a financial system biased against independent development and growth.

Naylor's view has been given some support in a footnote controversy involving H. A. Innis, J. H. Dales and E. P. Neufeld. In that controversy attention focused on the persistent income differential that has existed between Canada and the United States. Although he did not put the question that way, Naylor attributed the differential to stuck-in-the-commercial-stage Canadian financial institutions. John Dales attributed it to the effects of the protective tariff, and, in a long footnote he took H. A. Innis to task for suggesting that the tariff was not a protective, but a revenue device to facilitate development programmes.[13] In a shorter footnote, Ed Neufeld rejected Dales's explanation of the differential, suggesting instead, that it was a consequence of Canada's 'conservative' banking institutions.[14] This is not to say that Tom Naylor and Ed Neufeld saw 'eye to eye' on the question.

What was established in this three- or four-way discussion was the potential importance of the evolution of monetary institutions for the economics of Canada; and so, also, the importance of the monetary theories underlying those institutions. What the character of those institutions was, what their theoretical underpinnings were, and why they were what they were is what has to be shown in this chapter. That the rate and character of Canadian economic development can be understood only in the light of

96 *A history of Canadian economic thought*

answers to these questions has a bearing on the Urquhart–Chambers controversy over the staple theory, to which we must eventually give our attention (see chapter 11).

THE INSTITUTIONS

As important as it is to our story, we will leave it to others to account for the emergence of the gold standard, and of central banking in Britain and the United States in the nineteenth century.[15] We proceed to a summary of events insofar as they affected Canada.

The nineteenth-century currency controversy in Canada, Britain and the United States began with events surrounding the War of 1812. There had been attempts to set up banks in Canada prior to the War. Probably they are best explained as John Rae explained them (see chapter 4). During the War, by way of the British Army bills used to purchase supplies, Canada felt the effects of an increase in paper money in Britain. Prices rose in wartime prosperity. After the War the Army Bills ceased to circulate and prices fell as Britain returned to gold standard convertibility under Peel's Bank Act of 1819. From then until the last quarter of the century, in Canada, as in Britain and in the United States, there was constant controversy over the payments system. There were three questions to be answered. How centralized (monopolized) should the system be? How flexible (variable in quantity) should the currency be? Should the currency be convertible into gold on demand? Those in favour of decentralization were not identical to those in favour of a highly flexible (elastic) issue. In fact, any one of the four positions possible on the basis of combining degree of flexibility with degree of centralization could be found in combination with either a fiat or a fully backed currency proposal.

The lines of the debate in Canada were set by Governor-General Lord Sydenham very shortly after his arrival in Canada. The rebellions of 1837 had occurred during the monetary crisis of the same year. In both of the Canadas, banking monopolies had been on the rebels' list of alleged injustices. Following the Durham Report, Sydenham proposed to reform the banking system by setting up a provincial bank of issue based on the principles of the English Currency School. Sydenham was, in fact, George Poulet Thompson, and had been responsible for the substance of what was to be the British Bank Act of 1844. His proposal was not accepted, but, in certain quarters, his theories were, and there were further attempts to establish a public monopoly of currency issue in 1860, 1866, 1871 and 1881. After that the idea was abandoned, not to be revived until 1933. In 1841 Sydenham was supported, though not wholeheartedly, by Francis Hincks, opposed by a reform faction led by Isaac Buchanan, and defeated by the political power of the established banks.

In his early-twentieth-century summary of these events, Adam Shortt explained that in a country relying heavily on one or two primary product exports, wider fluctuations in the level of economic activity required a greater elasticity in the quantity of money than would be supplied by the banking system of the English Currency School. It was the first statement of that version of the staple theory in which the liberal economics and policies of advanced, industrialized Britain were judged inappropriate for the peripheral, Canadian economy.[16]

An important motivation in proposing the defeated provincial bank of issue had been the large capital that the scheme would have put at the disposal of the government. The provincial bank would have taken in a large amount of gold from the chartered banks, used only a fraction of it to back its paper issue, with the rest being available for public development projects. Following another financial crisis in 1847, the Canadian government established free banking on the New York plan; allowing the new banks to issue currency up to the value of their holdings of government bonds. It was another way to put the capital invested in banking at the disposal of the government. By tying up their capital in low-return assets the scheme so reduced the free banks' ability to compete that they were eventually absorbed into the established chartered banks.

The next two attempts to establish the provincial bank of issue were really stages in the most serious and critical attempt to set up a centralized, national banking system in Canada. The chartered banks had expanded in size and number during the railway-related speculations of the 1850s. They were to suffer the consequences. There was yet another crisis in 1858, once again leaving the government financially embarrassed, especially since its own bank, the Bank of Upper Canada, was equally embarrassed. It could hardly go to the government's assistance when it was, itself, desperately relying on the deposit of taxes just to stay afloat. In return for a sizeable loan, the government switched its account to the Bank of Montreal. The Bank of Upper Canada failed in 1866, and in the ensuing crisis the Commercial Bank of Kingston also failed. The two bank failures bracketed Confederation. Twice during this period the minister of finance, A. T. Galt, reintroduced the proposal for a provincial bank of issue. Twice it was rejected. After Confederation, at the time of the first decennial Bank Act, Galt's successor, John Rose, with the support of E. H. King, General Manager of the Bank of Montreal, made a last attempt to enact the proposed government bank.[17] Once again the scheme was opposed by Isaac Buchanan and his irredeemable currency faction. Once again the measure was defeated by the combined political power of the established banks. More than the reduction in their ability to issue currency, the banks rejected the centralization of banking that would have been a concurrent effect. Most especially, the interests of Toronto could not tolerate the raising of the Bank of Montreal to the position of a central bank. Established regionalism in the existing banking system triumphed over the national banking system proposed by the Government and the Bank of Montreal.[18]

It may be that changing the base of the currency, and adding a central bank and a bottom tier of local, unit banks, which was what was being proposed, would have been more appropriate for an economy about to develop its manufacturing sector. But it is not correct to say that the new scheme was rejected because established commercial interests did not want the existing, dependent, primary product exporting economy disrupted, as Naylor has said. It was regionalism, not commercialism, that defeated the national banking proposal; and, in any case, it has not been established that the existing economy was substantially dependent on primary product exports.

There was one more attempt to reconstruct the banking system. The losers in 1871 were those who wanted a fractionally based, centralized government issue. Those who wanted a national fiat currency took their turn at the time of the Bank Act of 1881. In the years building up to the mandating of the National Policy in 1877, Buchanan's irredeemable currency faction, now led by William Wallace, formed the Financial Reform League of Canada. They were a significant minority within the Conservative Party and they were able to have a national currency added to the proposed national tariff to form the National Policy platform on which the Conservatives ran in the election of 1887.[19] When the time came for the Bank Act revision, however, the national currency group received only a gesture in the form of a limited issue of small-denomination Dominion notes. Two factors were paramount in this final failure. The first was specific to Canada. The commercial banks, now including the Bank of Montreal, through an organization that was soon to become the Canadian Bankers' Association, lobbied hard against the change. The second was international. The United States, the last holdout against the gold standard, returned to convertibility in the late 1870s. The whole world was on gold and stayed that way until the First World War, when controversy over the payments system again flared up around institutional change.

THE THEORY

There seem to have been six polar positions in the widespread debates over money and banking in the middle years of the nineteenth century:[20] centralization and decentralization, government regulation and market regulation, currency as money and bank credit as money. In England specific combinations of these polar positions appeared in the Currency, the Banking and the Birmingham Schools. United States preference for a decentralized, market-controlled system was evident in frequent, though not universal, adoption of free banking by state legislatures.

At the risk of grave over-simplification, in order to keep our story within comprehensible bounds, the positions of the Currency, the Banking and the Birmingham Schools have to be given precise definitions.

The Currency School embraced the quantity of money theory of prices. Money was a medium of exchange. If its volume were expanded prices would rise and wasteful speculation would occur. Speculation would be followed by financial crisis, as 'true' values reasserted themselves. In the view of the Currency School, it was best to tie the quantity of money to the quantity of gold, thereby obviating wasteful speculation and disastrous economic crises.

The Banking School saw money as a means for servicing loans to worthy industrial ventures. It was preoccupied with maintaining the variability, that is, the 'flexibility' or 'elasticity' of the currency. The quantity of money should have expanded and contracted with the rhythm of business, and not with the irrelevant vicissitudes of the supply of gold.

Both the Currency and the Banking Schools wanted the quantity of money to be consistent with the volume of genuinely productive business. The one wanted to avoid an over-issue with attendant speculation. The other wanted to avoid the recurring crises associated with panic conversion of paper into gold.

The Birmingham School considered a gold-based currency to be an irrational binding of industry to the quantity of gold. Money was 'merely a veil for goods and services'. Its quantity ought to have been determined by the quantity of industry, that is the productive capacity of the economy.

In Canada the Currency School position was expounded first by Governor Sydenham. It would have been institutionalized in the proposed, but never achieved, provincial bank of issue. The Birmingham School position was expounded by Isaac Buchanan and the irredeemable currency faction. It would have been institutionalized in the proposed, but never achieved, national fiat currency. By 1881 Canada had a decentralized, though oligopolistic, private branch banking system, rooted in Banking School theory. All three interests, the government, the banks, and the currency reformers, at one time or another, borrowed from or appealed to United States theory and practice.

Had the provincial bank of issue been established, Vera Smith would have had a case to prove her contention that central banks were established to generate financial returns for governments.[21] Whether the events surrounding the eventual founding of the Bank of Canada between 1934 and 1936, support Goodhart's competing theory[22] is a story for another time.

MONETARY THEORY IN NINETEENTH-CENTURY CANADA

We may begin with Robert Gourlay's remarks during the economic slump that followed Peel's return to the gold standard ending the paper inflation of the War of 1812.

> Suppose Government had continued transactions and expenditure to the full extent in peace as in war; only with this difference, that those to whom they paid out money, had been employed profitably and not wastefully.... prices would have been kept high and all would have been prosperous.... Paper has not caused the present distress, but the cessation of that activity which kept it afloat.... Let profitable employment be found for all that are willing to work, let Government again issue its paper in every direction where it can yield a certain return, and undoubtedly mankind may flourish in peace as well as in war.[23]

Gourlay's term 'profitable employment' begs the central question about which monetary theory in Canada, as elsewhere, would turn.

Goodwin has recorded a number of Canadian commentaries on currency and banking in the period preceding the crisis of 1837,[24] including John Rae's. Rae was not concerned with crises and remedies for crises. His approach was microeconomic, and so his work is outside the range of the discussion here. Beyond that, there is nothing to be added to what Goodwin has said. We may take up the story with the views of Sir Francis Hincks.

Except for his birthplace and his specific interest in banking, Hincks was typical of the other immigrants to whom we have had occasion to refer. He arrived in Canada from Ireland to take his place as an importer and merchant in Montreal. He subsequently moved to York (Toronto) where he became a promoter and director of the Farmer's Joint Stock Bank. In 1835 he joined the Bank of the People, a chosen instrument of the Reform Party, and he was manager of that bank at the time of the Rebellion of 1837. In 1838 he became editor of the Toronto *Examiner*. Having been elected to the first Union Parliament, he was chosen by the new Governor as a special assistant in matters relating to money and banking.

Adam Shortt remarked that Hincks had written well on matters of currency in his newspaper, indicating Hincks's adoption of the Banking School position. We can turn to Hincks's own *Reminiscences*[25] for a first-hand assessment of his views.

Hincks allowed that he had been 'struck by the soundness' of the Currency School view.[26] He approvingly reproduced Sydenham's memorandum based on that view, calling for

Monetary theory and policy, 1812–1914 101

a prohibition of the issue of all notes payable on demand by any but a [proposed] Provincial bank.

The notes were to be based on a fractional reserve of gold, but issued up to the amount of gold received by the bank from the chartered banks in return for the notes. The reserve was to be 25 per cent of the gold received. The remaining gold was to be used to purchase public debt, that is, to be lent to the government. The advantages of the system were alleged to be: (1) a secure, convertible currency, free from 'injurious fluctuations' arising from 'over issue'; (2) the return of the 'profit' of the operation to the state; and (3) the placement of 75 per cent of the value of the issue at the disposal of the Province for the execution of public works.

With respect to the proposal, Hincks stated,

> I was of the opinion at the time ... that there was a fatal defect.... The bank loans to the commercial classes, to the extent that they were based on circulation, would necessarily [have had] to be withdrawn with serious loss and a commercial crisis would have been the inevitable result. this might have been guarded against, by permitting the existing banks to retain their issue to the extent of their average issue, a course adopted by Sir Robert Peel a few years later.[27]

Hincks favoured the Currency School position, but only as modified to accommodate Banking School considerations.

The importance of Hincks's view for the economics of Canada cannot be over-estimated. He was Minister of Finance when the free banks were established in the early 1850s, and he was called upon to replace John Rose as Minister of Finance in 1871 when the proposed central bank of issue failed to pass the Commons, and something else had to be put in its place.

As Chairman of the Select Committee on Currency and Banking in 1841, Hincks cast the deciding vote in favour of bringing Sydenham's proposal before the House. Among the dissenting members of the Committee were William Hamilton Merritt and Isaac Buchanan. Merritt, who promoted the Welland Canal by issuing a variety of financial instruments, was the champion of free banking in Canada, opposing the system of chartered banks because it seemed to limit banking enterprise to a privileged few. Buchanan, favouring an irredeemable currency, represented the Birmingham School.

Among the explicitly listed sources of Buchanan's economics we find H. C. Carey, Bernard Byles and Jonathan Duncan.[28] The question is, which of these is the true source of Buchanan's conception of the nature and functions of money?

Carey was as much a historian as a theorist. His conclusions were comforting and useful to Buchanan, but he did not have Buchanan's concept of money. Carey's long disquisition into money and banking as 'instruments of association' was an argument in favour of free banking in which it was shown, on historical grounds, that the established monetary institutions of England and the United States had not worked as well as other institutions might have worked. Here, as elsewhere in Carey's work, one looks hard to find any theoretical analysis.[29] Buchanan's theories did not come from H. C. Carey. In fact, Buchanan's economics was well formed long before Carey's work was published.

Bernard Byles's little book, *Sophisms of Free Trade and Popular Political Economy Examined*,[30] is a more promising ground for clues to the roots of Buchanan's economics. It has the arguments and the mode of argumentation that characterize Buchanan's pamphlets. Byles treats 'the tariff question' and 'the money question' as elements of a larger question concerning the fundamental error of the free trade proponents who, allegedly, passed themselves off as the guardians of reason and science in what was merely the elaboration of a preferred system of social organization. Bernard Byles was not the source of Buchanan's economics, which were well formed in 1837, some twelve years before Byles's book was published, but he points us in the right direction.

Bernard Byles and Jonathan Duncan were members of a recognizable school in British economics. Both were respectable citizens of comfortable means. Both earned a place in Smith's *Dictionary of National Biography*[31] as, among other things, currency reformers. Judging by the theoretical positions attributed to or expressed by them, both were members of the Birmingham School.[32]

Led by the Birmingham banker, Thomas Attwood, the Birmingham School first came into existence immediately after the War of 1812 as part of the Birmingham Political Union. Attwood was a proponent of the quantity of money theory of prices, on the basis of which he argued that the legal monetization of gold would destabilize prices. With the monetization of gold the supply of gold and speculation on changes in the purchasing power of gold would not be isolated from the currency and the general level of prices. The flaw in the free trade system was not that it was for free trade, but that it failed to apply the free trade principle to every commodity. Monetization of gold would frustrate market forces in the determination of the price of gold. Indeed, he asserted, if the price of gold were as free to vary as the price of any other commodity there would be no need for tariffs.

Hawtrey has given some examples of Attwood's theorizing.

The laws which make food dear, and those which, by making money scarce, make labour cheap, must be abolished.[33]

at a time of falling prices money laid by in a chest rises in value while that employed in business or in the purchase of goods is a loss.[34]

There is sense to what Attwood was attempting to say. If all prices rose, except the price of gold, it being legally fixed, external demand for goods would fall off and external demand for gold would rise. Commodity prices would fall and unemployment would be the result. Attwood saw the downside of the gold standard mechanism for balancing international trade. So, he concluded, the 'employment of our own people', as opposed to the employment of the people of countries with which England traded, could be achieved by the demonetization of gold. There should be, he said, laissez-faire in the price of gold. A commission should be established to issue currency in sufficient quantity to keep prices steady and employment at capacity. The quantity of money should be regulated to keep the level of wages constant.

If gold was in demand, and goods were not, then the price of labour would be down in relation to the price of gold. So if gold was 'dear', labour would be 'cheap', and the doctrine came to be expressed in terms of the 'money power' and the 'labour power' of England.

The position taken by the Financial Reform League of the late 1870s in Canada was that of the Birmingham School. The Birmingham School had grown out of the consequences of Peel's Act of 1819. Buchanan's recurring reference to that Act as the beginning of monetary problems is just one of many indications that Buchanan should be classified as a member of the School. Some of those associated with him in the Financial Reform League, particularly G. D. Griffin[35] and Walter Arnold[36] held views that were quite consistent with Attwood's, and, incidentally, Milton Friedman's. The only thing that separated these alleged 'inflationists' from the doctrines of modern Monetarism was the technical means that were to be used in fixing the quantity of money once the gold standard had been abandoned. But we must come to the connection between the Birmingham School, the Financial Reform League and Monetarism more slowly.

Consider the position taken by Buchanan on the occasion of Galt's second (1866) attempt to establish the provincial bank of issue,[37] a position which he claimed to have held from the time of the Rebellion in 1837. He accused Galt of being a Political Economist, and of attempting to re-enact Peel's Act of 1819.[38] The problem with the Political Economists, he wrote, was their application of the law of supply and demand to everything but the price of gold.[39] The English system, he alleged, might apply in countries in which trade preceded banking, but, in countries such as Scotland and Canada

104 *A history of Canadian economic thought*

banking had to precede trade. International trade was important, but it had to be reciprocal trade in goods. The tariff would not be necessary to ensure this if there were free trade in gold, that is, if the price of gold were freed by the institution of a fiat paper currency.

In the *Relations* Buchanan's doctrine on money begins with a statement of the Birmingham School position.

> The money power of England vs. the labour power ... dear money and cheap prices and wages [are] convertible terms.[40]

He repeats, or his editor, Morgan, repeats the statement that 'the money question and the employment question are the same'. The style is Bernard Byles. The economics is the economics of the Birmingham School.

> the circulation is based upon and in proportion to GOLD, the rich man's property, instead of upon labour, the poor man's property ... that this basis is therefore a thing that can be sent out of the country; instead, in a word, of money being the mere handmaiden of industry. The superstructure can never be continuously large when its basis (the golden basis of our inverted pyramid!) is allowed to become small....[41]

The members of the Birmingham School were referred to as inflationists because they proposed to keep prices up by issuing fiat currency, and they had no adequate answer to the question of how much currency should be issued. Buchanan denied the possibility of an over-issue of a fiat currency, because 'trade can only absorb money to the extent of its transactions',[42] but his explanation of this was unsatisfactory. He really had no answer. Attwood had suggested that currency be issued in sufficient quantity to keep money wages constant. Perhaps he should have said, to keep the general level of prices constant. The bias of Attwood's successors in favour of labour contributed to their eventual fall from credibility.

An acceptable answer was forthcoming, however; that is, if the answer given by twentieth-century Monetarists is acceptable. The absolute amount of currency is not the important thing. That sets a level of prices to which the system can become accustomed. The important thing is to have the money supply grow at the same rate as real income. That way there are no changes in the general level of prices. Milton Friedman's answer was to use an average of past annual growth rates of real income as a guide to the rate of increase in the money supply.[43] A *similar* answer was given by one of Canada's Currency Reform Leaguers as early as 1861. Walter Arnold, assuming that the 'stability and uniformity of [the currency's] value [was] almost as essential as the establishment of property itself', proposed the following,

> As regards the limit of the issue of a paper currency, due regard should be

had to the trade and business habits of a people, and an estimate should be made of the ratio that the amount of the currency should bear to population. This estimate once made, that ratio should always be observed; for as population increases business will also increase, and to keep up the relation between money and capital, an enlargement of the currency should take place. I believe no better plan can be adopted. By this means the currency would be steady in amount, and fluctuations in its value would depend only on a change in the ratio commodities bore to it. In a normal condition of things, this would be continually increasing and the movement of the currency would be towards a gradual increase in value; it would not be subject to those great rises and falls that now disconcert everyone. Opdyke in his *Political Economy*, published in 1851, and from statistics previous to 1846, says: 'The natural ratio of money, when expressed in dollars, to population in the United States is as 15 to 1.' That country may be considered as a fair standard by which to estimate the quantity of money required by this country; taking this ratio and our population to be 1,750,000, the Government might issue $41,250,000 of paper money and small change, and by this much reduce the public debt.[44]

Adherents of the Banking School found such views abhorrent. In their opinion the quantity of money should have been variable, depending on business conditions. The volume of credit was not something that could be determined once and for all. When confronted with a similar, non-Banking School assertion in Irving Fisher's proposed compensated dollar, Adam Shortt lumped the views of the 1850s and of the second decade of the twentieth century into one mistake. The idea that a managed currency could stabilize prices was an illusion in which people 'comforted themselves with theories of cause and effect which [could] be traced with mathematical accuracy, and with remedies that could be applied with mathematical precision'.[45]

Before leaving this general treatment of monetary thought in Canada West it is necessary to emphasize our admission that we have had to over-simplify in order to keep the story from falling into confusion. In fact, positions and factions were constantly changing, and never perfectly in line with the categories into which they have been put. For example, it was ironic that the final answer to the problems raised by the Birmingham School was as mathematical as the theories of the Political Economists whom they ridiculed for being mathematical in their approach to human behaviour. Indeed, many members of the Birmingham School would not have accepted Walter Arnold's answer. They were generally biased in favour of labour and of an increasing ratio of money to goods. They *were* inflationists. Hawtrey

106 A history of Canadian economic thought

attributed their demise as a recognizable faction to the rise in prices following the California Gold Rush of 1849. It eliminated the problem on which, after the departure of Attwood, they had chosen to focus their attention.

The same fluidity characterized American positions. Bray Hammond found that the attitude of the United States frontier states towards banking changed with the advent of capitalized, commercial farming. In the early half of the nineteenth century the frontier was conservative. The inflationist bias of populism did not appear until the second half of the century.[46] In Canada support for currency reform, that is for a national fiat currency, changed after the opening of the Prairies. The idea that radical currency reform moved west with an agricultural frontier[47] is insupportable. Currency reform in the middle years of the nineteenth century in Canada was an urban, business-oriented movement. Adam Shortt associated the National Currency League with an 'Agricultural Banking Scheme',[48] but he mentioned no farmers or farmers' organizations in support of the League, and contemporary accounts leave the impression that there were none.[49] Shortt's account, like those of so many others after the opening of the West, was shaped by contemporary problems, which he read into the more distant past. In any case, Shortt attempted to belittle the Birmingham position by associating it with late-nineteenth-century United States Populism. His opinions of the 'soft money' faction were hostile, and so, not to be trusted. Bray Hammond was right. It was not the sector of the economy that inspired fresh approaches to monetary institutions, but the structure of debt, in whatever sector.

The Birmingham School died out in England. In Canada it was kept alive by the Financial Reform League and the agrarian reformers of the new West. William Wallace was the principal spokesman of the movement from the founding of the Financial Reform League until the early twentieth century, when leadership passed to George Beavington and William Irvine of the United Farmers of Alberta, and eventually to William Aberhart of the Social Credit Crusade. Perhaps Major Douglas's ideas, originating as they did in England, also had their roots in the Birmingham School. If so, then the adoption of some of his terminology by the reformers of western Canada in the 1920s was a reunification of two streams of monetary thought that had separated about fifty years earlier.

Having dealt with the historical, institutional and intellectual context of nineteenth-century Canadian monetary and banking theory, and with the major schools of thought involved, we can now turn to treatment of some of the details.

FROM 1860 TO 1920

With some oversimplification, as we have admitted, the writers can be categorized into the accepted positions. In the Currency School there was G. Manigault and G. E. Casey.[50] In the Banking School, Francis Hincks, H. B. Willson, William Brown[51] and Adam Shortt. In the Birmingham School, everyone else, except Thomas Galbraith, who belongs with the promoters of the Crédit Fonçier movement in Quebec.

Galbraith proposed the following basis for the currency: the function of currency was to put the capital of a nation to work. Accordingly, money should be issued up to the value of the nation's capital. Since every farm is capital, every farmer should be able to borrow money, by way of an issue of currency, up to the value of his farm. Galbraith's proposal was a combination of the Birmingham School and the Crédit Fonçier ideas.[52]

Hugh Bowlby Willson, a lifelong friend of John Rae, will serve as an example of the Currency School. Willson was an annexationist who spent much of his time in the United States and in Britain. He wrote four pamphlets and a book on monetary policy, all intended for the wider Anglo-American audience.[53] Willson had a central proposal which he repeated several times. Banking ought to be separated from the issue of currency. The issue of currency should be the function of a department of government – other than the department of finance, to prevent conflict of interest. The currency ought to be convertible into gold. The government department, under a Board of Control, should operate so as to avoid 'the injurious effect from an indiscriminate issue of bank notes'.[54] As to what principle would guide the Board in its issuing currency to avoid injurious effects, Galbraith was never quite forthcoming. The Board 'will in a few years, be able to ascertain with tolerable accuracy the amount required by the law of supply and demand'.[55] Should independent, government control over the issue of currency have been established, Galbraith would then have been in favour of free banking.

The monetary theory of W. A. Thompson[56] exemplifies the consistency between the Canadian currency reform position[57] and the position of the Birmingham School. To some extent Thompson's position was influenced by the agrarian and development orientations of nineteenth-century Canada, but its core was the short-run, macroeconomic concerns of his British forerunners. The solution to the problem of recurring crises, according to Thompson, was an irredeemable, paper currency, issued by a 'Bureau of Production' in sufficient quantity to prevent unemployment and to remove the need for tariff protection. 'No people, under a natural money can produce more, in the aggregate, than it can consume'.[58]

There seems little doubt that the 'rag botheration' faction that had been ejected from the Birmingham Political Union by the Chartists in the 1840s survived in Canada in the form of the Financial Reform League, the so-called 'Rag Babies', of late-nineteenth-century Canada. Speaking in the House of Commons, the leader of the Financial Reform League insisted that the

108 A history of Canadian economic thought

expansiveness of money based on gold was 'not in equal ratio to the expansiveness of the industry of the world'. If the monetary system was to be adequate, he said, industry itself, that is, the productivity of labour, would have to be accepted as the basis of 'natural credit'. He pointed out that foreign money lenders had shown sufficient confidence in the productivity of Canadian labour. Could not the Canadian government show the same confidence? Why pay interest to foreign money lenders when the Canadian government could itself issue money to the labour, equipment and resources of the nation, thus eliminating depressions and permitting the nation to grow on its own capabilities. It would eliminate the need for the tariff, because 'Money which is not exportable, which cannot be sent to buy foreign goods, is the truest and best system of protection'.[59]

Of all the monetary views in Canada in the nineteenth century, that of the national fiat currency faction was at once the most persistently put forward and the least successful in the policy-making process. The Banking School faction, having the reactionary force of Canadian regionalism on its side, was the political winner. Thomas Naylor, making no reference to the theoretical roots of nineteenth-century Canadian institutions and policies, flattered the chartered banks when he suggested that by sheer political power they prevented reform in order to preserve an alleged dependent, commercial character of the economy. In fact, their position was respectably consistent with that of the Banking School. Their political strength was not theirs, but that of the natural fractionation of the Canadian economy. Apart from these distinctively Canadian considerations, the Currency School and the Birmingham School positions failed to carry the day in Canada for the same reasons that they failed everywhere in the industrialized world between 1880 and 1930.

The view that nineteenth-century Canadian monetary history is an account of the success of a reactionary, staple-export-oriented set of financial institutions ignores both the real economics and the informational environment in which the alleged reactionary success took place.

7 Some intrusions of history, 1890–1930

There were at least four major intellectual influences in Canadian economic thought between 1890 and 1930: neoclassical economics, historical economics, positive liberalism, and imperialism. The first three of these were elements in the informational environment of the whole of the industrialized world. The fourth was unique to the British Empire.

The impact on Canadian economic thought of the four intellectual influences, was dependent on two historical factors. The first of these was the geographic and political expansion of Canada. It occurred between 1867 and 1873, but it had its most dramatic effect on the economics of the country between 1890 and 1930. The second was the emergence of an economics profession, which, in conjunction with the other influences, changed the style and content of economic thought, though it produced little more than a *potpourri* of incomplete initiatives until after the First World War.

The terms used to describe the four intellectual influences have been much used. They carry different meanings to the adherents of different schools of thought. Perhaps they should not be used at all anymore. Still, it would be an impossible task to rewrite Canadian economic thought without using them, because the confusion and misunderstanding surrounding the terms is, itself, part of the story. So we must generate statements of the meanings that are to be attached to each of the four terms.

NEOCLASSICAL ECONOMICS

In our description of the nature and evolution of the neoclassical paradigm we will be relying on certain sources. We will be disciplined not by the content of our sources,[1] however, but by the nature and development of Canadian economic thought. The period covered will stretch from 1870 to 1940, to allow us to say what needs to be said to support our treatment of Canadian thought to the end of the Second World War. A further statement of the nature of neoclassical economics will be necessary for the period after the Second World War (see chapter 9).

The emergence of the neoclassical paradigm, sometimes called the marginalist revolution, was based on two innovations: an analytical technique, centreing on the use of first and second derivatives as defined in Calculus, to establish equality of costs and benefits in the maximizing process of human behaviour; and a theory of relative value dependent upon the interaction of market demand and supply. The perception that maximization is tautologically present in all human behaviour, regardless of individual goals, was only implicit in the paradigm at the time of its emergence, say, about 1870. Whether so directed by their innovations or not, the marginalists tended to focus their attention on the microeconomic behaviour of consumers and producers, and on the market structures within which that behaviour took place. That is to say, in short, that the marginalists undertook to establish the subjective and objective conditions of rational behaviour using static, partial equilibrium analysis. Establishing the subjective conditions took time and some aggressive prodding on the part of their critics. Eventually the principles involved were used to elaborate general equilibrium models of market systems.

The process by which neoclassical analysis purged itself of value-laden preconceptions inherited from classical Political Economy is particularly interesting insofar as the main thrust of Canadian economic thought in the nineteenth and early twentieth centuries was critical of Political Economy and of its preconceptions as they appeared, or appeared to appear, in the neoclassical paradigm. In all probability the Canadians did not choose sides on abstract theoretical grounds, but because they were concerned with a young and rapidly developing economy in which very long-run factors, outside the scope of Political Economy and neoclassical analysis, were paramount. Still they made their choice, and we have to note that the scientific underpinning of their approach was going to be downgraded when the neoclassical paradigm eventually purged itself of offending elements.

An historicist critique of the old Political Economy was alive in the German Historical School before the marginalist revolution occurred; and the revolution, though not generated by that critique, was profoundly shaped by it.[2] What Lionel Robbins reported in 1932[3] was the extraction of economic analysis from those things that the historicists had criticized in it; that is, from any reliance on Hedonism or individualistic legal institutions, or indeed, from any first instance reliance on specific values or empirically falsifiable propositions.

The evolution of the neoclassical paradigm under criticism did not stop with Lionel Robbins's *Essay*, however, it simply took another turn. Economic thought in Canada received the paradigm during this next turn.

For Robbins, neoclassical analysis was beyond falsification, because its general equilibrium models, based on presumptions of subjective and objective rationality, contained no empirical content to be tested. Not surprisingly, then, by the mid-1930s it had become fashionable to contrast the actual working of the economy with neoclassical abstractions assuming perfect competition and perfect knowledge. This was the source of the controversy over imperfect competition in which Joan Robinson first made an appearance. It was the source of J. M Keynes's analysis of the implications of irrational expectations in economic behaviour. In response to the new challenge, beginning with R. H. Coase's 'The Nature of the Firm',[4] those whom we shall call the New Institutionalists began analysis of market failures, non-market institutions, and decision-making in less than perfect informational environments. From discussions surrounding these concerns in their earliest days, H. A. Innis drew the economic theory underlying his study of the bias of communications – monopolies of knowledge, imperfect competition, and decision-making in biased information environments. After a neoclassical Keynesian paradigm had been displaced by yet other macroeconomic paradigms, that is, after 1970, the New Institutionalist neoclassical analysis emerged as a significant, if not dominant, element in Canadian economic thought.

But we are ahead of ourselves. In the 1890–1930 period it was not neoclassical analysis, but its critics, historical economists and old style Institutionalists, who influenced Canadian economic thought directly. Which is not to say that either the German Historical School or United States Institutionalism were accepted without modification.

HISTORICAL ECONOMICS

The German Historical School, in protest against the hypothetical abstractions and institutional biases of classical Political Economy, undertook inductive formulation of scientific laws of economic development. Society was to be described in terms of concepts similar to the stages of development posited by Adam Smith, that is to say, in terms of different 'styles' of behaviour or sets of values and institutions called 'ideal types'.[5] In its United States incarnation, the 'old Institutionalism', historical economics attempted to abandon all abstraction in favour of description of the economic effects of technical and institutional constraints. Thorstein Veblen assigned no scientific importance to indeterminate choice, treating everything in human behaviour as externally determined or mindlessly instinctive. A less radical attempt to reconstruct economics historically had appeared in England in the work of Cliff Leslie, J. K. Ingram and W. J. Ashley. First-generation Canadian professional economists, Adam Shortt and James Mavor were directly influenced by this group. W. J. Ashley held the first Chair in Economics at the University of Toronto. O. D. Skelton, another first-generation Canadian professional, studied under Veblen. Harold Innis and Stephen Leacock were also influenced by Veblen; but again we are getting ahead of ourselves.

POSITIVE LIBERALISM

A third important intellectual influence in Canadian economic thought between 1890 and 1930 was positive liberalism. Since we are about to define what we are to understand by this term we can use the value-laden term 'socialism' to designate what we mean by it. The socialism with which we are concerned was not Marxian socialism, opinions expressed at the time of the Winnipeg General Strike in 1919 notwithstanding. Marxian analysis did not appear as a significant element in Canadian economic thought until the 1930s, and had little academic respectability until the advent of the New Political Economy in the 1970s; but this will be dealt with elsewhere. The socialism with which we are now concerned is the positive liberalism that was recognized as socialism by Canadian economists before the 1930s. In Canada, as in the United States, socialist aspirations were rooted in neoclassical, not Marxian analysis. R. T. Ely's definition of socialism[6] was consistent with O. D. Skelton's[7] neoclassical critique.

Skelton defined socialism as a dozen indictments of the then existing social system. They fell into three categories. In the first category were criticisms rooted in the moral thrust of conscientious people hoping to improve human conditions in their immediate environment. These criticisms focused on such undesirables as poverty, slums, unhealthy working conditions, uncertain employment and income, and the disintegration of family life that accompanied these things. The second category of criticisms centred on what the New Institutionalists now call 'market failures': inefficiencies associated with common property, excess capacity in oligopolistic and competitive markets, non-informative advertising, the existence of fraud, theft and misinformation at every level of industrial and financial activity (moral hazard, asymmetric information and transactions costs), and the absence of a property right in labour. The third category consisted of a single indictment of the system, pervasive misinformed and mismatched decisions that induced recurring crises and bouts of unemployment. Positive liberalism was the ideology that held that social intervention should be used to remove these problems from the economic system. When it appeared in late-nineteenth-century Canada it was compounded with imperialism, international laissez-faire, and United States yellow journalism. We will have to trace its beginnings in free trade doctrines of the middle years of the nineteenth century.

IMPERIALISM

The fourth intellectual influence on Canadian economic thought was Imperialism. It was far more important in the informational environment of late-nineteenth-century Canada than its meagre contribution to economic thought would indicate. The Imperialists were Court Whigs who held gallantly to a positive concept of empire when 'little Englandism', free trade, and self governance for the colonies were in high fashion. The Imperialists saw the Empire as a constructive instrument in the advance of civilization. An active imperialism, in their view, would solve the problems of unemployment and social unrest 'at home' by adopting policies of constructive expansion in the colonies. Specifically, in the case of Canada, they promoted the construction of a transcontinental railway.[8] They also suggested protection of infant industries, and an issue of paper currency to finance expansion, but they were not in the same category as the members of the Nationalist or the Birmingham Schools in Canada. The Imperialists were not really Canadian, they were citizens of the British Empire who happened to be in Canada. They were not really theorists, even of the rank of the average theorist in Canada. They were promoters and doers.

Once the building of the railways began in earnest, the Imperialists generated propagandistic support for almost any kind of government intervention in the construction of the Empire, which they saw to be the construction of civilization.[9] The role of the United States engineer, William Van Horne, notwithstanding, it was Imperialists such as Sir Sanford Fleming who planned and built the railways and telegraph lines, and who projected the steamship lines that the railways complemented. Not only can the history of late-nineteenth-century Canadian expansion be told in terms of Imperial expansion, there seems to be no way to tell it without some reference to Imperialism.[10]

We come then to the first of the exogenous factors in the evolution of Canadian economic thought between 1890 and 1930, the geographic and political expansion of Canada from a 75-mile-wide strip along the lower Great Lakes and the St. Lawrence River to half a continent stretching from the Pacific to the Atlantic Ocean, and from the 42nd parallel to the geographic north pole.

GEOGRAPHIC AND POLITICAL EXPANSION

The acquisition of the Northwest Territories abruptly redirected the growth path of Canada. Thought and policy associated with the relative economic independence of mid-nineteenth-century Canada became inappropriate even as it was being embodied in the National Policy of 1876. Annexation of the Hudson Bay Territory was not part of an economic development plan according to which Canada was to grow on the basis of a wheat export from the Prairies, though it has been an irresistible temptation to tell the story as if that were the case. In one place, Ken Buckley asserted that in the 1870s it was 'widely expected' that wheat would be exported from the new west, and that central Canada would grow as a result of forward and backward linkages to the wheat export. To back up his statement he referred to a passage in W. A. Mackintosh's study for the late 1930s Royal Commission on Dominion–Provincial Relations, in which Mackintosh cited a Budget Speech delivered by Samuel Leonard Tilley on April 1, 1873.[11] So, what was 'widely expected' depends on whether Sam Tilley (heading into an election in which his government would be defeated, largely because it was caught accepting money from United States railway promoters looking for the contract to build the Canadian transcontinental) truly reflected the expectations of the time, or whether he was putting the best possible face on a policy to which his government was committed on other grounds. Despite Buckley's comment to the contrary, the opinion expressed by Tilley was not 'frequently expressed'. There was *hope* that *some* commercial development would follow from the building of the transcontinental railway, but the Liberals, who won the election, did not think it would be enough to cover the costs, and they tried to renege on the commitment. Even Cartier, Chairman of the Railway Committee of the House of Commons, saw the line as a political commitment to British Columbia that could not be met at too early a date without bankrupting the country. Buckley, himself, in another place, admitted that that had been the case.

> Expert opinions on the possibilities of the prairie region as an agricultural frontier were pessimistic. Support of government railway policy in the face of rather bleak economic facts revealed an excessive optimism and indifference to the implications of government debt.[12]

Penelope Hartland has pointed out that the *Economist* in London, as late as 1885, was advising investors to stay away from the Canadian Pacific Railway because it had poor commercial prospects.[13]

The Canadian Pacific Railway, and western expansion in general, were politically motivated. This is not to deny the existence of a faction that thought it could migrate to the West and do what had been done in agriculture in Ontario. It is an assertion that Confederation and the expansion of Canada was part of Imperial policy first, and secondarily part of Canadian policy. At the time of Confederation there were many in England who simply wanted to get rid of the colonies, but other opinions were on the rise. By 1870 it was becoming evident that Britain could fall behind in relation to developments in Europe and in the United States. A new defensive imperialism under Disraeli sought to unify the Empire against continental economies based on railway transportation. The Canadian Pacific Railway was part of a band of steel rails and steamships intended to hold the Empire strong against emerging rivals.[14]

The immediate goal for Canada was political. Achieving the immediate goal entailed a restructuring of the Canadian economy to meet the needs of an Imperial economy. Space, resources, technical and institutional infrastructure and population in the new Canada were such that independent, non-staple-export-oriented growth could not hold the place it had had in the Canadas before 1870. The federation was caught up in an Imperial venture, the demands of which exceeded by far the resources of the four original provinces. The regions appended to the old provinces were geographically ill-suited to self-sufficient agriculture, or not suited to it at all. Ontario and Quebec could not absorb the products of the new provinces if development was to take place on a scale that would make it viable, let alone commercially profitable. There had to be external capital and external markets. Those who hold other theories of why domestic capital was directed only to short-term commercial ventures, or why Canada lagged behind the United States even after the 'wheat boom', should give some consideration to the consequences of the lower St. Lawrence Basin and the Maritimes, in 1870, attempting to finance the development of half of a continent.[15] The country simply bit off more than it could chew.

Lest this account be misunderstood, I hasten to add that there were no regional objections to the acquisition of territory. Maritimes objections to Confederation carried over to become objections to the effects of the National Policy, as it worked out; but there were no prior objections to *expansion* from any region or group, including francophone Quebec. At the time each was as eager as the next to run after the main chance. Most certainly I am not asserting that Canada, or Quebec would have been better off without geographic expansion. There would have been no Canada, as we know it, and Quebec would still have depended on United States capital for its industrial development. But it would be a delusion to think that westward, and eastward, expansion of Canada in the late nineteenth century was a step into the wonderland of economic rationality.

Territorial expansion was accompanied by decentralization beyond what seems to have been intended in 1867. The burdens and benefits of expansion were preceived to have fallen unevenly on different regions. The Maritimes and Quebec complained that they were taxed for expansion in other parts of the country. The West protested against the monopoly that had to be granted

116 A history of Canadian economic thought

to get the railway built, and against the tariff that favoured the manufacturing 'East'. Ontario, complaining about being the 'milch cow of Confederation', pursued provincial autonomy and provincial territorial expansion, successfully contesting the jurisdiction of the central government over resources, hydroelectric development, and over anything that could conceivably come under its jurisdiction over property and civil rights. By 1910, provinces in every region were undertaking provincial 'national policies' based on resource exports to the United States. What began as a national policy of independent growth in 1876, was overlaid with a policy of dependent growth based on a wheat staple export, and undercut by a series of regionally oriented policies of dependent growth based on the export of minerals and forest products. This was the economics of Canada when, between 1890 and 1930, the natural fractionation of the country asserted itself against centralization associated with defensive imperial expansion.

As if to get every conceivable disruption over with at once, the period was also marked by the emergence of an economics profession. The professionals ignored, forgot or depreciated the economics that had preceded them in their own country, and started out on a new course to discover or construct the economics of Canada. The result was a major cleavage in Canadian economic thought about 1900. Prior to the turn of the century the old style of economics predominated. Afterwards it took a very second place to the work of the professionals, even though, in the beginning, the professionals had little to offer. To recount the last efforts in the old style it will be necessary to reach back into the middle years of the nineteenth century to pick up the thread of support for free trade, because, in the years of Imperial reconsolidation, free trade within the Empire, Imperial preference, became fashionable. Recounting the tedious disorder of the first years of the profession can be left for last.

FREE TRADE IN NINETEENTH-CENTURY CANADA

In the earliest years of the nineteenth century, Montreal had promoted free trade between Canada and the United States. Prior to the War of Independence in the New England colonies, the central plains of the continent had been the hinterland of Montreal. With free trade Montreal might have re-established that connection, to become the emporium of the United States Midwest.[16] Indeed, a degree of free trade was achieved in the 1840s, when the old British mercantile empire was being dismantled. It was free trade inside a measure of Imperial protection, however, so that when the barriers really came down with the end of the Corn Laws and the Navigation Acts, most of Montreal gave up on British North America and signed a manifesto calling for annexation to the United States. John Young, a business agent who had frequently travelled in the Midwest, took the opposite view. Canada could survive and prosper with free trade. Young gathered a core of like-minded Montrealers into a Free Trade Association that, for two years, filled *The Canadian Economist* with free trade statements by Smith, McCulloch, Malthus, Lauderdale, Say, Storch, Torrens, Sismondi, Garnier, Whatley and Bastiat.[17] As a practical matter, Young supplemented his appeal with secondary appeals for government support in the building of canals, harbour facilities and bridges. He was elected to the legislature and appointed Minister of Public Works during the prosperous years of the 1850s.

Towards the end of the 1850s the cause of free trade was taken up by a precursor of the professionals, a Professor of Natural History at the University of Toronto, the Reverend William Hincks, brother of Sir Francis Hincks. Having accepted Political Economy as 'scientific', and the competitive market as the best instrument for economic progress, Hincks attacked protection as a force for monopolization of markets and a generator of inefficiency.[18] There was nothing original about Hincks's theories. He understood the arguments of the classical Political Economists and presented them as making perfect sense in a trading nation such as Canada, which, of course, they did.

The real future of free trade in nineteenth-century Canadian thought was not to be in scientific analysis, but in political debate. In the early 1860s the cause was taken up by the editor of the Toronto *Globe*, George Brown, a towering figure in the Reform Party. His arguments were not elegant, but nonetheless made sense. The tariff was just one more way in which the privileged used their position to their own advantage at the expense of the Canadian farmer. Like so many other government interventions, the tariff was an instrument of corruption. The election of 1873, in which the Liberals defeated the Conservatives, was won on a platform of free trade and reduced government intervention in economic matters.

Throughout the half century following the Galt-Caley tariffs of 1857–8, reciprocal, Canada–United States free trade in natural products was a live issue. In the late 1880s, two cunning, would-be exporters of Canadian resources, Erastus Wyman and S. J. Ritchie, in concert with Canada's celebrated Manchester School journalist, Goldwin Smith,[19] toured Ontario and Quebec speaking in favour of 'unrestricted reciprocity' with the United States. They convinced those attending the rebellious Interprovincial Conference of 1887 to adopt an 'unrestricted reciprocity' resolution, and they precipitated an election over free trade in 1891. The Liberals and free trade lost.

The argument for free trade in the last decades of the nineteenth century was an argument for equity, not efficiency. It was part of the ill-formed but passionately held intellectual foundations of the new positive liberalism.

Henry George's single tax on the rent of land had many supporters in

118 A history of Canadian economic thought

Canada, especially in the newly settled west where it was thought that the tax would fall on land speculators. Its first and most articulate advocate, however, was a central Canadian school teacher, W. A. Douglass.[20] His core idea was that value depends on scarcity, not abundance, and that this was the source of a conflict between productivity and value. The larger the output, the lower the value per unit. Given the right elasticity of demand (a term not used by Douglass), rent, that is scarcity value, could be increased by a deliberate reduction of output. Further, any value created by increased effort or productivity would be drained into the rent earned by those whose products were not increasing as quickly. Apparently there were contradictions in the system. In Douglass's view, the protective tariff was just a device to create such scarcity value. Douglass's work was one of the sources of the increasingly widespread idea in Canada that the tariff, monopoly and other instruments to transfer wealth to the privileged were all consequences of a malfunctioning and unjust system.

The spirit of positive liberal reform and the kind of economics underlying the free trade movement in those years was best represented in the works of Edward Porritt.[21] Porritt lionized Richard Cartwright of the Liberal Party, calling him the Cobden of Canada, and the Political Economist of Canada, because Cartwright had defected from the Conservative Party on the tariff issue, and because he was denied the Ministry of Finance under Prime Minister Laurier for refusing to compromise on the issue. Speaking for free trade at the Liberal Convention of 1893, Cartwright attacked the tariff saying

> We are practically face to face with a vast and well organized conspiracy, with a conspiracy that controls the press in this country, which controls a very large part of the active wealth of the country ... whose motto is robbery and whose arms are force and bribery.[22]

In Porritt's account, Cartwright had attributed every evil in the country to the tariff: overproduction, unemployment, widespread fraud and poverty.

There were some less vituperative arguments to be found in Cartwright's position, if one looked hard enough. Canada lacked the necessary volume in its home market to make large-scale manufacturing pay. It would have to specialize in the production of those things in which it had a natural advantage. Cartwright was for 'free trade as far as our position allows it', and 'reciprocity on fair and equal terms' with the United States, because Canada was 'by necessity of its position an integral part of the Continent of North America'.

Porritts's advocacy of free trade was followed by that of the 'muck-raking' American journalist, Gustavus Myers. Myers's *History of Canadian Wealth*[23] had some influence among the professionals who were by this time a rapidly

Some intrusions of history, 1890–1930 119

growing force in the informational environment. We need only consider some chapter headings.

(1) Immorality, Theft, Murder (2) Effects of Debauching the Indians (3) Feudal Tributes and Servitudes Established (4) Squeezing the Vassals (5) Rum, Violence, Murder (6) Fixing Government Officials (7) Publicly Paid For but Privately Owned.

The book was noticed by W. J. A. Donald who brought it to the attention of his student, H. A. Innis. Innis used it as a text in a course on Canadian Economic History during his very first years at the University of Toronto (1920–22). His department head, James Mavor, withdrew him from teaching the course because he was teaching it 'along too radical lines'.

Once the twentieth century arrived, an interaction between the old economic thought and the work of the professionals occurred. Innis was interested in Myers, but, of course, his own work within an academic discipline was nothing like that of Myers. Adam Shortt devoted much of his time to showing that the proponents of the Birmingham position were simply wrong. The third generation of professionals would decide that Shortt was wrong, but by then the old style of economics would be recognized for what it became in the twentieth century, the economic thought of special interest groups. For example, J. J. Harpell waged a personal war on corruption in the insurance industry.[24] E. A. Partridge, at the 1920s emergence of that distinctive blend of regional, sectoral and class protest that was eventually called socialism in Canada, wanted western Canada to declare autonomy and to set up a co-operative commonwealth, that is, a non-capitalist, non-market economy.[25] Such works influenced the professionals by controlling the subject of attention.

THE PROFESSIONAL ECONOMISTS

The second exogenous factor, the sixth influence on economic thought in Canada between 1890 and 1930, was the emergence of an economics profession. This was a phenomenon of Euro-American civilization, not something unique to Canada, not even in its timing. It was a factor shaping economic thought in Canada, however, so it has to be accounted for. Having done so, we will not pursue a history of the profession and everything it has had to say in Canada. Our task remains centred on the economics of Canada, as defined, and economics insofar as it has been shaped by the Canadian experience.

A professional economist is a person who is paid to function as an economist, that is, someone who processes economic theory and facts for a financial return. The professional economist is distinguished from professionals in other social sciences by the unquestioned primacy with which he or she treats considerations of objective efficiency. Non-monetary factors, even non-economic factors such as political and sociological factors may be the subject of discourse in economics, but the economist's agenda, overt or hidden, bears on objective efficiency in human behaviour. The economics profession is the set of professional economists self-consciously interacting with one another as professional economists.

The economics profession appeared in the universities between 1870 and 1930.

> The magnificent dynamics of the philosophers, clergymen and stock brokers who wrote economics in the classical period was replaced in large measure by the more formalized rigorous statics of the professional economists beginning near the end of the nineteenth century.[26]
>
> In the early 1930's it seems that a considerable majority of university economists – and, in Britain, *very* few of any other kind existed....[27]

Between 1930 and 1950 the profession expanded its field of employment into the public service. After 1950 it expanded into a variety of private sector institutions. Of course there were forerunners, and exceptional individuals and periods.

The economics profession appeared in Canada at the same time that it appeared in Britain and the United States.[28] Its members in Canada, it seems, were distinguished by their reluctance to accept economic theory as scientific.[29] Since the empirical foundation of economics was still in doubt as late as 1980,[30] their reluctance may be considered prudent, rather than backward.

The economics profession in Canada was not a Canadian profession. Canada, as a society, was ill-defined in 1900. The Prairie Provinces, apart from a postage stamp covering Winnipeg, did not exist. Quebec and Ontario were separated by language and culture. The Maritimes and British Columbia were separated from the rest by intellectually untraversed geographic and historical distance. There was no Canadian academic community. There was a North American academic community, and an English-speaking North Atlantic community, and a French academic community, to which the Canadians belonged. For instance, A. W. Flux, one of the five 'Canadian' economists to be given space in the *New Palgrave Dictionary*, taught for nine years at McGill University in Montreal. During his stay he wrote a widely accepted text on neoclassical economics, and he contributed regularly to the *Journal of the Canadian Bankers' Association* on the nature of commercial crises. There was nothing distinctively Canadian about Flux. There was nothing distinctively Canadian about the whole profession in Canada, except, perhaps a touch of allegedly characteristic Canadian caution with respect to the scientific pretensions of their subject. F. W. Taussig taught Canadian students at Harvard who returned to teach in Canada and to write in the neoclassical tradition for publication in the United States and Canada.[31] For English-speaking Canadian economists, as a profession, there was no Canada–United States boundary.

Prior to 1928 there was no professional economics association in Canada. Everyone belonged to the American Economics Association. The *Geographical Index of Members and Subscribers* of the American Economics Association, supplemented by some commentaries on the early years of the profession, contains an approximate checklist of Canadian professionals between 1912 and 1928. At the beginning of the period 37 Canadians participated in the Association. Their numbers rose to 53 in 1919, and declined steadily thereafter to 45 in 1928. In 1912, at the Boston meeting of the American Economics Association, a number of Canadians formed the Canadian Political Science Association. It did not survive the First World War. In 1928, at the Chicago meeting of the American Economics Association, a number of Canadians, including some who had been present in 1912, again formed the Canadian Political Science Association. In the same year the periodical *Contributions to Canadian Economics* made its appearance, and from then on there was an organized subset of the profession in Canada.[32]

Development of Canadian professional economists was supported in the United States by interest shown in Canadian topics and Canadian students. Interest in Canadian history appeared in United States institutions about the same time as it appeared in Canada, and special facilities for the study of Imperial and Canadian topics multiplied rapidly south of the border.[33] At the University of Chicago four Canadians, competing in the category reserved for United States citizens, won prizes or honourable mention in the Hart, Schaffner, Marx awards programme. Persistent interest in Canadian economic history on the part of C. W. Wright at the University of Chicago made him one of the founders of the subject. He directed W. J. A. Donald's dissertation on the Canadian steel industry,[34] which was supposed to have been an introduction to Canadian economic development. Iron and steel were not the staples of Canadian development, so, when Donald attracted Innis's attention at McMaster and sent him off to Chicago, Wright directed Innis's *A History of the Canadian Pacific Railway*,[35] from which Innis moved to his classic study of the fur trade.

The Canadians in the profession did not do just what their United States colleagues did. For one thing, there were too many British-trained among them for that. The mixing of influences was evident in those who wrote the texts produced in Canada between 1912 and 1928. James Mavor's *Applied Economics*[36] was a melange of value theory and history. It was marked by a strong bias against government interference in the economy. S. A. Cudmore's *Economics for Canadian Students*[37] was a lesson book for Shaw's correspondence courses. R. E. Freeman's *Economics for Canadians*[38] made more use of neoclassical theory and used diagrams to explain the principles of economics and equilibrium prices. Freeman's work was biased towards a 'social point of view' and 'government involvement' in the economy. D. A. McGibbon, the only American-trained economist to produce a text, accomplished his task without the word 'utility'. The character of economics in Canada, as reflected in these works has to be modified by W. A. Mackintosh's remark that most upper-level students were taught from Taussig's *Principles*.[39]

It is unfair to judge Canadian economic thought on the basis of its published residue in a period in which publication was not as desperately sought as it later was to be. The written evidence does support the idea that the Canadians shied away from the theoretical economics typical of Harvard, and embraced history, which was typical of Chicago. Still, in commenting on the period W. A. Mackintosh, who was one of the important players, made the following remarks.

> In the early part of your period [1912–28] Chicago was a rather inferior place for economics. Veblen, who was stimulating rather than formative in his influence, and Davenport had left. Chester Wright was almost the only continuing link. Field was a competent statistician but L. C. Marshall was a busy second-rater. In this period, Chicago drew Canadian students primarily because of its summer quarter system, particularly convenient for young Canadian academics who could frequently get in two quarters a year. In the latter part of your period, the story was entirely different. J. M. Clark, Viner and Frank Knight gave it a new and great vitality while the Harvard group grew old despite the recruitment of Allyn Young.

> *Re* Skelton, he was never a student of Shortt. His undergraduate training was in the Classics and English. He always said he found Veblen stimulating but he was never a follower of Veblen. He had little interest in theoretical economics. His concerns were political science and welfare economics. His acknowledgement to Veblen was pretty much a matter of fact – Veblen's lectures at Harvard were the only fundamental consideration of socialism that had appeared before Skelton's book. Skelton's publications were influenced by the market. He had very little interest in Banking and his book on the Dominion Bank was done for a fee.

> Your reference to my low opinion of theoretical economics as a guide to policy is on the whole misleading. You quote a youthful and rather superficial article which I wrote when I was 23 and had worked a few

months in Ottawa but had not yet completed my graduate work. With more knowledge and more experience, my views changed.

I think we were all conscious of the lack of consideration of economics in Canadian history. About 1928, G. M. Wrong published a two volume history of New France in which the words furs or fur trade did not appear in the index. My interest in the staple theory, a term which I never liked, was in trying to answer the question, why Canadian development had been deferred even though the settlement at Port Royal had been as early as that at Jamestown. Callendar's thesis was only slightly elaborated from Adam Smith.[40]

There was some 'off the cuff' sniping at neoclassical economics. Skelton allowed that D. A. McGibbon's efforts had risen 'above the level of dry bones and dogmatic formulas' but not by much, and he questioned the wisdom of presenting young students with simplified versions of such 'highly controverted material'.[41] At one point H. A. Innis referred to neoclassical theory as 'a new form of exploitation with dangerous consequences'.[42] Stephen Leacock attempted a Veblenesque critique of neoclassical value theory, which, despite its lapses into first-class humour, was not pointless.[43]

When the time came, economists in Canada took to theory as keenly as did any other subset of the profession. In the 1890–1930 period, however, they constructed an account of the underlying, long-run factors in Canadian economic development. The necessary first step was to build the foundation; so the first and second generations of the profession in Canada had an historical orientation. The third generation, raised in the depression of the 1930s, turned to Keynesian and neo-Keynesian macroeconomic theory.

The first, native-born, professional economist in Canada, Adam Shortt, documented and interpreted the evolution of currency and banking in Canada from the earliest period to his own time. Throughout, he justified the view of the Banking School against the views of the Birmingham and Currency Schools. He demonstrated, contrary to received opinion, that Canadian banking institutions had been explicitly modelled on the Bank of the United States, and he was first to depict Canadian development as being shaped by reliance on a few primary product exports. H. A. Innis considered Shortt to be 'the founder of Canadian economics', and set out to build on the foundation he had laid.[44] At another point Innis seemed to say that he, Innis, was about to continue the work of Thorstein Veblen.[45] W. A. Mackintosh pulled it together with the comment that 'Veblen begat Innis out of Shortt'.[46]

O. D. Skelton, was responsible for the first economic history of Canada. Innis referred to it as a model of geographic interpretation.[47] Skelton's role as an adviser to governments, no less than his publications and his importance in the profession in Canada, would seem to place him next to Shortt as a 'founder of the subject'.[48]

Shortt and Skelton were the giants of the first generation of professionals. Innis and Mackintosh were the giants of the second generation. All four were economic historians dealing with long-run factors in Canadian economic development. The professionals did have other interests, however, the *potpourri* of the academics. We will consider it only as it pertains to the melange of borrowings and initiatives that characterized the recruitment stage of the profession. The first campaign was well under way by 1930, but that is another story.

A number in the profession showed interest in business cycles. G. E. Jackson and Humphrey Michell provided quantitative analysis under the heading 'Industry and Trade' in every issue of the *Canadian Forum* from the first in 1920 until 1927. They produced time series for Canada, and they reported on the work of William Berridge in England and Warren Persons of the Harvard Economic Service. After Michell made predictions on the basis of an hypothesized four-year agricultural cycle that proved to be incorrect, they abandoned their column in despair of ever solving 'the problem of leads and lags'. In January of 1928, Donald MacGregor used their space to review W. C. Mitchell's *Business Cycles*. MacGregor rejected the quantitative approach because it focused on symptoms rather than causes. V. W. Bladen and A. F. W. Plumptre were more receptive of Mitchell's approach. After 1927 Jackson turned for new ideas to the National Bureau of Economic Research in Washington.[49]

The historians produced two remarkable contributions to the analysis of business cycles. Adam Shortt pointed out the relationship between price fluctuations and bursts of government-supported railway construction.[50] O. D. Skelton took the next logical step, 'considering whether the principle of the government as the flywheel in the industrial machine could be appplied to Canada'.[51]

Only A. B. Balcom of Acadia University in the Maritimes approached business cycles by way of the quantity of money theory of prices.[52]

There was great interest in industrial organization between 1920 and 1930, but it was part of the elaboration of the staple thesis. It was industrial organization on a grand scale that sought an explanation of the structure of firms, of industries and of the whole economy, in response to very long-run factors. Developments in that kind of industrial organization were part of the first campaign. The recruitment process involved generating interest in a much narrower field. Vincent Bladen dutifully took up the subject of less than perfectly competitive markets.[53] It would be the 1950s before the profession as a whole in Canada would take that sort of enquiry seriously. There were two institutional studies of the labour movement.[54] Future Prime

Some intrusions of history, 1890-1930 125

Minister Mackenzie King produced his *Industry and Humanity*,[55] a sort of how-to-organize manual for those interested in social betterment. Lastly, there was James Mavor's critique of government ownership in Canada.[56]

International trade, as such, did not attract the attention one would have thought in a country so dependent on external markets. Still, what was done was of high quality. Jacob Viner produced his classic study of the working of the gold standard mechanism, *Canada's Balance of International Indebtedness:1900-1913*, during the period.[57] Theodore Boggs of the University of British Columbia had substantially anticipated the important chapter 12 of Viner's study some nine years earlier,[58] and he produced a widely accepted text.[59]

So much for the *potpourri*. There is little else to say before launching into the genesis and nature of the staple thesis of Canadian economic development. We may note a tendency for the professionals to finish their careers in government service. Prior to 1900 both J. B. Hurlbert and J. B. Cherryman left the classroom for the civil service. Adam Shortt and Oscar Skelton did the same. Cherryman, who received some attention from Goodwin, has more recently been celebrated in an excellent piece by Robert Dimand.[60] Cherryman was quite competent in the sort of economics for which Cournot has since become famous, and he recognized its importance long before it was recognized by the profession in general. We cannot leave the period without noting Goodwin's account of the role of R. H. Coats in the formation of the Dominion Bureau of Statistics in 1918, and in the collection of time series on the Canadian economy for some time before that.[61]

These were the formative influences and early beginnings in Canadian economic thought in the period from 1890 to 1930, the period of the legendary 'wheat boom', when the economics of Canada and economic thought in Canada were given a new start: theory and history, liberalism and imperialism, a continental wheat economy and an economics profession with a *potpourri* of little initiatives.

APPENDIX

Craufurd Goodwin has provided an account of the economics profession in Canada before 1912. After 1928 there was a professional organization and there were publications: *Contributions to Canadian Economics* from 1927 to 1934, and the *Canadian Journal of Economics and Political Science*, beginning in 1935, both carrying information about the profession. To fill in the lacuna between 1912 and 1928 I append a list of professional Canadian economists. The list indicates the universities at which their last degrees were earned, and the Canadian university with which I found them affiliated. The

126 *A history of Canadian economic thought*

names are drawn largely from the American Economics Association membership list.

Chicago

W. C. Kierstead, New Brunswick; S. B. Leacock, McGill; O. D. Skelton, Queen's; W. J. A. Donald, McMaster; K. W. Taylor, McMaster; H. A. Innis, Toronto; S. J. McLean, Toronto; G. A. Elliot, Manitoba; W. W. Swanson, Saskatchewan; D. A. McGibbon, Alberta.

Harvard

A. B. Balcom, Acadia; W. R. Maxwell, Dalhousie; J. C. Hemmeon, McGill; W. A. Mackintosh, Queen's; W. C. Clark, Queen's; W. T. Jackman, Toronto; A. F. McGoun, Alberta; H. S. Patton, Alberta.

Wisconsin

J. A. Estey, Dalhousie; L. C. Gray, Saskatchewan.

Yale

T. H. Boggs, British Columbia.

Columbia

E. H. Oliver, Saskatchewan.

Edinburgh/Glasgow

A. Shortt, Queen's; J. Mavor, Toronto; R. M. McIvor, Toronto; R. E. Freeman, Western Ontario; W. B. Hurd, Brandon.

Cambridge

G. E. Jackson, Toronto; G. I. H. Loyd, Toronto; C. R. Fay, Toronto.

London

H. R. Kemp, Toronto; R. McQueen, Saskatchewan.

Leeds

H. Heaton, Queen's.

Birmingham

C. A. Ashley, Queen's.

Heidleberg

H. Michell, McMaster; L. A. Wood, Western Ontario.

Economists in government

R. H. Coats, M. C. MacLean, R. M. Fisher, D. McArthur, M. J. Patton, B. M. Stewart, H. Marshall, J. Bonar.

Others

B. C. Bordon, Mount Allison; J. E. Todd, Dalhousie; A. McPhail, McGill; C. A. Curtis, Queen's; F. A. Knox, Queen's; C. E. Walker, Queen's; C. H. Bland, Queen's; A. L. McCrimmon, McMaster; A. J. Glazebrook, Toronto; J. M. McEvoy, Western Ontario; T. H. Fraser, Manitoba; A. L. Burt, Alberta.

Remainder from the American Economics Association listings for 1914–28, by place of residence. Some of these would not have been professional economists.

Halifax, B. C. Hunt; St. John, J. Sealy, I. S. Isaacs, C. K. Ganong; Fredericton, W. S. Kierstead; St. Lambert, B. K. Sandwell; Macdonald College, M. A. Jull; Sherbrook, L. S. Patterson, H. E. Goodhue; Montreal, R. D. Bell, G. Creak, E. H. Fitzhugh, N. W. A. McNaughton, C. Riorden, J. Turnbull, A. J. DeBray, R. H. Cohan, G. F. Steele, H. R. Wood, J. Clurgh, R. R. Johnson, D. M. Marvin; Kingston, G. Y. Chown, B. K. Sandwell; Ottawa, R. L. Bordon, A. H. G. Grey, G. Iles, J. White, W. L. M. King, R. J. McFall, F. J. Horning, M. H. Staples, G. Bouchard; Toronto, G. H. Locke, S. H. Frame, F. B. Hayes, W. O. Mathews, W. R. Marson, R. Williamson, A. Brady, C. L. Burton, S. C. Norsworthy; Wakerville, T. Walker, H. H. Walker; Hamilton, A. V. Young; St. Catherines, H. Swindley; Woodstock, A. E. Izzard; Rockwood, J. J. Brennan; Winnipeg, C. S. Freeman, J. A. McLean, A. J. Gaillard, N. P. Lambert, L. F. J. von Riemsalijk, J. B. Sinclair, A. H. Benton, R. F. Jones, J. M. Ward, A. Cairns; Portage La Prairie, W. A. Hendry;

Brandon, W. B. Hood; Saskatoon, D. Maclean; Carnduff, T. C. Bereton; Edmonton, T. C. Boyd, A. E. Guy, J. M. Cassels; Lenfield, W. Wallace; Vancouver, H. W. Dyson, J. A. Campbell, E. B. Ross, W. H. Maddock, F. M. Sylverster; Victoria, C. H. O'Halloran.

8 The staple thesis, 1920–40

In the 1930s it was a staple thesis. It became a theory at the hands of Wynne Plumptre at the end of the 1930s, but even then it looked nothing like what came to be called the staple theory in the 1960s. The thesis was complete long before Keynsian economics was understood, let alone accepted, in Canada. It was complete before Canadians took an interest in international trade as something other than an opaque, uncontrollable external force. It was conceived in the context of an historical critique of neoclassical economics in a period when neoclassical economics went far in accommodating the critique, purging itself of unconscious value judgements and then accommodating the non-market and imperfect market institutions of historical reality. It was an attempt to *make* theory in the context of history, so that as neoclassical theory accommodated historical reality its accommodations were, after a fashion, absorbed into the thesis. The staple thesis was a microeconomic general disequilibrium analysis of a specific economy.

The forces in the information environment directing the evolution of the staple thesis have been powerful, complex and unrelenting. A recent episode in the debates among Canadian Marxists may serve as an example.

RESHAPING THE STAPLE THESIS

Long after the staple thesis had been transformed into a theory and presented in a number of different versions, Mel Watkins stated that W. A. Mackintosh had integrated the staple theory with Keynesian disequilibrium analysis.[1] Without pretending to be perfectly faithful to Watkins's statement we may reconstruct his argument in the following way. To achieve full employment in an open economy, assuming a Keynesian world, external demand and foreign investment have to be controlled. The alternative would be a restructuring of the economy to eliminate dependence on foreign markets. With independence, domestic monetary and fiscal policy would be sufficient.

Watkins alleged that at the end of the 1930s depression, when the concern was to keep demand and investment up, Mackintosh had suggested that maintaining full employment would require stimulating external demand for and foreign investment in Canada's staples; that is, Mackintosh had suggested a further shift in the direction of economic dependency.

Any suggestion that further reliance on international capital might be a good thing would be abhorrent to a western Marxist nationalist such as Watkins, but he may have had a more complex agenda. To those among Canadian Marxists who adopted legitimization crisis theory, Keynesian policy was an internally contradictory attempt to buy off the workers with their own money while leaving the class structure intact. When they first made this contention they did so by rejecting the sort of dependency theory that had motivated Marxian nationalists up to that point, causing a marked division in the Marxist camp.[2] But, if Keynsian policies were to be carried out by increasing external dependence, there was no contradiction between legitimization crisis theory and dependency theory in the Canadian case, and there was no theoretical basis for the division within the Marxist camp. Reshaping the staple theory had its uses.

The point is not that the Marxists revised the staple theory, because everyone revised the staple theory. The point is that the staple theory was never a fixed thing even when it was still a thesis, and the rate of change accelerated after it became a theory. With so much useful emendation intervening it is not a simple thing to reconstruct the staple thesis as it was in the early 1930s.

RECONSTRUCTING THE STAPLE THESIS

Some elements in Canadian economic thought between 1920 and 1940 were more important than others in the construction of the staple thesis. Economic history, industrial organization and public finance were the important fields. Aggregate economics, international trade and the economics generated by positive liberalism were not. On the one hand, what has to be shown is that economic history in Canada was not devoid of theory, that the theory involved was a certain kind of industrial organization theory, and that public finance in Canada was an extension of that theory to the organization of the entire economy. On the other hand, it has to be shown that macroeconomics, that is, Keynesian theory, and international trade theory were relatively underdeveloped among Canadian professional economists prior to the Second World War. The economic thought generated by positive liberalism during the 1930s was an important part of the informational environment, but it was not part of the staple thesis.

THEORY IN HISTORY

To say that economic history in Canada had a significant core of economic theory would seem to challenge the gods. In summing up economics to 1932, O. D. Skelton remarked,

> It cannot be said that any substantial new contribution to pure economic theory has yet come out of Canada. It has rather been in economic history and in the study of taxation, of tariffs, of transportation, of trade unions, of agricultural organizations and of money and banking, that our most distinctive work has been done.[3]

In summing up economics to 1943, A. R. M. Lower remarked

> But few Canadian social scientists have gone much beyond the state of analysis. So far no wide-ranging books have appeared. (The first Canadian book on theoretical economics has appeared in May 1942.)[4]

Considered closely, however, these statements are not rejections of theory. They are statements that economics in Canada had been an application of theory. During the 1930s, when the Keynesian revolution was taking place, a comment that textbook theory was to be scorned was really a comment that theory was too alive and changing to be adequately presented in textbook form. Such comments could be misconstrued. For example Wynne Plumptre's comment:

> Now unfortunately economic theory, for the most part, consists of the unlovely and inanimate skeletons of economic controversies of the past. The simpler the exposition, the barer the bones, and the less likely are the skeletons to bear any resemblance to the robust arguments of the past or to the evolving problems of the present. On the other hand, that economic theory which relates to contemporary opinions upon matters of national policy is usually far too complex and always far too controversial to receive adequate treatment in a textbook.[5]

Theory had its place, but Canadian economists, in general, were not interested in pure theory for its own sake. So what was the nature and role of theory in economic thought in Canada between 1920 and 1940? Consider C. R. Fay's comments on theory in Canadian economics.

> some Canadians suspect that when they do write their economic history it has got to be their economic theory as well.... The method is the opposite of that followed, let us say, in the Macmillan Report on Finance and Industry. There you have such bits of history as a dominant theory allows to ornament the preface. Here you have history as the substance.... [The concluding chapter of Innis's *The Fur Trade in Canada*] extracts from the

detail that has gone before something that one wants to call laws, the Laws of Staple Production in an area of a given latitude with a given geography and racial stock. There is more theory in it than in all the question-begging rigmarole of English political economy on the subject of Diminishing Returns in Agriculture. And there is almost enough matter in the book for another chapter of conclusions which would be equally important to theory concerning the economics of barter trade.[6]

Fay must not be taken too seriously, because he tended to ascribe to the Toronto historians what he, himself, was doing. Indeed, any attempt to systematize Innis[7] must not be taken too seriously, because it may have been that systematization was contrary to the nature of his scientific project. Innis's theory was something like neoclassical economics without perfect knowledge, without continuous substitutability, without known utility and production functions, and without a prohibition on consideration of very long-run factors in the advance of Euro-American industrialization. But we may let him speak for himself, in this case from his notes for a guest appearance in Vincent Bladen's seminar, probably in the late 1920s.

> I shall warn you in the beginning that I am not sure that rent is the subject about which I am going to talk to you nor am I certain that any other term will cover the subject matter which I have in mind....
>
> The facts about which we are concerned are very briefly the virgin natural resources of Canada and the late stage of Canada's industrial development....
>
> The problem of interest to the economic theorist and the economic historian is the disposal of the profits arising from this situation. What is the character of the profits? In the case of wheat, costs of production being lower with virgin soil, it might be expected that the price of wheat sold in the European market would decline, but the evidence suggests that the increasing industrialization of England kept par or more than kept par with the supply of wheat....
>
> Perhaps we are more interested in a theory of profits than of rent. The gigantic scale on which capital has been poured into Canada to undertake our transcontinental type of development has made unpredictable any definite returns.... One of the results of the surplus arising from the cashing in of natural resources is the speed with which capital has poured into the country and with which it has developed. Overhead costs present a continuous unpredictable situation in which mines, pulp and paper mills and power built up in a former non-traffic producing area give fresh contributions of.... To offset the increase in returns accompanying reduction of overhead costs the speed of development involves numerous extra expenditures in terms of duplication of track facilities. In any case it gives

rise to a situation which is beyond the power of prediction and beyond private enterprise. This is a first result of the surplus which has arisen from virgin natural resources.

What are the results of a situation in which the profit index ceases to operate or operates too efficiently, and the engineer is allowed to run loose, so that the swiftness of development and its unpredictable character are beyond the scope of normal economic theory? Ordinarily the results would become evident in the failure of the enterprises concerned....

We are forced to turn to other devices in this pathological study.

If government support or government ownership is essential to the economic development of new countries because of the unpredictability of the results and the immensity of the immediate demands for capital the effects of capital investment differ materially from the gradual involvement of labour and capital for which economic theory is accustomed to allow in a discusion of the dynamic state. Violent swings are set in motion according to the prediction of unpredictableness. In the main these swings are the result of the intensified application of the machine industry at a mature stage of technique to vast virgin natural resources. Low cost of production is responsible for large profits and rapid expansion. It becomes the immediate task of the government to take advantage of the upward swings to secure returns in compensation for the burden involved in the heavy initial outlay.[8]

Not all the economists in Canada were engaged in this kind of theory making. Perhaps no one but Innis was; but somehow they took enough from what he was saying, or reacted on their own in the same informational environment, to put together a generally accepted staple thesis describing the nature and development of the Canadian economy.

There is a temptation to leap from C. R. Fay's comment about the theory of barter trade to J. C. McManus's analysis of the institutions of the North American Indians in the fur trade,[9] which was a thorough piece of post-1970 New Institutionalism. There is a similarity between Innis's approach and that of the New Institutionalists. Both look at historical practice and at the existing structure of economic institutions first. Theory comes later. But the difference is this: Innis, like the old Institutionalists, like the Historical School, was looking for theory. He was discovering theory. The New Institutionalists have their theory ready-made in neoclassical analysis. There is much in Innis that is suggestive of the New Institutionalism,[10] but there is a hiatus between the two, a hiatus in time, in doctrine and in personal connections.

Still, a comparison of Innis's work with that of the New Institutionalists is instructive. Innis looked at the structure of institutions. His history was a study of industrial organization. Insofar as the institutions of government were correctives for market failures, and that was how he saw Confederation, Innis turned to public finance as an aspect of industrial organization. There were junctures at which he argued for the superior efficiency of non-competitive market structures and of non-market economic institutions, much as the New Institutionalists do. *The Diary of Alexander James McPhail*[11] was an account of transactions costs in co-operative grain marketing in western Canada. Innis's 'Introduction' to R. H. Fleming's *Minutes of Council, Northern Department of Rupert Land, 1821–1831*[12] was an account of the superior efficiency of monopoly over competition in the harvesting of a common property resource. But, there is no reference to optimization or to the equation of marginal costs and marginal benefits in Innis. He was too conscious of the consequences of objective irrationality, that is 'unpredictableness', to think that much could be learned about historical outcomes from the undoubted fact of subjective rationality.

At the beginning of the New Institutionalist economics Ronald Coase developed the theory of the firm. It was a general theory applying to any firm. Innis came close to developing a theory of the modern industrial state that would have applied to any modern state.[13] In general, however, his attention went the other way. He produced an analysis of a particular case.

Innis was an old-style institutionalist with a bias against government interference in the economy. He did not, as it is alleged of other institutionalists, jump on the Keynesian bandwagon because it justified intervention.[14] Indeed, he did not jump on it at all. He was invited to Chicago to be with the founders of New Institutionalism, but he did not go. He cannot be identified with the New Institutionalism any more than he can be identified with the New Canadian Political Economy. The one is neoclassical, the other neo-Marxist, and Innis was neither.

There were theoretical elements in economics in Canada quite apart from those entailed in the staple thesis. Lionel Robbins's definitive *Essay on the Nature and Significance of Economic Science*,[15] appearing in 1932, made the point that economics, neoclassical economic theory, was devoid of value judgements, and abstracted from anything that could be empirically falsified.

> 'Economics', says Mr. Hawtrey, 'cannot be dissociated from ethics'... [but, in fact] Economics deals with ascertainable facts; ethics with valuations and obligations.[16]

For the next five years a stream of articles worrying over the role of values in economics appeared in Canada, mostly from the pens of heads of departments of economics and presidents of the Canadian Economics and Political Science Association, and from Frank Knight.[17] After 1937 the debaters turned from economics to the newer discipline of sociology. Only

Urwick, former Head at Toronto, and Frank Knight, from among the economists, stayed at their podiums.

Some of the protagonists in this rather nasty exchange over the objectivity of social science did think objectivity possible. Innis thought that objectivity could be reached by studying bias itself. This was the beginning of his departure from Canadian economic history for the history of communication media. Mackintosh thought the new aggregate economics to be objective, and he began his departure in that direction.

There were contributions in history quite apart from those that searched the reaction of Canadians to their geographical and technological circumstances for an economic theory of institutions and policy. The *interbellum* period was a great period in the writing of Canadian history. It was a period when Idealism was giving way to Materialism, and Imperialism to nationalism in Canada. A revolution occurred in the writing of Canadian history, quite apart from anything economic theory contributed.[18] Historians can find the beginning of the staple thesis in the work of Marion Newbigin,[19] but that was not economics.

The sort of economic history that produced the staple thesis was distinguished by its empirical description and theoretical explanation of industrial organization in both the private and public sectors. It was distinguished from standard industrial organization theory which dealt with idealized forms of market organization, in the short- and in the long-run, first, and empirical application second. That is not the economics of institutional formation in either the New Institutional or the old Institutional traditions.[20] Some outstanding examples of Canadian economic history are H. A. Innis's *A History of the Canadian Pacific Railway*,[21] *The Fur Trade in Canada*,[22] *Settlement and the Mining Frontier*,[23] and *The Cod Fisheries*;[24] D. G. Creighton, *The Commercial Empire of the St. Lawrence*;[25] A. R. M. Lower, *The North American Assault on the Canadian Forest*;[26] S. A. Saunders, *An Economic History of the Maritime Provinces*;[27] W. A. Mackintosh, *The Economic Background of Dominion-Provincial Relations*;[28] G. E. Britnell, *The Wheat Economy*;[29] A. F. W. Plumptre, *Central Banking in the British Dominions*;[30] and W. A. Carrothers, *The British Columbia Fisheries*.[31]

There were economic histories that did not contribute to the staple thesis; for example, D. C. Masters's *The Reciprocity Treaty of 1854*[32] and G. N. Tucker's *The Canadian Commercial Revolution: 1845–51*.[33] Masters subsequently used N. S. B. Gras's stages theory to describe the growth of Toronto.[34] Masters was right, of course, not to use the staple theory in that instance. Agriculture and manufacturing in Quebec and Ontario were not included among the industries studied in the construction of the staple thesis.

Economic history in the staple thesis was microeconomic theory of a sort, but, for the students of the period[35] it was theory in which the mechanisms of general equilibrium were severely clogged. The long-term capital commitment necessary to implement modern industrial techniques was ill-fitted to the price cycles of primary product exports, particularly wheat exports. Output prices fell, but debt and other costs did not. The adjustment to equilibrium was slow and uneven. Add to this the effects of government intervention in increasing costs and encouraging activities in sparsely populated areas in which there was no room for competition, and further rigidities were added to the structure of prices. When goverments were called upon to relieve those who were victims of the uneven adjustment in prices, they did so by further interfering with the adjustment of prices. The staple thesis was a case study of the interaction of government policy, industrial technique and geography in general economic disequilibrium.

There was little interest in standard industrial organization theory among Canadian professional economists in the 1930s. There was more interest, both inside the profession and out, in that extension of industrial organization theory called economic systems; not an empirical interest, but a policy interest. Its issue was other than but not unrelated to the staple thesis, which was a case study of a particular economic system. Discussion of socialist and fascist systems was an important element in the information environment in which the staple thesis took shape.

ECONOMIC SYSTEMS

There were people in Canada in the 1930s who advocated communist social control of business enterprise. There had been Marxists in Canada since the late nineteenth century, though the earliest publication of Marxist views by a Canadian, appearing in 1887,[36] made no reference to Canada. Gustavus Myers's work may be considered a piece of radical socialist literature, though Myers makes no mention of Karl Marx. Certainly, from 1890 on, there were Marxian socialists in Canada whose primary goal was to educate Canadians, and whose instruments, *inter alia*, were selections from Karl Marx, including *Value, Price and Profit*, *Wage Labour and Capital*, *The Communist Manifesto* and *Socialism, Scientific and Utopian*.[37] It would be difficult to establish the importance of these activities, or of the pamphlets and periodicals produced by the Marxian socialist groups. Whatever it may indicate in this regard, there were professional economists who were quite exercised about Marxian socialism. James Mavor wanted the elimination of all government ownership, all trade unions, and indeed, anything that even suggested socialism.[38] R. M. MacIver, who succeeded Mavor as Head of the Department of Political Economy at the University of Toronto, suggested a degree of social control as a defence against socialism,[39] as did O. D. Skelton.

Every tax-dodging millionaire, every city slum, every instance of shady high finance or of overworked and underpaid employees is an argument for socialism. Remove the greivances, and there are many... and the socialist has lost his best ammunition.[40]

After 1917, the year of the Bolshevik Revolution in Russia, and of the manifesto of the British Labour Party, *Labour and the New Social Order*, socialism in Canada separated itself into Communism and Democratic Socialism. The latter came to be the more influential of the two.

In a general way both kinds of socialists voiced the same critique of capitalism. The system was judged to be inefficient. What the socialists meant by the term efficiency was not clear, and they could have used the neoclassical definition with effect. Their basic complaint was the existence of excess capacity; that is, too many firms and too much capital in particular industries, with consequent overproduction leading to periodic depressions. The system seemed to advance in chaos and waste, producing an abundance of silly things while basic wants went begging. If it was controlled at all, it was controlled by a few very large firms and by an elite of disproportionately wealthy owners of those firms. It was monopoly capitalism, fighting within itself for international hegemony, and pulling nations into war behind it.[41]

The proposed solution to these problems was either enforcement of healthy competition or social control through public commissions, public regulation and public ownership. To the democratic socialist the beginnings of social control were already recognizable in provincial government ownership of utilities, and in the railway and tariff commissions of the federal government. It was recognizable in the variety of price-fixing and market-sharing arrangements into which private enterprise retreated from the inefficiencies and losses associated with excessive exploitation of particular markets. According to Francis Hankin and T. W. L. MacDermot of McGill, the answer was to recognize the end of the competitive era, repeal the Combines Act, which only perpetuated the outmoded system, and build a system of co-operation co-ordinated by commissions appointed by the Government from candidates nominated by the users of the industries involved.

Their proposal was comprehensive. They wanted rationalization of existing arrangements under a national Economic Council representing government and business. The Council, supported by a professional research team, would provide information, co-ordination, advice and an overall plan. There would be an unemployment insurance scheme to replace the existing 'dole'. There would be a privately owned central bank. Nationalization of banking was rejected because 'Bureaucratic centralization of commercial banking would wreck the efficient work of the banks on the rocks and sands of political interference.'[42] The goal was 'efficiency, equity and social welfare'. Unlike the alleged authoritarian systems proposed by socialists and fascists, Hankin and MacDermot's system was to achieve its goal by combining the motive of self-seeking with the tendency to co-operate for a common purpose.

Canada's first economic council was established in British Columbia under the direction of a professional economist, W. A. Carrothers, during the 1930s; but a national system of consultative planning bodies, similar to the Hankin-MacDermot proposal, did not come into being until the 1960s. By then the goal had changed to growth and regional development.

A second, more celebrated, plan for social control was produced by the League for Social Reconstruction. The League was the intellectual wing of the new democratic socialist party, the Co-operative Commonwealth Federation. There were professional economists involved. Its manifesto, *Social Planning for Canada*,[43] contained the same critique as, and followed the general outline of, the Hankin-MacDermot book. A different solution was proposed: government ownership and operation of the main industries of the nation. There was to be central planning of a sort that would require political centralization of the federation; not necessarily at once, but without hesitation if necessary. The banking system was to be 'socialized'. Patents were to be suppressed. There were to be unemployment and medical insurance schemes. The tone of the League's manifesto was much more aggressive and partisan than that of Hankin and MacDermot's calmly reasoned proposal.

Hankin and MacDermot came down on the side of private enterprise. The League came down on the side of public enterprise. The 1937 Royal Commission on Price Spreads, marshalled by Lester Pearson and his 'expert staff of economists',[44] came down on both sides of its question. The commission was to

> inquire into and investigate the causes of the large spread between the prices received for commodities by the producer thereof, and the price paid by the consumers therefore; and the system of distribution in Canada of farm and other natural products, as well as manufactured products.

This it did, leaving behind a remarkable collection of detailed market studies. Its conclusion was a set of recommendations concerning the working of the Combines Investigation Act and other methods of social control of economic enterprise, all of which, it said, ought to be gathered into a new Federal Trade and Industry Commission. The Commission's goal would be 'the socialization of monopoly and the civilization of competition'.[45]

INDUSTRIAL ORGANIZATION

Work done on the other sort of social control, that is the preservation of healthy competition, was a very minor element in the informational environment of the depression years in Canada.[46] It was standard industrial organization theory updated by the more recent contributions of Kaldor, Robinson and Chamberlin in that field. Economists in the United States were more interested in Canadian competition policy than were Canadians. The crowning study of the period, L. G. Reynolds's *The Control of Competition in Canada*[47] was a complaint by an expatriate Canadian that the Canadian government had done more to eliminate than to promote competition. Nonetheless, Reynolds was able to gather an interesting bibliography of industry studies in Canada, many of them reports of Royal Commissions, and to complete a standard study of price fixing, market sharing and other monopolization devices.

Taking the field as a whole, the point with respect to industrial organization is that a group of Canadian economists, particularly at the University of Toronto, integrated a number of concepts, such as overhead costs, imperfect competition and the development role of government, into an analysis of the effects of capital-intensive, advanced techniques in the exploitation of international markets for primary products. They observed the consequence to be unevenly rigid prices inhibiting the processes of equilibration that would have returned the system to full employment and an even distribution of returns over all sectors and regions of the economy. This was the staple thesis. It described the unique factors in the Canadian case. There was no consensus on policy among the professionals who developed the thesis, even in the depths of the depression. Socialists, mostly not professional economists, and, until the mid-1930s, mostly not academics, who had long held clear ideas about the imperfections of the market system, were able to build their general analysis into the circumstances of the depression, and to generate a justification for social control of economic activities. The economic systems they proposed as solutions were not based on the unique factors in the Canadian case.

AGGREGATE ECONOMICS

With respect to aggregate economics the point is that a group of professional economists, mostly at Queen's University in Kingston, was able to integrate a number of concepts, such as the equation of exchange, the multiplier and the categories of aggregate expenditure and output, into an analysis of the generally depressed economic conditions of the 1930s. Monetary reformers, not professional economists, and mostly located in Western Canada, who had long held clear ideas about the imperfections of the existing monetary system, were able to build their analysis, which also used these concepts, into the circumstances of the depression to generate a justification for social control of money and banking, and, indeed, for an increase in the money supply as a cure for the depression. The professionals were much slower than the reformers in accepting these ideas, doing so largely as a result of contact with J. M. Keynes's *General Theory*.[48] The professionals had a clear understanding that the policy proposals coming out of the *General Theory* would not work in an economy that was heavily dependent on external commodity and capital markets.

The Industrial Organization – Monetary Theory split between Toronto and Kingston was not without overlap. W. A. Mackintosh, an authority on co-operative marketing of wheat, was at Queen's, and A. F. W. Plumptre, an authority on central banking, was at Toronto.

Development of aggregate economics and its relation to fiscal and monetary policy in Canada has been definitively described for the inter-war period in Irving Brecher's *Monetary and Fiscal Thought and Policy in Canada, 1919-1939*.[49] The people who made the connection between thought and policy have been most effectively described in Jack Granatstein's *The Ottawa Men: the Civil Service Mandarins, 1935-1957*.[50] Nothing needs to be added to what they have said beyond the usual sort of caveat that not all of the mandarins were from Queen's, and not all Queen's men became mandarins. O. D. Skelton, W. C. Clark and W. A. Mackintosh all taught at Queen's before entering public service. All were professional economists. C. A. Curtis and Frank Knox taught at Queen's and made important contributions to aggregate economics in Canada, but they were not in Granatstein's group of Ottawa men. Louis Rasminsky and Wynne Plumptre were Ottawa men, but not from Queen's.

A few citations from Brecher's account give the highlights of the story as seen from the late 1950s when the neo-Keynesian paradigm was in an early phase of its ascendency in Canada.

> For the most part, those individuals and institutions representing the so-called 'radical' point of view demonstrated a greater capacity for understanding economic principles and problems than those following the 'conservative' approach.[51]

The 'radicals' were men like William Irvine, George Beavington and J. S. Woodsworth, who represented those groups in Parliament that coalesced into the Co-operative Commonwealth Federation and the Social Credit Crusade. The 'conservatives' were the bankers, above all, but also the professional economists. The bankers, quite stupidly in Brecher's view, clung to the Banking School real bills doctrine.[52]

> the controversy involved little more than inadequate exposition of ... the contemporary Fisher-Keynes version of the 'quantity theory' of money

by the Labour and Progressive members of Parliament, and denial of the validity of that theory by the bankers.[53]

With the exception of the statements of J. F. Parkinson of the University of Toronto, who was 'strikingly Keynesian and unorthodox in 1933',[54]

> One probes the economic journals and other published sources in vain, in search of thoroughgoing discussion of the economics of employment.[55]

That is to say, there was no Keynesian discussion of the economics of unemployment. With the exception of J. F. Parkinson, the professional economists were slow to pick up on the idea of compensatory fiscal policy, taking until 1939 to suggest its use.[56]

> The economists' crucial contribution ... was mass entry into the final stages of the central bank controversy. Their contribution was strongly on the side of creation of a central bank....[57]

The rationale for setting up the central bank was not found in Keynesian theory. Swanson of Saskatchewan and Montpetit of Laval, favouring the gold standard over a fiat currency, were opposed. Curtis, Knox and Mackintosh of Queen's were in favour, as were Professors Creighton, Day, Plumptre and Parkinson. The argument was, in general, that the gold standard mechanism was defunct, and that something ought to be put in its place; and, that, in any case, Canada needed an instrument for international monetary co-operation.[58] With the exception of Parkinson, no one had Keynesian policy goals in mind.

The reluctance of professional economists to accept Keynesian theories needs explanation. Consider the case of Wynne Plumptre who had been in Keynes's seminar at Cambridge in the early 1930s and had had some influence in the future Keynesian mandarin, Bob Bryce, studying under Keynes.[59] Plumptre understood Keynesian theory and its implications for both fiscal and monetary policy. His cautious approach with respect to Canadian policy was a consequence of the open nature of the Canadian economy. Unless external demand increased, any stimulation through monetary expansion or fiscal pump priming would only cause further over-production and falling prices.[60] Plumptre's concern was echoed in the opinions of Frank Knox, who had a 'virtually exclusive concern with the international orientation of the Canadian economy'.[61] Whether this reluctance continued after 1939 remains to be seen. According to Brecher, the changes in monetary thought and policy in the 1930s were only a 'forerunner of the more spectacular developments which occurred during and after World War II'.[62]

The Queen's traditions of committed public service and conservative monetary policy did not begin with O. D. Skelton and Clifford Clark. They began with Adam Shortt and his work on the Civil Service Commission, that is, his pre-First World War attempt to turn the civil service into a merit-based professional organization. The macroeconomic monetary and fiscal policy favoured by the mandarins, in the 1930s, was consonant with Shortt's refusal to accept the monetary theories of the Birmingham School as they surfaced in the agrarian politics of his time. Shortt first elaborated the staple thesis in his explanation of the folly, as he saw it, of Sydenham's Provincial Bank of Issue. He used Canada's dependence on external markets to argue against the inflationist proposals of the 'Populists' of the early twentieth century. But on the other hand, monetary policies that, perhaps, made sense in a developed, relatively mature economy, were not suited to the Canadian case in which aggregate demand and aggregate investment depended on uncontrollable external factors. In essence, this was the position taken by Plumptre, Knox and Mackintosh with respect to monetary and fiscal expansion in Canada in the 1930s. It reflected the sensible side of Banking School theory. Unless there was profitable industrial activity to be undertaken, increasing the quantity of money would be merely inflationary; but if the basis on which bills were issued was really real, then increasing bank credit and currency would increase real income.

THE ENVIRONMENT OF THOUGHT

Irving Brecher has done a masterful job in capturing what he calls 'the shallowness of the environment of monetary thought in which public policy was implemented' in the 1930s.[63]

The general informational environment of the early 1930s was captured in *Queen's Quarterly* during the last few years preceding the first issue of the *Canadian Journal of Economics and Political Science* in 1935.

In Volume 40 (1933) there appears the article, 'The Proposal for a Central Bank',[64] which received much attention in late-1980s discussion of the virtues of free banking, deregulation, and other moves to undo the policy consequences of alleged misunderstanding of events in the 1930s. Of course, the article advocates the establishment of a central bank; but what is notable is that it is one of a series of four articles, prepared jointly by the Departments of Economics and Political Science at Queen's, dealing with all aspects of the contemporary problems of Canada. The first, 'Financial Manipulation: a Project of Reform',[65] alleges a significant level of fraud and foolishness in the financial structure of Canada, much of it related to Provinces competitively easing regulations in order to induce companies to reside in their jurisdictions. The third article, 'Financial Problems of our Federal System',[66] outlined the growing importance of government in all aspects of economic life, and the growing gap between responsibilities and revenues with respect to federal and provincial jurisdictions. The fourth article, 'Canadian Trade Policy in a World of Economic Nationalism',[67] rejected the economic nationalism of Keynesianism in favour of freer international trade. Following these commentaries on the nature of the Canadian economy and the Canadian state, there were articles on the role of the state in general,[68] in praise of fascism,[69] and in praise of socialism.[70] These articles were one root of the discussion of national purpose and the objectivity of economic theory that filled the war-shadowed pages of the *Canadian Journal of Economics and Political Science* after 1935.

The articles submitted by the Departments of Economics and Political Science at Queen's may have been influenced by Norman McLeod Rogers. Rogers was a stout defender of provincial rights against the onslaught of Frank Underhill and other socialists who considered the provinces to be feudal remnants standing in the way of central planning in Canada. Underhill likened Rogers to Calhoun and other defenders of slavery and the right of secession during the American Civil War. He called the professional economists purveyors of 'bourgeois homiletics'. There can be no doubt that the political passions of the times pressed hard on the professional economists, yet the staple thesis, the period's important contribution to economics, was a cold, empirical thing.

PUBLIC FINANCE

Because the problems of the Canadian federation were acute, because the structure of the federation was at the heart of the problems, and because the political heat generated was intense, public finance became a preoccupation of the professional economists. In this area there were contributions to theory, whether the rest of the world noticed or not, to the theory of fiscal federalism, and to the theory of public finance in general. In public finance, more than any other field of economics, the coterie of professionals was pan (English-speaking) Canadian: J. A. Maxwell in the Maritimes, D. C. MacGregor in Ontario, A. B. Clark in Manitoba, W. W. Swanson in Saskatchewan, G. A. Elliot in Alberta, W. A. Carrothers in British Columbia. The list is not exhaustive. Their accomplishment was the cumulative effect of their collective effort.

First there was reflection on increasing provincial demands for federal subsidies, and on the possible need for a revision of taxing powers.[71] Then came the studies detailing the reasons why. The responsibilities of the provincial governments – health, education, welfare and roads – were outgrowing their revenues.[72] From 1932 on, at the latest, Dominion-provincial conferences were marked by discussions concerning which jurisdiction should have the income tax and which the corporation tax.[73] Political concern

144 *A history of Canadian economic thought*

became intense with the publication of the *Jones Report*,[74] containing Norman McLeod Rogers's measure of the very uneven interregional burden of the tariff.

In an appendix to the *Report*[75] R. A. Mackay showed that federal-provincial financial arrangements could be changed, and had been changed frequently, and for a variety of reasons: need, impairment of sources of revenue, inequality, and the national interest. These changes, achieved by Act of the British Parliament, while showing change to be possible and desirable, fell short of the fundamental changes that seemed necessary. There would have to be amendments to the British North America Act.

There was no procedure for amending the British North America Act.[76] Still, change seemed necessary.

> Nova Scotia entered voluntarily (though possibly under undue influence) into Federation. It seems to me only reasonable to suppose that this implies a guarantee of her right to continue as a community. In this sense there seems to be a 'compact', and that compact involves a right to earn roughly the Canadian standard of living within the boundaries of the province, if reasonably possible. No province can be expected to accept the position of a colony to be exploited, nor to accept, except in the last resort, the migration or transfer of its people to the other provinces.[77]

What was true for Nova Scotia was true for the Prairie Provinces and for British Columbia, and, indeed for the constituent parts of a number of federations in the Empire.[78] And nowhere was there an easy solution, because the required degree of economic centralization was politically unacceptable. There was not even assurance about the economic aspect of the solution, because the theory of public finance had nothing to say about the basic problems involved.

> The great extensions of government activities in all industrialized countries since the War have not been balanced by an equivalent development of the Theory of Public Finance.... [It has yet to incorporate] new knowlege of monetary systems, of business cycles, of imperfect competition and of short-time analysis.... The studies of public finance made by Edgeworth, Marshall and Professor Pigou are based on the particularist method of approach, as opposed to the general equilibrium approach of Walras and Pareto.[79]

Donald MacGregor had anticipated some of these ideas, but Stewart Bates of Dalhousie stated the whole case. Taxes, expenditures and debt could no longer be considered in isolation from one another. The effect of the budget in redirecting economic activity and on the general level of output would have to be taken into account. Mr. Keynes's investment multiplier and Mr.

Kahn's employment multiplier would have to be incorporated into the analysis. The effects of large government activities on the *ceteris paribus* conditions of microeconomic activity, the effects of policy on expectations and initiative, and the implications of socialized consumption would all need consideration.[80]

Solutions were proposed: transfer of powers between federal and provincial jurisdictions, writing down of debts, repudiation of debts, grants in aid, and unconditional grants. None seemed to provide the requisite formula. As early as 1936, W. C. Clark, Graham Towers and O. D. Skelton were suggesting a Royal Commission to consider the question.[81] Eventually there was a commission and it reported, but the degree of centralization recommended was never achieved.[82]

But what had this to do with the staple thesis? In the staple thesis the political structure of Canada was an institutionalization of the needs of the economy. The problems of federal–provincial relations had grown out of the exigencies of developing a national economy with heavy reliance on staple exports.

INTERNATIONAL TRADE

The problem of international trade was at the core of the staple thesis, because the thesis depicted Canada as a small part of the industrialized Euro-American economy; but the *theory* of international trade had no part in the staple thesis, and very little part in Canadian economic thought in general. Canadian economic thought was very inward-looking in the 1930s.

There was some interest in international trade theory. Review articles kept the profession abreast of developments in the field as they proceeded in the work of Taussig, Viner, Haberler, Yntema, Ohlin and Harrod.[83] Data on international trade were published and international trade agreements, with their implications for free trade and the structure of the tariff, were closely followed: The Imperial Conference of 1932, the agreement reducing trade barriers between Canada and the United States in 1935, and the Canada–United States–United Kingdom free trade agreement of 1938. For the most, however, Canadians were interested in their domestic scene.

The big events for the economists were the Royal Commission on Banking and Currency in 1933, The Royal Commission on Price Spreads, 1934–1937, The Nova Scotia Royal Commission of Provincial Economic Inquiry in 1934, an administrative body, the National Employment Commission, set up in 1936, and, more than any other, the (Rowell-Sirois) Royal Commission on Dominion–Provincial Relations, the *Report* of which embodied the staple thesis of Canadian economic development.

146 *A history of Canadian economic thought*

THE STAPLE THESIS

The *Report* of the Royal Commission on Dominion–Provincial Relations and its associated studies mark the highpoint of that period in the history of economic thought in Canada that was dominated by the staple thesis.

> Canadian social scientists, long caught up in the problems of building a transcontinental economy in the face of regional divisions and the threat of United States penetration at key points, had found the way to a sound interpretation of Canada's 'old industrialism' of railways and wheat, iron and tariffs. National autonomy was to rest on a prairie agriculture geared to European markets, an eastern Canadian industry protected by high tariff walls against competition from the south, and a railway network that provided the economic ties of federal unity. This was the structure of the old fur trade writ large. To the 1930s it had all the appearance of a successful response to the challenge faced by Canada's first nationbuilders. Wheat was king, and railway investment, industrial protection, and transAtlantic trade bowed to this staple's leadership in national development.[84]

The first statement of the staple thesis antedates Adam Shortt, but Shortt, writing in the first decade of the twentieth century, used the thesis to justify rejection of Sydenham's Currency School banking proposals in 1840. The thesis pervaded O. D. Skelton's 'General Economic History of the Dominion: 1867–1912',[85] but was not explicitly stated therein.

In the early 1920s a number of scholars were working towards an economic history of Canada. James Mavor, Head of the Department of Political Economy at Toronto when Innis arrived, attempted a reconstruction of Canadian development in terms of the stages that the Historical School had inherited from Adam Smith.[86] C. R. Fay, a colleague of Innis in the 1920s, amended Mavor by defining the stages of Canadian development in terms of successive staple exports.[87] G. E. Jackson pointed to the importance of wheat as a factor in the level of GNP in Canada.[88] W. A. Mackintosh, taking his lead from the frontier thesis of F. J. Turner in the United States, wrote his classic 'Economic Factors in Canadian History',[89] in which he depicted Canadian development as a search for an export staple until wheat was produced on the Prairies. But there was still no general treatment of Canadian economic development.

Innis undertook his study of the fur trade. It was published in 1930, subtitled *An Introduction to Canadian Economic History*. With the publication in 1933 of *Problems of Staple Production in Canada*[90] Innis and his Toronto colleagues had elaborated the thesis of the *The Fur Trade* to take in, in a general way, the effects of more advanced transportation technique on institutions, and, in particular, on the nature and functions of government ownership in Canada. A year later, in *The Canadian Economy and Its Problems*,[91] they filled it out with respect to the financial arrangements of the federation, differences in regional economies, and the role of the business cycle and of monetary and financial institutions. The staple thesis was a description of the causal relationships between a number of factors in a particular economy dependent on a few primary product exports. Causation ran from geography and technology, and from aspirations imported from more advanced centres of industrial civilization, to dependence on staple exports and institutions to facilitate dependence.

By 1935 the substance of the staple thesis could be found in the work of Innis, but he had not stated it as a theory. In 1936 Mackintosh tied the idea of staple-driven cycles in Canada to the macroeconomic disequilibrium theory of J. M. Keynes.[92] This, more or less, applied the thesis to a class of phenomena, implying that it was a theory of business cycles in a staple producing economy, rather than an historical thesis, though Mackintosh did not elaborate on this.

A theory is an explanation of some general phenomenon. It explains a class of events, rather than a single event. The staple thesis explicitly appears as a description of a class of events in Plumptre's 'The Nature of Political and Economic Development in the British Dominions'.[93] The class of events included 'the economic, political, and social life of Australia, New Zealand, South Africa and Canada'. The thesis was set out in ten constituent elements that applied to all four instances in the class. Plumptre made no attempt to reconcile the thesis with either neoclassical theory or Keynesian theory. Neo-Keynesian and neo-Marxian theory did not exist at the time.

The ten elements that Plumptre listed as constituting a theory applicable to the British Dominions were the following:

(1) The pivotal place of a very few staple exports in the economic political and social life of the countries.
(2) The dependence of successive waves of development upon changes in the prices of staple exports.
(3) The dependence of successive waves of development upon the discovery either of new sources of materials or of new techniques of exploitation and transport.
(4) The extreme waves of optimism and pessimism which result from the peculiar difficulty of estimating the probable gains and losses of development.
(5) The import of capital and the problems arising from foreign debt.
(6) The necessity for intervention and assistance by the governments in connection with all major developments.

(7) The crystallization and immobilization of the fixed charges, incurred by heavy developmental expenditures, into government debts.
(8) The emergence of economic nationalism in the form of demands for economic diversification and, in particular, for secondary industries.
(9) Sectionalism, arising out of the divergent interests of widely separated economic areas; which fosters political jealousies, creates constitutional problems, and impedes the formulation and execution of national policies.
(10) Imperialism.

In this formulation the staple thesis had become an implicit theory. It had yet to be given the cause and effect logical structure of a theory. Innis had used theory, stretching it to its limits, to analyse a particular case. Plumptre applied the analysis in the form of description to a number of cases. In 1942 A. W. Currie gave the implicit theory a neoclassical formulation,[94] but that takes us beyond the period under consideration.

Returning to the question raised by Watkins, and discussed at the opening of this chapter, what was the relationship between the staple thesis and Keynesian theory? Both dealt with general disequilibrium, but Keynes's contribution was a macroeconomic theory. The staple thesis elaborated the microeconomic foundations of a particular, open, regionalized economy. They led to different policy conclusions. In fact, the staple thesis stated a problem, not a solution. Those who considered Keynesian theory in the context of the staple thesis concluded that Keynesian policies were not the solution in Canada.

9 Pensée économique, vingtième siècle

Etienne Parent (1846), Léon Gérin (1894), Edouard Montpetit, Esdras Minville, François-Albert Angers et plusieurs autres ont tous, tour à tour, déploré la faiblesse de la participation des Canadiens français à la vie économique. Le problème est toujours le même aujourd'hui.[1]

So wrote the authors of Quebec's projected economic plan under the Government of René Lévesque's separatist *Parti Québécois*. No doubt the plan had the guidance of the Minister of Finance, Jacques Parizeau, and so, at one remove it was influenced by the interventionist economist, François Perroux, under whom Parizeau had studied in Paris in the early 1950s. The constitutional referendum on the separation of Quebec from Canada (sovereignty-association) was only a year away. It was time to start planning.[2]

We resume our account of what was distinctive in the economic thought of francophone Quebec, remaining, until the 1940s, more or less under the guidance of François-Albert Angers and the nationalist (provincialist) tradition of *la pensée économique*. After 1940, in part a result of the intrusion of positive economics into Quebec, the nationalist tradition transformed itself into a new kind of *sociologie économique*.

The twentieth century was a new age for Quebec. Having developed relatively slowly in the late nineteenth century, Quebec stirred under the influence of advances in the use of electricity, a growing United States market for primary products, and the enhanced role of provincial governments in an increasingly decentralized federation. Quebec assumed the tasks of a welfare state while passing from a conservative agrarian to a modern industrialized society. The new age implanted itself in the social sciences with the work of the sociologist Léon Gérin, whose intellectual roots reached back to France and whose influence branched forward to the economics of Robert Errol Bouchette.

THE NEW NATIONALISM: GÉRIN AND BOUCHETTE

Frédéric Le Play was the intellectual father of the new age in French Canada. His importance in regard to the work of Antoine Gérin-Lajoie in nineteenth-century Quebec has been mentioned. His most forceful channel of influence, however, was the new sociology of Gérin-Lajoie's son, Léon. Unlike his father, Léon was a 'second generation' disciple of Le Play. That is to say, he was biased more to objective analysis than to social reform.[3] In adapting Le Play's methods to objective observation of the Quebec case, he developed internationally acclaimed research techniques.

Gérin held, and attempted to substantiate, the thesis that there was such a thing as a 'supériorité social des Anglo-Saxons' in Canada. By this he meant that they were, in fact, more competent than the French; that in some sense, the 'Anglo-Saxons' were deserving of the superior position they seemed to hold. The sociological foundation of their superiority, according to Gérin, was the aggressive individualism taught in the English schools, on the one hand, and the traditionalism of education and rural life among the French, on the other. Where Etienne Parent had accounted for the situation of the French by pointing to the Conquest, Léon Gérin accounted for the Conquest by pointing to the situation of the French.[4]

> La conquête du Canada par les Anglais s'explique donc, du point de vue social, par le triomphe d'une société particulariste sur une société exagèrement centralisée.

The specific hypothesis was new, though the idea of using social science to solve the problems of the French in Canada was not. The idea was accepted by a group of French-speaking, federal civil servants centreing on the person of Errol Bouchette, Chief Clerk of the Library of Parliament in Ottawa. Bouchette launched the project into the field of economics, where it was subsequently anchored by the work of Edouard Montpetit.

Robert Errol Bouchette (1863–1912) shifted the focus of the nationalist movement in Quebec from agriculture to manufacturing. He achieved this in the course of private conversations, in public addresses and in the writing of three books: *Emparons-nous de l'industrie*,[5] *Etudes sociales et économiques sur le Canada*,[6] and *L'indépendance économique du Canada français*.[7] His work is one of the intellectual roots of the modern separatist movement in Quebec.

Bouchette accounted for Canada's problems by pointing to the superiority of the United States in attracting people and capital. He accounted for Quebec's problems by pointing to traditionalism and conservativism rooted in Quebec's predominantly rural communities, in its educational system, and in an alleged penchant for soft and quiet living. His solution was a mild form

Pensée économique, vingtième siècle 151

of democratic socialism in which government support for development, particularly of hydroelectric power, would prevent both the under-use and the exhaustion of natural resources. But government support in Bouchette's scheme was to be largely indirect, that is, confined to improving the educational system. The task of government was to support the natural and the social sciences with a view to creating a 'bourgeois class', that is a technical and economic elite, that would initiate and direct industrialization.

Unlike his predecessors, Bouchette attempted to work out the economics of industrial development, which he thought to be divided into two principal elements: (1) the transfer of resources from consumer's goods to producer's goods industries, and (2) technological progress. The first entailed a reduction in the relative share of workers and farmers in the national product. The second, if it were capital saving, could eliminate the need for a reduction in either the relative or the absolute share of labourers and farmers. In Bouchette's view, all the burden of growth could be put on technological advance. Technological advance was dependent on the advance of science, so government action could be reduced to various forms of education. The 'problem of labour', the possibility that labour costs would choke off industrialization, was dismissed with an assertion that productivity gains would outpace wages. 'C'est la question de l'influence de la science sur les prix.'

Growth required capital and capital required knowledge and organization. Bouchette defined capital as 'natural', rather than 'private', and therefore, contrary to the doctrine of Adam Smith, it could not be equated with savings. Following J. K. Rodbertus, he defined the capital of a nation as the sum of its resources and abilities. To become productive it need only pass through an intermediate stage. It was this intermediate stage, this industrial experience, that was lacking in Quebec. The capital was there. What was wanting was a 'politique industrielle'. In 1979 the Parti Québécois would claim to present the first such 'politique économique', but Bouchette had had something to offer in 1914.

Bouchette suggested an ill-defined, government banking scheme. The state would organize and conserve the national capital, in much the same way that private corporations gathered capital from various sources through organizational devices. It then would portion it out to private enterprise to carry out the detail of industrialization. There would be no need to interfere with small businesses or agriculture, of which Bouchette was very protective. He wanted a 'balanced growth' that would include all sectors of the economy. Tariffs would be used only in those cases in which the industries in question would be internationally competitive. He gave as an example the dairy industry's contemporary advance into the production of cheese, which, he said, represented Rodbertus's intermediate stage. In that case government credit was being used to organize orderly production.

ELEMENTS OF THE NEW NATIONALISM

Bouchette initiated the change from 'Emparons-nous du sol' to 'Emparons-nous de l'industrie', but his effort was only one element in a general change in the informational environment in Quebec. The new mood became evident following publication of the Papal Encyclical, *Rerum Novarum* in 1891.[8] In 1907 l'Action Sociale Catholique was organized to spread Catholic social doctrine by means of the press. In 1911 the Jesuits founded a similar organization, L'Ecole Sociale Populaire. Finally, in 1920 Papin Archambault founded Les Semaines Sociales du Canada to train a social elite and to focus attention on the problems of French Canada.

Some of the doctrinal content of the popular movement may be inferred from the work of Arthur Saint-Pierre, who was one of the founders of the Ecole Sociale Populaire, and a heavy contributer to its monthly publication. He began to clarify his position in 1909[9] by noting the effects of immigration on the United States and Canada. The proportion of the French in Canada was declining and the 'melting pot' process of the United States made any prospect of annexation increasingly objectionable. At the same time, Canada's connection with Britain was visibly weakening and the American connection was growing stronger. To Saint-Pierre this meant that the cause of Confederation was being lost. It would be wrong to say that he turned to separatism as the only acceptable alternative, but certainly he drew attention to the possibility of a separate existence for Quebec. He worked for a Christian social order, for 'la mission de notre race; établir chez nous un ordre social chrétien'.[10] In his earlier writings on the history and organization of labour unions, he had pleaded for separate, Catholic organizations, in the expectation that irreligious international unions would leave the door open to socialism, or even anarchy.

A significant section of the new generation was not religious in orientation. Some, like Olivar Asselin,[11] continued in the tradition of the anti-clerical secularists who had appeared in the nineteenth century. About the time that some English-speaking Canadians were deciding that the 'old line political parties' were bankrupt, some French-speaking Canadians were deciding the same thing. In Quebec, of course, there were special circumstances. Prime Minister Laurier had badly settled the Manitoba School Question, and he had acquiesced in the Boer War. A generation later, when the conscription issue, increasing American ownership of business, and the problems of the 1929 depression had been added to the scale, disenchantment crystallized into a new political party, the Union Nationale. Olivar Asselin had worked hard in that direction. Having received his initiation into politics in the 'exile' Franco-American press during the Muck-Raking Era in New England, he had brought its methods home to put them at the service of French Canadian nationalism.

Asselin's aims included the nationalization of hydroelectric power, government conservation of natural resources, and an educational programme geared to the exploitation of Quebec by Québécois. Indeed, according to Gagnon,[12] he followed Léon Gérin and preceded Bouchette in calling for the economic independence of Quebec. Asselin was not an economist, except in the sense defined by F.- A. Angers (see chapter 3). He was a journalist who was concerned with economic policy; as were Henri Bourrasa, Edmond de Nevers and others connected with the early years of *Le Devoir*. By 1938 the economic aspect of his position was distinguishable from that of Errol Bouchette only by its strong bias towards 'Achat chez nous'.[13]

L'ECOLE DES HAUTES ETUDES COMMERCIALES

An important consequence of the new age's attitude was the establishment of the Ecole des Hautes Etudes Commerciales (H. E. C.) in 1911, and, in 1925, the birth of its journal, *Actualité économique*. H. E. C. was largely the result of Bouchette's hope that a commercial education would direct French Canadians into business careers. *Actualité économique* was the voice of the faculty of H. E. C., a forum for opinion on economic policy, serving in Quebec purposes similar to those of the *Canadian Forum* in English-speaking Canada. The general level of prices, banking, and industrial concentration dominated discussion in the first eight years.

Three economists associated with the Ecole des Hautes Etudes made distinctive contributions: Henry Laureys, Raymond Tanghe and Esdras Minville. Tanghe and Laureys were Europeans. They showed little of the characteristic patriotism of French Canadian writers. Esdras Minville, the most voluminous publicist of the three, was a norm in the mainstream tradition of *la pensée économique au Québec*.

Laureys was born in Belgium and studied economic geography at Louvain. He came to Canada in 1911 when H. E. C. was founded, and became Director of the School in 1916. His first book, *Essai de géographie économique du Canada*[14] was descriptive economic geography. His last book, *La technique de l'exportation*[15] was a text for commerce students, in no way a theory of international trade. It was an account of advertising, selling, credit and transportation instruments. *La conquête des marchés extérieurs*[16] his most important work, was an account of Canadian international trade, a plea for increased exportation of Canadian goods, and a set of practical suggestions as to how marketing and credit procedures could be improved.

Raymond Tanghe, like Laureys, was an economic geographer. He published more than Laureys, and did work in other fields. Two works,

Géographie humaine de Montréal and *Géographie économique du Canada*[17] probably represent his most solid contribution. During the 1929–39 depression he showed interest in the question of government control of credit, and in 1948–9 he gave a series of radio lectures on economic thought and policy in the nineteenth century. They were subsequently published as *Théories Economiques et Réalisations Sociales du XIXe Siècle*.

Esdras Minville, a native Canadian, received his licentiate at H. E. C. in 1922. After five years in the business community and part-time teaching, he accepted a full-time position at H. E. C. He was one of the founders of *Actualité économique*. He became Dean of H. E. C. in 1938. For some time he was an adviser to the Quebec Minister of Commerce.

Much that Minville produced was simply economic geography of the most rigorously descriptive sort. His outstanding work was the series *Notre Milieu*,[18] which he edited and to which he made a contribution. As Minville explained in the preface to the first volume, the series was not intended to include probative, analytic or even problem-oriented material. Each volume was a comprehensive description of some sector or division of the Quebec economy.

In the worst of the 1929–39 depression, Minville issued a sort of manifesto, *La politique qu'il nous faut*,[19] expressing his belief in a back-to-the-farm doctrine. The city ate people like wheat, so the doctrine ran, and produced neither. The country, however, was the source of capital, of food and of vitality. Still, the pace of urbanization was accelerating. Something had gone wrong with the organization of modern industrial society, something that ought not to be copied in Quebec. Economic advance was desirable, but if it meant relying on the United States for capital and skills, then it meant too much urbanization. What he saw as Quebec's basic need was an elite, an entrepreneurial class, that would assume responsibility for the economic development of agriculture and of small industries, without adopting Anglo-Saxon, individualistic organization, which he held to be foreign to the value system of the society he was trying to preserve.

Minville returned to this subject twice: in 1939, under the title 'L'avenir de notre bourgeoisie'[20] and in 1948 in *Invitation à l'étude*.[21] In 1942 a group of prominent French Canadians, including F.-A. Angers and Minville, had come together in an informal institute of social and economic research. Their prime concern had been the problem of Quebec. In *Invitation à l'étude*, the institute's first publication, Minville wrote of an American economic invasion of Canada, and again called for a French Canadian bourgeoisie to undertake the programme outlined by Errol Bouchette, but in a Quebec less closely tied to the rest of Canada.

Si, faute de capitaux, faute de solides institutions de crédit, de cadres économiques généraux assez suissants, nous ne pouvons, comme nous l'avons dit déjà, fondé des entreprises du type capitaliste capable de résister à la concurrence des entreprises anglo-canadiennes et américaines qui sont déjà installées chez nous, nous pouvons, grâce à notre nombre, et par la practique de solidarité nous soustraire quand même à leur dépendance. Incapable de récourir a l'association de capitaux nous pouvons en effet récourir à l'association de personnes...[22]

THE BEGINNINGS OF A POSITIVE APPROACH

Some of the work done in Quebec in the 1920-50 period paralleled the economic history approach that typified the emergence of the staple theory in English-speaking Canada. Paul-Emile Renaud, a student of Edouard Montpetit and a contemporary of H. A. Innis, drew on the work of Adam Shortt to tell the story of New France in terms of the establishment of private property, and the conditions surrounding the advent of exchange and specialization.[23] Gustave Lanctôt was another who showed an interest in economic history, but Lanctôt was also an economist in the fashion of F.- A. Angers, a patriotic historian concerned with the social and economic advancement of French Canada. J.- N. Fauteux, particularly in his *Essai sur l'industrie au Canada sous le régime français*,[24] made a heavy contribution to economic history in Canada. The tradition continued into the 1950s in the work of Albert Faucher and Charles Lemelin. All of these rightly have been cited for their contributions to economic history in Canada as a whole.[25] Their work also had significance for *la pensée économique au Québec*, and we will return to that.

MAINSTREAM PENSÉE ECONOMIQUE

The most representative spirit for the period from 1900 to 1940 was Edouard Montpetit. He received his B. A. from Laval in 1899. In 1908 and 1914 he acquired diplomas from l'Ecole Libre des Sciences Politiques, and from le Collège des Sciences Sociales in France. In 1920 he became Director of the School of Social, Economic and Political Science at the University of Montreal. In 1914 he was elected Fellow of the Royal Society of Canada and in 1924 he was made Chevalier de la Légion d'Honneur. His work included a remarkably long list of publications. His work in economics after 1910 was published in a three volume collection, *La conquête économique*.[26]

Montpetit set out with deliberation to elaborate an economics for francophone Quebec. Charles Gide, under whom he had studied, had insisted on introducing into economics what Montpetit called an element of humanity, that is, some means of measuring values other than by their expression in prices. The values in which Montpetit was interested were those of French Canada. He sought a compromise between what he called English practicality and French cultural superiority, a set of institutions that would bias prices and private enterprise towards French rather than English or American values. He wanted to combine the French genius for planning with English pragmatism to create an economics for Quebec.[27]

In his practical proposals Montpetit showed himself in the line of Parent, Gérin and Bouchette. He made a plea for mutual economic support among French Canadians in the form of a voluntary *achat chez nous* programme. Like the others he insisted on the need for improved education to ensure the conquest of the Quebec economy by *les Québécois*. 'Pour le moment, créons un élite qui repondra, par l'exemple et par la parole, les idées sur lesquelles nous nous serons accordées.'

In regard to both the tariff and capital accumulation his position was virtually the same as that of Bouchette.[28] Perhaps his emphases were different. He was more willing to accept state enterprise, stressing the need for a government development bank, and for government ownership of transportation facilities. In general, however, he was not in favour of public intervention in economic matters. Montpetit's approach may best be summed up in his own words.

> On disait autre fois: Emparons-nous du sol; on a écrit hier: Emparons-nous de l'industrie; disons a notre tour: Emparons-nous de la science et de l'art.[29]

THE IMPACT OF DEPRESSION AND WAR

The problems of the 1930s gave an urgency to economics everywhere in Canada. In English-speaking Canada an indigenous style of economic history came to some sort of completion, and there was fresh importation from abroad in the form of Keynesian macroeconomics, at least. In French-speaking Canada Bouchette's doctrine of economic nationalism was restated with a more aggressive intent. Keynesian economics, because it implied a more centralized federation, caused a new kind of division in French Canadian economic thought.

The year of destiny was 1936 when J.- H. Marcotte issued his manifesto, *Osons! Notre émancipation économique et national l'exige*, and Victor Barbeau wrote *Mesure de notre taille*. According to Marcotte, the American economic invasion of Canada had been an obvious success. *Les Québécois* had done nothing to prevent it. They had encouraged it. He suggested withdrawal from Confederation and a policy of complete economic independence. Barbeau was less definite in his separatism, but otherwise he had little to add to or delete from Marcotte's statement, except an extended substantiation of the proposition that French Canadians did not own the greater part of industry in Quebec. He summed up the situation by endorsing the view of Léon Gérin. A traditionalist society had overlooked its opportunity. To correct the error he urged, 'Emparons-nous de l'industrie'.

There was a new insistence in the tone of these assertions, and they contained a new idea of how the French Canadian project might be carried out. Marcotte repeated the old ideas about increasing the quantity of economics and science being taught in the schools, and about activating a French Canadian business class. As for capital, he again asserted that there was sufficient if only it could be centralized and properly directed. Barbeau took almost the same stand. 'Au commencement de notre misère il y a l'école; au commencement de notre libération, il y a l'école.'[30] But Barbeau despaired of any help from the French-speaking business elite. The bourgeoisie of French Canada had failed. Their time was past. In their place the schools would produce a new kind of elite, an elite of politicians and civil servants. Barbeau thought in terms of government rather than private enterprise.[31]

Changes in the attitude of the Church, and in the attitude of *les Québécois* towards the Church, were important factors in the preparation of post-Second World War Quebec. The Church accepted socialization in economic matters, removing any objection, from a certain point of view, to nationalization (provincialization) of industry. Nationalization was one way in which industry could be 'seized' without the adoption of 'Anglo-Saxon attitudes' and institutions. The pamphleteering of Richard Arès, S. J. illustrates how Church doctrine interfaced with changing attitudes. In 1938 Arès was sufficiently impressed with the sorry state of the economy to suggest the need for fundamental institutional reform.[32] After 1945, when economic problems were being addressed through new initiatives in Ottawa, he turned his attention to the 'national question' in Quebec, and to the working of Confederation.[33] In 1962, a year after Pope John XXIII issued his encyclical on Christianity and social progress, *Mater et Magistra*, Arès outlined the implications of the new ideas in *Le rôle de l'état dans un Québec fort*.[34] Had he foreseen even ten years ahead to the cultural revolution of the late 1960s and to the Quiet Revolution in Quebec, he might have written on the very diminished role of the Church in the New Quebec. After 1970 Roman Catholicism had no explicit place in economic thought in French Quebec.

Until the Second World War most economic thought in Quebec was economics according to the definition we have received from F.- A. Angers, but there was often some of the other kind of economics mixed in with *la pensée économique*. There was economic history, as noted, and there was some discussion of monetary economics, theory and policy.

MONETARY ECONOMICS BEFORE KEYNES

In the 1920s Beaudry Leman, one-time President of the Banque Canadienne Nationale, was a strong spokesman for the traditional view of credit, that is, he was opposed to government interference. It was part of his argument, however, that the banks responded to more than the possibility of profit, and, therefore, that credit in Quebec should be controlled by *les Québécois*.[35] Looking back in 1952,[36] he admitted some room for government control, but he did not surrender the gold standard.

> L'argent est un instrument d'échange, c'est là du moins son rôle principal, et sa valeur se mesure à ce qu'il permet d'acheter.... Depuis quand hérite-t-on de ses descendants? ... une économie qui répose sur l'épargne est beaucoup plus stable qu'une économie qui s'appuie sur le crédit.

Charles Rist would have been pleased. Raymond Tanghe and Edouard Montpetit agreed. 'Une autre forme de crédit qui a fait florès depuis quelques vingt ans, c'est le crédit à l'etat, la grande illusion ou l'impôt camouflé.'[37]

Roger Vezina did not agree. Vezina wanted a national credit scheme to lift the weight of the depression, much as did the Social Credit advocates of the West.[38] In Quebec, as in the rest of Canada, a full understanding of modern money and banking theory did not come until later.

POSITIVE ECONOMICS: THE LAVAL VISION

After the Second World War positive economics deepened its intrusion into the informational environment of francophone Quebec, and of Canada. The substance of what happened is clear. Positive economics, at that time in Quebec frequently associated with Keynesian economics, offered a new and apparently scientific foundation for analysis, judgement and policy, thereby threatening a host of entrenched values.

What happened in Quebec was similar to what happened across the country. At Toronto in the late 1930s the question of value-laden, as opposed to positive, economics lay at the heart of Innis's resignation from the University during a contest for the chairmanship of his department. Innis, of course, was not Keynesian, and, in fact, associated Keynesian policy with value-laden social science. At the University of Saskatchewan reaction took the form of the Chairman of the Department of Economics and Political Science refusing to hire or promote anyone who would not adhere to the quantity theory of money and the gold standard, that is, any Keynesian. Mabel Timlin emerged from that crucible. The intensity of the experience was still evident thirty years later in the way Ken Buckley would assert that, despite the confusions of those years, 'Timmy knew'.

Pensée économique, vingtième siècle 159

In Quebec, where positivism and centralization in line with Keynesian policies contradicted the entrenched, value-oriented *pensée économique*, and, indeed, seemed to write off its values as those of an obsolescent 'folk society',[39] acrimonious interpersonal relationships, with all that they entailed in the struggle for promotion, position, courses and curriculum content within the universities, was more than just intense.

It was in these cirumstances that the Department of Economics at the University of Montreal was introduced to neoclassical economics by Roger Dehem, and the Faculty of Social Science at Laval developed under Father G-. H. Lévesque. At Laval, in particular, positive social science, neoclassical economics, Keynesian economics and a Canadian national perspective found a tolerant environment. It was not that these elements were analytically compatible with one another. What could have been more diverse than the neoclassical, Currency School conservatism of Roger Dehem,[40] the Keynesian interventionism of Maurice Lamontagne,[41] and the German Historical School approach of Albert Faucher?[42] What they had in common was incompatibility with the established informational environment.

The group at Laval represented the spectrum of intruding elements, and because they held their positions in opposition to a most strongly pressed set of values, they saw and articulated the values of a reconstructed Canadian economy more urgently than their English-speaking counterparts. Their vision, which, for a time, was to be an implicit assumption of most Canadian economics, was clear. Constrained by geography and technology, the country had grown on the basis of primary product exports. The consequence had been advance, but advance had been accompanied by periodic depression and regional income disparities. With the advent of positive liberalism and Keynesian enlightenment, the advance could be continued without the depressions, with a social welfare net, and with inter-regional equalization. The advance of the Canadian nation stimulated by the National Policy of 1878 could continue into a period of industrialization and high income under a new, more scientifically founded and humane, national policy.

The explicitly entailed proposition was that, having benefited from Confederation in the past, Quebec would continue to benefit from it in the future.

In English-speaking Canada a similar perception was formed against a different constellation of opposing interests. It was implicit in the changes in Bladen's introductory text between its 1941 and 1956 editions.[43] Monetary theory and policy were taken from the appendices and given a place with the analysis of staple exports. It was latent in Mark Inman's post-Samuelson Canadian text.[44] The macroeconomic policy was there, but analysis of Canadian economic development was not extended beyond 1940. Fowke had revealed the vision quite clearly as early as 1952,[45] but it was not until Tony Scott wrapped the staple theory into neo-Keynesian growth theory and late

1960s macroeconomic fine tuning, that the vision decended to the lowest common denominator of the established informational environment.[46]

Lamontagne's work appeared two years after Fowke's article, but it was prepared independently, and developed the vison in much greater detail. It immediately became part of the general informational environment in Quebec, informing the views of his non-neo-Keynesian colleague, Roger Dehem, until the late 1960s, at least.[47] Its substantive content challenged in Quebec a more radical regionalism than existed in the rest of the country.

The Laval vision was not analytical. It was synthetic. Given the values of modern liberal civilization, and the possibilities, however limited, of positive social science, it projected a reasonable programme of social reconstruction for Quebec and for Canada. The aspirations of those who made the commitment were beyond reproach. It is regrettable that the naïve Keynesianism with which the vision became associated proved to be so vulnerable, and that, having been rooted in a theory of dependent export-led growth, it lost credibility when the theory was called into question.

The details of this story, of course, will have to be told from inside Quebec by someone with a wider knowledge and a keener sense of the informational environment.[48] Indeed, this is epecially true in the present instance, because the economics of Canada as described in this history of economic thought, although neither intended to be, nor, in fact, an argument for separatism, contradicts the economics of Canada that has been presented as one of the arguments in favour of Quebec's remaining in the federation.[49]

REACTIONS IN THE AGE OF POSITIVISM

Positivism and 'pan-Canadianism' prodded the tradition of *pensée économique* into a self-conscious flowering,[50] just before it transformed into *sociologie économique*. Minerva's owl took flight, especially in the work of François-Albert Angers.

Three articles, in particular, have been designated by Gilles Paquet as summing up economic thought in Quebec since 1945. They are Jean-C. Falardeau's 'Perspectives',[51] André Raynauld's 'Recherches économiques récentes sur la Province de Québec',[52] and his own 'La fruit dont l'ombre est la saveur: réflections aventureuse sur la pensée économique au Québec'.[53] For economy of presentation, and to prevent uncontrolled deviation from what francophone establishment *Québécois* have considered to be *la pensée économique au Québec*, we can anchor our consideration of post-Second World War economic thought in Quebec in these articles and in the forums and volumes in which they first appeared.

The first volume, *Essais sur le Québec contemporain*, contains two relevant essays, neither of which is so much a history of economic thought as a presentation of contemporary conclusions in two streams of economic thought. The first, 'History of Industrial Development',[54] by Albert Faucher and Maurice Lamontagne, was a summary of the economic development of Quebec taking the approach of the Toronto School in the 1920–50 period. Innis and Lower were cited, as were other English- and French-speaking historians, in a nice summary of the changing fortunes of Quebec in response to changes in technology and world demand for Quebec's resource-based output. The pace and character of development were seen to be independent of political or cultural factors within Canada or within Quebec. The essay filled out an aspect of Quebec's development that only indirectly had been suggested in Minville's earlier account of the development of Quebec.[55]

The second relevant essay, J.-C. Falardeau's 'Perspectives', filled in the institutional aspect of development, the evolution of the corporation from an instrument of 'captains of industry' in the late nineteenth century to the large, impersonal, multinational institution of the mid-twentieth century. Despite the pleas of Parent, Bouchette and Montpetit, there had been no seizing of industry by francophone Québécois. Indeed, Falardeau saw no place for a traditional, ethnocentric philosophy in the modern economic order.[56] Quebec had relied on a domestic supply of inexpensive labour and raw materials, an outside supply of capital, and Anglo-Canadian and American enterprise, in a post-1900 sprint to industrialization. As Minville had put it, 'A population that was four-fifths rural and nine-tenths self-sufficient had become three-quarters urbanized and seven-tenths dependent.'[57]

Ten years later it seemed that the essential point of Falardeau's 1953 summary was that external forces had brought about irrevocable economic change, and that the inevitable, consequent social adjustments had yet to be made.[58] How such a post-mortem could be interpreted would depend on where the coroner stood on the national question.

When André Raynauld produced his 1962 essay on recent economic research in the Province of Quebec, he gave no explicit recognition to the Minville–Angers tradition in *la pensée économique au Québec*.

ON THE NATURE OF POSITIVE ECONOMICS

By 1962 Keynesian economics had been extended into positivist growth theory. R. F. Harrod's *Towards a Dynamic Economics* was published in 1948. Paul Samuelson's application of Logical Positivism to the field of economics, his *Foundations of Economic Analysis*, had been published as far back as 1945. All the essays in Milton Friedman's *Essays in Positive Economics* were completed by 1952. Leontief's application of inter-industry input–output analysis in *The Structure of the American Economy* had already drifted into the category of an early work. In short, economics had become oriented to general equilibrium. It had become technical, and, in a word, positivist.

Positivist economics is 'operationally viable economics'. It sets out hypotheses for quantitative falsification. The hypotheses take the form of mathematical models, that is, sets of equations, the empirical content of which is to be judged by whatever statistical tests are appropriate. Not all of positivist economics passes itself through all of the implied steps of scientific method, but all of it has or assumes, mathematical statements suited for statistical testing, at least in principle. Positivist economics is technically sophisticated, either in its elaboration of models or in its data gathering and processing methods. It is capable of efficient statement of the complex logical relationships that characterize even the simplest models. For the sake of discussion here, economics that only verbally describes the relationships between agents or 'variables' of a micro or macro sort, that uses only charts or graphs of time series to corroborate conjectured relationships, is not to be considered positivist.

The expression of post-war, positivist economics in Canada can be traced in the pages of the *Canadian Journal of Economics and Political Science* to 1967, and in the pages of the *Canadian Journal of Economics* thereafter. There was no positivist economics in the *Canadian Journal of Economics and Political Science* before 1943. Thereafter there were one or two pieces, articles or notes, in almost every volume until 1963. Many were contributed by United States residents. The Canadians making such contributions were, in chronological order: J. C. Weldon, Benjamin Higgins, Roger Dehem, Harry Johnson, Murray C. Kemp, Gideon Rosenbluth, Mac Urquhart and Gordon Bertram. In 1963 the *Journal* carried three positivist articles. By 1970, non-positivist articles were close to non-existent in the *Journal*.

André Raynauld's 1961 *Croissance et structures économiques de la Province de Québec*[59] represented the cutting edge in the application of positivist economics to practical questions. It used Harry Johnson's work[60] to apply growth theory to the very open Quebec economy. It surpassed Hood and Scott's application of Kuznets's and Harrod's analyses to the Canadian economy[61] by incorporating a Leontief-type inter-industry analysis and the growth-pole analysis of François Perroux. It was a triumph in the application of the latest in economic thought.

Raynauld presented his conclusions in chapter VII of *Croissance et structures*, and in his 1962 essay on recent economics in Quebec, in which he confined himself, almost exclusively, to contributions along the lines of his own work.

Those industries in which Quebec had a comparative advantage, resource export industries and labour-intensive industries with a domestic Canadian market, either had weak interlinkages with the rest of the Quebec economy or were low-productivity, slow-growth industries. Ontario had the capital-intensive, high-productivity, tertiary manufacturing industries that Quebec lacked. In seeking an explanation, Raynauld rejected the view, taken by Faucher and Lamontagne in 1952, that directing forces in the development of Quebec were to be found outside the province. Citing evidence uncovered by John Dales,[62] he singled out cultural factors, working through a highly elastic domestic supply of labour, a phenomenon that Arthur Lewis had noted in the underdeveloped countries of the Third World.[63]

Not only the older, value-oriented *pensée économique*, but even earlier forms of positive economics lost ground to the new fashions. In an excellent statement of the tasks of economic history as seen by a member of the German Historical School in the mid-twentieth century,[64] Albert Faucher flanked Raynauld's comments with a lament that history was being crowded out of economics departments to make room for Keynesians, macro model builders, mathematicians, statisticians and those historians of the future, the development economists;[65] which, as we have noted, did not align Faucher with the Minville-Angers tradition.

Proponents of traditional *pensée économique* faced the new economics in a state of shock. From the point of view of policy, the early years of positivist economics in Canada were characterized by the national political centralization proposed by the (Rowell-Sirois) Royal Commission on Dominion–Provincial Relations, and by the 1945 White Paper on Employment.[66] The latter, at least, was strongly influenced by Keynesian theory. Economists in the tradition of *la pensée économique* simply rejected them. In response to the Commission on Dominion–Provincial Relations, Quebec had its own Royal Commission of Inquiry on Constitutional Problems. Chapter IX in Section III and appendices 5 and 11 of the report were the work of François-Albert Angers.

FRANÇOIS-ALBERT ANGERS

Angers's motivation was explicit. He intended to discredit what was known in Quebec as the 'centralist thesis'. That was the view, attributed to the authors of the federal (Rowell-Sirois) commission's report and to the civil service elite in Ottawa, that taxation, particularly taxation of income, was an unlimited right of the federal government, that it should be an unlimited right because it was an instrument not only of revenue but of stabilization policy, and that stabilization policy was a matter of federal jurisdiction because the British North America Act had given the federal government full responsibility for the economic condition of the federation as a whole. The alternative 'thesis', which was not given a name, was the assertion that it was the task of the federal government to ensure the social and economic viability of the federation's constituent parts, and that it should do so by ensuring that provincial governments could carry out their responsibilities. Quebec was not the first province to assert this thesis, but it was its turn to assert it at the time of the provincial (Tremblay) commission's report. Quebec, of course, was concerned about the threat to French Canadians as an identifiable linguistic and cultural group, and to their position in the economic structure of the federation. Angers put it in the following way. The New Federalism would be responsible for

> causing the Canadian State to lose its political character and of being transformed into an economic society, which, above all else, would be concerned with material well-being and technical efficiency.... There must be other, more cogent, motives than administrative simplification, technical efficiency or even economic stabilization.[67]

Angers presented an argument that Keynesian compensatory fiscal policy, especially with the income tax as its instrument, would be neither efficient nor equitable. Whatever his motivation, Angers made his case, with erudition, on theoretical and practical economic grounds. In its lucidity and substance, his performance is to be compared with Charles Rist's *History of Monetary and Credit Theory*:[68]

> Let us not forget that we have, within the past half century, witnessed the political bankruptcy of two theories in which our modern world, or at least certain parts of it, had placed its hopes – the liberal theory of economic equilibrium and the quantitative theory of money in its mathematical form. ... They leave behind them principles and experiences which are definite acquisitions for human knowledge and wisdom, but none to defend their integral application as policies.[69]

In his critique of the Keynesian proposition, Angers invoked a host of authorities: Pigou, Robertson, Haberler, Ohlin, Chamberlin, Leontief, Hawtrey, Rist, Nogaro, Perroux, and others, from whom he drew his theoretical arguments.[70] His three practical arguments, though virtually dismissed in his own time, would be highlighted in standard texts of the 1980s.[71] He outlined all of the informational problems associated with attempts to fine-tune an economy.[72] He pointed to the efficiency and equity problems that would be entailed in applying a uniform stabilization policy to an economy as regionally diversified as Canada's.[73] He used the problems associated with Keynesian policies in an open economy to show that arguments purporting to demonstrate that the federal government was the suitable locus for expenditure and demand control really showed that control of Canadian counter-cyclical policy should be located in Washington.[74]

Angers's attack on the income tax was an extended argument showing the superiority of an expenditures tax, which he would have associated with provincial governments. The argument betrays no knowlege of the work of Henry Simon or of Carl Shoup and those around him in the United States who, at that time, were making a case for a value-added tax. Angers worked on his own, citing everyone who had ever had anything to say about the relative merits of income and expenditure taxes. For example, J. S. Mill, on the income tax:

> This tax, while apparently the most just of all modes of raising revenue, is, in effect, more unjust than many others which are prima facie more objectionable.[75]

In brief, his argument was that the income tax was a tax on the conscientious, that is, those who worked hard and did not falsify their income reports. It was a tax on saving and on investment. It was a tax easily evaded by lobbying for tax law loopholes, and by contriving to pass on the incidence. In practice it was regressive, whereas an expenditures tax was not regressive in principle, and could be made non-regressive in practice. Whatever else might be said of the case that Angers made, his arguments for an expenditures tax were well put. It is a telling comment on the role of good judgement and sound reasoning in public policy that it took the policy makers of any jurisdiction in Canada another thirty-three years to acknowledge these arguments. To say this, of course, is not to agree with any corporatist views that Angers may have held.[76]

LA SOCIOLOGIE ECONOMIQUE AND THE NEOCLASSICAL PROJECT

The arrival of positivist economics in Canada by 1970 was contemporary with the arrival of what has been called the New Political Economy, or, in Quebec, '*la sociologie économique*'. While an economist cannot speak with authority about the nature of another discipline, it is necessary to set out the assigned meaning of a term that is to be used. The New Political Economy arrived in Canada in the 1970s following demands during the student unrest of the late-1960s for a value-oriented and critical social science. It was fed by the writings of A. G. Frank, with respect to the problem of economic underdevelopment, and later by the writings of Ralph Miliband in Europe, which dealt with the legitimization crisis of modern capitalism. The latter influence does not seem to have been as strong in Quebec as in Ontario.

Much of *la sociologie économique* can be categorized as Western Marxism. It is an explicit protest against neoclassical economics as, in its view, an ideology. As a value-oriented social science, *la sociologie économique* is post-positivist; so it is also a protest against the technically sophisticated, positivistic methodology of post-Second World War economics. It involves little explicit reference either to the more technically economic works of Marx, or to post-positivist philosophies of science such as those of Imre Lakatos or Paul Feyerabend. Its focus is on social structures, such as class and class factions, and on power relationships, and it is much more at home in departments of sociology and political science, than in departments of economics.

The repeated, open attacks on neoclassical economics by the practitioners of *la sociologie économique*, rarely, if ever, contained a statement of the neoclassical project as a scientific endeavour. To clarify what is meant by that phrase here, it is necessary to add to the earlier over-simplified statement on the nature of neoclassical and positivist economics.

The neoclassical project, as the term is used here, is an attempt to establish the conditions of objective rationality in the use of material resources for the realization of individual values. Its whole analytical apparatus could be turned to the establishment of conditions necessary for the realization of some communal value, however that might be established, but that would not be the neoclassical project. The essence of the definition of objectivity in the neoclassical project lies in the reduction of value judgements to the level of the individual, thus removing them from explicit consideration in the analysis. What is measured is relative material cost, which has a physically enumerable value and is, therefore, objectively measurable in a positivist sense. The value judgement at the core of the project is the assertion that the cost of achieving individual realization should be minimized, or, alternatively, that, given limited material means, realization should be maximized. This abstract criterion of efficiency, carefully defined as Pareto Optimality, is unmixed with any other value, preference or taste.

Neoclassical analysis is of no use to individuals in the conduct of their daily economic affairs, because subjective rationality is tautologically based on subjectively perceived values and constraints. It is of fundamental importance to social action in which the organization of behaviour must be based on explicit information sharing among individuals, that is, the objective specification of values and constraints. Neoclassical theory has two functions: to establish the conditions for objective rationality in an absolute way, and to establish the details of organization that achieve rationality under specific constraints. The first provides criteria for altering constraints in the direction of efficiency. The second provides criteria for altering behaviour in the direction of efficiency. Both provide objective rules for the advance of civilization, defined as the realization of individual human potential. No room is left for the consideration of group values defined by culture, language, race, or any other criterion.

Whatever the failures of individual neoclassical economists, or whatever the limitations of neoclassical analysis at some stage in its development, in the past or at present, the validity and importance of the neoclassical project as a field of social science is unquestionable.

The arrival of *la sociologie économique* in the 1970s was contemporary with the embarrassment of Keynesian orthodoxy (see chapter 10). So there was a paradoxical situation in which Keynesianism was crowded by a positive economics, more firmly rooted in the neoclassical project, on the right, and a new and ill-defined paradigm, political economy or *sociologie économique*, on the left.

THE HISTORICAL CONTEXT, 1970–90

The effect of these fundamental changes on social science in Quebec took place in the context of, and was influenced by, the changing long- and short-run conditions of the Canadian economy. Post-war expansion in North America ended with the recovery of Europe and Japan in the late 1950s. After some hesitation, another period of strong growth was associated with the advance of industrialization in Asia. By 1970, however, North America had entered a period of 'deindustrialization' and 'stagflation' in which it adjusted to the consequences of its own expansionary policies, natural and contrived supply shocks, and the presence of newly industrialized competitors. Following a severe downturn in 1981–3, there was a return to growth, apparently based on massive innovation in the field of telematics, and on the continuing spread of industrial civilization. All of these events had effects on economic thought in Quebec.

In Canada, and in Quebec, the course of events had distinctive elements. The rise of multinational enterprise occasioned much discussion of the ownership of Canadian industry and of the consequences of ownership, a topic that had been of special interest to the practitioners of *la pensée économique au Québec*. The energy crisis, which was part of the supply-shock situation of the 1970s, caused a boom in the petroleum industry in western Canada, but added to the problems of deindustrialization and stagflation in Ontario and Quebec. Relative decline in certain aspects of United States industry, in consequence of the continuing spread of industrialism throughout the world, was the occasion of increased protectionism in Canada's primary external market. To head off this threat the federal government negotiated a free trade treaty with the United States.

In Quebec itself there was a sequence of events that was distinctively Québécois, and cannot be ignored in any account of economic thought in the province. In 1960 the Rassemblement pour l'Indépendance Nationale was formed, Jean Lesage's Liberal government was elected, and the Quiet Revolution got under way as the state became an instrument to achieve the long-cherished aspiration, 'emparons-nous de l'industrie'. In 1967 Charles de Gaulle made his 'Vive le Québec libre' remark in Montreal, prematurely terminating his official visit to Canada. In 1968 René Lévesque's *Option Québec* was published, leading up to the founding of the Parti Québécois. In 1970 Pierre Laporte's assassination by members of the Front de Libération du Québec was followed by the October Crisis, during which Quebec was placed under the War Measures Act. In 1976 the separatist Parti Québécois formed the government in Quebec. In 1980 a referendum on Sovereignty Association (separation) was defeated by a majority of 59.6 per cent. In 1984 the Parti Québécois abandoned, at least temporarily, the goal of separation from Canada.

THE PASSING OF *LA PENSÉE ECONOMIQUE*

La pensée économique, as defined by F.- A. Angers, evaporated when positivistic neoclassical economists, referred to as the 'plumbers', separated economics from the more value-oriented traditional approach.[77] At the same time the new discipline, *la sociologie économique*, with its value-oriented focus on dependency, development, class structure, power and control, was a natural home for consideration of the nature and role of the Quebec bourgeoisie, and of the structure and relative position of the Quebec economy. The policy agenda of *la pensée économique* fell to those in the Parti Québécois who were bent on transforming the 'pius and nationalistic wishes' of the past into concrete proposals as the state reformed, or attempted to reform, the economy.[78]

When a forum was organized at Laval in 1984 to take stock of the state of the social sciences in Quebec, discussion of economics fell to André Sales, a sociologist, who did passably well, despite his evident distaste for the subject, and to Gilles Paquet, who had the genius to see the possibility of holding the melange of new beginnings together in a 'meso-analyse', without being able to convince anyone else of the merits of so doing.[79] Neither was in sympathy with the positivist neoclassical project.

Both Sales and Paquet began by noting that economics in Quebec was preoccupied with the fields of international trade, urban and regional economics, and mathematical economics and econometrics. In his comment on Sales's address, Gérard Bélanger suggested that these preoccupations were not unique to Quebec.[80] He made a comparison with work done in British Columbia, implying that such interests were natural in an regionally differentiated, open economy in which the bulk of the professional economists were trained in the United States.

The 1960s had been years of economic planning in Quebec, as elsewhere in Canada, and an enormous amount of economic literature was produced in that connection, for example, by the Bureau d'amenagement de l'est du Québec. Some of it was theoretically interesting, as well as administratively useful. Of course, it was regional economics.[81]

Regional development was related to the question of foreign ownership. The Québécois had been interested in foreign ownership by Anglo-Canadians and United States companies for decades. The new fashion in studies of foreign ownership that caught on in the rest of Canada in the late-1960s was quickly absorbed and put to use in the cause of Quebec nationalism.[82]

In their 1979 economic manifesto the Parti Québécois[83] elaborated one more in the long series of attempts to describe the nature and causes of the perceived unfavourable position of the Quebec economy and of the French population within it. Characteristics attributed to the economy were those described in André Raynauld's *Croissance et structure* with the addition of a rate of growth that was falling even in relation to Ontario's falling rate of growth. Allegedly, the cause was not the Conquest, nor traditional French culture, nor geography and technology, as had been suggested in the past. According to the manifesto, it was the policies of the federal government, favouring Ontario and denying Quebec control of its own destiny, that inhibited its entrepreneurial initiative.

At last the more intense and complex regionalism (nationalism) of Quebec had brought it around to a view of national policy similar to that accepted by British Columbia, the Prairies, and the Maritimes much earlier; with the difference that in Quebec separatists seriously proposed a solution by way of autonomy, rather than by way of increased federal support. Once autonomy was achieved, said its proponents, the rest would depend on the 'will to act of autonomous individual economic agents',[84] and on the ability of the state to co-ordinate activity and encourage it through provision of information, of financial aid, of infrastructure, training, regulation, deregulation, and all the other instruments of state initiative that seemed acceptable in the age of democratic planning.

Economists addressed the question of the economic consequences of separation with a mass of published material,[85] but without coming to any generally accepted conclusion.[86] In the middle of the debate, the profession in Quebec formed its own, French-speaking association, perhaps in preparation for separation, but the economists of the Maritimes also formed a regional association about the same time. Regionalization reflected the state of development of the profession in North America, as much as anything special to Quebec.

As politics split into an extreme right and an extreme left, spokespersons for both sides appeared in Quebec's cadre of social scientists. The left seems to have been more numerous, perhaps because *la sociologie économique* was a more appropriate approach to the topics that most interested Québécois. A

170 A history of Canadian economic thought

smaller group of economists, working in the tradition of Buchanan and Tulloch in the field of public choice, and, perhaps, with the Coase-Williamson, New Institutionalist approach, was best represented by Jean-Luc Migué.[87]

Migué deftly applied the criterion of efficiency to elements of Quebec's nationalist, interventionist policies. Of particular interest was his foray into language policy.[88] The economics of language, as part of the economics of information, was an area in which significant contributions could be made to the discipline of economics in general.

The left may have been best represented by Jorge Niosi,[89] who articulated its apprehensive preoccupation with international capitalism, the international corporation and the United States economic empire. It was possible for the left to note that 'francophones now occupy a majority of the management positions and hiring positions in the large private enterprises' of Quebec.[90] Their appreciation of the Quebec bourgeoisie changed accordingly. The long-awaited bourgeoisie was now designated a 'class, not only in itself, but for itself'.[91]

Approximately eighty people listened to André Sales deliver his account of contributions to the economics of Quebec. Only one was an economist. The sole economist, Gérard Bélanger, suggested that one could better discover who was making what contributions to economics in Quebec by reading the *Social Science Citation Index*. To correct the bias of the Sales and Paquet accounts I checked the *Index*, using the names of the members of the Economics Departments of the University of Montreal, Laval and the University of Quebec in Montreal for 1987, and the citations and sources for the years 1977, 1982 and 1987. The method has little scientific validity. I merely sketch the results.

The Department at Montreal was most prolific, and was highly academic and neoclassical, as Gilles Paquet had suggested. The Department at Laval showed no indication of being biased towards Keynesian doctrine and economic history, as Paquet had suggested for the earlier years of the period. It was not unusual for members of the two departments to publish in non-Quebec journals. A number of French-language journals in Europe were named. The *Canadian Journal of Economics* and *Canadian Public Administration*, both of which accepted articles in French, were frequently named, particularly the latter. Those publishing in English in non-Canadian journals, *Econometrica, American Economic Review, Advanced Studies in Theoretical and Applied Economics*, and others, were producing 'technical' and econometric studies.

Little can be achieved by attempting to record the specific substance of these studies. Some of it will come to light when the state of economic thought in Canada as a whole is reviewed for the period (see chapters 10 and 12). Much of it was good, positivist, pushing back of the margins of knowledge in the process of 'normal science'. As Schumpeter would have said, its authors were solid builders, adding to what they had received and providing something for others to build on. But to correct the impression left by Sales and Paquet some detailed reference would seem to be in order. In 1982, M. Dagnais of the University of Montreal was cited five times, four in English-language journals; and had published 'A General Approach for Estimating Econometric Models with Incomplete Observations'. J-. M. Dufour was cited eight times, and had published 'Recursive Stability Analysis of Linear Regression Relationships – an Exploratory Methodology'. G. Dionne had published 'Moral Hazard and State Dependent Utility Functions' in the *Journal of Risk Insurance*. In 1987, M. Boyer was cited fourteen times and had four articles published, including 'On Stackleberg Equilibria with Differential Products – the Critical Role of the Strategy Space' in the *Journal of Industrial Economics*. All of these from the University of Montreal. J. T. Bernard had published 'The Probability-Distribution of Future Demand – the. Case of Hydro Quebec', in the *Journal of Business Economics* in 1987. Bernard was a member of the Department at Laval. From the University of Quebec in Montreal, C. D. Fluet had published 'The Sharing of Total Factor Productivity Gains in Canadian Manufacturing – a Price Accounting Approach, 1965–1980' in *Applied Economics*. This is by no means the end of the list, but, perhaps, the point has been made.

With respect to the general subject of the present work, the economics of Canada, it may be unnecessary to remark that, the work of Fauteux, Faucher and André Raynauld indicated the importance of primary product exports only in twentieth-century industrialization in Quebec. Raynauld subtantiated his conclusion that linkages between resource industries and the rest of the economy were weak, but he made no attempt to measure the importance of primary product exports in relation to non-export primary production or the production of manufactured goods for domestic consumption as elements in Quebec's economic growth. Traditional *pensée économique* was concerned with non-francophone ownership of enterprise, but that had no theoretical connection to staple exports. Indeed, traditional *pensée économique* was affronted by the positivism of the staple thesis. *La sociologie économique* might in some way be related to the staple theory in some of its later versions, but its value orientation precluded positivistic measurement of anything. Verification of the proposition that the staple theory explained what happened in Quebec, or was thought by *Québécois* to have explained what happened in Quebec, the Laval vision notwithstanding, is simply not possible on the basis of the literature produced in Quebec.

10 Keynes in a small open economy

There have been two broad periods in post-Second World War Canadian economics. The first, roughly from 1957 to 1970, was a period of British influence. The second, after 1970, a period of United States influence. The first is associated with Keynesian macroeconomics, the second with Monetarism, neoclassical microeconomics and positive economics in general. But this puts it too simply.

What happened in economic thought over the midpoint of the century paralleled what had happened to the economy over the turn of the century. Before 1896, integration of the Canadian economy into the United States economy proceeded at a measured pace. During the Wheat Boom period there was a massive, though temporary, reintegration of the Canadian and British economies, both with respect to markets and with respect to capital flows. Not that integration with the United States stopped. It did not. But, for a time, until the end of the First World War, the British connection was the more active. After the First World War, reversion to the late-nineteenth-century pattern of integration with the United States was rapid and definitive. So it was with economic thought over the midpoint of the century. Before 1939, integration of Canadian into United States economic thought proceeded at a measured pace. In part because the economies were integrating into a North American market, and in part because, in a world of capital deepening, a common technology tended to dominate the effects of geography and history in economic activity. During the post-Second World War period there was a sudden and massive reintroduction of British economic thought into Canada. Neo-Keynesian thought, the United States version of what was imported from Britain, began to take hold, but it was not until the high period of the Keynesian paradigm had passed that United States neo-Keynesianism appeared as the alternative to Monetarism and New Classical Economics, which were also generated in the United States. Since then, with widespread acceptance of a positivist approach, there has been no substantial distinction between Canadian and United States economics.

Keynes in a small open economy 173

In this chapter we will be concerned with the period before 1970 when Canadians attempted to adapt Keynesian economics to a small open economy. Keynes had assumed a closed, mature economic system. By introducing considerations relating to development and trade into Keynesian general equilibrium analysis Canadians, particularly in the person of Harry Johnson, made major contributions to the development of economics.

THE MOTHER OF INVENTION

In the late 1940s an influential subset of Canada's economic policy-making elite set out to establish the Keynesian paradigm. They faced a number of problems. To begin with, it was not crystal clear what that paradigm was, and intellectual war soon broke out between a classical, perhaps Marxian, interpretation and a neoclassical, that is, neo-Keynesian interpretation. In addition to this, applying Keynesian economics to Canadian circumstances was problematic. Keynes had developed his theory on the assumption of a balanced, homogeneous, closed economy in a unitary state. The Canadian economy was open, regionally diversified, relatively dependent on primary product exports, and governed by a federated state. There would be questions raised about Canada's reliance on primary product exports, but no one questioned the open character of the economy. To accommodate this situation theoretically Canadian economists integrated Keynesian macroeconomics and international trade theory, dominating trade theory in the process. A number of expatriate Canadians were involved. We review only the literature that comes under our definition of Canadian economic thought.[1]

THE EARLY PERIOD OF PARADIGM SHIFT

The new paradigm did not slip into place immediately. During and after the war the economics profession was as distracted as other agents in the economy. The *Canadian Journal of Economics and Political Science*, generally speaking, contained a few items left over from the problems of the Depression, and a number of articles on the wartime organization of the economy. Following the war the rate of publication in economics fell off in a period of uncertainty that lasted into the mid–1950s.[2] When recovery did come it seemed to accentuate the uncertainty. A dozen or so books, topped by Easterbrook and Aitken's masterful summary,[3] rounded out the historical work of the 1930s; but, the pious hopes of economic historians notwithstanding,[4] the period of dominance of the staple paradigm had passed. H. A. Innis was in his later period of communication studies. His work was immediately relevant to the economics of information,[5] but it was embodied in a form that was alien to the emerging discourse among economists. The Keynesian character of the immediate future in economic thought was still not evident.[6]

Studies of Canadian banking unconsciously pointed out the limitations of Keynesian theory in Canada by recording the attempts of the Central Bank to live up to its demands as embodied in the White Paper on Employment.[7] Given the open, regionalized character of the economy, the Bank found it increasingly impossible to conform,[8] and began to build an alternative paradigm, based, in part, on the distinction between credit and capital that had been so useful to Adam Shortt[9] in his debates with pre-Keynesian, easy money interests. It took a full-scale rebellion on the part of the economics profession,[10] and a Royal Commission[11] to get the Bank back into line.

Practical problems and perverse central bankers did not prevent the new paradigm from capturing the loyalty of most professional economists. Mabel Timlin, and others, restated it and defended it from the intellectual imperialism of right-wing, neoclassical economists and left-wing Marxists, making it clear that the new paradigm was not just Keynes, and not just neoclassical welfare economics, but general equilibrium analysis, put in the service of a very carefully defined regime of public interference in the economic life of the nation.[12] The Canadians insisted on seeing Keynes through their own eyes and in terms of their own policy preferences, and not through the eyes of Lawrence Klein, Don Patinkin, Abba Learner, Oscar Lange, Paul Samuelson or anyone still at Cambridge. After all, when Keynes had lectured in the 1930s, members of the Canadian profession's establishment had been there.[13]

In 1948 R. F. Harrod's *Towards a Dynamic Economics* drew a new theory of growth from Keynes's *General Theory*. At the same time, the very evident phenomenon of development in the Third World demanded a theory of economic development. Together, growth theory, development theory, and trade theory, all necessary to reconcile Keynes to the Canadian case, were going to produce the economics of Harry Johnson, but, during the post-war readjustment, measured absorption of United States economics continued.

This was true of general equilibrium and trade theory, too, but there the challenge of the Canadian situation was going to make a difference. The Canadians vaulted the pedestrian processes of importing theory by turning their attention to the 'lively frontier areas' in which international trade theory was emerging from consideration of current events in small developing countries and in large developed countries forming customs unions.[14] In other fields the absorption of United States economics was more readily accepted.

THE UNDERLYING NORTH AMERICAN DISCOURSE

The phrase 'absorption of United States economic thought' is inaccurate. Its counterpart, 'penetration of United States ideas' is just as inappropriate to what happened. The economics profession in Canada integrated itself into a discourse that was emerging in North America, taking from it and contributing to it at the same time. For example, it can hardly be said that United States economics penetrated resource economics in Canada, even though resource economics turned for the first time to neoclassical theory, because initiative and leadership in the application of neoclassical theory to this field belonged to Canadians.

By happy accident, within a year of one another, Anthony Scott and H. Scott Gordon produced highly complementary, seminal works in the economic theory of natural resources. The one was a simple, but forceful use of capital theory in explanation of the efficiency of market forces in directing resource exploitation.[15] The other was a simple, but forceful demonstration that, in the absence of private property, market forces would not be efficient in resource exploitation.[16] Under a barrage of immediate criticism,[17] Anthony Scott admitted that there was room for consideration of what have since been called market failures, thereby laying the foundation for an enormous expansion of analysis in the field of resource economics. Neither the *Tragedy of the Commons* literature nor the *Limits to Growth* literature that followed can be understood without reference to analysis rooted in these two seminal works. The volume of literature on the economics of the fishery, stemming from these beginnings, is awesome.[18] It was a solid foundation, not surprisingly laid in Canada; and, not surprisingly, Canadians continue to make contributions in this now highly technical[19] and, sometimes, profoundly disturbing field.[20]

Not all forays into the new discourse were as innovative as that in resource economics. Canadian developments in the field of standard industrial organization theory were more derivative, though they were accompanied by the same stirring in the profession.

Controversy began with Gideon Rosenbluth's use of concentration ratios to describe the industrial structure of the Canadian economy,[21] which he showed to be more concentrated than the American. In a debate that turned on nice points in statistical method, optimal analytical approaches, and, one suspects, personal animosity, Rosenbluth's efforts survived the critical acumen of Stephen Stykolt.[22] Rosenbluth having survived, those who used variants of his approach in ploughing the field of industrial organization went on to consider policy and the difficulties of fitting economic analysis to rules of evidence and other practices of the courts charged with enforcing anti-combines legislation.[23]

In the field of public finance the emerging North American discourse was accepted at the level of general theory and for teaching purposes in the universities, but research was another matter. The distinctive character of Canadian political institutions and problems required Canadians to find their own way.

With wide acceptance of state intervention in the economy after the Second World War, almost every field of economics elaborated itself into policy applications. Public finance seemed to encompass the whole of the discipline. Indeed, after 1959, the accepted text in public finance was a *tour de force* through all of allocation, distribution, stabilization, and growth theory.[24] Canadian researchers retreated from these wider horizons, though not from their interest in the problems of federalism, about which the accepted text had nothing to say. They focused on the one area that distinguishes the student of public finance, taxation. Outstanding scholars, John Due, Milton Moore, Robert Clark and J. H. Perry, under the aegis of the Canada Tax Foundation, described and analysed every aspect of the Byzantine plots of federal and provincial tax makers,[25] adding to what was already known about the structure and evolution of the Canadian tax system.[26]

THE DARK SIDE OF THE DISCOURSE: REGIONALISM, NATIONALISM

Not everything about modern, high-technology, industrialism is good. It has generated a capability for evil as well as good, and its arrival was disruptive, generating losses as well as gains. It has a dark side where it is difficult to distinguish between the emergence of new, constructive institutions and the loss of human values. Declining economic regions and shifts in political power, consequent upon the emergence of new arrangements, generated reactions in Canada.

By the late 1950s the new Keynesian paradigm had displaced the concerns of the 1930s: inter-regional income disparities and absence of control over essential external markets.[27] These were facts in the environment that would generate their own economic analyses as regionalists and nationalists also made their appearance.

Keynesian policy instruments were placed in the hands of the central government and could not be used to meet the divergent needs of dissimilar regions. Neoclassical theory, rooted in the idea of allocational efficiency in the nation as a whole, gave cold comfort to the residents of declining areas. So, in the 1960s, regional development enthusiasts would turn to A. O. Hirshman, Gunnar Myrdal and François Perroux. In the period of readjustment after the Second World War they had only theoretically incoherent statements of needs, and a set of demands for political initiatives.

Keynes in a small open economy 177

There was a move on the part of francophone Québécois to control and develop their provincial economy. In comparison with others, they were latecomers to the field of economic development. Ontario had pioneered government ownership of hydroelectric distribution before the First World War. After the Second World War, Saskatachewan undertook a number of business ventures, ranging from the packing of horse meat to the production of steel forms. In 1944, Ontario set up a Department of Planning and Development that opened offices in the United Kingdom to seek out markets and to encourage British firms to locate in Ontario. It screened potential immigrants to provide air fare for those who would aid in the further development of manufacturing. The Ontario Planning Act of 1946 was intended to foster manufacturing. Ontario had passed through the stage of reliance on staple exports.[28] The Maritime Provinces did not originate regional development, they originated the idea of doing it with federal money. When Quebec took it up, regional economic development was a widely accepted political activity, without an economic rationale.

A similar thing was true of economic nationalism. Indications of dissent from postwar liberal, Keynesian policies came with the realization that there was a new institutional form in international trade, the multinational firm. It was *not* characterized in its foreign subsidiaries by a separation of ownership from control, and the increasingly close relationship between Canada and the United States was dominated by such firms.[29] Apprehension was expressed first within the Liberal Party, which had seemed to support the New Economics in the immediate postwar period. As a governing party with its fortunes sagging in the economic distress of the late 1950s, the Liberals set up a Royal Commission on Canada's Economic Prospects in the hope of discovering a more electable economic policy. The Commissioner, Walter Gordon, reported that Canada's problem was exposure to the United States, and, particularly, to the effects of foreign ownership. In quick succession a second alarm sounded from within the Bank of Canada, presumably a principal instrument of Keynesian policy. The Governor, James Coyne, refused to ease monetary conditions in a period of relatively high unemployment. The problem was, he said, not insufficient aggregate demand, but regional and structural distortions, caused by an uneven penetration of United States interests into the Canadian economy.[30]

FOREIGN OWNERSHIP AND NEO-MARXIAN ANALYSIS

It is a kind of proof of the hypothesis that Canada was not 'penetrated' by United States economics, but, rather, integrated itself into an emerging, common, North American discourse, that nationalists, opposed to 'American domination', aligned themselves with, or made common cause with, socialists, opposed to both national and international capitalist organization. The nationalists were opposed to something that was happening in Canada. Which is not to say that all Canadian nationalists and regionalists were socialists, or even 'bourgeois interventionists', nor is it to say that they were just reactionaries. They had valid points to make.

In the mid-1960s Walter Gordon asked Mel Watkins to report on the structure of Canadian industry.[31] Steven Hymer, a member of the appointed Task Force, would earn his place with the other four Canadians in *The New Palgrave* dictionary for his work on international corporations in underdeveloped countries. His work, *An Odyssey to Marxism*, was one root of the early 1970s spate of Canadian literature on the evils of international capitalism.

Hymer's analysis of the consequences of expanding internationalism for national policy had a direct bearing on the applicability of Keynesian policy in the Canadian case. He, too, was concerned about the limitations of Keynes in a small, open economy.

Starting as 'a conventional business economist of the antitrust school',[32] he analysed multinational corporations from the point of view of neoclassical efficiency, noting that social control of monopoly power, an instrument to compensate for inefficiencies within a nation state, was impossible on a global scale. He also noted that the division of tasks in the multinational corporation was causing an international division of labour in which upper-level administration and control were polarized into the larger metropolitan areas of the already developed world. This left the lower, dependent and less well-paid activities for the underdeveloped nations. The demands of efficiency in the multinational corporations, given the oligopolistic nature of the world market, dictated rapid growth and polarization, rather than slower growth and a more even spread of the benefits of growth.

> The advantage of national planning is its ability to remove the wastes of oligopolistic anarchy: i.e. meaningless product differentiation and an imbalance between different industries within a region. It concentrates all levels of decision making in one locale and thus provides each region with a full complement of skills and occupations.[33]

> ...if each country loses its power over fiscal and monetary policy due to the growth of multinational corporations (as some observers believe Canada has), how will aggregate demand be stabilized? Will it be possible to construct super states? Or does multinationalism do away with Keynesian problems?[34]

One could say much more about Steven Hymer's contributions, and of his gradual conversion to the New Political Economy of neo-Marxism. It is rare to be able to watch the process of choice as one reads, in chronological order, the works of an author; and to see, to some extent, the influences and the logical steps of a fundamental redirection of thought. First, the belief that the nation state might, through regulation and prohibition, through industrial development policies, counteract a perceived dark side of growing internationalism. Then the conclusion that the new internationalism, itself, was sapping the strength of the nation state so to do. The shift in focus from efficiency to equity. The perception that an unfortunate institutional structure could be corrected only by political means, and that political means entailed the mobilization and readjustment of classes of people. It all added up to a change of perception from that of economics to that of political science and sociology, from neoclassical analysis to neo-Marxian analysis, from acceptance of the established order of things, to 'radicalism'.

Steven Hymer's ideas were root elements in the *Report* of the Task Force on Foreign Ownership and the Structure of Canadian Industry,[35] and in subsequent work by Mel Watkins.

> Monetary-fiscal policies remain important weapons to facilitate Canadian growth along the American growth path, but a neo-Keynesian National Policy – "let the price system work and lean against cyclical winds" – must not be confused with policies designed to create, or even maintain, Canadian independence vis-à-vis the American system. More bluntly, the capacity of the Canadian government to create jobs and keep inflation under control is negligible.[36]

If one wanted to trace the conversion of another economist to the New Political Economy, another citation from the work of Mel Watkins in this period would be warranted. It illuminates the alliance of interests hoping to modify the effects of continentalization, indeed, globalization, associated with technical and economic advance.

> A capitalist is also a citizen and liberals who argue that a capitalist is merely a capitalist are vulgar Marxists unwilling to face the reality of nationalism. Canada is committed to the capitalist path of development, and, in the final analysis, Canadians should prefer home-brewed capitalists over alien capitalists.... a case can be made for a *Canadian bourgeoisie* whose competence and initiative are of a high order.[37]

THE HIGH PERIOD OF KEYNESIAN INTERNATIONALISM

With financial support from the Private Planning Association, an organization of interests favouring closer economic ties with the United States,[38] the economics profession, *not* to a man, rallied to give Canadian

Keynesianism a clear and perhaps unamendable statement. Once again, Minerva's Owl took flight in the gathering storm.[39] In the 1960s we come to the best and the worst of Canadian Keynesianism; and to the arrival of the forces of its disintegration; that is, the ravages of history, and a positivist, conservative revival.

The counterattack against seemingly myopic special interests among the efficiency-blind nationalists and regionalists took place on two levels, polemic and analytic. Work on the level of polemics may be characterized as naïve Keynesianism. On the level of analytics the Keynesian counterattack found its best expression in the work of Harry Johnson.

The naïve Keynesians seemed to lose all sense of history. Recall the contention of Adam Shortt, that there was no room for domestic manipulation of the money supply in Canada because of the open nature of the Canadian economy. Recall the generally held view at the end of the Depression, that the open and regionally diversified nature of the Canadian economy would inhibit, if not prohibit, the use of Keynesian policies in Canada. The naïve Keynesians were vaguely aware of the situation. In 1965 Scott Gordon declared that, in Canada, throughout the 1940s and 1950s, 'Keynesian statements were confined to the abstract plane of discourse; they were not connected with actual policy'.[40] In noting the official rejection of Keynesian-type expansionary fiscal policies in 1960, he said the government 'focused attention on two things: the structural characteristics of the unemployment problem, and the dominating significance of the international sector'.[41] The naïve Keynesians simply failed to recognize the meaning of these things. After a long discussion of the function of Keynesian fiscal and monetary stabilization policies, with no reference at all to the open and regionalized character of the Canadian economy, Scott Gordon suggested that James Coyne should be fired for taking such things into account. I hasten to add that Scott Gordon was not alone in this. Twenty-nine other economists joined him in writing a letter to this effect to the Minister of Finance.[42] When Harry Johnson reviewed Ben Higgins's *What Do Economists Know?*,[43] in which a similar confidence in the Keynesian paradigm was expressed, he responded that all we can say is that 'Economists know more about economics than non-economists', implying that they did not, necessarily, know more about the economy.

Harry Johnson's assessment of monetary policy in Canada was of a different order. I introduce it here both to throw light on the state of economic thought in Canada, and to introduce Johnson's contribution to Canadian economics and to the discipline in general.

HARRY JOHNSON: GENERAL EQUILIBRIUM, GROWTH AND TRADE

His assessment was set out in a report to the 1962 (Porter) Royal Commission on Banking and Finance.[44] Johnson preceded his comments with a statement that monetary policy had had an unsatisfactory record in Britain and the United States as well as in Canada, and that this had led to a reassessment of principles by the American Commission on Money and Credit, and by the British Radcliffe Committee. Clearly the problem in Canada might not be accounted for in terms of the particulars of Canadian experience. The banks had probably done all they could, especially in Canada, where what was unique in the situation worked against the central bank's ability to do anything at all.

> It can be argued that the openness of the Canadian economy to the world economy, and particularly the dependence of the Canadian economy on the American industrial complex for markets for Canadian resource products and on the American capital market ... restricts the possibilities of economic stabilization by domestic economic policy.[45]

In any case, he did not think that 'the existing state of economic knowledge' held out 'much prospect of significant improvement in the practical achievement of stabilization in the near future'.[46] Johnson then proceeded to distance himself from the opinions of the signers of the letter to the Minister of Finance, noting that the main evidence for the circumstances they had alleged was the fact that they had alleged them.[47] In short, he lifted the discussion from the level of personalities, placed the Canadian problem in its international context, noted the distinctiveness of the Canadian situation in that context, and proceeded to a discussion of the relevant circumstances and theory.

It has been alleged that Harry Johnson thought he could have written a better *General Theory* than Keynes. Applying the counter-factual technique of the New Economic History we can ask, What if Harry Johnson had written *The General Theory*? I answer, it would have been a better one.

Johnson's contribution, from the perspective of Canadian economics, was a direct reflection of the position of the Canadian economy in the immediate post-Second World War period. The increased and increasing internationalization of trade, in consequence of improved communications and the spread of industrialization throughout the world, exposed the open Canadian economy to competitive pressures, in part from new entrants into the world economy, and in part from the formation of trading blocs, such as the European Common Market. At the same time, the effects of the recent depression, in the production of Keynes's *General Theory* and of Keynesian counter-cyclical stabilization policies, demanded that the Canadian government employ national instruments to maintain full employment and stable prices. Johnson's contribution was the reconciliation of these two demands, at least on the level of theory. First, he adapted Keynesian-type general equilibrium theory, mediated through Harrod's application of it to growth theory, to international trade theory.[48] Second, with a generous assist from Lipsey and Lancaster, he elaborated the theory of trading blocs.[49] In addressing these policy relevant questions in general equilibrium and international trade theory, Johnson did more for economic theory, and economic science, perhaps, than he was able to do for the Canadian economy.

With other purposes in mind, Harrod had established that the growth rate in any economy is the rate of saving multiplied by the ratio of output to capital, assuming the savings to be invested and the output to capital ratio to be constant.

$$g = \frac{s}{k}$$

In an open economy the drain of expenditure into savings would be augmented by a drain out of the economy for imports, and the expenditure due to investment would be augmented by an inflow in return for exports.

$$I + X = sY + mY$$

where s and m are the rates of saving and importing out of income, and I is investment, X is exports, and Y is National Income. The statement with respect to the growth rate then becomes

$$g = \frac{(s + m - \frac{X}{Y})}{k}$$

or, in reduced form,

$$g = \frac{(s - b)}{k}$$

From there it was (for Harry Johnson) simply a matter of further elaboration into the enormous complexity of the conditions of international trade.

His interest in this matter never fell off, though his treatment of it changed over the years. The subject, a general equilibrium approach to international trade, looked quite different when, having lost confidence in growth theory, he presented it in the second-to-last chapter of his last text;[50] but the importance of the subject to him, which is the point here, was evident in the frequency with which he applauded Harrod's *Towards a Dynamic Economics* as the only contribution of Cambridge (England) to economics, after Keynes; and in the viciousness with which he attacked Meade's *The Balance of Payments*.[51]

Johnson had been working on the adaptation of general equilibrum theory to an international context since 1950. It was to be his major contribution. Meade's book came out in 1952, and was, as Johnson elsewhere acknowleged, an extention of Keynesian analysis to international trade. It was not just that Meade's statement violated the cannons of scientific economics, on which Johnson insisted as conscientiously as his 'greatest teacher in economics, Harold Innis'.[52] It was an invasion of Johnson's turf.

The point with respect to the economics of trading blocs was basically simple, but of great policy relevance in the 1950s and 1960s. The formation of customs unions entailed the elimination of tariffs between the members of the union, and the raising of a common tariff against the rest of the world. Whether there would be a welfare gain would depend on the balance of gains and losses from the simultaneous lowering and raising of tariffs, and this, in turn, would depend on a host of empirically verifiable specific conditions. It was a very Johnsonian point that pure theory could prescribe nothing in the absence of knowledge of the conditions in which it was being applied.

Quite apart from the field of international trade, which was his, Harry Johnson mastered general equilibrium theory, not so much by being an innovator as by doing what others did, only better, and by bringing together what others had done. In his last three texts, *Macroeconomics and Monetary Theory*,[53] *The Theory of Income Distribution*,[54] and *General Equilibrium Analysis*[55] he displayed a comfortable ability to use simple mathematical formulas and complex geometric illustrations in getting all the pieces of the models right, in manipulating them, and in not confusing them with the real world.

He was able to go beyond interpretation of *The General Theory* to a presentation of the analysis in its most advanced state. He explained the general theory, where it came from, where it fell short and was a tract for its times, and in what respects it had been improved upon. In his view the heart of the Keynesian model was a contribution to monetary theory.

> Anyone competent to think clearly knows that Keynes was a quantity theorist, as all monetary theorists must be, in the sense that his theory gave a crucial role to monetary policy and changes in the quantity of money. His novel contributions were to shift the focus of analysis from changes in prices (with 'full employment' output) to changes in output and employment (with 'sticky wages') [which was more appropriate in 1920–

1940, than after 1945].... and in monetary theory proper, to shift the analysis from the mechanical frame of velocity to the role of money as an asset alternative to other assets, and the influence of expectations on money holding.[56]

Keynes had integrated monetary and capital theory,[57] but there were confusions that had to be cleared up by others, including Milton Friedman, who had gone 'far in providing a synthesis of Keynesian and classical approaches to the demand for money in capital theory terms'.[58]

When Asimakopulos suggested that Harry Johnson had not agreed with the Cambridge (England) interpretation of Keynes, or more specifically, Cambridge (England)'s version of Keynesian growth theory,[59] it was a polite understatement on two counts. Johnson abhorred the approach and the views of the post-Keynesians under the apparent leadership of Joan Robinson, and he considered all of growth theory not really policy relevant. Nonsense was nonsense, and Cambridge (Mass.) should have left it alone, and not reconstructed it until the mistakes became evident.

> It must be observed, however reluctantly, that by abstraction from those factors that determine the growth rate of the economy the analysis of this [growth] model – and others like it – fails to consider the very problem that appears to be of greatest interest ... abstraction is an indispensible element of scientific investigation but ... not abstraction from the problem at hand.[60]

In repeated comments Johnson attributed growth to the more subtle forces of technological advance, particularly when they took the form of human capital. Referring to empirical work on the sources of growth, he gave primacy to factors other than the rate of formation of physical capital. He pointed to the weakness of planning for development in Third World countries when these other factors had not been taken into account.[61]

His views on planning for growth and development were policy relevant in Canada. During the economic slow-down that characterized North America between 1957 and 1963, there was much talk of economic planning in Canada. Europe, under a kind of co-ordinative planning, was doing well. With provincial-level economic councils and departments of development springing up across the country, serious consideration was given to national planning in Canada. Jacques Parizeau, speaking from the privileged position of a future leader of the separatist party in Quebec, denied the possibility on political grounds.[62] Once again pointing out that the more important factors of economic growth 'lie beyond the scope of national planning of investment', Harry Johnson suggested that planning of the type practised in some other countries might even retard growth.[63] A national planning body, the Economic Council of Canada, was established, none the less.

Harry Johnson's contribution, as others have pointed out, was not, like that of J. M. Keynes, a revolutionary new paradigm. Along with others, he drew heavily on the Keynesian paradigm to give new meaning, life and applicability to the core of generally accepted doctrines in economics. He was a genius of Kuhn's 'normal science'. His vision of the neoclassical project as a scientific endeavour, and his estimate of its importance in the rebuilding of the liberal order[64] never diminished.

Johnson acquired his strong preference for a positivist approach in social science in H. A. Innis's lectures at Toronto just before the Second World War. Given the marked differences between their work this requires some explanation. The economics of Innis was incommensurable with the economics of Harry Johnson. In the tradition of the Historical School, Innis dealt with the economic effects of changes in technical and institutional constraints. In the tradition of the neoclassical school, Johnson dealt with the logic of rational choice assuming those constraints not to change. Innis was acutely conscious of the limitations of neoclassical theory in handling the very long-run factors with which he was concerned. Johnson accepted the general substance of Innis's analysis, and moved to consideration of long- and short-run factors. What Innis and Johnson, and John Rae for that matter, had in common was a passion, if that is a permissable descriptive in this case, a passion for scientific analysis. It was on this ground that Rae attacked Adam Smith; and Innis's repeated criticisms of works on the grounds of their lack of a scientific approach has been documented.[65] Harry Johnson carried this aspiration directly from his contact with Innis. Anyone who has read Innis on discussion in the social sciences, who appreciates what Innis thought of the economist as 'sandwich-man' (as 'public adversary', in Johnson's more tempered phrase), and who has read the last 125 pages of *The Shadow of Keynes*,[66] knows that Innis's discussion of the dionysian forces of unreason in economics, with which he was fully occupied when Johnson was an undergraduate at Toronto, were taken up again by his best student. The demons were still alive in 'fuel policy, regional policy, science policy, subsidies to investment in chosen industries, government purchasing policy, and other expressions of national purpose'.[67] In this matter Johnson took Innis's approach in the pursuit of scientific economics. 'Above all, no zeal', except the zeal for science itself.[68] It is fair to say that the subject, the role of values in social science, became an obsession with Innis, and was a major factor in the direction of his later studies on communications. With this Johnson disagreed.

The problem of values is to be overcome, not by investigating values themselves, and attempting to develop a 'value-free' social science, but by applying the tests of scientific experimentation and proof. In short, it is the community of scholars policing and accepting or rejecting each other's work, according to scientific standards of verification, not the individual scholar researching his own soul, that produces a social science that is genuinely scientific and not propagandistic.[69]

Economics was scientific if it was scientific, that is if it subjected itself to scientific testing, and only then. The theory without testing was not scientific. Johnson spoke of

the pretentious and misleading conception of the possibility of 'scientific' economics particularly characteristic of the adolescent phase of the new welfare economics. ... There are any number of reasons for doubting that the static Paretian approach of modern welfare economics formulates the problem of economic policy in a useful way.[70]

BEYOND HARRY JOHNSON AND OUT OF THE SHADOW OF KEYNES

There were Canadian contributions to international economics and growth theory beyond those of Harry Johnson and Richard Lipsey, some compatible, some not. Clarence Barber developed a measurable concept of the rate of effective tariff protection, by focusing on value added in the protected firm, and by including the total effect of all relevant tariffs.[71] H. E. English demonstrated the 'miniature replica' effect of tariff protection in Canada, the industrial structure of which had become a miniature replica of that of the United States. It had the same structure without the size to generate the same economies of scale.[72] Indeed, there were a number of studies examining the effect of the tariff with respect to the degree of oligopoly and economies of scale.[73] They laid the groundwork for one side in the free trade debate of the 1980s.[74]

Outside the Johnson-type work, most Canadian efforts in the field of growth were empirical studies based on the works of Sir Roy Harrod and Edward F. Denison,[75] but there was some work of the Cambridge (England) type.[76]

Many in the profession sided with Harry Johnson in viewing the multinational corporation as the most efficient institutional arrangement for exploiting international technologies, any inefficiencies associated with oligopoly and the disruption of obsolescent national arrangements notwithstanding. A. E. Safarian's path-breaking *Foreign Ownership of Canadian Industry*,[77] for example, attempted an empirical measurement of the relative behaviour of foreign and domestic firms, and found no significant differences. But the studies of the 1960s were only a preliminary to the avalanche of paper that fell on the subject after 1970.[78]

Regional Economics

Regional economics, which was really distinct from the regionalism depreciated by Johnson and Grant Reuber, expressed itself primarily in national conferences. I select only one to illustrate what was happening in the field, the 1965 conference at Queen's University, *Areas of Economic Stress in Canada*.[79] It was paid for largely by the federal and Ontario governments, and its agenda was drawn up in consultation with the Department of Industry in Ottawa and the Department of Economics and Development in Toronto. The conference was attended by a fair representation from all the regions (provinces) of the federation, including a strong representation from French-speaking Quebec.[80]

The conference's goal was a theoretically sound, administratively feasible, regional policy. Some speakers adopted a neoclassical, national point of view, stressing the importance of facilitating market forces in the readjustment of declining regions.[81] Others adopted an eclectic approach that stressed maximization in the context of separate regions. Those taking the latter approach assumed that regional development policies were a fact of life, and that the purpose of regional economics was to make them as reasonable as possible.[82] After all, the federal government had always transferred moneys to the provinces, and would continue to do so. The only new element was the transformation of the rationale for the transfers, from compensation for the inequities of Confederation and the National Policy of 1878, to grants on the basis of fiscal need in provincial attempts to maintain national standards in social welfare services.[83] The more eclectic type of regional economics was the more politically successful in a decade that ended with the establishment of the federal Department of Regional Economic Expansion. The crowning work of the decade, T. N. Brewis's *Regional Economic Policies in Canada*,[84] argued that any type of interference ended in development policies, so one might as well get on with the work of designing the best policies possible.

Regional economics, urban economics, and the economics of science policy were all attempts to build up a body of theory in areas in which the governments seemed bent on spending money to please sectoral interests, regional interests, or the voters in general.[85] They were really attempts to rationalize the system of corruption by which the federation was still being held together almost a century after the influence of the Scottish Enlightenment and the Court Whigs might have been presumed to have ended.

PUBLIC FINANCE

In the 1970s public finance shared a very Canadian problem with regional economics, that is, the unresolved question of which welfare function(s) was (were) to be maximized, that of the nation as a whole, or those of the provinces. F.- A. Angers had stated the problem, in a non-theoretical way. A. D. Scott had given it its first formal statement[86] in an attempt to show how a spending authority could be made responsible for raising taxes. Establishing this responsibility was the justification for *conditional* grants from one jurisdiction to another. The need to respect the jurisdiction of the grantee, was the justification for *unconditional* grants. Albert Breton's path-breaking contribution to the design of economically optimal constitutions was impaled on the horns of this dilemma;[87] which is not to depreciate his theoretical breakthrough in exploiting the concept of a 'public good' to advance the economic analysis of institutions. His idea was to map political jurisdictions onto the geographical extension of the publicness of goods. This, it seemed, would justify taxation and expenditure for each public good in one jurisdiction only.

The high point for public finance during the 1960s had not to do with the somewhat peripheral issue of optimal constitutions, but with hard-core taxation economics. It is a further indication of the continuing, measured integration of Canadian economics into an emerging Euro-American discourse that the Carter Commission *Report*[88] was hailed by Richard Musgrave and Arnold C. Harberger as a model for the world;[89] Milton Moore's objections notwithstanding.[90] The *Report* called for a complete, consistent restructuring of the tax system along the lines of Henry Simon's *Positive Programme for Laissez Faire*. Taxation was to be on the basis of ability to pay, and the income tax was judged best suited to the task, with the family unit as the income-earning unit. Capital gains were to be included in income, and the corporation and income taxes were to be integrated. That is, all income was to be taxed, but only once. Some expenditure taxation was to be retained, but the hidden manufacturers tax was to be replaced with a federal sales tax that was to be integrated with provincial sales taxes. Despite the painstaking efforts, typical of public finance economists, to trace out in detail every possible virtue of the new tax as it ramified throughout the economy, the proposals were not enacted into law. The *Report*, nevertheless, was a remarkable achievement in the application of theory, and a number of the younger members of the profession cut their teeth on its studies.

Somewhere between international trade theory, regional economics, and public finance there is an area in the economic theory of institutions called the economics of nationalism. With the forces of technology and economics shrinking the world and reducing established institutions to obsolescence, it was inevitable that the national question in Canada and in Quebec would come to the fore. The distinctive characteristics of the Canadian situation were the occasion of the distinctive elaboration of Keynesian theory in Canada. The same characteristics, openness and internal fractionation, were the occasion of reaction against the tendency of technological and economic advance to remove the meaning of national and provincial boundaries. It can hardly be surprising that one of the contributions of Canadians has been the economics of nationalism, and that its outstanding economists have been involved. Indeed, whether the integration of Canadian economics into a broader North American discourse was an acceptable part of these changes was, itself, debated in the profession.

THE ECONOMICS OF NATIONALISM

The economics of nationalism began with an article by Harry Johnson,[91] in which he repeated his contention that economic internationalism was on the rise, and that Canada must react positively to the new circumstances, particularly to the formation of international trading blocs, or history would pass it by. He damned the reactionary rise of protectionism and the anti-foreign ownership campaign for being the products of despicably small-minded Canadian chauvinism. At the end of the article he suggested that Canadian nationalism was the exploitation of emotion to improve the welfare of a few Canadians at the expense of the nation as a whole.[92]

Three years later, Albert Breton gave this idea a theoretical statement in which nationalism was treated as a 'public good', purchased by the nation as a whole, but generating material benefits only for the middle class.[93] Nationalism was depicted as an instrument for transferring wealth within a nation, not between nations.

> Subsequently Johnson fleshed out Breton's analysis from two sources. First, he appealed to Becker's economic theory of discrimination and showed that the analogue to Becker's 'taste for discrimination' (the sacrifice of economic gain by discriminators for a psychological gain) is a 'taste for nationalism'. Secondly, he appealed to Downs's economic theory of democracy, from which a number of things follow, specifically that although the net benefits of nationalist policies are negative there is an asymmetry between the distribution of benefits and costs such that the former are concentrated in the hands of specific producer interests and the latter are thinly dispersed over the mass of consumers, which works to facilitate the winning of political support for such policies.[94]

There were theories on the other side. Abraham Rotstein described national boundaries as a sort of failsafe device to prevent costly disturbances from spreading unimpeded over an increasingly interconnected world, just as sealed bulkheads prevent a damaged ship from flooding.[95] After a period of waffling,[96] Mel Watkins combined regionalism, science policy, and nationalism with the intricate class analysis of the New Canadian Political Economy, to construct an anti-Johnson, anti-continentalist position.[97]

In the 1970s, as the paradigms of the postwar period lost currency, the debate over nationalism switched grounds. Jean-Luc Migué applied the economic theory of information to the question of French Canadian nationalism and the absence of francophones in the upper echelons of business in Quebec.[98] His point was that the critical importance of information flows at the decision-making level of business enterprise, and economies of scale in the production of these flows consequent upon the adoption of a common language and culture by those involved, dictated either the co-option or the exclusion of francophones with respect to these levels of operation. It was this factor, he conjectured, not the Conquest, or the educational system, or geography and technology, or cultural traits of any kind, or biased federal policies that (had) accounted for the absence of a francophone bourgeoisie in Quebec.

A much broader application of this kind of analysis to internal and external Canadian nationalism, that is, a more complete use of the point of view and methodology of the New Institutionalism, appeared in English shortly thereafter.[99] It was characterized by the droll humour of those Canadians who, without understanding them, must live with the set of collective passions, regionalist, nationalist and continentalist, that rules the politics of their country.

But the economics of nationalism was a secondary contribution of Canadian economics between 1945 and 1970. Its principal contribution was to the theory of trade and development in the context of Keynesian general equilibrium analysis. The staple theory was still important, but for most in the economics profession, it had become a fading, implicit element in the information environment.

11 The economics of the West

The economics of western Canada turns on primary product exports. It is no surprise that major contributions to resource economics and to fisheries economics have been associated with the University of British Columbia and Simon Fraser University (see chapter 10). It is a little surprising, however, that major contributions to the staple theory are associated with the Prairie Provinces, because the pivotal role of Innis in the development of the staple thesis, and the important role of M. H. Watkins in the development of the staple theory, are undeniable, and both belong to southern Ontario. Still, others associated with the theory, particularly with positivist analysis of the theory, are westerners: Vernon Fowke, Ken Buckely, Ted Chambers, Mac Urquhart, Ken Norrie and Marvin McInnis.

In this chapter the topic is the staple theory in the post-Second World War period of positivist economics in Canada. It features the economics of the Prairie Provinces and the contribution of western Canadian economists.

Vernon Fowke's histories of agricultural policy in Canada do not have the characteristics of the positivist period of economics, even though they appear in the post post-Second World War period.[1] They were part of the general wrap-up of the work of the 1930s that occurred as the staple paradigm was about to give way to a Keynesian paradigm towards the end of the decade following the war. Nonetheless, Fowke produced a simple and powerful conceptualization of the economy that lent itself to modelling and quantitative testing, so that the positivist debate over the role of primary product exports in Canadian development became, in fact, a debate over whether Fowke was right.

Fowke depicted agriculture as an economic sector exploited first

> as a means for the defence of territory and trade routes; second, as a provisioner of the great staple trades, and, third, as a provider of investment opportunities on the agricultural frontier.[2]

Agriculture was aided, not because it was the chief colonial activity, but

192 *A history of Canadian economic thought*

in order that it might more fully contribute towards the chief colonial activities.[3]

Between 1870 and 1930, according to Fowke, the role of agriculture was to serve 'the so-called "purposes of the Dominion"' in the period of continentalization and build-up of manufacturing in the St. Lawrence Lowlands of central Canada. In short, the country had been built on the backs of western farmers for the benefit of commercial, manufacturing and financial interests located, consequently, in the more prosperous regions of the country; and it was time to repay the debt with an agricultural policy designed for the benefit of western agriculture, and not for its despoliation.

His account of Canadian economic history was simple and powerful, an account of thoughtless, crippling exploitation of one staple after another, with agriculture in tow until agriculture itself became the sector to exploit, by a self-serving set of commercial interests. It recalled Innis's pleas for steps to be taken to redress the effects 'which are characteristic of exploitation without afterthought'.[4] Its depiction of the common man being exploited by a commercial, colonial elite recalled the mythology associated with the rise of responsible, democratic government in Canada. Its appeal was irresistible. Its inevitable effect in economics was the conceptualization of the development of the economy as nothing but a series of staple exports.

THE THEORETICAL QUESTION

Positivistic formulation of the staple theory (as distinct from the staple thesis), and questioning of it, began in the United States in a 1955 controversy between Douglas North and Charles Tiebout.[5] North wanted to show that per capita income, and not structural development, was the criterion of prosperity. He wanted to show that economic progress did not involve a sequence of stages, as the Marxian paradigm presumed, and that the neoclassical paradigm of specialization and exchange was adequate for understanding regional economies, even when the region was politically a sovereign state. Canada, allegedly having developed into the world's fourth wealthiest nation on the basis of successive specializations in primary product exports, was given as an example. Tiebout's response said nothing about Canada. He pointed, rather, to the limitations of the theory as such. A staple export could be developed and could feed back into the further growth of an economy only if the economy had sufficient non-staple development to support and utilize the staple export activities. Indeed, the causal relations could be reversed. Export development could be a forward linkage from non-export activities. Tiebout did not put it in such terms, but he depicted North's error as being that of the Physiocrats, and of Karl Marx; that is, the error of looking at a system of interdependent elements from the point of view of only one element, and seeing all things in relation to that one. All wealth comes from land. All wealth comes from labour. All wealth comes from primary product exports. He was suggesting that apparent cases of development based on primary product exports, in substance, might be cases of development and growth beginning in and feeding back to secondary and tertiary internal domestic development, that is, cases of independent development and growth involving international trade.

THE THIN EDGE OF THE WEDGE OF DOUBT

These theoretical developments in 1955 were accompanied by the first placement of the thin edge of empirical questioning of the staple theory in Canada. Penelope Hartland pointed out that the success of the National Policy, which she understood to be a policy of development based on a wheat staple export, did not come until other staples, pulp, paper, non-ferrous metals, and a non-export staple, hydroelectricity, were in place; and that some quantitative amendments to the simple Fowkean model were in order.[6]

The main thrust of Hartland's piece was well within the staple export paradigm. What she wanted to establish was a certain parallel between the pattern of development in the 1850s and that of the first decade of the twentieth century. Both periods enjoyed staple export export-based expansion, in her view, and both were followed by periods of 'consolidation'. During the expansions, GNP per capita grew at a more rapid rate, and during the consolidations consumption per capita grew at a more rapid rate. Her model accounted for observed continued growth during the 1870s and 1880s when there was contraction in staple exports, and would have accounted for a similar continued growth in the 1910–30 period had she actually produced figures to make the corroboration in the latter period of 'consolidation'.

Figures for the period, 1910–30, appeared in a much larger study by Jack Firestone, figures that failed to corroborate Hartland's hypothesis or any other dependent growth, staple theory. According to Firestone, during the 1910–30 period real per capita consumption rose by an annual rate of 0.33 per cent, as compared with 1.76 per cent from 1870 to 1880, 1.64 per cent from 1890 to 1910 and 1.77 per cent from 1930 to 1950. His estimates indicated no consolidation, in Hartland's sense of the word, after the expansion of 1900–10.[7] Ken Buckley registered the general response to Firestone's time series.

> According to the estimates, national income per capita in Canada increased at an average annual rate of 1.59 per cent from 1870 to 1890, 1.95 per cent from 1890 to 1910, but at a *zero* rate from 1910 to 1930 (p. 171).

> I find this hard to believe.... Among the results which I would question is a level of GNP in constant dollars at a considerably higher level during the latter 1870's than during the earlier '70's (p. 276), although Firestone himself refers to a 'severe economic slump from 1874 to 1880...'(p. 146).[8]

Firestone had produced estimates that rejected the generally accepted, though, as yet, unarticulated, *theory* of dependent staple export growth. His account contained inconsistencies and the estimates were questionable, but that only reinforced the importance of his work in setting the cleometric agenda in Canada for the next thirty years.

Buckley's disbelief was scientific. He quickly turned to the question implicit in Firestone's estimates and produced a preliminary report.[9] Its concise introductory summary of the work of H. A. Innis was a demonstration that 'Innis did not subscribe to a staple theory of economic growth'. The body of the report was a statement that neither did Buckley.

> But after 1820, when fur was replaced by timber and wheat, the possibility of other sources of national economic growth and change cannot be ignored. It is difficult, for example, to relate the enormous growth of the French Canadian labor force in the nineteenth century to the new staples.... It is one thing to assert that a great deal of domestic capital formation was induced by the emergence of the wheat economy and to list some of the regions and industries in which it must have occurred. But when all the measurable capital formation is there before you, the inescapable question is how much of it was so induced and where?[10]

Buckley's question was straightforward enough, but the dating of the end of reliance on staple exports was an easier subject to grasp; so, for those working in the field, the simple, and incorrect, question became, 'when did the Canadian economy's substantive dependence on primary product exports end?' Buckley had suggested 1820. In their contemporarily published text, Easterbrook and Aitken suggested 1930. Working on a different, but related, research agenda, Walter Rostow suggested some time between 1896 and 1914.[11] Gordon Bertram responded to Rostow's answer with evidence that the end of reliance had not occurred when Rostow said it had.

Bertram made two points. First, Rostow's stages model was inappropriate for an economy dependent on primary product exports, and, second, growth in late-nineteenth-century Canada had been gradual. There was no period of acceleration and take-off into self-sustaining growth.[12] This was, perhaps, a correct answer to an incorrect question.

HOW MUCH DEPENDENT GROWTH AND WHERE?

Buckley's question, How much dependent growth and where?, was not explicitly raised in Bertram's article, but it was there implicitly, appearing in the form of an inconsistency. Bertram was aware that there had been no decline in the growth of manufacturing in Canada between 1870 and 1890.[13] It was the steadiness of growth of manufacturing, in fact, that provided the basis for his rejection of a sudden take-off in the 1896-1914 period. The other ground for rejecting the hypothesis was the fact that the staple theory more clearly described the Canadian economy than did Rostow's stages theory, and much of Bertram's article was given over to a rather elaborate presentation of a Douglas North-type staple theory, and an extended discussion of what was 'probably' linked to what.[14] The contradiction appeared in the form of a statement in the article's 1967 version.

> Part of this growth [in manufacturing] may be attributed to the influence of staple industries analysed here, while a further significant portion may be attributed to the intensive development of secondary manufacturing within the region of Central Canada.[15]

Towards the end of the article, Bertram provided clear and definite corroboration for the proposition, which he had not made, that there was independent development and consequent growth, unrelated to staple exports, in central Canada between 1870 and 1890.[16] The inconsistency lay between the two grounds on which he rejected the take-off hypothesis: the more appropriate fit of the staple theory, and the constant rate of growth of manufacturing; because a 'significant portion' of the growth of manufacturing could not be accounted for in the context of the staple theory. He could not have a wheat export boom and a staple theory explanation of growth, and still have a constant rate of growth over the 1870-1914 period, much of it not related to exports, and he knew it.

> The western wheat boom was unquestionably a highly significant event in the development of the Canadian economy. However, one can suspect that the dramatic quality of the event and the considerable scholarly attention devoted to it have obscured the significant industrial growth that had already occurred in eastern Canada.[17]

The thin edge of the empirical wedge of doubt was beginning to penetrate, but it threatened a proposition encased in an ever-thickening crust of theory. Bertram's own relatively extensive statement of the staple theory was a pale reflection of what was being said elsewhere, and what would eventually be said in Canada. The profession was about to witness the transformation of the staple thesis of Canadian development into a staple theory of growth.

A STAPLE THEORY OF GROWTH

The first step was taken by two residents of the United States, R. E. Caves and R. H. Holton. Their study came very shortly after the *Report* of the (Gordon) Royal Commission on Canada's Economic Prospects, when the shock of the report's anti-foreign ownership proposals prompted the Private Planning Association's efforts to increase Canadian–American trade. It was commissioned by private enterprise in Canada, and arranged through the good graces of J. K. Galbraith at Harvard. Whatever its explicit intent, the Caves and Holton study made it clear that the Canadian economy was increasingly dependent on American markets. There was some evidence that Canada was less reliant on staple exports than in the past, but, certainly, the staple explanation of Canadian growth was alleged to have made very good sense right up to the time of the writing of the book.[18] The staple theory, in appropriate form, was as useful in justifying a close Canadian–American relationship in the mid-twentieth century as it had been in justifying a close Canadian–British relationship somewhat earlier.

The study was quantitative, but not of the sort that Buckley had called for, nor of the kind that Bertram and Chambers had undertaken. Caves and Holton demonstrated that periods of growth in Canada, defined in the short-run Keynesian paradigm as fluctuations in Gross Investment and Gross National Product, were correlated with exports. There were problems, of course. The correlation between exports and income was much higher in depressed times, and they had difficulty explaining the decline in the share of wages and salaries in GNP, and the decline of per capita consumption in the early 1920s, when exports and investment were high as a proportion of GNP,[19] and they found that growth of GNP picked up in the late 1920s when investment was not so much related to exports, or financed from foreign sources.[20] They made no attempt to distinguish staple from non-staple exports, or to measure net staple exports, or empirically to trace the relationship between capital formation and staple exports to answer Buckley's question, how much capital formation was related and where?

The Caves and Holton result tended to remove doubt about the continued applicability of what had become a staple theory to the Canadian case, and gave Mel Watkins the ground he needed to elaborate the theory in great detail.[21] Watkins's classic article was a masterful taxonomy of different possible linkage contexts and institutional environments in which staples might be exported, and of the consequent variety of growth paths. The whole was elaborated with extensive reference to the work of R. E. Baldwin, A. O. Hirshman, C. P. Kindleberger, W. W. Rostow, W. Arthur Lewis and a number of lesser lights, all of whom were interested in the rise of the Third World during the hottest period of the Cold War between the United States and the USSR, and the most rapid cooling of relations between Cambridge, England and Cambridge, Massachusetts, in the matter of growth theory. In this informational environment there was little room for the nagging doubts of one or two Canadian economic historians about a theory touted to be 'Canada's most distinctive contribution to political economy'.[22]

Buckley had criticized the staple approach because of its tendency 'to ignore any section once the staple which created or supported it is no longer expanding'. Here is Watkins's answer.

> His point has some validity, at least so far as Quebec is concerned, but the neglect is not inherent in a properly stated staple theory of economic growth.[23]

Watkins concluded, nonetheless, that the case of Quebec was unexplained, even in a 'properly stated staple theory'.[24] With respect to the proposition that there was significant growth in the 1870–90 period when there was little expansion in staple exports, he asserted that growth in real income could be attributed to the export sector anyway, without offering quantitative evidence.

AN ANALYTIC GAP

'Growthmania' became a worldwide passion in the mid-1960s, with theories of growth, and measurement of the components of growth, multiplying beyond control. These studies began with a broader question. What, in general, are the factors in growth, and what importance have they had in historical growth? The answer was reached by assuming that an Harrodian or a neoclassical model of growth fairly represented the historical process. By assuming that certain equilibrium conditions were met, at least for all practical purposes, the return to the factors of production could be taken as their contribution to output.

There were, at least, three such studies in Canada.[25] One might think that they would have cast some light on the debate over the role of staple exports in Canadian growth, but they did not. Only one of the studies referred to the question at all. Harvey Lithwick asserted that the primary product export-led theory of growth was a matter of faith, apologizing that 'we ... have very little knowledge of the role played by natural resources as factors of production'. 'This analytic gap', he confessed, 'is rather disconcerting'.[26] It was not just that a growth model using the quantity and productivity of general categories of inputs could not distinguish staple export activities; but, coming at the matter from the point of view of supply only, it had no conceptual room for a demand-determined leading sector.

In the late 1960s, 'growthmania' was followed by the 'New Economic

History', a combination of neoclassical theory and time series relating to long-run factors in economic development.

THE NEW ECONOMIC HISTORY

The New Economic History was explicitly positivist. It focused on rejection of established hypotheses by way of quantitative testing. Historical processes were stated in the form of a model, in practice, a neoclassical model. In this form, with all the relevant factors specified, it was possible to ask and answer the question, what if the values of specific variables were different? History, depicted as the working out of a neoclassical model, was subject to the counter-factual question, what if a certain factor had had a different value? What, for example, if there had been no railways in the United States, only canals? How much would the economy have grown? And the answer to that question provided an estimate of the contribution of railways to economic growth in the United States.

And so, with the Chambers and Gordon question: 'Let us imagine, for example, what would have happened if all the land that was brought under cultivation between 1901 and 1911 had been impenetrable rock.'[27] What would happen in the Chambers and Gordon model was not very different from what did happen in the Chambers and Gordon version of historical fact, indicating to its builders that growth in the Canadian economy in the wheat boom period was largely dependent on something other than wheat exports. They did not show what that other something was, or how it related to growth. They only demonstrated that a theory of dependent growth related to exports was inadequate to explain the development and growth of the Canadian economy, if wheat exports during the 1901–11 period were the exports on which growth depended.

The initial response to the Chambers and Gordon proposition was rejection.

> for both technical and conceptual reasons, the theoretical apparatus the authors use is inappropriate to test any proposition, regardless of its ontological status.... The result does not come within light-years of qualifying as an 'empirical measurement' of anything that economic historians have ever said – or would ever want to say – about the Canadian wheat boom.... All of the odd assumptions and empirical oversights of the model pale into insignificance beside that truly preposterous hypothesis: 'Let us imagine, for example, what would have happened if all the

land that was brought under cultivation between 1901 and 1911 had been impenetrable rock.'[28]

The critics went on to defend the staple theory of growth and development in the Canadian case.

Subsequent responses attempted to justify a respecification of the model to allow for the accrual of some of the gains from exporting wheat in forms other than the net farm rents measured by Chambers and Gordon.[29] These could be added to net farm rents to swell the contribution of wheat exports to growth. An auxiliary goal was to improve the estimates of farm rents and of other sources of farm income[30] to get the contribution up from Chambers and Gordon's 5-8 per cent to Caves and Bertrams's 20-30 per cent.[31]

In the process of making these revisions, the revisionists identified the Chambers and Gordon position with the model specified in their article.

> If export-led growth is seen only as the venting of surplus resources in the long run, as I believe Chambers and Gordon tend to see it, then the real-income gains reduce primarily to rents on perpetual assets, and other effects that have been hypothesized within the framework of the model are disposed of as inconsistent with long-run purely competitive equilibrium.[32]

But this was not Chambers's model of growth in the Canadian economy. This was the model that he alleged did not explain growth in the Canadian economy. The critics pointed out that if the model had contained scale effects outside the export sector, and efficiency gains in the 'gadget sector', induced domestic savings, etc.,[33] the measure of growth would be much higher. But this was Chambers's point in the first place. The only difference is the causal relation. Does export of the staple cause productivity advance outside of its own immediate sphere, or does the independent capability of the rest of the economy to capitalize on an increase in exports make the greatest contribution to growth?

INVERSION OF THE STAPLE THEORY

It was a curious thing that it was possible to criticize Chambers and Gordon, and support them at the same time. Vickery introduced his piece by saying that it contradicted the Chambers and Gordon result. He then went on to substantiate the proposition that in six of ten periods between 1851 and 1930 Canada had grown with technological and organizational advance in industry as the driving force, and only in four out of ten with staple exports as the driving force, the 1901-11 period *not* being one of the latter.[34] In fact, Vickery substantiated Chambers and Gordon in the period with which they were concerned, broadened the approach to include a test for an alternative explanation of growth, extended the analysis to nine other periods, and concluded that Chambers and Gordon were right six out of ten times.

Gordon Bertram produced superior measurements of farm rent and of the additional factors suggested by the critics, but when it came to the point at issue he was surprisingly cautious.

> While the rate of manufacturing growth in central Canada in the period 1870–90 might have continued at its satisfactory rate in 1900–10, if there had been no West, even a cursory investigation suggests that additional per capita income growth from manufacturing might have been missing in the absence of the wheat boom. There is an assumption in C-G [Chambers and Gordon] that the next best alternative use of resources after wheat would have yielded only a slightly lower rate of return, but it is equally probable that, after wheat, alternative rates of return might have fallen sharply.[35]

From this it would seem that both Chambers and Gordon, and Bertram assumed a pre-existing surplus that could have been put to uses other than the production of a primary product export. For whatever reason, as they mentioned the alternative uses of the surplus, they did not list all the logical possibilities. The alternative use could have a slightly lower rate of return, a much lower rate of return, the same rate of return, a slightly higher rate of return, or a much higher rate of return. It is more surprising that Chambers did not notice this, because he had the idea that growth originated with technological advance in the non-staple-export sector. Indeed it is quite surprising that anyone familiar with Canadian history would not have considered the possibility of a lower rate of return in Prairie farming, because there is a very viable case to be made that the opening of the West was a political, nation-building exercise, undertaken despite the economic cost; that is, despite the alternative cost of not using the resources involved to expand higher-return activities in central Canada. If this was the case, however, the staple theory would be inverted, if that is the phrase. Wheat export activity would be a drag on the rest of the economy. The more of GNP that could be attributed to it, the lower the overall rate of growth in the economy. Of course, as the economy shifted to the new, lower-equilibrium rate of growth, there would be an investment boom, a temporary lifting of the rate of growth, but the rate of growth after the boom would be lower than it would have been. Despite the support given to this interpretation by the estimates of Firestone, and Chambers and Bertram, and Caves and Holton, it would have been very rash to suggest that this interpretation had any validity, but it was suggested.

Actually, two economists suggested that opening of the West for settlement may have reduced, or did reduce, the long-run growth rate of the

Canadian economy. Clive Southey, noting that the homestead system of giving away land reduced farm land to a common property resource, suggested that the rents were competed away, settlement was excessive, and that the increase in wheat prices over the turn of the century could have raised the cost of living throughout the whole economy.[36] There seems to have been no direct response to Southey, perhaps because his was, by his own admission, primarily a theoretical exercise, uncomplicated by historical data. Much earlier, and much more pointedly, John Dales had denounced the National Policy of tariffs, railroad subsidies and immigration subsidies as an unfortunate interference with market forces that may or may not have contributed to extensive growth, but certainly had not contributed to increases in per capita income.[37] He kept his attack focused on government policy, however, especially on the tariff, so it was not immediately evident that he was deploring the effects of policy in the opening of the West. Indeed, he may have been suggesting that the western wheat economy would have been developed anyway, that is, without the National Policy, and that development would have been much more efficient, but that needed proof, and it still left him saying that the western wheat economy was inefficient and a drag on the rest of the country.

There never was any question about the importance of settling the west, of wheat exports, or of the massive reorientation of the economy to accommodate the new realities of a coast-to-coast system. The question was, rather, to what extent was the latter-day National Policy a political act? To what extent had politically motivated subsidization increased the extent of the economy at the expense of efficiency?

It seems out of place to talk of subsidization of western Canada in the face of a century of western complaints about being exploited for the benefit of eastern railway and financial interests. Yet, Dales was comfortable in suggesting that subsidization of immigration and settlement 'did much short-term and long-term harm in Western Canada'.[38] Could it have been as Innis said, that subsidization, by moving the system away from efficiency, led to demands for more subsidization?[39]

THE CLUSTERING OF RELATED STUDIES

When younger cliometricians turned to the question they corroborated the inverted staple theory with respect to all three pillars of the latter-day National Policy: the railroads, land settlement and the tariff.

Addressing the question of economic discrimination against the Prairie region, Ken Norrie concluded that

> it would appear that the benefits to westerners in the form of real income

outweighed any possible adverse impact on industrialization. ... as a minimum the prairies probably were at least as well off with the transportation features of the national policy as they would have been under the next most likely system.... If the markets for land were reasonably efficient, the purchaser for his part would have been indifferent between a situation with tariffs and lower purchase prices or no tariffs and a higher price. The only real 'losers' in this case were the agencies with land to sell – the CPR, the Hudson's Bay Company and the federal government itself.[40]

Norrie was supported by Peter George, who concluded that the CPR had been excessively subsidized, and would not have returned a normal profit without about 50 per cent of the subsidy;[41] and by Lewis and MacKinnon, who concluded that the Canadian Northern Railway could not have been built without government loan guarantees, and that the result was a debt-to-equity ratio that ended in bankruptcy.[42]

Papers dealing with land settlement were not as pointed with respect to the economic efficiency of the wheat economy, still, they are not without interest. Studness began the discussion with an assertion that the rate of settlement was determined by government policy, slowed down, in fact, by government policy.[43] Norrie replied that the slow-down had to do with the rapid filling up of sub-humid lands first, and the slower subsequent spread of dry-land farming technique; that is, that the rate of settlement was determined by economic factors.[44] Then Marr and Percy found that the rate of settlement correlated with government subsidization in the form of railway expansion and settlement expenditures.[45] Finally, Frank Lewis pointed out that, within the constraints given by the institutional setting, settlers responded to economic considerations,[46] which allowed him to have it both ways.

The point was that the rest of the economy had subsidized the West. The wheat economy had survived with transfers from central Canada, contrary to what one would have thought from reading Vernon Fowke.

There was another, more interesting set of studies, more clearly in the spirit of Buckley and Chambers, dealing with areas of the economy not undergoing staple export-induced expansion. All had to do with agriculture in Ontario and Quebec. Their thrust was summed up in the title, 'The Wheat Economy in Reverse: Ontario's Wheat Production 1887–1917'.[47] Contrary to the simple staple theory, which had Ontario expanding under the impetus of its own wheat exports until Western wheat came on stream and *then* shifting to mixed farming and cheese exports, the shift from wheat to mixed farming in Ontario was completed by 1870, long before settlement in the West. Adjustments in crops were controlled by a dominant domestic market, and not by the prices of exported products.[48] Even in the first half of the century Upper Canadian expansion could not be shown to have depended on external markets for wheat. Staple export booms appeared 'less as the cause than as the result of growth', because wheat production was part of the technical process by which land was cleared.[49] With respect to agriculture in Quebec, W. J. Eccles reported that Innis, and, by implication, Fowke, simply had misconstrued the place of the fur trade and its inter-relationship with agriculture in New France.[50]

While all this chipping away at the details of the staple theory was going on, Mac Urquhart, in company with others, was preparing a revised set of estimates of Gross National Product. In his comments on the results, John Dales presented a measured account of the debate over staple export and non-staple export factors in Canadian development.

> Urquhart makes no claim that his new estimates settle this debate. He thinks the new figures may give marginal support to the traditionalists, ... [The figures have not yet been deflated but] in the meantime we do have a more accurate picture of the western boom than we have had in the past. Urquhart shows that it was at first primarily an investment boom, and that wheat exports did not explode until after 1910.[51]

This reinforced an earlier conclusion of Bob Ankli's that

> if one is restricted to analyzing the period 1901–11 there was no export boom. Rather this was a period of investment boom, a tooling up, based in part on export growth between 1896 and 1900, but at least as important was the belief that it was Canada's turn to take its place as an economic power.[52]

It gave substance to Morris Altman's contention that, contrary to the earlier Chambers and Bertram conclusion, as he saw it, there really was a structural break in the development of Canadian manufacturing over the period 1870–1910, with heightened development taking place in the last decade in those areas of manufacturing which, through excessive expansion in connection with the wheat economy, were about to go into relative decline, if not formal bankruptcy.[53]

The literature indicates that the staple theory, fortified with political considerations, explains the development of the whole Canadian economy only in the period from 1890 to 1940, though it explains the growth of some regions of the economy over their entire period of European settlement.

12 A North American discourse

It is only a conjecture that economics in Canada, after 1970, was not simply absorbed into some putative United States cultural imperialism, but, rather, integrated itself into an emerging, dominant, North American, if not global, discourse. Even suggesting the lines of an hypothesis would require an excursion into the generality of modern economic thought that is well beyond the scope of an history of Canadian economics. It is possible, however, to explore the conjecture by recounting Canadian economic thought as if the conjecture were correct. If the facts and events so recounted do not violate the rules of observation and reason, then we have an indication that the conjecture is worth consideration.

We must not expect too much. There were some in the Canadian profession who did not participate in the dominant discourse. Their presence will support the conjecture insofar as they make explicit that they are reacting against the dominant, positivist discourse, that is, that they are taking a 'critical', or value-oriented approach, as the proponents of the New Canadian Political Economy did. And we must expect that there were some old conservatives who, having seen more than one grand theory fall into disrepute, turned to a less impassioned search for something more fundamental. There will have been mavericks, and some with purely local interests.

We look only for indications. For example, it is an indication that the conjecture has substance, that even the internationalist, Harry Johnson, eventually lamented the importation of economic thought from Britain and the United States. Like the nationalists, against whom he had laboured, when the dominant discourse was not to his liking, he abused its international character by labelling it an evil intrusion from a foreign source.

> Canadian academics with either insufficient professional competence by present standards or a taste for easy popularity among the masses to take the ready route of imitating and regurgitating the unscholarly and rabble-rousing pseudo-intellectual outpourings of their opposite numbers in

A North American discourse 205

foreign countries, predominantly in the United States but also in the failed and bitterly jealous quondam rival empires of the United Kingdom and France.[1]

Johnson was referring to the consequences of recourse for funding to the Canada Council and other, private, research institutions. Most, if not all, such institutions in Canada had counterparts throughout the Euro-American community, established to meet needs similar to those they were intended to meet in Canada. Had he foreseen the extent to which research institute funding and internationally accepted paradigms were to dominate the succeeding years of Canadian economic thought, Johnson might have been even more pessimistic than he was. The emerging discourse, in whatever country, failed to meet his standards.

Apart from the marked effect of telematic communication technique on the form and content of research in all branches of science throughout the world, the main factors influencing the evolution of economic thought in Canada after 1970 were those arising from within the discipline in consequence of the failure of Keynesian theory to answer the problems of stagflation and slow productivity growth, and those arising from within the discipline in Canada in consequence of the secular trend to political decentralization within the federation and economic integration with the United States. The latter were local, Canadian concerns, but they were taken up in paradigms developed in view of current conditions everywhere in the Euro-American community.

The situation, generated by the failure of neo-Keynesian theory to meet the problems of stagflation, was described by John Graham in his presidential address to the Canadian Economics Association.

> We have the paradox of being well on the road to developing a fully articulated body of theory and findings much of it irrelevant as a basis of policy because the economic system to which it pertains is no longer ... appropriate to our society.[2]

In response to this situation Canadians turned to the neoclassical analysis, the New Institutionalism and the New Classical macroeconomics that was used to meet the situation in the United States. Those who opposed Milton Friedman's Monetarism did so with the instruments of neo-Keynesian theory, rather than the Canadian Keynesianism of the mid-century.

Conservatives, now called NeoConservatives, (but really reincarnated Whigs) decided that the cause of stagflation and slow growth was too much socialism. Socialists, speaking through European legitimization crisis theory, as adopted by the New Canadian Political Economy, decided that the root problem was a failure to fundamentally change the structure of the economy.

There was still too much capitalism. Persisting inflation and the failure of the social welfare system to equalize the distribution of wealth were important elements in the underlying explanations of both positions. The NeoConservatives captured the commanding heights of policy in the late 1970s, insofar as they are capturable in Canada, but the point is that both sides treated the problem as a local variant of a problem common to the whole industrialized world.

THE NEW CANADIAN POLITICAL ECONOMY

It is beyond the scope of a history of economic thought to deal adequately with the New Canadian Political Economy that appeared in the disciplines of Political Science and Sociology in the 1970s. Its substance can be gleaned from a relatively small number of publications: L. Panitch, *The Canadian State: Political Economy and Political Power*;[3] *Rethinking Canadian Political Economy*;[4] and W. Clement and G. Williams, *The New Canadian Political Economy*.[5]

Debate over policy clustered around events. Wage and price controls in the middle of the 1970s focused the debate over macroeconomic policy. In 1978 a Royal Commission on Corporate Concentration had the same effect on industrial organization theory. The energy crisis and the New Energy Policy of the federal government focused the debate over deindustrialization and federal–provincial relations into the 1980s. A severe, allegedly policy-induced, recession preoccupied the profession in the early 1980s, and the mid-1980s were taken up by the Royal Commission on Economic Union and Development Prospects for Canada, which, like the 1939 Royal Commission on Dominion–Provincial Relations, and the 1957 Royal Commission on Canada's Economic Prospects, was a federal government attempt to outline a new national policy when the old one seemed no longer electable. It was, among other things, a preliminary to the free trade debate and election of 1988.

Debate clustered around events. Like-minded debaters clustered around research institutes.

THE WAR OF THE INSTITUTES

The C. D. Howe Research Institute was the oldest, having been the product of a 1973 merger between the C. D. Howe Memorial Foundation and the Private Planning Association. The Private Planning Association, modelled on a research institute of the same name in the United States, had been established to counteract a wave of protectionism in the late 1950s.[6] The C. D. Howe Research Institute continued to take this Continentalist view of

Canadian–American trade, sharing it with the Economic Council of Canada.[7] When the free trade debate flared up in the mid-1980s, the Howe Institute was still in the fray.[8]

In most matters the Howe Institute took a clear stand, but the inter-regional problems of the federation left it at a loss. Having at first temporized on wage and price controls,[9] it soon shifted to a Monetarist position with respect to monetary and fiscal policy in general. The studies were a cut above popular debate. T. J. Courchene, modelling his approach on Paul Wonnacott's *The Canadian Dollar, 1948–62*,[10] elaborated a mini-history of monetarism in an open economy, stressing the role of exchange-rate policy and government deficits in leading the central bank into interventionist manipulation of credit conditions.[11] The Howe Institute was mildly in favour of deregulation, and clearly opposed to any criticism of multinational corporations.

With its head office in Montreal, the Howe Institute found the problems of Quebec in Canada to be a matter of practical concern.[12] In one study it was pointed out that firms with head offices in Quebec, but with major operations outside the province, would find the best response to legislation requiring French in the work place to be the removal of head office operations and the establishment of a local operation for Quebec. The Institute, itself, adopted this strategy in the early 1980s, moving its head office to Toronto.

The Science Council of Canada was a government-created research institution emerging from the recommendations of a Royal Commission. It seems that Canada had a *de facto* science policy and it was thought that it should be given centralized co-ordination. In its first Annual Report (1966), the Council accepted a mandate to facilitate science policy. It sponsored at least one study by an economist,[13] but such studies were not its major thrust.

The Council's campaign for an industrial strategy peaked in intensity between 1977 and 1983. Virtually all of the relevant studies were variations on the same theme.[14] The analysis was not economics. Indeed, it explicitly rejected 'orthodox economics'. The topic was economic policy, however, and what was said certainly generated a response from economists.

According to the Science Council, the problems of the Canadian economy were structural; that is, Canada was not sufficiently advanced from a technological point of view. The country suffered from low productivity and a trade deficit in high-tech end-products. The enervating effects of foreign ownership and failure to finance small, innovating, job-creating, domestically owned Canadian firms, it was alleged, were turning Canada into a low-wage, technologically dependent region. 'Canadian manufacturing [did] not suitably self-adjust through the mechanism of a flexible exchange rate',[15] so the government should have issued a 'statement of principles or guidelines, which would have outlined the way manufacturing companies... both foreign and domestic... should behave'.[16] The Council denounced

208 A history of Canadian economic thought

Canada's pervasive, 'unnecessary consumption',[17] and suggested an industrial strategy of subsidization and regulation directed towards technological independence.

Neither the Fraser Institute nor the Ontario Economic Council was established to counter the Science Council, but both represented the new wave in neoclassical theory, and both took sight on the Science Council's pronouncements.[18]

The Fraser Institute, modelled on free enterprise 'think tanks' in England and the United States, presented the concerns of the dominant North American discourse in economic analysis. Milton Friedman was right, and J. K. Galbraith, wrong. Market power and market failure were not the cause of inflation. Inflation was a monetary phenomenon. Wage and price controls, that is, incomes policy, would not work because this did not affect the underlying cause of inflation, and they distorted market decisions by preventing the adjustment of relative prices.[19] The real trade-off was not between inflation and unemployment, but between public goods and income, and employment and growth. Canada was suffering from 'the British disease', too much socialism.

Herbert Grubel's *Free Market Zones* was a comprehensive statement of the Fraser Institute's position on microeconomic policy.[20] The propositions can be listed.

(1) Government interference with the market disturbed the constancies assumed when policies were put in place, making the results of policy unpredictable.
(2) Regulated industries tended to capture regulatory agencies, with consequent politicization in favour of the regulated, at the expense of economic efficiency.
(3) Apparent monopoly was not an adequate excuse for regulation, because markets only had to be 'contestable' to be efficient.
(4) The presence of externalities might suggest the need for regulation, but motivation in government bureaucracies was not likely to generate an efficient equation of costs and benefits. The problem of government failure was as serious as any problem of market failure.
(5) All insurance schemes generated the 'moral hazard' of 'adverse selection'. For this reason, universal, government insurance schemes, with the secondary purpose of social welfare and income equalization, tended to be far more costly than their benefits warranted.

Unions and the idea of tripartism or so-called industrial democracy, that is, worker control through participation in management, or through the agencies of a corporate state, came in for particular criticism in Fraser Institute publications. Unions might not cause inflation directly, that is, by demanding higher wages, but their lobbying the government to undertake excessive expenditures forced it to have recourse to the Bank of Canada for funds, and that caused inflation; and, certainly, through their contracts against inflationary losses, unions ensured that inflation would spread rapidly. Any benefits from unions creating harmonious work conditions, and so improving productivity, were seen to be offset by the impact of higher wages on the profits of small, innovative, job-creating firms. Where it had been tried, industrial democracy generated decisions that had benefited the workers directly, and not industry or society as a whole. The result was inefficient firms surviving on government loans. Tripartism, that is, corporatism, only eased the way for special interests to manipulate the economy for their own benefit, to the detriment of the public good.[21]

In line with contemporary practice, Fraser Institute studies frequently employed and quantitatively tested reduced form mathematical models. Some of the studies were more an explanation of current market behaviour, than a complaint about inappropriate policies. One study, for example, explained contracting out as a phenomenon occurring when services became sufficiently standardized to be more efficiently acquired at arms length in the market.[22] The authors did not extend their analysis to contracting out by government, a form of 'privatization', but the implication can be seen.

The Ontario Economic Council sponsored at least seven studies on industrial policy. All rejected it. All were examples of the new, positive approach. Daly and Globerman, for example, constructed a model of the Johnson-Breton analysis of nationalist economic policy, and put it to a quantitative test.[23] E. G. West applied a quantitative test to the Baumol–Bowen hypothesis concerning frozen productivity levels in performing arts.[24] Mathewson and Quirin used what they called a 'two sector-firm pseudo-empirical model' to test the freedom of multinationals to manipulate transfer prices, and succeeded in defining conditions in which their freedom would be significantly limited.[25]

These are only examples, but they illustrate the extent to which the conservative side in the new conservative–old liberal debate of the period accepted the structure of the emerging dominant discourse. The Canadian Institute for Economic Policy, on the other side of the debate, was less *au courant* with the latest, positivist fashions, but nonetheless well within the dominant, North American discourse in most of its studies.

The Canadian Institute was associated with the names of Walter Gordon and Abraham Rotstein, and so with the Committee for an Independent Canada. Sid Ingerman characterized the Canadian Institute's studies as the products of 'Post-Keynesian Interventionists', ('die-hard neo-Keynesians'), and 'Traditional Canadian Tinkerers', ('bourgeois nationalists').[26] Those of the Institute's studies that could be classifiable as economics were in the dominant economics discourse.

The counter-attack on Monetarism illustrates the point. It was well organized into a theoretical statement, an empirical refutation of counter claims, and a general statement of where policy should move in the future. Inflation was structural, a product of organized market power and fortuitous supply shocks. Accordingly, it required a structural solution, that is, an incomes policy, specifically, a tax based incomes policy of the type being proposed in the United States. Wastes entailed in unemployment were too large to tolerate, but, if aggregate demand were increased, the non-competitive structure of the economy would generate inflation as institutions with economic power used the opportunity to raise prices and wages. The solution was to control wages and prices by raising taxes on those benefiting from inflated wages and prices. The alternative, macroeconomic control by fine-tuning the money supply, was seen to be an insuperably difficult task, plagued by the ever-changing nature of money and by unstable markets.[27]

Clarence Barber and John McCallum's empirical refutation of Monetarism was archetypical.

> The whole of the 1.5 percentage point increase in the unemployment rate between 1975 and 1978 can be explained by the delay in the exchange rate depreciation resulting from a tight monetary policy.[28]

> The gross inefficiency and waste of a policy of inflation-fighting by means of monetary restraint alone ... such a policy has large and persistent effects on unemployment combined with small erratic effects on inflation.[29]

> In every one of the eleven years between 1964 and 1974 the government sector as a whole ran a surplus, yet it was precisely during this period that we moved from an inflation rate of about 3 per cent to double-digit inflation. Further more, between 1972 and 1974, the period of most rapid acceleration of inflation, there were large *increases* in government surpluses relating to GNP. This is true for all measures of the budget balances.[30]

Their theory was not neoclassical, but they respected all the cannons of positive economics. The material was Canadian, but the discourse was such that a conference featuring Sydney Weintraub, J. K. Galbraith and Lester Thurow addressed the issues involved.[31]

The Institute for Research on Public Policy can be filed into the conjecture about the emergence of a dominant global discourse because its establishment was preceded by an extensive review of United States and European research institutes. All were seen to be meeting needs commonly experienced thoughout the Euro-American community.[32]

Many of the Institute's publications were not in the field of economics, but it did sponsor Irving Brecher's excellent account of Canada's Competition Policy,[33] to which the present account will return, and it sponsored a popular version of Breton and Scott's exciting work on economically optimal constitutions.[34]

Having considered these research institutes, it would be unCanadian not to give some further consideration to the Canadian Center for Policy Alternatives, founded by the socialist, New Democratic Party. By its own admission it looked for economic guidance to Michael Kalecki, J. M. Keynes, Karl Marx and Joan Robinson. The Center was a forum for combative, left-wing economics[35] where one could describe the assumption of rational expectations as 'academic idiocy', with complete impunity.[36] Its policy interests were Canadian, but like the other research institutes, the Center communicated in the context of a more general paradigm.

There were many other research institutes, and hundreds of other studies; and no claim is made that studies and institutes chosen for special consideration here were chosen on a scientific basis. Among the institutes not mentioned were: The Economic Council of Canada (at least 500 studies), The University of Toronto Institute for Policy Analysis, le Centre de Recherche et Développement en Economique at the University of Montreal, The North–South Institute, the Pacific Group for Policy Alternatives, le Centre d'Etudes et de Recherches en Economique Philanthropique, and the Atlantic Provinces Economic Council. Indeed, in the 1970s and 1980s everything seemed to multiply. Regional economics associations, with separate meetings, were set up in Atlantic Canada and in Quebec. A new journal, devoted to policy in Canada, *Canadian Public Policy – Analyse de Politiques* appeared in the mid-1970s. Subject-based groups in theory, economic history, and regional and development economics separated from the Canadian Economics Association to hold their own meetings. Add to this all the economic studies produced by all the relevant departments of all the governments, and the need for some other approach to economic thought in Canada becomes unquestionable.

ECONOMIC HISTORY

There were two new texts in economic history.[37] Although they were very different from one another, and very different from the classic Easterbrook and Aitken text, they shared some fundamentals. The one through compendious accounts of the sectors of the economy, the other through a rather tight focus on alternative theories of development, came to the conclusion that the staple theory of Canadian economic development was not supported in the context of the new, positivist discourse. Indeed, economic history in general shied away from the distinctively Canadian staple theory, and turned to regional topics, as did history and economic history throughout North America, thereby supporting the general conjecture of this chapter.[38] Works in the western Marxist tradition made the point by using the staple thesis, suitably reinterpreted, to attack what they admitted to be a dominant, North American, discourse.[39] Eventually, even the Marxists abandoned the staple theory for ideas generated by Ralph Miliband in Europe.

THE NEW INDUSTRIAL ORGANIZATION

After a half century of resistance, Canadians finally accepted standard industrial organization theory. Indeed they contributed heavily to the development of the more advanced 'New Industrial Organization Theory'; but the story of this integration of the Canadian profession into the more general, positivist discourse was interesting from a number of points of view.

The new developments emerged in the context of the Coase-Williamson tradition in microeconomic analysis. They grew out of a concern with the determinants of the number of firms in a market, and with a definition of 'the firm' that would facilitate analysis of those determinants. The new theory perceived market structures to be a rational response to elements in specific technological and informational environments.[40] With the new approach came a new set of terms: state variables, pre-emption, credible commitments, contestable markets, principal–agent problems, strategy space, and transactions costs; all of which helped to explain 'What it is that firms can do that markets, either through prices or through a broader range of contracts cannot do (or can do, but at a greater cost)'.[41] Where 'traditional theory', starting from given market structures, proceeded to the negative welfare effects of certain business practices, the new analysis was able to show that it was wrong to generalize welfare conclusions on the basis of structure and behaviour. 'Arguments for [anti-combines] policy based on traditional competitive analysis [were] inappropriate'.[42]

The new market analysis was immediately relevant to the economics of Canada, and contributions by Canadians, by Frank Mathewson in particular, integrated discussion into the mainstream of Euro-American discourse,[43] but what was also evident, even from casual contact with the literature in this tradition,[44] was that it assumed considerable knowledge of theoretical and mathematical technique, a condition that put it beyond the reach of most businessmen, lawyers and politicians.

The arcane character of the new industrial relations theory, combined with the importance of the information environment in policy formation, ensured continuation of some problems, despite integration into the new global discourse.[45]

In 1970, competition law needed upgrading and teeth. It needed to encompass the 'dynamic' considerations of what was then the new analysis, that is, Schumpeterian views on the benefits and stability of monopoly. It needed to be extended to services at a time when services were outgrowing commodities in everyday transactions. Mergers and trade practices needed to be removed from the criminal code in order to be dealt with by a tribunal of economists and lawyers under the rubrics of civil law. Not least, competition policy needed to be seen by the business community as an alternative to regulation, not as another form of regulation.[46]

According to Irving Brecher, one thing that stood in the way of meeting these needs in the 1970s was the indifference of most economists. Two works appearing in 1976, *Dynamic Change and Accountability in a Canadian Market Economy*[47] and *Canadian Industrial Organization and Policy*[48] did not indicate a general interest on the part of the profession. That came with the Royal Commission on Corporate Concentration and its background studies, even though the Report[49] selectively ignored the studies.[50] So interest was aroused in the 1980s, and a number of enlighted texts appeared, for example, Dunlop, McQueen and Treblicock's *Canadian Competition Policy*;[51] but policy remained bogged down in the consequences of a self-selection process among top civil servants, and of the 'arcane' character of the new analysis;[52] both of which, according to Brecher, contributed to a 'state of intellectual drought' among upper-level civil servants, and to the 'intellectual fog' that surrounded competition policy for both politicians and the public. There were other factors. Increasing internationalization of the economy led some economists to suggest that free trade was all that was needed to ensure competitive conditions. Others argued that mergers were necessary to achieve competitive status in the new international economy. Lastly, the business community was unable to see the difference between competition policy and industrial strategy.

Stumbling from one legislative disaster to another, a few, old-school, industrial-organization economists persisted: Irving Brecher, Ted English, Larry Skeoch and David McQueen. The Competition Act of 1987 met virtually all their demands. A year later, the long-sought-after civil tribunal was put in place to apply the new rules. By then, however, analysis had so far outreached practice as to require much more time in application than the need for expeditious judgements would allow, and it was no longer believed that the benefits and costs of seeming anti-competitive behaviour could always be identified, let alone measured.

MACROECONOMICS, MONEY AND BANKING

The last word in the debate over macro models and policy goes to Richard Lipsey,[53] whose assessment of the integration of Canadian Keynesian theory into the newer paradigms was clear. The crisis in macroeconomics was 'a crisis of policy, not a crisis of our understanding of the world of our experience'.[54]

> early Keynesians typically thought in terms of downward inflexibility of money *wages*. No doubt it was the Monetarists with their expectations augmented Phillips curve who really jolted Keynesians into thinking about rates of change of individual prices relative to expected rates of change of all prices. But once that point was accepted – and it took nearly half a decade for the absorption to really happen fully – it became clear that the logic of Keynes's argument extends to this situation.[55]

His point was that neo-Keynesian theory was a viable research programme, able to absorb and explain new facts, and to outpredict with reasonable accuracy its rivals. There was the point about inertial and rational expectations, of course, but Lipsey thought the theory could accommodate a reasonable form of rational expectation. He should have added that we will no longer assume that parameters remain constant through changes in policy, that policy changes will not be evaded so that effects are reduced or even eliminated, or that definitions of unemployment (and money) need not be updated with structural changes in the economy.

Battered, altered, perhaps improved, perhaps integrated into a broader discourse, but certainly no longer what it had been, Keynesian theory had survived the attacks mounted from the University of Western Ontario: first the Monetarist attacks of David Laidler,[56] then the more 'fundamentalist',[57] New Classical attacks of Michael Parkin. Lipsey selected Parkin's presentation as the most formidable, recognized its content as an important contribution to economic analysis, and dismissed it as a basis for policy because it was not consistent with observed reality.[58] Laidler and Parkin's colleague, Peter Howitt, dismissed it because he could see situations in which the assumed equilibrium of New Classical theory would not obtain.[59]

Whatever the content of monetary theory, before or after the Monetarist counter-revolution, Canadian monetary policy, according to Ron Shearer,[60] had always been a sort of half pragmatic business that rarely took theory into account, even in the *Report* of the (Porter) Royal Commission on Banking and Finance in 1964. Presumably this fuzzy position, accompanied by a concern for the problems of banking in an open and regionally diverse economy, continued to be the position of Canadian monetary policy thereafter; because Shearer, having noted that the real departure in the Porter

A North American discourse 215

Commission *Report* was its concern for microeconomic issues, said no more about it, except to make a brief contradictory assertion, supported by a citation from Irving Brecher's account of the *inter bellum* period, that the Real Bills Doctrine, associated with Adam Shortt, was the Canadian tradition in policy.[61]

The Porter Commission's preoccupation with competitive conditions in financial intermediation was consonant with the new Euro-American conservative preoccupations of the 1970s and 1980s; preoccupations that were epitomized in Chant and Acheson's much published demonstration that non-market, non-policy directed motivations determined the behaviour of the central bank.[62] These preoccupations appeared first in Bill Hood's study for the (Gordon) Royal Commission on Canada's Economic Prospects. Under his direction, they pervaded the background studies of the Porter Commission.

The Porter Commission *Report* recommended competition, disclosure, and inspection, rather than regulation, as the route to efficiency in banking. Any necessary regulation was to be by function, rather than by institution, in order to remove institutional barriers to the provision of whatever services the market demanded. Irremoveable regulations were to be centralized in order to put provincially incorporated near-banks on the same footing as federally incorporated banks. A subsequent study by the Economic Council carried this thrust further by suggesting deposit insurance for all financial intermediaries, federal and provincial, premiums being variable with risks rather than type of institution or jurisdiction of incorporation. In general the idea was to minimize regulation and reduce barriers to entry, while not opening the door to self dealing through concentrated ownership in either the financial intermediation sector or any other sector.[63]

The Bank Acts of 1967 and 1980 did not solve the problems outlined in the Porter Commission *Report*. Deposit insurance, while reducing the need for regulation, may have encouraged inefficient levels of risk. Homogenizing the regulation of banks and near banks by removing interest rate ceilings on bank loans, and permitting banks into non-banking markets, strengthened the position of the banks. Making it easier for near banks to get into banking proper did increase competition, or, at least, it increased the number of banks. What also occurred, however, was a political campaign for regional banks, and a resource boom in western Canada. Over-expansion resulted in bank failures, massive losses to depositors,[64] a run on the new banks, and a series of mergers. In the end the number of domestic, chartered banks returned to where it was before Porter. Perhaps Adam Shortt had been right after all. Very long-run market forces had shaped the Canadian banking system and would continue to do so. Substantial structural interference was ill-advised. Real competition came from international financial intermediation, which,

216 *A history of Canadian economic thought*

in the 1980s telematic revolution, became even more intense. There were cases in which more attention to Canadian conditions, and less attention to the categories of global discourse, were in order.

PUBLIC FINANCE

The 1970s–1980s trend to normative neoclassical theory and positivist testing of mathematically articulated models was evident in the field of public finance, but public finance in Canada had to deal with the intractable problems of federalism in a difficult case. The accepted texts of the period[65] did not give a clear picture of developments.

At the very beginning of the period Richard Bird summed up the state of the field in Canada and made some suggestions for future research.

> An adequate positive theory of public expenditure is needed to permit the effective implementation of our normative theories of what goods 'should' be provided publicly and which public activities 'should' be expanded and which cut.[66]

He could not have foreseen the difficulties. He correctly saw the possibilities emerging from the theory of public goods and from developments in the theory of non-market public choice, but he did not see the way in which those possibilities would be realized. He failed to predict the great growth in normative theory that, in fact, occurred. It was one thing to run a quantitative test of the extent to which some ideal state was not being realized. It was another to elicit from the data an explanation of what *was* being realized, whether it conformed to the ideal or not. Pure positivism required less biased curiosity and a different, more exacting discipline. A decade later Bird was unable to report any progress towards a positive theory of growth in government spending.[67]

Pure positivist considerations of the sort called for by the intractable problems of the Canadian federation were swamped by the high fashion of positivist testing of normative neoclassical analysis. Eventually even the leaders in normative theory, Robin Boadway and Tom Courchene, bowed a little to political reality,[68] but they seemed unaware of the agenda of the small group who accepted Bird's challenge.

Attempts to work out a pure positivist theory of public finance can be traced to the early work of Irwin Gillespie who pointed out that the norms of compensatory fiscal policy and income equalization did not describe the realities of the Canadian case.[69] Subsequently he and two of his Carleton University colleagues, Walter Hettich and Stan Winer, formalized and applied a positive approach.[70]

Application of neoclassical welfare considerations to public finance in

Canada in the 1970s and 1980s was spearheaded by Robin Boadway. The style was that of the day, mini models and microcomputer corroboration. The concern was optimal taxation in a general equilibrium context that allowed for market failures, public goods, and production in a non-market-driven public sector. The place was Queen's University, a centre of excellence in this research project,[71] the most disturbing conclusion of which had to do with the central topic of Canadian public finance, fiscal federalism.

Political federalism, a consequence of economic and cultural regionalism in Canada, has attracted the attention of economists because it is a source of undoubted inefficiencies in the Canadian economy as a whole. The inefficiencies grow out of provincial interference with trade,[72] and, allegedly, out of the transfer payments made by the federal government to 'have not' provinces. These policies, according to Tom Courchene, perpetuated a misallocation of resources and generated 'transfer dependency'. There is little point in citing Courchene's numerous works in support of this contention. Richard Bird referred to Courchene as 'one of the most important analysts and commentators on the ongoing saga of Canadian federalism'. Anything that might be said here would be dwarfed by such a statement from that source.

In a surprising turnabout, Robin Boadway and Frank Flatters suggested that equalization transfers might be efficiency generating.[73] For those who needed theories to justify policies unavoidably adopted on other grounds, the suggestion was a godsend.[74] For policy commentators it was a bonanza.[75]

The equalization payments 'flap' has to be seen in context. Quebec had just come out of the referendum on separation. Separation was voted down, but everyone was sensitized to federal–provincial arrangements. New equalization payment arrangements were due to be put in place in the year in which the 'flap' occurred. The energy crisis and the mistaken expectation of $40.00-per-barrel oil had completely upset the expected balance between have and have-not provinces. Was Alberta to become rich while others became poor because of the price of oil? Some kind of compensation seemed to be in order. Boadway and Flatters suggested that in regions with high resource revenues fiscal burden would be very low, inducing in-migration to a point where the marginal product of labour would be below that of other regions. Transfer payments, inhibiting the migration, would prevent this misallocation of resources. That the argument was contrived did not escape the commentators, but it was all a tempest in a teapot anyway. The resource boom collapsed, thousands of Maritimers left Alberta, and the new equalization formula ignored the arguments of the economics profession.[76]

There was a third thrust in public finance in the 1970s and 1980s, an attempt to elaborate the logic of choice in the context of historically extant non-market institutions, and to extend it to public choices of a seemingly non-economic character. The complexities of Canadian confederation and its constant state of crisis made it inevitable that Canadians, especially from the francophone community, would make relevant contributions to the discipline in this regard, and Albert Breton did. He was not alone,[77] but the others worked in reference to his output. Breton's work on federalism, a natural extension of his economic analysis of nationalism and language, was a successful attempt to explain the rationality and irrationality of certain political choices.[78]

There was much change in Canadian public finance in the 1970s and 1980s, and we cannot leave it without noting a subtle shift of opinion away from the income tax towards some form of value-added, general sales tax,[79] on grounds of both equity and efficiency. The influence of Carl Shoup finally had its effect as the economics profession in Canada integrated itself into the more general modern discourse in yet another matter.

REGIONAL ECONOMICS

Regional economics had started out in the 1950s as a policy looking for a theoretical justification. It ended in the 1980s with two justifications, pointing in two contradictory directions, and with its credibility as a basis for policy in doubt.[80] There was more at work in this than a change in the character of the dominant discourse, but the change in discourse was also a factor.

When regional policy failed to make much of a dent in regional disparities, satisfying politically motivated regional demands lost some of its appeal. The economic rationale was dropped. So regional economics was reduced to an appeal against the immediate costs of long-run efficiency, and Michael Bradfield quoted Donald Savoie who, quoted Tom Courchene, to the effect that 'an unrelenting pursuit of national efficiency is simply not acceptable in Canada. The cost in adjustment and in personal hardship would be prohibitive.' [81] Regional economics was one area that could not be comfortably integrated into the general North American and European informational environment. Donald Savoie described the situation most aptly by suggesting that neo-Marxist, neoclassical and regional dependency theories were 'other worldly' with respect to the real budgetary process that dominated government planning and expenditure in Canada.

When André Raynauld took his turn at summing up a national conference on regional policy in 1974,[82] he did not report a neoclassical –non-neoclassical split in opinions. He did have Roland Parenteau's repetition of the old complaint that it was impossible to achieve regional (read provincial) development by elaborating structures, and spending money in federal jurisdictions.[83] Neoclassical sentiment appeared at points in Harvey Lithwick's 1978 summary of the state of things.[84] Perhaps policy could assist adjustments dictated by market forces. At yet another conference at the University of Ottawa, in 1980, the division was evident with Tom Courchene taking a national and neoclassical position, and Michael Jenkin, of the Science Council, taking a provincial and non-neoclassical position.[85] The final maturing of generally accepted regional economics into what one outstanding expert called 'an empty set' became fully evident in two volumes appearing in the late 1980s,[86] in which François Perroux, himself, elaborated the state of growth pole theory, André Raynauld displayed the latest econometric results, and Tom Courchene and James Melvin expounded a neoclassical approach. In that same year regional dependency theory appeared in an elaborate, not explicitly Marxist, statement by Michael Bradfield.[87] According to Bradfield some regional underdevelopment could be explained in the context of the neoclassical paradigm, if market failures were taken into account, but the main problem was the exercise of economic and political power by developed regions. Counter-exercise of that kind of power, even at the expense of national growth and development[88] was seen to be in order.

THE MACDONALD ROYAL COMMISSION

There was little in the field of international trade in the 1970s and 1980s that would be of interest here that has not already been mentioned, except for what showed up in the (Macdonald) Royal Commission on the Economic Union and Development Prospects for Canada.[89]

The *Report* recommended free trade with the United States. This was not remarkable given the new character of Canadian economics. The Commission envisaged Canada exporting manufactured goods. The time for reliance on primary product exports was over. Resources industries were in decline and suited only for policies of conservation. If Canada was to keep up with world development it would have to open itself to trade in the expectation that exporting firms would develop in, and markets would develop for, the manufacturing sector.[90] The significance of this for the staple theory of Canadian economic development, that is, for the economics of Canada, will form part of the subject of the next and concluding chapter.

APPENDIX

To sample the information environment with respect to the continentalization of the economics profession by means of an unscientific survey, I asked the following question of 17 professional economists working in central Canada.

To what extent are departments of economics in Canadian universities 'farm teams' or 'branch plants' of departments of economics in United States universities; and to what extent can the relative rise and decline of departments of economics in Canada be accounted for in terms of such relationships?

Needless to say, the sample was heavily biased by the predominant presence of English-speaking central Canadians.

The responses were wide ranging, but not, on the whole, inconsistent with each other. Only one respondent considered the subject of the question 'a non-issue' and 'not interesting'. The others scattered themselves between a refusal to accept the connotations of the terms 'farm team' and 'branch plant', to those who plunged into a history of the rise and decline of 'cloned' centres of research interest in North America–Canada being treated, without apologies, as an undifferentiated part of the whole.

Five theories of the inter-relationship between departments of economics surfaced. First, migration of students and faculty tends to be confined within continentally defined regions, rather than nationally defined regions: easterners stay in the east, westerners in the west, francophones return to Quebec, United States graduates of United States departments consider positions in Canada (only in second or third choice), and so on. Second, Canadian departments of economics expand at different rates, expanding departments becoming over-representative of the more fashionable United States departments and schools of thought during the period of their expansion. Third, the market for publications being in the United States, and Canadian publishers failing to show interest in material aimed at an international readership, Canadian economists not dealing with local Canadian subjects are forced to accept United States interests and standards. Just how this third factor results in relationships between particular departments, as opposed to the general continentalization of the profession, was not elaborated. The remaining two theories will be stated in a specific context.

Respondents whose last degree was received prior to 1970 looked back to the immediate post-Second World War period when Canadian departments were thought to have drawn their inspiration, and their faculties in some instances, from Oxbridge and the L.S.E. There was, in their view, no question of Canadian departments being 'branch plants'. It was just that the best economics was being done in England. After the 1950s, in their view, Canadian departments became more independent, and more oriented towards centres of excellence in the United States. This group measured the independence of the economics profession in Canada in terms of numbers of doctorates produced and numbers of Canadian doctorates competitively chosen for positions in Canadian departments. Even within this group of respondents, however, there were admissions that it was probable that Canadian students would go to United States departments for their final degrees, because United States departments had 'more resources, greater depth and more people'. Students were more likely to find the best possible supervision in the United States. Respondents whose last degree was received after 1979 tended to be unselfconsciously part of an undifferentiated North American profession.

Detailed comment by the respondents can be broken down by region: the Maritimes, Quebec, Ontario, the West. I begin with the Maritimes.

All but one of the respondents had to be asked specifically about Maritimes departments before offering a comment. Dalhousie was uniformly thought to be among Canada's significant departments. Memorial was described as a 'branch plant' of Toronto, and U.P.E.I as a 'branch plant' of Carleton. Whatever connection Maritimes departments might have with United States departments was beyond the interest and knowledge of all respondents.

Departments in francophone universities were more commented upon than those of the Maritimes, but, again, it usually took a specific question to elicit a response. The department at the University of Montreal was generally thought to be 'good', 'rising', 'good in theory' and neoclassical in its approach. It was thought to hire in a wide range of specializations, having access to, but limited to, the best in Quebec, and for that reason, having connections with no special group of departments in the United States. One of the best of the world's francophone departments, it was said to have connections with the University of Social Sciences at Toulouse, the best in France. Both the department at the University of Montreal and the department at Laval were thought to have strong connections with continental Europe. The University of Quebec received no attention, but a number of respondents admitted to having no knowledge of any of the francophone departments.

McGill was no more in the field of consideration of the respondents than were the francophone departments. It was generally said to have had a post-Keynesian connection with Cambridge, though not a 'branch plant' relationship. Some reported that it had not 'kept up' with more recent work, others, that it had found money and was making a comeback. Its connections with the United States were below the consideration line.

Most respondents were sufficiently at home in talking about Ontario and western departments to offer confident rankings and assertions as to which were 'rising' relative to others. The rankings were quite consistent. British Columbia and Western vied for first place. Queen's and Toronto were selected as third or fourth. McMaster, Carleton and Simon Fraser competed for fifth place. British Columbia and Western were thought to have risen in relation to Toronto and Queen's over the previous two decades, but their positions had stabilized, and Waterloo and Simon Fraser were now 'rising'.

In general, the respondents rejected the terms 'branch plant' and 'farm team', preferring to describe the relationship with United States departments as 'intellectual', rather than 'institutional'; a consequence of the natural networking that occurs between scholars working on related topics; or a consequence of an historically determined 'old boy' network – a social, rather than an institutional or intellectual relationship. Canadians were not thought to be special in this. Everyone looked to the United States. Dissatisfied United Kingdom and Australian economists were migrating to the United States in search of a better work environment. The United States was where the best economics was being done in the 1970s and 1980s.

The department at Queen's drew unsolicited comment from all respondents. It was ranked middle of the road in the conservative–liberal continuum, and was thought to be neo-Keynesian in macroeconomics. This was consistent with its assumed strong connection with Ivy League departments just to the south. Having had a broad, policy-oriented approach during the time of Urquhart, Deutsch and David Smith, it was said to have moved towards a more fashionable concentration on techniques of analysis. The department at Trent University was supposed to be its wholly-owned subsidiary. It was thought to be in relative decline, to have a fear of graduating anyone, and was depreciated for being 'a center of rest in Canada'.

If the department at Toronto was a 'branch plant' then it was a branch plant of departments at Chicago, Harvard, M. I. T., and perhaps Yale, in one or other of its many parts. It was thought to have world-class scholars in Industrial Organization and in utility theory. The department at Toronto, and perhaps the University of Toronto, in general, was thought to have lost its chance during the 1950s, when it hired on the 'American plan', but taught and graduated on the 'British and European plan', It hired PhDs, but did not consider the doctorate to be the normal teaching degree, and did not think of graduating any.

Having 'risen from nothing' in the 1970s, the department at Western Ontario was associated with Chicago, Monetarism, rational expectations and New Classical Economics. Of course, it was categorized with the 'conservative institutions'. When rational expectations moved from Chicago to Minnesota, when theory and econometrics moved from Chicago to Wisconsin and the University of California at San Diego, and, eventually, when 'Minnesota macro' became a term of derision, it was alleged, Western took up interest in analytic and research technique, following the lead of the University of Rochester to the point of being dubbed 'Rochester times three'. The department at Western was known to have a variety of good people, and was accorded the rank of a good United States department in 'quality', but not in depth and breadth of cover.

The rise of the Department of Economics at the University of British Columbia was thought to have begun in the late 1950s. In the time of Gideon Rosenbluth and Tony Scott, U. B. C. had a broad policy approach, but, it had turned since to analytics and technique. Having achieved world leadership in duality theory, the department had become bogged down, despite its connections with west coast United States departments, and despite its general success in keeping up with current fashion.

A fast riser among Canadian economics departments, Simon Fraser was associated by some with Chicago and by others with U. C. L. A. and Washington. The story was given to me as the following.

When Chung and Coase were at Chicago, and Alchian was at U. C. L. A., U. C. L. A. was, in fact, more 'radical' than Chicago. Then Chung and Barzel 'turned up' at Washington, and the department at Washington became a 'clone' of U. C. L. A.'s department, insofar as Industrial Organization was concerned. Subsequently an M. I. T. group emerged at Washington, and two members of the department moved to S. F. U. in Burnaby. S. F. U. then became a 'clone' of Washington and U. C. L. A. at earlier periods, other influences from the New Industrial Organization tradition having arrived at S. F. U. by other routes.

In a kind of first-look check on these assertions, I drew up a list of Canadian departments of economics and their members' institutions of last degree, as reported in the Canadian Economics Association *Membership Directory* for 1990.

Memorial, Carleton, McMaster, York, Toronto, Wisconsin, Notre Dame, Upsala.
St. Mary's, 2 Toronto, S. F. U., U. B. C., Clark, Boston College, Brown.
Dalhousie, 3 U. B. C., 2 Yale, 2 Dalhousie, 2 Brown, Stanford, Texas A. & M., Rochester, Columbia, Cornell, Berlin, Bonn.
U. N. B., 3 Queen's, 2 McMaster, 2 Western, 2 S. F. U., London, Toronto.
Laval, 2 Louvain, 2 Pennsylvania, 2 Laval, Texas A. & M., Western Ontario, Carnegie-Mellon, Princeton, Montreal, Wisconsin, U. C. L. A., Sherbrooke.
U. Q. A. M., 3 Montreal, 2 Laval, 2 Berkeley, McGill, Concordia, Rochester, Stanford, Toronto, Princeton, L. S. E., U. Q. A. M.
H. E. C., 3 Montreal, 2 Queen's, 2 Toronto, York, Laval, Chicago, H. E. C., McGill, U. B. C.
Montreal, 3 Princeton, 2 Louvain, 2 Chicago, 2 Queen's, 2 Yale, Geneva, Brussels, N. Y. U., U. B. C., M. I. T., Paris, Stanford, Minnesota, Berkeley, Manchester, Carnegie-Mellon, Montreal, North Western.
Concordia, 3 McGill, M. I. T., McMaster, Berkeley, Paris, Western Ontario, New School of Social Science N. Y., Cornell, Toronto, Syracuse, Pennsylvania.
Ottawa, Berkeley, U. B. C., Bryn Mawr, Harvard, Pennsylvania, Paris, Laval, Louvain, Cordoba, Princeton, Rotterdam.
Carleton, 4 Johns Hopkins, 4 M. I. T., 3 Western Ontario, 2 McGill, 2 Harvard, 2

224 *A history of Canadian economic thought*

Pennsylvania, Queen's, London, Minnesota, Duke, Indianna, S. F. U., Carleton, Toronto, Chicago, Dalhousie, U. C. L. A., Cornell.
Queen's, 9 Queen's, 3 Harvard, 3 U. B. C., 3 Chicago, 2 Princeton, 2 Michigan, Cambridge, Rochester, London, Pennsylvania, Essex, Oxford, Saarbruchen, Alberta, Stanford, Cornell, Southampton, L. S. E.
Trent, 3 Queen's, 2 McMaster, Carleton, McGill, Toronto, Western Ontario.
York, 2 McMaster, 2 Queen's, 2 Chicago, 2 London, Yale, Berkeley, M. I. T., Oxford, Wisconsin, L. S. E., Carleton, Minnesota, Duke, Western Ontario, U. B. C., Indianna, Harvard, Princeton, U. C. L. A., McGill.
Toronto, 5 Harvard, 5 Berkeley, 4 Princeton, 4 Chicago, 3 Toronto, 2 M. I. T., 2 Wisconsin, 2 Cambridge, 2 Columbia, Duke, Yale, London, Sorbonne, S. U. N. Y., Western Ontario, U. B. C., Stanford.
Brock, 3 Western, 2 U. B. C., Essex, McGill, Chicago, Carleton, Yale, Oxford, Queen's, S. U. N. Y.
McMaster, 4 Minnesota, 3 Western Ontario, 3 Toronto, 2 McMaster, 2 London, Purdue, Cambridge, Queen's, Ohio, 2 Essex, Rice, U. B. C., M. I. T., McGill, Brown, Wisconsin, Berkeley, Harvard.
Western, 3 Chicago, 2 Wisconsin, 2 Toronto, 2 Boston College, 2 Queen's, 2 Yale, 2 Rochester, Minnesota, Manchester, M. I. T., Stanford, Purdue, Harvard, Columbia, Princeton, Western Ontario, U. B. C., Northwestern.
Guelph, 4 L. S. E., 4 Queen's, 3 U. B. C., Minnesota, Duke, M. I. T., Australian National, La Trobe, Essex, Iowa, Toronto.
Waterloo, 4 Western, M. I. T., 3 Queen's, Toronto, U. B. C., Cal. Tech., S. F. U., Michigan, McGill, McMaster, Brown, Pennsylvania, Duke, U. C. L. A., Berkeley.
Wilfrid Laurier, 2 Western Ontario, 2 Alberta, Queen's, Carleton, Toronto, McMaster, Washington, Harvard, Cornell.
Windsor, 3 Western Ontario, Toronto, Michigan, Pennsylvania, McGill, L. S. E., Wayne State, Bryn Mawr, Alberta, York, Condordia, Queen's.
Manitoba, 3 Manitoba, 2 Toronto, Wisconsin, Alberta, L. S. E., Rotterdam, Australian National, Columbia, Michigan, Leeds, Iowa.
Saskatchewan, Berkeley, 2 Minnesota, 2 Queen's, Cornell, Vienna, McGill, Ohio, Maryland, Western Ontario, Utah, Brown, S. F. U., (Regina Campus) 4 Western Ontario, 2 Queen's, Ohio, Oxford.
Lethbridge, Colorado, Queen's, Concordia, Washington, Alberta, Purdue, McGill, S. F. U..
Calgary, 4 Queen's, 2 McMaster, U. B. C., Vanderbilt, L. S. E., Minnesota, Penn. State, Alberta, Columbia, Birmingham, Western Ontario, Michigan, Prague, Utah, Cambridge.
Alberta, 4 U. B. C., 2 Princeton, 2 Berkeley, 2 Western, 2 Queen's, 2 Essex, M. I. T., 2 Cornell, Minnesota, Fribourg, Johns Hopkins, Yale, Ottawa, Oxford, Columbia, Chicago, Birmingham, L. S. E., Michigan, Ohio, Manchester, Toronto.
S. F. U., 2 Harvard, Princeton, Indianna, Berkeley, Michigan, Carleton, Duke, London, N. Y. U., S. F. U., Yale, U. B. C., Brown, Wisconsin, Minnesota, L. S. E., Ames Ohio.
U. B. C., 5 Harvard, 5 Stanford, 4 Wisconsin, 2 Chicago, 2 Queen's, Ohio State, George Washington, Toronto, Michigan, Oregon, M. I. T., Pennsylvania, Princeton, Berkeley, Brown, Northwestern, Edinburgh, Western Ontario, Washington, L. S. E., London, Johns Hopkins, Rochester, Warwick.
Victoria, 2 Harvard, 2 Washington, Purdue, Queen's, Carnegie-Mellon, Durham, Toronto, Yale, S. F. U.

Information on Canadian degrees granted in Economics, broken down by institution, regions and/or provinces, between 1919 and 1986, can be found in W. D. Wood, L. A. Kelly and P. Kumar, *Canadian Graduate Theses: 1919–1967*: (Kingston, Industrial Relations Centre, Queen's University, 1970); the Canadian Association of Graduate Studies *Annual Report* for the years 1968 to 1975; and Statistics Canada series after 1976. Changes in the numbers of degrees granted seems to vary more with the reporting source than with anything else. In general, however, the available numbers do not contradict the impressions given by the respondents to my question, with respect to universities west of Montreal.

Two excellent studies of the structure of the profession in Quebec have been reproduced in Gilles Paquet's, *La pensée économique au Québec français*: Bernard Bonin's 'Une mesure de notre taille', and Pierre Fortin's 'La recherche économique dans les universités du Québec français: les sources de rupture avec le passé et les défis de l'avenir'.[91] Fortin's study supports, in the case of economics in Quebec, the interpretation of economics in Canada as a whole found here. The discourse in economics in Quebec, of course, may not be the dominant discourse in Quebec, as it may not be the case in Canada as a whole. Bonin's study focuses on the content of *Actualité Economique* in more recent times.

13 Conclusion

Economic thought in Canada has been influenced by three distinct factors: (1) a unique geographic endowment, (2) different cultural influences in different regions, and (3) unscreened exposure to the elements of modern industrialism, including Euro-American economic thought.

The Canadian historical experience has been that of a new country on the frontier of European civilization during Europe's period of industrialization. In consequence, the attention of those interested in Canada's economics has been directed to theories of growth and development. Because Canada is not geographically or culturally homogeneous, its processes of growth and development have not been uniform. In some regions, and in the whole country in one period, development has been, and was, dependent on primary product exports. In other regions, and other times, development has been, and was, a domestic process. In no case have the processes of dependent and independent development been totally isolated from one another, but they have been distinguishable. Out of this experience have come the economics of John Rae, a theory of independent development and growth, and the economics of H. A. Innis. Around both contributions there have been clusters of related works: those of the Nationalist School in the nineteenth century, and the many versions of the staple theory in the twentieth century.

The Canadian experience has not produced distinctive contributions to monetary theory, but there has been a typical, that is, a characteristic Canadian position – that of the nineteenth-century British Banking School. There have been differences, of course, especially insofar as the primary consideration in Canada, as pointed out by Adam Shortt and those who followed him, has been the open character of the economy. Certainly, other positions have been proposed in Canada. Perhaps the majority of those concerned with money and banking proposed something else, as was the case when the Birmingham School position was held by so many in nineteenth-century English-speaking Canada. What establishes the Canadian position in this case is the consistency of national policy, and the fact that, throughout the twentieth century, it has had support from some economists, despite changing fashions in monetary theory.

A case can be made for the one time existence of a distinct economics among the English-speaking of what is now central Canada, that is, in southern Ontario. It was not fundamentally indigenous, having roots deep in the Scottish Enlightenment and in other elements in the historical development of the British Empire. It was distinguished, nonetheless, by its opposition to nineteenth-century British Political Economy, and by its separation from the development of economic thought in the United States. Its 'theory' of value was drawn from David Hume, its method from Francis Bacon.

The distinct economics of Quebec, existing well into the twentieth century, was entirely a product of the historical experience of the French in Canada. Its 'theory' of value was drawn from the collective aspirations of the French to survive as a distinct society. Its method was value-oriented.

Neither of these distinct economics survived the emergence of a positivist, North American economic discourse in the mid-twentieth century. There were transitional figures in both cases. H. A. Innis accepted the positive methods of the German Historical School, mediated by American Institutionalism. His 'theory' of value, by which I mean his position on the role of values in social science, was an obsession of his later years. F.- A. Angers rejected positive economics, but used economic theory to support positions taken in *la pensée économique au Québec.* By the 1980s the concerns of Quebec's distinct economics emerged in *la sociologie économique.* English Canadian concerns about economic development, having been transformed from the distinctive economics of the Nationalist School in the nineteenth century to the economics of the staple thesis, were transformed, once again, into the post–1970 debates over the meaning and validity of the staple theory. By then, both of these special concerns, each in its own way, was outside the common North American discourse into which economics in Canada had integrated itself.

It is a corollary of these 'conclusions' that economics in the Maritimes and in western Canada, in some definable way, has been distinct from economics in Ontario and Quebec. Of course, there was no economics in western Canada before 1900, but the experience of both regions has been a marked, continuing dependence on primary product exports; and their economic thought has centred on that. Despite this distinctive concern, the theory and methods used in both regions have become those of the common, positivist, North American discourse.

Notes

PREFACE

1 Toronto, University of Toronto Press, 1979.
2 London, George Allen & Unwin, 1982.
3 New York, Macmillan, 1973.
4 *Journal of Econometrics*, 1982, vol. 18, pp. 295–311.

1 THE ECONOMICS OF SETTLEMENT

1 R. E. Caves, '"Vent for Surplus" Models of Trade and Growth', in R. E. Baldwin et al., *Trade, Growth, and the Balance of Payments: Essays in Honour of Gottfried Haberler*, Chicago, Rand McNally and North-Holland Publishing Co., 1965, pp. 95–115.
2 *Histoire véritable et naturelle des productions de la Nouvelle France*, Paris, 1664.
3 W. J. Eccles, *France in America*, New York, Harper, 1972. L. R. Macdonald, 'France and New France: The Internal Contradictions', *Canadian Historical Review*, 1971, vol. 71, pp. 122–143.
4 *The Description and Natural History of the Coasts of North America*, Paris, 1672.
5 D. G. McFetridge, 'Preface', G. F. Mathewson and R. A. Winter, *Competition Policy and Vertical Exchange*, Toronto, University of Toronto Press, 1985.
6 *History of the Government of the Island of Newfoundland*, London, 1793.
7 Reeves, op. cit., p. 45.
8 K. Mathews, 'Historical Fence Building: a Critique of the Historiography of Newfoundland', *Newfoundland Quarterly*, 1978, vol. 99, pp. 21–30.
9 *The Newfoundland Journal of Arron Thomas, 1794*, J. M. Murray, ed. Don Mills, Longmans, 1968.
10 *The Newfoundland Journal of Arron Thomas, 1794*, op. cit., p. 164.
11 H. A. Innis, *The Cod Fisheries*, Toronto, University of Toronto Press, 1954, pp. 93, 212, 486–488.
12 M. Blaug, *Economic Theory in Retrospect*, Home Wood, Richard D. Irwin, 1968, p. 80.
13 L. D. Milani, *Roberty Gourlay, Gadfly, Forerunner of the Rebellion in Upper Canada*, Thornhill, Ampersand Press, 1971.

Notes 229

14 Milani, op. cit., pp. 268-270.
15 ibid.
16 C. D. W. Goodwin, *Canadian Economic Thought*, London, Cambridge University Press, 1961, pp. 9-19.
17 London, 1822.
18 Goodwin, op. cit., p. 18.
19 *Statistical Account....* op. cit., pp. cxlix-cli.
20 ibid., p. clxxxiv.
21 ibid., pp. ccxxxii, cccxxxiii-cccxxxiv.
22 ibid., pp. cclxxiv-ccclxxvii.
23 Goodwin, op. cit., p. 14. J. Bouchette, *The British Dominions in North America*, London, 1832.
24 ibid., vol. 2, pp. 220-221.
25 ibid., vol. 2, p. 222.
26 Gourlay, *Statistical Account*, p. cccxxxvii.
27 *Report on the Affairs of British North America from the Earl of Durham*, 1839. Goodwin, op. cit., p. 22.
28 'The Art of Colonization', *England and America*, London, 1833, vol. 2, pp. 61-262.
29 ibid., p. 103.
30 ibid., p. 110.
31 ibid., p. 150.
32 ibid., pp. 190-192.
33 ibid., Note xi, pp. 47-60.
34 Chester Martin, *'Dominion Lands' Policy*, Toronto, McClelland and Stewart, 1973, p. 134.
35 *Appendix B*, op. cit., p. 113.
36 *The British Dominions in America*, London, 1831, vol. 2, Chapters XIV, XV, pp. 205-247.
37 *Considerations on the Past, Present and Future of the Canadas*, Montreal, 1839.
38 Fernand Ouellet, *Economic and Social History of Canada: 1760-1850*. Toronto, Gage, 1980, pp. 332-369.
39 G. Paquet and J-. P. Wallot, *Patronage et pouvoir dan le Bas Canada: 1794-1812*, Montréal, Les Presses de L'Université du Québec, 1973.
40 D. McCalla, 'The Wheat Staple and Upper Canadian Development', *Canadian Historical Association, Historical Papers*, 1978, pp. 34-46. 'Commercial Politics of the Toronto Board of Trade: 1850-1860', *Canadian Historical Review*, 1969, vol. 50, pp. 51-67.
41 'The Staples Thesis, Common Property, and Homesteading', *Canadian Journal of Economics*, 1978, vol. 11, pp. 547-559.
42 *"Dominion Lands" Policy*, Toronto, McClelland and Stewart, 1979, pp. 116-150.
43 ibid., p. 145.
44 'Snarkov Island', R. F. Neill, *A New Theory of Value*, Toronto, University of Toronto Press, 1972, pp. 146-149, pp. 148-149.
45 'A Defence of the Tariff', R. F. Neill, op. cit., pp. 149-159, p. 157.
46 Chester Martin, op. cit., pp. 128-139.

2 THE ECONOMICS OF THE MARITIMES

1 London, 1747.
2 ibid., no pagination.
3 Anon., *An Account of the Present State of Nova Scotia*, London, 1786, pp. 72–73.
4 See N. Macdonald, *Canada: 1763–1841, Immigration and Settlement*, Toronto, 1939.
5 J. Stewart, *An Account of Prince Edward Island in the Gulf of St. Lawrence*, London, 1806.
6 D. C. Harvey, 'The Intellectual Awakening of Nova Scotia', *Dalhousie Review*, 1933–34, vol. 13., A. A. Lomas, *The Industrial Development of Nova Scotia, 1830–1854*, M. A. Dissertation, Dalhousie University, Halifax, 1950.
7 *The Stepsure Letters*, Toronto, McClelland and Stewart, 1960.
8 *The Letters of Agricola*, Halifax, 1920.
9 M. Blaug, *Economic Theory in Retrospect*, op. cit., p. 26.
10 *The Letters...*, op. cit., p. 451.
11 ibid., p. 461.
12 ibid.
13 T. C. Haliburton, *A General Description of Nova Scotia*, Halifax, 1832; *An Historical and Statistical Account of Nova Scotia*, Halifax, 1829; *Historical and Descriptive Sketches of the Maritime Colonies in America*, London, 1828. Robert Cooney, *A Compendious History of the Northern Part of the Province of New Brunswick and of the District of Gaspé*, Halifax, 1832. R. M. Martin, *History of Nova Scotia*, London, 1837. John Crosskill, *A Comprehensive Outline of the Geography and History of Nova Scotia*, Halifax, 1838. W. C. Atkinson, *A Historical and Statistical Account of New Brunswick, B. N. A., with Advice to Immigrants*, Edinburgh, 1844.
14 op. cit, 1829.
15 *The Clockmaker*, Halifax, 1836.
16 See Lomas, op. cit.
17 Lomas, op. cit., p 110.
18 London, 1847.
19 Halifax, 1849.
20 op. cit., 1849, pp. 6–8, 21, 218, 288.
21 ibid., p. 218.
22 ibid., p. 218–219.
23 R. G. Haliburton, *A Review of British Diplomacy and its Fruits*, London, 1872.
24 R. G. Haliburton, *Inter-Colonial Trade our Only Safeguard against Disunion*, Ottawa, 1868, p. 40.
25 *Speeches and Public Letters*, Halifax, 1909, vol. 1, pp. 8 ff.
26 ibid., vol. 1, pp. 82–122.
27 ibid., vol. 1, pp. 646–647.
28 ibid., vol. 2, pp. 77.
29 ibid., vol. 2, pp. 104–193.
30 Charles Tupper, *Political Reminiscences*, London, 1914, p. 45.
31 F. B. McCurdy, *Nova Scotia's Right to Live*, Halifax, 1924; *A Statement of Nova Scotia's Position*, an address to the Canadian Club of Toronto, Apr. 27, 1925. Canada, *Report of the Royal Commission on Maritime Rights*, Ottawa, 1926. Nova Scotia, (Jones) *Report of the Royal Commission of Economic Enquiry*, Halifax, 1934. Canada, *Report of the Royal Commission on Financial Arrange-*

ments between the Dominion and the Provinces, Ottawa, 1935. A. B. Balcom, 'The Jones Report, an Interpretation', *Dalhousie Review*, 1935–36, vol. 15, pp. 1–13. E. R. Forbes, *Maritime Rights: The Maritime Rights Movement, 1919–1927*, Kingston and Montreal, McGill-Queen's, 1979.
32 C. R. Fay, 'The Problems of the Maritime Provinces', *Dalhousie Review*, 1924–25, vol. 4, pp. 438–451; 'The Economic Development of the Maritime Provinces', *Cambridge History of the British Empire*, London, 1930, vol. 4, chapter 24, pp. 657–671; *Life and Labour in Newfoundland*, Toronto, 1956. S. A. Saunders, 'The Maritime Provinces and the National Policy (Comments on Economic Regionalism in Canada)', *Dalhousie Review*, 1936, vol. 16, pp. 87–89; *The Economic Welfare of the Maritime Provinces*, Wolfville, 1932; *The Economic History of the Maritime Provinces*, Ottawa, 1939.
33 'The Problems of the Maritime Provinces', op. cit., pp. 440.
34 See H. G. Johnson, *The Antigonish Movement*, Antigonish, 1944. A. F. Laidlaw, *The Campus and the Community: The Global Impact of the Antigonish Movement*, Montreal, 1961. M. M. Coady, *Masters of their Own Destiny*, New York, 1939. George Boyle, *Democracy's Second Chance: Land, Work, and Co-operation*, New York, 1941. A. F. Laidlaw, *The Antigonish Movement in Retrospect*, an address given at the University of Toronto, December 9, 1967.
35 John Graham, *Fiscal Adjustment and Economic Development: A Case Study of Nova Scotia*, Toronto, 1963.
36 S. A. Saunders, op. cit., 'The Maritime Provinces and the National Policy'. J. A. Maxwell, 'Aspects of Canadian Federalism', *Dalhousie Review*, 1936, vol. 16, pp. 275–284.
37 Canada, Royal Commission on Dominion Provincial Relations, *Report*, Ottawa, 1939.
38 Nova Scotia, Royal Commission on Provincial Development and Rehabilitation, *Report*, Halifax, 1944.
39 B. S. Kierstead, *The Economic Effects of the War on the Maritime Provinces* mimeo., no date, pp. 212 ff. p. 224.
40 Canada, Royal Commission on Provincial Development and Rehabilitation, *Report*, Ottawa, 1944.
41 Halifax, 1965.
42 T. N. Brewis, *Regional Economic Policy in Canada*, Toronto, 1969.
43 *Evolution of Economic Research in Regard to the Atlantic Region*, Fredericton, 1967.
44 ibid. p. 42.
45 A. C. Parks, *The Economy of the Atlantic Provinces: 1940–1958*, Halifax, 1960. A. K. Cairncross, *Economic Development and the Atlantic Provinces*, Fredericton, 1961. T. Wilson, *Financial Assistance with Regional Development*, Fredericton, 1964. L. E. Poetschke, 'Problems and Policies', a paper delivered at the joint Canadian Economics Association, Canadian Council on Rural Development Conference, Winnipeg, Nov. 14, 1970. Atlantic Provinces Economic Research Center, *Industrial Development Policy in the Maritime Provinces*, Prepared under the direction of A. C. Parks for the (Deutsch) Royal Commission on Maritime Union, 1970. Royal Commission on Maritime Union, *Report*, Halifax, 1970.
46 R. F. Neill, 'The Old Economics and the New National Policy', *A. C. E. A. Papers*, 1982, vol. 11, pp. 147–154.
47 R. C. Montreuil, 'Canada's National and Regional Economic Development

Strategies'. T. J. Courchene, 'Aspects of Regional Policy in the 1970s', Barry Weller, ed. *National and Regional Economic Development Strategies; Perspectives on Canada's Problems and Prospects*, Ottawa, University of Ottawa Press, 1981, pp. 12–24, 69–76.

48 George de Benedetti, 'Conflicting Federal Policy in the Development of Atlantic Canada', *A. C. E. A. Papers*, 1987, vol. 16, pp. 1–4. R. C. Le Blanc and M. Desilleres, 'Réforme de la taxation des biens au Nouveau-Brunswick', ibid., pp. 54–68. L. Eden, 'The Impact of Equalization of Municipal Fiscal Capacity: A Comparison of the Maritime Provinces', ibid., 1986, vol. 15, pp. 84–107. J. R. Winters, 'Economics, Politics, and Regional Transfers', ibid., pp. 9–19. W. J. Woodfine, 'Regional Development Policy, a 25-Year Perspective', ibid., pp. 127–131.

49 M. Kabir and N. Ridler, 'A model for the Allocation of Public Funds to Develop a Multi-Species Aquaculture', ibid., 1987, vol. 16, pp. 165–178. M. Aynul Hasan, 'Time Series Forecasting Models: Some Canadian Provincial Economy Experiences', ibid., 1986, vol. 15, pp. 156–171.

50 C. M. Li and A. L. Levine, 'Interpersonal Comparability of Cardinal Utility, and the Social Welfare Function', ibid., 1986, vol. 15, pp. 172–182. A. L. Levine, 'Toward a New Theory of Non-Tatonnement', ibid., 1987, vol. 16, pp. 125–143. N. H. Morse, 'The Nature of European Intrusion and the Subsequent Development of the Western Hemisphere', 1982, vol. 11, pp. 119–128.

51 E. R. Forbes, 'In Search of Post Confederation Maritime Historiography, 1900–1967', *Acadiensis*, 1978, vol. 8, pp. 23–31. E. W. Sager, 'Newfoundland's Historical Revival and the Legacy of David Alexander', *Acadiensis*, 1981–83, vol. 11–12, pp. 104–115. T. W. Acheson, David Frank, J. D. Frost, *Industrialization and Underdevelopment in the Maritimes, 1880–1930*, Toronto, Garamond Press, 1985.

52 J. Goulding, *Newfoundland in Crisis*, Ottawa, Sisyphus Press, 1982, pp. 3, 56.

53 J. F. Kearney, *Common Tragedies: A Study of Resource Access in the Bay of Fundy Herring Fisheries*, Halifax, Institute of Resource and Environmental Studies, Dalhousie University, 1983.

54 C. Lamson and A. J. Hanson, eds, *Atlantic Fisheries and Coastal Communities: Fisheries Decision-Making Case Studies*, Halifax, Dalhousie Ocean Studies Programme, 1984. *Fisheries, Journal of Canadian Studies*, 1984, vol. 19, pp. 3–177.

3 PENSÉE ÉCONOMIQUE, DIX-NEUVIÈME SIÈCLE

1 G. Paquet, J.-. P. Souque and J. Trent, eds, *Social Science Research in Canada. Stagnation or Regeneration?* Ottawa, Science Council of Canada, 1985, pp. 98–115.

2 F.- A. Angers, 'Naissance de la pensée économique au Canada français' *Revue de l'histoire de l'Amerique français*, 1961, vol. 15, pp. 204–229, p. 205.

3 F.- A. Angers, 'Preface', Esdras Minville, *L'économie du Québec et la science économique*, Montréal, Fides, 1979, pp. 24–28.

4 P. E. Gosselin, *Etienne Parent*, Montréal, 1964.

5 Esdras Minville, 'L'économique, facteur de deviation de la politique provinciale', *Le Citoyen Canadien Français*, Montréal, Fides, 1946; republished as chapter 4, 'Economique et culture: deviations des orientations culturelles' in

L'économique de Québec et la science économique, Montréal, Fides, 1979, pp. 239-261.
6 E. Parent, *Importance de l'étude de l'économie politique*, Montréal, 1846.
7 *De l'importance des devoirs du commerce*, 1852.
8 ibid., p. 14.
9 ibid., p. 17.
10 ibid., p. 20.
11 Fernand Ouelette, *Economic and Social History of Quebec, 1760-1850*, Toronto, Gage, 1980.
12 *Conversations sur l'agriculture par un habitant de Varennes*, Quebec, 1834.
13 *De l'abolition des droits féodaux et seigneuriaux au Canada*, Montreal, 1849.
14 *Le canadien émigrant*, Québec, 1851.
15 *La question de la tenure seigneurale de bas-Canada ramenée à une question de crédit fonçier*, Montréal, 1852.
16 J. I. Cooper, 'Some Early French Canadian Advocacy of Protectionism', *Canadian Journal of Economics and Political Science*, 1937, vol. 3, pp. 530-540.
17 J. Fournier, *Le Canada: son présent et son avenir politique et finances*, Montréal, 1865. C. D. W. Goodwin, op. cit., pp. 49-51, 82-83.
18 J. A. Mousseau, *Le tarif, protection et libre-échange*, 1876.
19 C. Beausoleil, *Système Protecteur ou de la necessité d'une réforme du tarif canadien*, Montréal, 1871.
20 *La reciprocité*, Québec, 1891. *Vive la protection*, Montréal, 1891.
21 *Protection et libre-échange; quelques statistiques*, Montréal, 1879.
22 Hector Fabre, *Confederation, indépendance, annexation*, address to the Canadian Institute at Quebec, March 15, 1871.
23 J. Tassé, *Philemon Wright, colonisation et commerce en bois*, Montréal, 1891.
24 *Discourse de l'Honourable M. Chapleau, prononcé à Ste Thérèse le 3 Novembre, 1881*, Montréal, 1881.
25 M. Chapleau, *Discourse en proposant la vente du Chemin de Fer Québec, Montréal, Ottawa et Occidental, à l'assemblée legislative*, Québec: 1882.
26 Chester Martin, *'Dominion Lands' Policies*, Toronto, McClelland and Stewart, 1973, p. 172.
27 Québec, 1863.
28 Québec, 1864.
29 op. cit., *Coup d'oeil...* pp. 29-30.
30 *Etudes sur les industries du Québec*, Québec, 1870.
31 Québec, 1870-81.
32 B. A. Testard de Montigny, *Manuel d'économie domestique*, Montréal, 1896; *La colonisation, le nord de Montréal à la région Labelle*, Montréal, 1895.
33 *La Vallée de l'Outaouais*, Montréal, 1873.
34 Montréal, 1874.
35 Montréal, 1876.
36 L. Beaubien, *Agriculture et colonisation*, Montréal, 1894.
37 *Etoffe du Pays*, Montréal, 1901.
38 *La conquête économique*, Montréal, 1939, vol. 1, pp. 259-291.
39 *Pour rester au pays*, Québec, 1926. *Le vrai remède*, Québec, 1931.
40 J. A. N. Provencher, 'Crédit fonçier', *La Révue Canadienne*, 1864, vol. 1, pp. 7-20.
41 Québec, 1863.
42 *Biographie de François Vezina, Caissier de la Banque Nationale*, Québec, 1867.

43 ibid., p. 82.
44 J. C. Langelier, op. cit.
45 A. Desjardins, *Le Caisse Populaire*, Montréal, 1912.

4 THE ECONOMICS OF JOHN RAE, 1822-34

1 J. A. Schumpeter, *History of Economic Analysis*, New York, Oxford University Press, 1954, p. 468.
2 Two volumes, Toronto, University of Toronto Press, 1965.
3 D. McCalla, 'The Wheat Staple and Upper Canadian development', *Canadian Historical Association, Historical Papers*, 1978, pp. 34–46. 'The Canadian Grain Trade in the 1840s', *Historical Papers*, Toronto, The Canadian Historical Association, 1974. 'The Commercial Politics of the Toronto Board of Trade, 1850–1860'. *Canadian Historical Review*, 1969, vol. 59, pp. 51–67. D. McCalla and P. George, 'Measurement, Myth, and Reality: Reflections on the Economic History of Nineteenth Century Ontario', *Journal of Canadian Studies*, vol. 21, no. 3, pp. 71–86. R. L. Jones, *History of Agriculture in Ontario, 1613–1880*, Toronto, University of Toronto Press, 1946. V. C. Fowke, *Canadian Agricultural Policy: the Historical Pattern*, London, Oxford University Press, 1946.
4 C. D. W. Goodwin, op. cit., pp. 56–57, 126.
5 H. A. Innis, 'Imperfect Regional Competition and Political Institutions on the North Atlantic Seaboard', *Commerce Journal*, Toronto, University of Toronto, 1942, pp. 21–26.
6 Eatwell, (*et al.*, *The New Palgrave: a Dictionary of Economics*, New York, Stockton, 1978, vol. 1, pp. 327–333, 345–347, 357–368.
7 S. Leacock, *The Unsolved Riddle of Social Justice*, Toronto, 1920.
8 James, op. cit., vol., 2, pp. 131–137.
9 ibid., p. 122.
10 ibid., p. 264.
11 London, Macmillan, 1932.
12 James, op. cit., pp. 63–66.
13 ibid., p. 67.
14 ibid., p. 94.
15 ibid., pp. 352–357, 185–197.
16 ibid., p. 119.
17 ibid., pp. 86–89.
18 ibid., p. 87.
19 ibid., pp. 91–94.
20 ibid., pp. 93–94.
21 ibid., p. 168.
22 ibid., p. 172.
23 ibid.
24 ibid., pp. 118–129.
25 ibid., p. 264.
26 ibid., pp. 173, 260.
27 ibid., pp. 172–173.
28 ibid., pp. 193–196.
29 ibid., p. 197.
30 ibid.

31 ibid., pp. 263.
32 ibid., pp. 65–66.
33 ibid., p. 261.
34 ibid., pp. 43–46.
35 ibid., p. 55.
36 ibid., pp. 57–59.
37 ibid., pp. 300–304.
38 ibid., p. 71.
39 ibid., pp. 72, 304.
40 ibid., pp. 229, 253, chapter X.
41 ibid., pp. 305–312.
42 ibid., p. 262.
43 ibid., pp. 384–385.
44 ibid., pp. 328–351.
45 ibid., pp. 183–184, pp. 397–412. Craufurd Goodwin, *Canadian Economic Thought*, London, Cambridge University Press, 1961, pp. 92–97.
46 ibid., p. 408.
47 R. Warren James, op. cit.
48 ibid., p. 69.
49 'The Classical Theory of International Trade and the Underdeveloped Countries', *Economic Journal*, vol. 68, 1958, pp. 317–337.

5 THE NATIONALIST SCHOOL, 1830–90

1 S. D. Clark, *The Developing Canadian Community*, Toronto, University of Toronto Press, 1968, *passim*.
2 E. J. Chambers and G. W. Bertram, 'Urbanization and Manufacturing in Canada, 1870–1890', *Canadian Political Science Association Conference on Statistics*, Toronto, 1964, pp. 225–258.
3 C. D. W. Goodwin, op. cit., pp. 42–70.
4 R. C. Brown, *Canada's National Policy*, Princeton, 1964.
5 Canada, *Debates of the House of Commons*, March 7, 1876.
6 Adam Shortt, *Adam Shortt's History of Canadian Currency and Banking: 1600–1880*, Toronto, Canadian Bankers' Association, 1987, pp. 707–708.
7 P. J. Smith, *The Ideological Genesis of Canadian Confederation*, PhD. Dissertation, Department of Political Science, Carleton University, Ottawa, 1983. A. Chitnis, *The Scottish Enlightenment*, London, Croom Helm, 1976; *The Scottish Enlightenment and Early Victorian English Society*, London, Croom Helm, 1986. K. D. McRae, 'Le concept de la société fragmentaire de Louis Hartz et son application à l'exemple Canadien', *Canadian Journal of Political and Social Theory*, 1979, vol. 3, pp. 69–82. G. Horowitz, 'Conservatism, Liberalism and Socialism in Canada', *Canadian Journal of Economics and Political Science*, 1966, vol. 32, pp. 143–171. R. L. Meek, *Social Science and the Ignoble Savage*, Cambridge, Cambridge University Press, 1976.
8 G. J. Stigler, 'The Economics of Carl Menger', J. J. Spengler, ed. *Essays in Economic Thought: Aristotle to Marshall*, Chicago, Rand McNally, 1960, pp. 656–671. J. A. Schumpeter, *History of Economic Analysis*, New York, Oxford University Press, 1954, pp. 844–855.
9 J. P. Smith, op. cit., pp. 197–199.

236 *A history of Canadian economic thought*

10 *The Wealth of Nations*, London, J. M. Dent and Sons, 1933, vol. 1, p. 403.
11 ibid., p. 329.
12 ibid., vol. 2, p. 264.
13 ibid., vol. 2, p. 212.
14 J. B. Hurlbert, *Protection and Free Trade*, Ottawa, 1882, p. 68.
15 Carl Berger, *The Writing of Canadian History*, Toronto, Oxford University Press, 1976, p. 22.
16 op. cit., p. 42.
17 Upper Canada, House of Assembly, Select Committee appointed to inquire into the state of the trade and commerce of the Province of Canada, *Report, Journal*, Appendix no. 11, 1835.
18 op. cit., p. 45.
19 *Sketches of Celebrated Canadians*, Montreal, 1863, pp. 553–581.
20 There is no adequate intellectual biography of Buchanan. Morgan's account is brief, premature, and without analysis. Doug McCalla's *The Upper Canadian Trade; 1834–1872: a Study of the Buchanans's Business*, 1979, is just that, a study of the business.
21 *The Relations...*, pp. 1–57.
22 ibid., p. 59.
23 ibid., p. 59.
24 ibid., pp. 77–87.
25 ibid., p. 61.
26 ibid., p. 61.
27 ibid., pp. 63–65.
28 ibid., p. 70.
29 ibid., pp. 70–71.
30 ibid., pp. 70–73.
31 ibid., p. 73.
32 ibid., p. 74.
33 *Protection and Free Trade*, Montreal, 1867. *The Complete Tariff Hand Book*, Toronto, 1880. 'Provincial Toryism', *This Week*, 1884, vol. 1, pp. 407 ff. 'The True Solution of the Silver Problem', *This Week*, 1884, vol. 1, pp. 263 ff. 'Two of a Trade', *This Week*, 1884, vol. 1, pp. 135 ff. 'The Women Question in Relation to Progress', *This Week*, 1884, vol. 1, pp. 214 ff. 'This Growing Country', *This Week*, 1884, vol. 1, pp. 712 ff.
34 *Collection of the Products of the Waters and Forests of Upper Canada*, Montreal, 1862. *Britain and Her Colonies*, London, 1865. *Field and Factory Side by Side, or How to Establish and Develop Native Industries*, Montreal, 1870. *The Climates, Resources and Productions of Canada*, Montreal, 1872. *Physical Atlas of the Dominion*, Montreal, 1880. *Protection and Free Trade with Special Reference to Canada and Newly Settled Countries: History of Tariffs and What They Teach*, Ottawa, 1882.
35 Compare J. B. Hurlbert, op. cit., *Protection and Free Trade...* pp. 70–73. I. Buchanan, op. cit., *The Relations...* pp. 63–73.
36 For a more recent, but very similar critique of the methods of the classical economists see Marc Blaug, *The Methodology of Economics*, Cambridge, Cambridge University Press, 1980, pp. 58–86.
37 J. B. Hurlbert, *Protection and Free Trade* ... op. cit., pp. 65, 86, 100–101. J. Maclean, *Protection and Free Trade* ... pp. 18, 36.
38 J. Maclean, op. cit., pp. 40, 42.

39 ibid., p. 54.
40 J. B. Hurlbert, ibid., pp. 80, 85, 93–95.
41 J. B. Hurlbert, ibid., pp. 1–50, 68, 107.
42 J. Maclean, *Protection and Free Trade* ..., pp. 17–27.
43 ibid., p. 59.
44 J. B. Hurlbert, *Protection and Free Trade* ..., pp. 62–64.
45 ibid., p. 65.
46 J. Maclean, *Protection and Free Trade*..., p. 41.
47 ibid., p. 50.
48 ibid., pp. 56–57. J. B. Hurlbert, *Protection and Free Trade* ..., op. cit., pp. 53–54, 74–75.
49 ibid., pp. 11–27.
50 ibid., pp. 105–106.
51 ibid., pp. 107–108.
52 ibid., p. 27. J. Maclean, *Protection and Free Trade* ..., p. 43.
53 R. B. Brown, 'D'Arcy McGee and the Economic Aspects of the New Nationality', *Canadian Historical Association Annual Report*, 1967, pp. 95–104.
54 See O. D. Skelton, *The Railway Builders*, Toronto, 1916; *The Life and Times of Sir Alexander Tilloch Galt*, Toronto, 1920.
55 A. T. Galt, *Canada, 1849–1859*, London, 1860.
56 D. G. Creighton, *John A. Macdonald*, Toronto, 1955–56.
57 Sir John A. Macdonald, *Debates of the House of Commons*, March 7, 1876.

6 MONETARY THEORY AND POLICY, 1812–1914

1 Goodwin, op. cit., pp. 71–106, 133–135.
2 *Adam Shortt's History of Canadian Currency and Banking*, Canadian Bankers' Association, Don Mills, 1987.
3 Toronto, Macmillan, 1972.
4 Toronto, 1958.
5 R. M. Breckenridge, *The Canadian Banking System, 1777–1890*, Toronto, 1894.
6 Adam Shortt, op. cit., pp. 476–479.
7 W. T. Easterbrook and H. G. J. Aitken, *Canadian Economic History*, Toronto, Macmillan, 1958, p. 374.
8 H. C. Pentland, *Labour and the Development of Industrial Capitalism in Canada*, Toronto, University of Toronto Press, 1960. R. Pomfret, *The Economic Development of Canada*, Toronto, Methuen, 1981, pp. 122–146.
9 K. Buckley, 'The Role of Staple Industries in Canada's Economic Development', *Journal of Economic History*, 1958, vol. 18, pp. 439–452.
10 G. W. Bertram, 'Economic Growth in Canadian Industry', *Canadian Journal of Economics and Political Science*, 1963, vol. 29, 159–184.
11 R. T. Naylor, 'The Rise and Fall of the Third Commercial Empire of the St. Lawrence', G. Teeple, ed., *Capitalism and the National Question in Canada*, Toronto, University of Toronto Press, 1972, pp. 1–41. *The History of Canadian Business, 1867–1914*, Toronto, James Lorimer, 1975. K. Levitt, *Silent Surrender*, Toronto, Macmillan, 1970. M. Watkins, 'The Staple Theory Revisited', *Journal of Canadian Studies*, 1977, vol. 12, pp. 83–96.
12 R. T. Naylor, op. cit., *The History of Canadian Business*, vol. 1, pp. 74, 79, 84–85. Adam Shortt, op. cit., pp. 707–727.

238 *A history of Canadian economic thought*

13 J. H. Dales, *The Protective Tariff in Canada's Development*, Toronto, University of Toronto Press, 1966, pp. 145–147.
14 E. P. Neufeld, op. cit., *The Financial System of Canada*, pp. 60–61.
15 Charles Rist, *History of Monetary and Credit Theory*, London, George Allen and Unwin, 1940. John Jay Knox, *A History of Banking in the United States*, New York, Bradford Rhodes, 1903. Bray Hammond, *Banks and Politics in America*, Princeton, Princeton University Press, 1957. C. Goodhart, *The Evolution of Central Banks*, London, London School of Economics, 1985. Vera C. Smith, *The Rationale of Central Banking*, London, P. S. King, 1936.
16 op. cit., p. 407.
17 E. H. King, 'The Policy of the Bank', in M. Denison, *Canada's First Bank*, Toronto, 1966, vol. 2, pp. 152–155. John Rose, *Speech of the Honourable John Rose, Minister of Finance, Canada, on Introducing the Resolutions on Banking and Currency*, Ottawa, Hunter and Rose, 1869.
18 Adam Shortt, op. cit, p.608. 'Legislative Development of the Canadian Banking System', V. Ross, *A History of the Canadian Bank of Commerce*, Toronto, Oxford University Press, 1920–1934, vol. 2, pp. 389–417. See also V. Ross, op. cit., vol. 1, pp. 1–65. D. C. Masters, 'Toronto vs. Montreal', *Canadian Historical Review*, 1941, vol. 22, pp. 133–146.
19 Adam Shortt, op. cit., pp 627–660, p. 640.
20 On the advice of Schumpeter I am following Charles Gide, op. cit., *History of Monetary and Credit Theory*.
21 Vera Smith, op. cit., *The Rationale of Central Banking*.
22 C. Goodhart, op. cit., *The Evolution of Central Banks*.
23 Robert Gourlay, op. cit., pp. ccclxxv–ccclxxvi.
24 op. cit., pp. 71–77, 87–97.
25 *Reminiscences of His Public Life*, Montreal, William Drysdale, 1884.
26 op. cit., p. 70.
27 op. cit., p. 71.
28 Buchanan, op. cit., *The Relations...*, pp. 73–74, 92.
29 H. C. Carey, *Principles of Social Science*, Philadelphia, B. J. Lippincott, 1858–59, vol. 2, pp. 393–480.
30 Philadelphia, Henry Carey Baird, 1872. First published in England in 1849.
31 Oxford, 1917.
32 See C. Rist, op. cit., pp, 181–184. R. G. Hawtrey, 'Inflationism', *Trade and Credit*, London, Longmans Green, 1928, pp. 64–81.
33 Cited in Hawtrey, op. cit., p.71.
34 ibid., p. 73.
35 *Important Information on Banking*, Hamilton, 1883.
36 *Money and Banking*, Toronto, 1861.
37 *A Government Specie-Paying Bank of Issue and other Subversive Legislation Proposed by the Minister of Finance*, Hamilton, 1866.
38 ibid., p. 14.
39 ibid., pp. 7–8.
40 op. cit., p. 9.
41 ibid., p. 99.
42 ibid., p. 102.
43 'The Role of Monetary Policy', *American Economic Review*, 1968, vol. 58, pp. 1–17.
44 W. Arnold, *Money and Banking*, Toronto, 1861, p. 28–29.

45 Adam Shortt, 'Railroad Construction and National Prosperity: An Historic Parallel', *Proceedings and Transactions of the Royal Society of Canada*, ser. 3, sec II, 1914, vol. 8, pp. 295-308, p. 295.
46 op. cit., pp. 622-630.
47 R. F. Neill, 'Social Credit and National Policy', *Journal of Canadian Studies*, 1968, vol. 3, pp. 1-12.
48 op. cit., pp. 707-712.
49 *The Mail*, Toronto, January 29, 1879. *The Globe*, September 30, 1879.
50 Goodwin, op. cit., pp. 85-86.
51 Goodwin, op. cit., p. 99.
52 Thomas Galbraith, *A New Chapter Added to Political Economy Pointing Out a 100 Millions Dollar Capital*, Toronto, 1882. *New Monetary Theory*, Montreal, 1863. *Bensalem or the New Economy*, New York, 1874.
53 R. W. James, op. cit., vol. 1, pp. 129-30.
54 T. Galbraith, *A Plea for Uncle Sam's Money*, New York, 1870. p. 18.
55 ibid., p. 14.
56 C. D. W. Goodwin, 'A Forgotten Forerunner of Social Credit, William Alexander Thompson', *Journal of Canadian Studies*, 1969, vol. 4, pp. 41-45.
57 Robert Davis, *The Currency, What It Is and What It Should Be*, Ottawa, 1867. John McCormick, *The Conditions of Modern Labour and Modern Civilization*, Toronto, 1880. G. D. Griffin, *Important Information on Banking*, Hamilton, 1883. A. Husbandman, *Money and the Money Question*, Toronto, 1897.
58 Goodwin, op. cit., p. 43.
59 Canada, House of Commons, *Debates*, 1880, pp. 1729-1734.

7 SOME INTRUSIONS OF HISTORY, 1890-1930

1 J. J. Spengler, 'Marginalism and Neoclassicism', J. J. Spengler and R. D. Allen, eds, *Essays in Economic Thought*, Chicago, Rand McNally, 1960, pp. 534-552. G. J. Stigler, 'The Development of Utility Theory', G. J. Stigler, *Essays in the History of Economics*, Chicago, University of Chicago Press, pp. 66-165. T. W. Hutchison, *On Revolutions and Progress in Economic Thought*, Cambridge, Cambridge University Press, 1978, pp. 58-120. Lionel Robbins, *An Essay on the Nature and Significance of Economic Science*, London, Macmillan, 1952.
2 T. W. Hutchison, op. cit., pp. 77-79, 86-89. J. A. Schumpeter, *Economic Doctrine and Method*, R. Aris trans., New York, 1954, chapter IV.
3 op. cit., *An Essay on the Nature and Significance of Economic Science*.
4 *Economica*, 1937, vol. 14, pp. 386-405.
5 Arthur Spietoff, 'The Historical Character of Economic Theories', *Journal of Economic History*, 1952, vol. 12, pp. 131-139. 'Pure Theory and Economic Gestalt Theory: Ideal Types and Real Types', F. C. Lane and J. C. Riemersma, eds, *Enterprise and Secular Change*, Homewood, Richard D. Irwin, 1953, pp. 431-463. Fritz Reidlich, 'Arthur Spietoff on Economic Styles', *Journal of Economic History*, 1970, vol. 30, pp. 644-652.
6 *Socialism and Social Reform*, New York, Thomas Y. Crowell, 1894.
7 O. D. Skelton, *Socialism: a Critical Analysis*, New York, 1911, pp. 1-40.
8 R. Carmichael-Smythe, *The Employment of the People and the Capital of Great Britain in Her Own Colonies*, London, 1849. F. A. Wilson and B. A. Richards, *Britain Redeemed and Canada Preserved*, London, 1850.

240 *A history of Canadian economic thought*

9. T. C. Keefer, *The Philosophy of Railroads and Other Essays*, H. V. Nelles, ed., Toronto, 1972. *Free Trade, Protection and Reciprocity*, Ottawa, 1876.
10. L. J. Burpee, *Sanford Fleming: Empire Builder*, London, Oxford University Press, 1915. Carl Berger, *Imperialism and Nationalism, 1884-1914: a Conflict in Canadian Thought*, Toronto, 1969. *The Sense of Power: Studies in Canadian Imperialism, 1867-1914*, Toronto, University of Toronto Press, 1970.
11. Kenneth Buckley, *Capital Formation in Canada, 1896-1930*, Toronto, McClelland and Stewart, 1974, p. 3. W. A. Mackintosh, *The Economic Background of Dominion-Provincial Relations*, Toronto, McClelland and Stewart, 1964, p. 25.
12. op. cit., p. 40.
13. P. Hartland, 'Factors in Economic Growth in Canada', *Journal of Economic History*, 1955, vol. 15, pp. 11-22, p. 18.
14. J. McGibbon, *Steel of Empire*, Toronto, 1935. N. Penlington, *Canada and Imperialism*, Toronto, 1965. R. C. Brown, *Canada's National Policy*, Princeton, 1964.
15. T. Naylor, *The History of Canadian Business*, Toronto, 1975. G. Williams, *Not for Export*, Toronto, McClelland and Stewart, 1983. E. P. Neufeld, *The Financial System of Canada*, Toronto, Macmillan, 1972. J. H. Dales, *The Protective Tariff in Canada's National Development*, Toronto, University of Toronto Press, 1966.
16. D. C. Creighton, *The Commercial Empire of the St. Lawrence*, Toronto, 1937.
17. Goodwin, op. cit., p. 110.
18. W. Hincks, 'On the True Aims, Foundations and Claims to Attention of the Science of Political Economy', *The Canadian Journal*, 1861, vol. 6, pp. 20-28. 'An Enquiry into the Natural Laws which Regulate the Interchange of Commodities between Individuals and Nations and the Effects of Interference with Them', *The Canadian Journal*, 1862, vol. 7, pp. 180-190. 'Notes on Some Practically Interesting Questions in Economical Science Bearing on the Prosperity of Countries Situated Such as Ours', *The Canadian Journal*, 1866-67, vol. 11, pp.96-113.
19. *Canada and the Canadian Question*, (reprint) Toronto, 1971.
20. 'Wages', *Proceedings of the Canadian Institute*, November 27, 1884. 'Canadian Problems and Politics', *Westminster Review*, 1912, vol. 177, pp. 39-404. 'Rent, a Criticism of Professor Walker's Work on that Subject', *Proceedings of the Canadian Institute*, December 12, 1885. 'The Antagonism of Social Forces', *Proceedings of the Canadian Institute*, February, 19, 1887. Goodwin, op. cit., p. 34.
21. *The Revolt in Canada Against the New Feudalism*, London, 1911. *Sixty Years of Protection in Canada, 1846-1912*, Winnipeg, 1912. *The Evolution of the Dominion of Canada*, New York, 1920.
22. E. Porritt, *Sixty Years of Protection in Canada: 1846-1907*, London, 1907, p. 376.
23. Chicago, Kerr, 1914.
24. *The Canadian National Economy*, Toronto, 1911.
25. *A War on Poverty*, Winnipeg, 1925.
26. J. J. Spengler, *Essays in Economic Thought*, Chicago, Rand McNally, 1960.
27. T. W. Hutchison, op. cit., p. 165.
28. Goodwin, op. cit., pp. 152-196.
29. ibid., pp. 184, 186, 191.
30. Mark Blaug, *The Methodology of Economics*, Cambridge, Cambridge University Press, 1980.

31 W. C. Clark, 'Shall Maximum Prices Be Fixed', *Bulletin of the Departments of History and Political and Economic Science at Queen's University*, no. 27, 1917. A. F. McGoun, 'The Nature of Interest and the Causes of its Fluctuation', *Quarterly Journal of Economics*, 1916–17, vol. 31, pp. 547–570. 'Higher and Lower Desires', *Quarterly Journal of Economics*, 1923, vol. 37, pp. 291–301.
32 H. A. Innis, 'The Teaching of Economic History in Canada', M. Q. Innis, ed. *Essays in Canadian Economic History*, Toronto, University of Toronto Press, 1956, pp. 34–46. 'The State of Economic Science in Canada', *Commerce Journal*, February, 1936, pp. 24–30. 'Notes and Comments', *Contributions to Canadian Economics*, 1929, vol. 2, pp. 5–7. O. D. Skelton, 'Fifty Years of Political and Economic Science in Canada', Canadian Political Science Association, *Fifty Years in Retrospect: Canada, 1882–1932*, Toronto, 1932, pp. 85–90. K. W. Taylor, 'Economic Scholarship in Canada', *Canadian Journal of Economics and Political Science*, 1960, vol. 26, pp. 6–18. C. R. Fay, 'The Toronto School of Economics', *Economic History*, 1934–37, vol. 3, pp. 168–171. W. T. Easterbrook, 'Trends in Canadian Economic Thought', *South Atlantic Quarterly*, 1959, pp. 91–107. V. W. Bladen, 'A Journal is Born', *Canadian Journal of Economics and Political Science*, 1960, pp. 1–6. A. R. M. Lower, 'The Development of Canadian Economic Ideas', J. F. Normano, *The Spirit of American Economics*, New York, Day, 1943, vol. 1, pp. 211–241. C. B. Macpherson, 'The Social Sciences in Contemporary Canada', Julian Park, ed. *The Culture of Contemporary Canada*, Ithaca, 1967. C. D. W. Goodwin, op. cit. S. M. Wickett, 'The Study of Political Economy at Canadian Universities', *Appendix to the Report of the Ontario Bureau of Industries, 1897*.
33 R. G. Trotter, 'Canadian History in the Universities of the United States', *Canadian Historical Review*, 1927, vol. 8, pp. 190–207.
34 *The Canadian Iron and Steel Industry*, Boston, 1915.
35 London, 1923.
36 New York, 1914.
37 Toronto, 1912.
38 Toronto, 1928.
39 W. A. Mackintosh to R. F. Neill, December 8, 1965.
40 W. A. Mackintosh to R. F. Neill, December 8, 1965.
41 O. D. Skelton, Review, D. A. McGibbon, *An Introduction to Economics for Canadians*, *Canadian Historical Review*, 1925, vol. 6, p. 87.
42 H. A. Innis, 'Teaching of Economic History in Canada', *Contributions to Canadian Economics*, 1929, vol. 2, p. 54.
43 S. B. Leacock, *The Unsolved Riddle of Social Justice*, Toronto, 1920.
44 R. F. Neill, 'Adam Shortt: a Bibliographical Comment', *Journal of Canadian Studies*, 1967, vol. 2, p. 53. Nancy J. Leman, 'Introduction', *Adam Shortt's History of Canadian Currency and Banking*, Toronto, Canadian Bankers' Association, 1987.
45 H. A. Innis, 'A Bibliography of Thorstein Veblen', *South Western Political and Social Science Quarterly*, 1929, vol. 10, pp. 56–68.
46 W. A. Mackintosh, 'Innis on Canadian Economic Development', *Journal of Political Economy*, 1953, vol. 61, pp. 185–195. 'Adam Shortt', *Canadian Journal of Economics and Political Science*, 1938, vol. 4, pp. 164–176.
47 H. A. Innis, 'The Teaching of Economic History in Canada', op. cit., p. 10, n. 4.
48 O. D. Skelton, *Socialism: a Critical Analysis*, New York, Houghton Mifflin, 1911; *The Life and Times of Sir A. T. Galt*, Toronto, 1920. *The Railway Builders*,

Toronto, 1916. *General Economic History of Canada*, Toronto, 1913. *The Life and Letters of Sir Wilfrid Laurier*, Toronto, 1913. *The Canadian Dominion*, Toronto, 1919. *The Dominion Bank: Fifty Years of Banking Service, 1871–1921*, Toronto, 1922. 'Galt and the Draft of the Canadian Constitution', *Proceedings and Transactions of the Royal Society of Canada*, 1917, vol. 11, sec. II, pp. 99–108. *Our Generation: Its Gains and Its Losses*, Chicago, 1938. 'Canada's Rejection of Reciprocity', ' Reciprocity: the Canadian Attitude', *Journal of Political Economy*, 1911, vol. 19, pp. 77–97, 726–801. 'Canada and the Most Favoured Nation Treaties', *Bulletin of the Departments of History and Political and Economic Science of Queen's University*, no. 2, January, 1912. 'Federal Finance', *Bulletin of the Departments of History and Political and Economic Science of Queen's University*, no. 16, 1914–1915, no. 29, 1917. 'Presidential Address', Canadian Political Science Association, *Proceedings of the Canadian Political Science Association*, 1931, vol. 3, pp. 67ff.

49 V. W. Bladen and A. F. W. Plumptre, 'Analysis of Price Indexes in Canada', *Canadian Historical Review*, 1927, vol. 8, p. 246. G. E. Jackson, 'Cycles of Employment in Canada, *Contributions to Canadian Economics*, 1928, vol. 1, pp. 40–55.

50 'Railroad construction and National Prosperity: an Historic Parallel', *Proceedings and Transactions of the Royal Society of Canada*, 1914, vol. 8, pp. 295–308.

51 'Federal Finance', *Bulletin of the Departments of History and Political and Economic Science of Queen's University* no. 16, 1914–1915.

52 A. B. Balcom, 'The Rise in Prices', *University Magazine*, 1920, vol. 19, pp. 16–23.

53 V. W. Bladen, 'Operating Combinations in Canadian Industry as Revealed by the Census of Manufacturing', *American Economic Review* 1927, vol. 17, pp. 601–604. 'The Size of Establishments in Canadian and American Industry', *Contributions to Canadian Economics*, 1928, vol. 1, pp. 56–61.

54 B. M. Stewart, *Canadian Labour Laws and the Treaty*, New York, 1926. H. A. Logan, *The History of Trade Union Organization in Canada*, Chicago, 1928.

55 Boston, 1918.

56 *Government Telephones; The Experience of Manitoba, Canada*, New York, 1916. *Niagara in Politics: A Critical Account of the Ontario Hydro Electric Power Commission*, New York, 1925.

57 Cambridge, Mass. 1924.

58 'Capital Investments and Trade Balances within the British Empire', *Quarterly Journal of Economics*, 1915, vol. 768–993.

59 *International Trade Balance in Theory and Practice*, New York, 1922.

60 'An Early Canadian Contribution to Mathematical Economics: J. B. Cherryman's Review of Cournot', *Canadian Journal of Economics*, 1988, vol. 21, pp. 610–616.

61 op. cit., pp. 140–141.

8 THE STAPLE THESIS, 1920–40

1 M. Watkins, 'The Political Economy of Growth', W. Clement and G. Williams, eds, *The New Canadian Political Economy*, Kingston, McGill-Queen's, 1989, p. 19.

2 *Rethinking Canadian Political Economy, Studies in Political Economy*, 1981, vol. 6.
3 'Fifty Years of Political and Economic Science in Canada', *Fifty Years Retrospect, an Anniversary Volume*, The Royal Society of Canada, 1932, pp. 85–90, p. 88.
4 'The Development of Canadian Economic Ideas', J. F. Normano, *The Spirit of American Economics*, New York, John Day, 1943, pp. 213–241, p. 240. B. S. Keirstead, *Essentials of Price Theory*, Toronto, 1942.
5 A. F. W. Plumptre and A. E. Gilroy, 'Review of Economic Textbooks for Use in Canadian High Schools', *Contributions to Canadian Economics*, 1934, vol. 7, pp. 123–124.
6 C. R. Fay, 'The Toronto School of Economic History', *Economic History*, 1934–37, vol. 3, pp. 168–171.
7 R. F. Neill, *A New Theory of Value, the Canadian Economics of H. A. Innis*, Toronto, University of Toronto Press, 1972, chapter 4.
8 H. A. Innis, 'Two Unpublished Papers', R. F. Neill, *A New Theory of Value: the Canadian Economics of H. A. Innis*, Toronto, University of Toronto Press, 1972, pp. 146–148, 150.
9 'An Economic Analysis of Indian Behavior in the North American Fur Trade', *Journal of Economic History*, 1972, vol. 32, pp. 36–53.
10 R. F. Neill, 'Rationality and the Informational Environment: a Reassessment of the Work of Harold Adams Innis', *Journal of Canadian Studies*, 1987–88, vol. 22, pp. 78–91.
11 Toronto, 1940.
12 Toronto, Publications of the Champlain Society, 1941, pp. xi–lxxvii.
13 'Government Ownership in Canada', *Schriften des Vereins für Sozial-politik*, 1931, vol. 176, pp. 241–279.
14 E. W. Kitch, 'The Fire of Truth', *Journal of Law and Economics*, 1983, vol. 26, p. 173.
15 London, Macmillan, 1932.
16 ibid., p. 148.
17 F. H. Knight, 'Social Science and the Political Trend', *University of Toronto Quarterly*, 1934, vol. 3 pp. 280–287. S. Leacock, 'What is Left of Adam Smith', *Canadian Journal of Economics and Political Science*, 1935, vol. 1, pp. 41–51. E. J. Urwick, 'The Role of Intelligence in the Social Process', *Canadian Journal of Economics and Political Science*, 1935, vol. 1, pp. 64–76. H. A. Innis, 'The Role of Intelligence; Some Further Notes', *Canadian Journal of Economics and Political Science*, 1935, vol. 1, pp. 280–287. F. H. Underhill, 'The Conception of a National Interest', *Canadian Journal of Economics and Political Science*, 1935, vol. 1, pp. 396–408. D. A. McGibbon, 'Economics and the Social Order', *Canadian Journal of Economics and Political Science*, 1936, vol. 2, pp. 68–73. W. R. Maxwell, 'Economic Theory and National Purpose', *Canadian Journal of Economics and Political Science*, 1936, vol. 2, pp. 119–127. E. J. Urwick, 'The Ethics of Competition', *Canadian Journal of Economics and Political Science*, 1937, vol. 3, pp. 250–263. W. A. Mackintosh, 'An Economist Looks at Economics', *Canadian Journal of Economics and Political Science*, 1937, vol. 3, pp. 311–321.
18 Carl Berger, *The Writing of Canadian History*, Toronto, Oxford University Press, 1976.
19 *Canada, The Great River, the Lands and the Men*, London, 1926.

20 R. H. Coase, 'R. H. Coase Lectures', *Journal of Law, Economics and Organization*, 1988, vol. 4, p. 33.
21 Toronto, 1923.
22 New Haven, 1930 *Settlement and the Mining Frontier*.
23 Toronto, 1936.
24 Toronto, 1940.
25 Toronto, 1937.
26 Toronto, 1938.
27 Toronto, 1939.
28 Ottawa, 1939.
29 Toronto, 1939.
30 Toronto, 1940.
31 Toronto, 1941.
32 Toronto, 1937.
33 New Haven, 1936.
34 *The Rise of Toronto*, Toronto, 1938.
35 I. M. Biss, 'Overhead Costs, Time Problems, and Prices', H. A. Innis, ed. *Essays in Political Economy*, Toronto, University of Toronto Press, 1938, pp. 11–26.
36 Phillip Thompson, *The Politics of Labour*, New York, Belford Clark, 1887.
37 N. Penner, *The Canadian Left, a Critical Analysis*, Scarborough, Prentice Hall, 1977.
38 *Niagara in Politics*, New York, Dutton, 1925.
39 *Labour in A Changing World*, Toronto, 1919.
40 'Are We Drifting into Socialism?', *Monetary Times*, January, 1913.
41 F. Hankin and T. W. A. MacDermot, *Recovery by Control*, Toronto, J. M. Dent, 1933.
42 F. Hankin and T. W. L. MacDermot, *Recovery by Control*, Toronto, J. M. Dent and Sons, 1933, p. 190.
43 Toronto, Thomas Nelson & Sons, 1935.
44 L. B. Pearson, *Mike*, Toronto, University of Toronto Press, 1972, p. 72.
45 Canada, Royal Commission on Price Spreads, *Report*, Ottawa, 1937, p. 275.
46 V. W. Bladen, 'Combines and Public Policy', *Proceedings of the Canadian Political Science Association*, 1932, vol. 4, pp. 168–70. J. A. Ball Jr., *Canadian Anti Trust Legislation*, Baltimore, 1934.
47 Cambridge, Harvard University Press, 1940.
48 *The General Theory of Employment Interest and Money*, London, Macmillan, 1936.
49 Toronto, University of Toronto Press, 1957.
50 Toronto, Oxford University Press, 1982.
51 op. cit., pp. 20–21.
52 op. cit., p. 33.
53 op. cit., p. 35.
54 op. cit., p. 99.
55 op. cit., p. 98.
56 op. cit., pp. 207–216.
57 op. cit., p. 142.
58 op. cit., pp. 144–154.
59 Granatstein, op. cit., pp. 49, 256.
60 Brecher, op. cit., pp. 119–121, 148–150.
61 ibid., p. 146.

62 op. cit., p. 108.
63 op. cit., p. 45.
64 pp. 424–440.
65 1933, vol. 40, pp. 264–283.
66 1933, vol. 40, pp. 580–598.
67 1934, vol. 41, pp. 81–98.
68 F. A. Knox, 'Leviathan or Octopus', 1934, vol. 41, pp. 493–498.
69 H. M. Thomas, 'The Corporate State', 1935, vol. 42, pp. 242–252.
70 F. R. Scott, 'The Efficiency of Socialism', 1935, vol. 42, pp. 215–225.
71 H. R. Kemp, 'Is A Revision of Taxing Powers Necessary', *Proceedings of the Canadian Political Science Association*, 1931, vol. 3, pp. 185–201.
72 J. A. Maxwell, 'Expenditures of Canadian Provincial Governments', *Contributions to Canadian Economics*, 1931, vol. 4, pp. 41–52.
73 R. B. Bryce, *Maturing in Hard Times: Canada's Department of Finance through the Great Depression*, Kingston and Montreal, McGill-Queen's, 1986, pp. 200–201.
74 Nova Scotia, Royal Commission of Provincial Enquiry, *Report*, Halifax, 1934.
75 op. cit., 'Memorandum on Financial Relations between the Provinces and the Dominion with particular reference to Nova Scotia', 'Appendicies', pp. 18–40.
76 N. McL. Rogers, 'The Compact Theory of Confederation', *Proceedings of the Canadian Political Science Association*, 1931, vol. 3, pp. 205–230.
77 V. W. Bladen, 'The Economics of Federation', *Canadian Journal of Economics and Political Science*, 1935, vol. 1, p. 350.
78 R. McQueen, 'The Economics of Federalism', *Canadian Journal of Economics and Political Science*, 1935, vol. 1, pp. 351–367. W. A. Carrothers, 'Problems of the Canadian Confederation', *Canadian Journal of Economics and Political Science*, 1935, vol. 1, pp. 26–40. W. J. Wains, J. A. Maxwell, J. S. M. Allely, 'Federal Public Finance: Canada, Australia, South Africa', *Canadian Journal of Economics and Political Science*, 1937, vol. 3, pp. 181–209.
79 S. Bates, 'Classificatory Note on the Theory of Public Finance', *Canadian Journal of Economics and Political Science*, 1937, vol. 3, pp. 163–180.
80 ibid., *passim*.
81 R. B. Bryce, op. cit., p. 191.
82 ibid., p. 215–216. Canada, Royal Commission on Dominion-Provincial Relations, *Report*, Ottawa, 1940.
83 V. F. Coe, 'The Gains of Trade', *Canadian Journal of Economics and Political Science*, 1935, vol. 1, pp. 588–598. G. A. Elliot, 'Transfer of Means of Payment and the Terms of Trade', *Canadian Journal of Economics and Political Science*, 1936, vol. 2, pp. 481–492. O. J. McDiarmid, 'Imperfect Competition and International Trade', H. A. Innis, ed. *Essays in Political Economy*, Toronto, University of Toronto Press, 1938, pp. 117–146.
84 W. T. Easterbrook, 'Recent Contributions to Canadian Economic History', W. T. Easterbrook and M. H. Watkins, *Approaches to Canadian Economic History*, Toronto, McClelland and Stewart, 1967, p. 261.
85 A. Shortt and A. B. Doughty, eds, *Canada and its Provinces*, Toronto, 1914, vol. 9, pp. 25–247.
86 James Mavor, 'An Introduction to Canadian Economic History', *Contributions to Canadian Economics*, 1928, vol. 1, pp. 7–16.
87 'Mearns and the Miramichi: An Episode in Canadian Economic History', *Canadian Historical Review*, 1923, vol. 4, pp. 316–320.

88 'Wheat and the Trade Cycle', *Canadian Historical Review*, 1922, vol. 3, pp. 256–274.
89 *Canadian Historical Review*, 1923, vol. 4, pp. 12–25.
90 Toronto, Ryerson Press, 1933.
91 Canadian Institute of International Affairs, Toronto, 1934.
92 'Some Aspects of a Pioneer Economy', *Canadian Journal of Economics and Political Science*, 1936, vol. 2, pp. 457–463.
93 *Canadian Journal of Economics and Political Science*, 1937, vol. 3, pp. 488–507.
94 *Canadian Economic Development*, Toronto, Nelson, 1942.

9 PENSEE ECONOMIQUE, VINGTIEME SIECLE

1 Québec, *Bâtir le Québec: énonce de politique économique*, Editeur officiel du Québec, Québec, 1979, p. 36.
2 ibid., p. 8.
3 J.-C. Falardeau, 'Problems and First Experiments of Social Research in Quebec', *Canadian Journal of Economics and Political Science*, 1944, vol. 10, pp. 365–371.
4 L'abbé Bédard, 'Le Play et la réforme sociale', *La Revue Canadienne*, 1984, vol. 30, pp. 664–694. A. Saint-Pierre, 'Léon Gérin, un disciple Canadien de Frédéric Le Play', *Proceedings and Transactions of the Royal Society of Canada*, ser. 1, sec. 1, 1954, vol. 48, pp. 91–103. H. Carrier, *Le sociologue Canadien, Léon Gérin: 1863–1951*, Montréal, 1960.
5 Ottawa, 1901.
6 Montréal, 1905.
7 Montréal, 1913.
8 A. Faucher, 'L'enseignement des sciences sociales au Canada de langue française', *Royal Commission Studies*, a selection of essays prepared for the Royal Commission on National Development in the Arts, Letters and Sciences, Ottawa, 1941, pp. 191–203.
9 *L'avenir du Canada français*, Montréal, 1909.
10 A. Saint-Pierre, *Questions et ouvres sociales de chez nous*, Montréal, 1914.
11 M-. A. Gagnon, *La vie orageuse d'Olivar Asselin*, Montréal, 1962.
12 ibid.
13 O. Asselin, 'L'industrie dans l'économie de Canada français', appendix to *L'achat chez nous*, Montréal, 1938.
14 Brussels, 1914.
15 Montréal, 1935.
16 Montréal, 1927.
17 Montréal, 1947.
18 Montréal, 1942–45.
19 Montréal, 1933.
20 *La bourgeoisie et l'économique*, Montréal, 1939.
21 Montréal, 1948.
22 *Invitation à l'étude*, op. cit., p. 157.
23 Paul-Emile Renaud, *Du travail en Nouvelle France*, Montréal, 1923. *Les origines économique du Canada*, Mamers, 1928.
24 Québec, 1927.

25 W. T. Easterbrook, 'Recent Contributions to Economic History in Canada', *Journal of Economic History*, 1959, vol. 19, pp. 76–102.
26 Montréal, 1939–1942.
27 E. Montpetit, 'Pour une économie canadienne-française', *Proceedings and Transactions of the Royal Society of Canada*, ser. 3, sec. 1, 1939, vol. 33, pp. 193–217.
28 E. Montpetit, 'Errol Bouchette et l'indépendance économique du Canada français', op. cit., *La conquêt économique*, vol. 1, pp. 193–215.
29 'L'indépendance économique du Canada français', op. cit., pp. 193–295.
30 V. Barbeau, *Pour Nous Grandir*, Montréal, 1937, p. 191.
31 V. Barbeau, *L'avenir de notre bourgeoisie*, Montréal, 1939. L. Robitaille, *Présence de Victor Barbeau*, Montréal, 1962.
32 R. Arès, *Catechisme de l'organization corporative*, Montréal, 1938.
33 R. Arès, *La confédération, pacte ou loi?*, Montréal, 1949.
34 Montréal, 1962.
35 B. Leman, *Les institutions de crédit*, Montréal, 1920.
36 B. Leman, *Hier et demain*, Montréal, 1952.
37 R. Tanghe, *Le crédit au Canada*, Montréal,1935.
38 R. Vezina, *La monnaie et le crédit*, Montréal, 1941.
39 P. Harvey, ' Preface', Albert Faucher, *Histoire économique et unité canadienne*, Montréal, Fides, 1970, pp. ix–xv.
40 *Précis d'économie international*, Paris, Dunode, 1982, pp. 227–229. *Précis d'histoire de la théorie économique*, Québec, Les Presses de l' Université Laval, 1978, pp. 230–235.
41 *Le Fédéralisme Canadien*, Québec, Les Presses Universitaires Laval, 1954, pp. 105–234.
42 op. cit., 1970.
43 *An Introduction to Political Economy*, Toronto, University of Toronto Press, 1941 and 1956.
44 *Economics in a Canadian Setting*, Toronto, Copp Clark, 1959.
45 'The National Policy – Old and New', *Canadian Journal of Economics and Political Science*, vol. 18, pp. 271–286.
46 P. A. Samuelson and A. D. Scott, *Economics: an Introductory analysis*, Toronto, McGraw-Hill, 1966, pp. 771–805, 827–853.
47 R. Dehem, *Planification économique et fédéralisme*, Genève, Librarie Droz, 1968, pp. 159–185.
48 More, but not all of the story can be found in Gilles Paquet's *La pensée économique au Québec français*, Association canadienne-française pour l'avancement des sciences, 1989.
49 M. Lamontagne, *The Double Deal*, Montreal, Optimum Publishing Co., 1980. R. Dehem, *On the Meaning of 'Economic Association'*, Montreal, Howe Research Institute, 1978.
50 F.- A. Angers, 'Naissance de la pensée économique au Canada français', *Revue d'histoire de l'Amérique français*, 1961, vol. 15, pp. 204–229. 'L'économie de Québec et la science économique', Esdras Minville, *Vie économique*, Montréal, Fides, 1979, vol. 1. 'La pensée économique d'Esdras Minville', *L'action national*, 1976, vol. 65, pp. 727–761. 'Le sens d'une vie', *L'action national*, 1976, vol. 65, pp. 800–803. G. Garon, *La pensée socio-économique de Mgr. Jean Langevin*, Thèse de M. A. (Histoire) Université de Sherbrooke, 1977. J. Grube, 'La libération économique du Québec', *L'action national*, 1980, vol. 70, pp.

293-317. P. Perrault, *Errol Bouchette: sa pensée – son oeuvre*, Thèse de M. A. (Lettres) Université du Québec à Trois Rivières, 1976. J. Belec, *La pensée socio-économique de l'association de la Jeunesse Canadienne-française, 1904-1935*, Thèse de M. A. (Histoire) Université de Montréal, 1972. R. Blais, *L'idéologie économique de la Confédération des Syndicats*, Thèse de M. A. Sciences Sociales (Relations Industrielles) Université de Montréal, 1971. G. Durand, 'Lá pensée socio-économique d'André Laurendeau', R. Comeau, ed. *Economie québecoise*, Montréal, Presses de l'Université du Québec, 1969, pp. 485-495. P. Southam, 'La pensée économique d'Olivar Asselin', R. Comeau, ed., *Economie Québecoise*, Montréal, Presses de l'Université du Québec, 1969, pp. 394-404.

51 J.- C. Falardeau, ed. *Essais sur le Québec contemporain*, Québec, Les Presses Universitaires Laval, 1953, pp. 239-257.

52 Dumont et Martin, eds, *Situation de la recherche sur le Canada français*, Québec, Presses Universitaires Laval, 1962, pp. 55-64.

53 *Recherches sociographiques*, 1985, vol. 26, pp. 356-398.

54 Falardeau, op. cit., pp. 23-37.

55 Esdras Minville, 'L'économique, facteur de déviation de la politique provincial' F. A. Angers, ed. *L'économie du Québec et la science économique*, Montréal, Fides, 1979, pp. 239-261.

56 ibid., pp. 255.

57 Esdras Minville, 'Conditions de Notre Avenir', J.- C. Falardeau, op. cit., pp. 231-238, p. 237,

58 Charles Lemelin, 'Commentaire', Dumont et Martin, op. cit., pp. 65-74, p. 67.

59 Ministère de l'Industrie et du Commerce, Province de Québec, Québec, 1961.

60 H. G. Johnson, 'Equilibrium Growth in an International Economy', *Canadian Journal of Economics and Political Science*, 1953, vol. 19, pp. 478-500.

61 *Output, Labour and Capital in the Canadian Economy*, Ottawa, 1955.

62 'A Comparison of Manufacturing Industry in Quebec and Ontario, 1952', Mason Wade, ed. *La dualité Canadienne*, Québec, Presses Universitaires Laval, 1960.

63 W. A. Lewis, 'Economic Development with Unlimited Supplies of Labour', *The Economics of Underdevelopment*, New York, Oxford University Press, 1963, pp. 400-499.

64 A. Faucher, *Histoire économique et unité Canadienne*, Montréal, Fides, 1970. Gilles Paquet, 'Albert Faucher, économiste-historien'; 'Bio-bibliographie d'Albert Faucher', *Actualité économique*, 1983, vol. 59, pp. 395-400.

65 A. Faucher, 'L'histoire économique de la Province de Québec jusqu'à la fin du XIXe siècle', F. Dumont et Y. Martin, op. cit., pp. 45-53.

66 Canada, Department of Reconstruction, *Employment and Income*, Ottawa, 1945.

67 Quebec, Royal Commission of Inquiry on Constitutional Problems, *Report*, Quebec, 1956, pp. 174-281.

68 London, George, Allen and Unwin, 1940.

69 Angers, op. cit., p. 297.

70 op. cit., Appendix 11, pp. 131-141.

71 R. Lipsey, *Economics*, 5th Canadian edition, New York, Harper, 1985.

72 ibid., p. 202.

73 ibid.

74 ibid., p. 299.

75 Angers, op. cit., Appendix 5.

76 G. Paquet, *La pensée économique au Québec français*, Montréal, 1989, p. 38.

77 P. Fortin, 'La recherche économique dans les universités du Québec français: les sources de rupture avec le passée et les défis de l'avenir', G-. H. Lévesque, *Continuité et rupture, les science sociales au Québec*, Montréal, PUM, 1984, vol. 1, pp 161–171.
78 J. Parizeau, 'La recherche en sciences économiques', L. Beaudoin, ed. *La recherche au Canada français*, Montréal, PUM, 1968.
79 André Sales, 'La construction sociale de l'économie québécoise', *Recherches sociographiques*, 1985, vol. 26, pp. 319–360. Gilles Paquet, 'Le fruit dont l'ombre est la saveur: réflections aventureuses sur la pensée économique au Québec', *Recherches sociographiques*, 1985, vol. 26, pp. 365–389.
80 'La lecture des économists, est-elle si pauvre?', *Recherches sociographiques*, 1985, vol. 26, pp. 361–364.
81 B. Higgins, F. Martin, A. Raynauld, *Les orientations de développement économique regional dans la province du Québec*, Ottawa, Ministère de l'expansion économique régional, 1970.
82 André Raynauld, 'La propriété et la performance des entreprises établies au Québec', *Etudes internationales*, 1971, vol. 2, pp. 81–109. Le Gouvernement de Québec, *Le cadre et les moyens d'une politique québécois concernant les investissements étrangers*, Quebec, 1973. Maurice Saint-Germain, *Une économie à libérer*, Montréal, PUM, 1973.
83 Gouvernement de Québec, Développement économique, *Bâtir le Québec: énonce de politiques économiques*, Editeur officiel de Québec, 1979.
84 ibid., p. 79.
85 Sales, op. cit., p. 332.
86 Paquet, op. cit., 1985, p. 392.
87 Jean-Luc Migué et Gérard Bélanger, *Le prix de la santé*, Montréal, Hurtubise, 1972. Jean-Luc Migué, *L'économiste et la chose publique*, Québec, Les Presses de l'Université de Québec, 1979. *Nationalistic Policies in Canada: an Economic Approach*, Montréal, C. D. Howe Research Institute, 1979.
88 'Nationalisme et langues au Canada', *L'économiste et la chose publique*, op. cit., pp. 91–125.
89 *Le control financier du capitalisme canadien*, Montréal, PUQ, 1978. *La bourgeoisie canadienne*, Montréal, Boreal Express, 1980. *The Decline of the American Economy*, Montreal, Black Rose Books, 1988.
90 Sales, op. cit., p. 359.
91 Pierre Fournier, 'Les nouveaux paramètres de la bourgeoisie québécoise', *Le capitalisme au Québec*, Montréal, Albert Saint-Martin, 1978.

10 KEYNES IN A SMALL OPEN ECONOMY

1 H. G. Johnson, Review of M. C. Kemp, *The Pure Theory of International Trade*, Englewood Cliffs, Prentice-Hall, 1964, *Canadian Journal of Economics and Political Science*, 1965, vol. 31, pp. 139–144. 'Canadian Contributions to the Discipline of Economics since 1945', *Canadian Journal of Economics*, 1968, vol. 1, p. 143.
2 K. W. Taylor, 'Economic Scholarship in Canada', *Canadian Journal of Economics and Political Science*, 1960, vol. 26, p. 16. W. T. Easterbrook, 'Trends in Canadian Economic Thought', *South Atlantic Quarterly*, 1959, vol. 26, pp. 102–104.

250 *A history of Canadian economic thought*

3 W. T. Easterbrook and H. G. J. Aitken, *Canadian Economic History*, Toronto, Macmillan, 1956.
4 H. G. J. Aitken, 'The Present State of Economic History', *Canadian Journal of Economics and Political Science*, 1960, vol. 26, pp. 87–95.
5 R. F. Neill, *A New Theory of Value, The Canadian Economics of H. A. Innis*, Toronto, University of Toronto Press, 1972, chapter 8. 'Rationality and the Informational Environment: a Reassessment of the Work of H. A. Innis', *Journal of Canadian Studies*, 1988, vol. 22, pp. 78–92.
6 Easterbrook, op. cit., 'The Trend ...', failed to give H. G. Johnson more that a footnote reference, and simply missed Anthony Scott's *Natural Resources, The Economics of Conservation*, Toronto, University of Toronto Press, 1955.
7 Canada, *Employment and Income*, Department of Reconstruction, 1945. I. Brecher, *Monetary and Fiscal Thought and Policy in Canada, 1919–1930*, Toronto, 1953. R. C. McIvor, *Canadian Monetary, Banking and Fiscal Development*, Toronto, Macmillan, 1958. E. P. Neufeld, *Bank of Canada Operations, 1935–54*, Toronto, University of Toronto Press, 1955.
8 The Governor of the Bank expressed himself on the point several times in the late 1950s and early 1960s. I cite only J. E. Coyne, 'Money and Growth', Remarks prepared for delivery at a meeting of the Canadian Club of Montreal, Nov. 16, 1959; and 'Credit and Capital', Remarks prepared for delivery at a meeting of the Investment Dealers Association of Canada (Ontario District), Toronto, Dec. 14, 1959.
9 Coyne, op. cit., 'Credit and Capital', p. 12.
10 See H. S. Gordon, *The Economists versus the Bank of Canada*, Toronto, Ryerson, 1961.
11 Canada, Royal Commission on Banking and Finance, *Report*, Ottawa, 1964.
12 M. F. Timlin, *Keynesian Economics*, Toronto, University of Toronto Press, 1942. 'The Economics of Control', *Canadian Journal of Economics and Political Science*, 1945, vol. 11, pp. 258–293. 'Price Flexibility and Employment', *Canadian Journal of Economics and Political Science*, 1946, vol. 12, p. 204 ff. 'General Equilibrium Analysis and Public Policy', *Canadian Journal of Economics and Political Science*, 1946, vol. 12, pp. 483 ff. See also H. G. Johnson's review of R. Dehem, *L'Efficacité du système économique: Criteriologie de la politique économique*, Louvain, E. Nauwelaerts, 1952, *Canadian Journal of Economics and Political Science*, 1955, vol. 21, pp. 102–104.
13 As a tribute at the time of his death, Keynes was memorialized at the meetings of the Canadian Economics and Political Science Association by M. F. Timlin, A. F. W. Plumptre, G. A. Elliot, R. B. Bryce, and W. A. Mackintosh, *Canadian Journal of Economics and Political Science*, 1947, vol. 13, pp. 363–378. Plumptre and Bryce had studied under Keynes. Harry Johnson, who attended only one seminar given by Keynes after the war, was, as yet, not part of the Canadian academic establishment.
14 H. G. Johnson, Review of M. C. Kemp, *The Pure Theory of International Trade*, Englewood Cliffs, Prentice-Hall, 1964. *Canadian Journal of Economics and Political Science*, 1965, vol. 31, pp. 139–144.
15 A. D. Scott, 'Conservation Policy and Capital Theory', *Journal of Economics and Political Science*, 1954, vol. 20, pp. 504–513. *Natural Resources: The Economics of Conservation*, Toronto, University of Toronto Press, 1955.
16 H. S. Gordon, 'The Economic Theory of a Common Property Resource: The Fishery', *Journal of Political Economy*, 1954, vol. 62, pp. 124–142.

17 G. Goundry, 'Conservation and Capital Theory: A Comment', *Canadian Journal of Economics and Political Science*, 1956, vol. 22, pp. 92–97. J. N. Wolfe, 'Conservation and Capital Theory: A Second Comment', *Canadian Journal of Economics and Political Science*, 1956, vol. 22, pp. 98–99. A. D. Scott, 'Conservation and Capital Theory: Rejoinder', *Canadian Journal of Economics and Political Science*, 1956, vol. 22, pp. 99–102.
18 A. D. Scott, 'Development of Economic Theory on Fisheries Regulation', *Journal of the Fisheries Research Board of Canada*, 1979, vol. 36, pp. 725–741.
19 See G. R. Munro, 'Fisheries, Extended Jurisdiction and the Economics of Common Property Resources', *Canadian Journal of Economics*, 1982, vol. 15, pp. 405–425.
20 P. Copes, 'The Market as an Open Access Commons: A Neglected Aspect of Excess Capacity', *Discussion Paper 82–04–2*, Simon Fraser University, Burnaby, British Columbia.
21 G. Rosenbluth, 'Industrial Concentration in Canada and the United States', *Canadian Journal of Economics and Political Science*, 1954, vol. 20, pp. 332–346. *Concentration in Canadian Manufacturing*, Princeton, Princeton University Press, 1957.
22 S. Stykolt, 'The Measurement and Causes of Concentration', *Canadian Journal of Economics and Political Science*, 1958, vol. 24, pp. 415–419. 'Comment', *Canadian Journal of Economics and Political Science*, 1959, vol. 25, pp. 200–204, pp. 454–541. K. A. H. Buckley, 'On Rosenbluth's Concentration in Canadian Manufacturing Industries' *Canadian Journal of Economics and Political Science*, 1959, vol. 25, pp. 195–200. G. Rosenbluth, 'A Note on the Concentration Controversy', *Canadian Journal of Economics and Political Science*, 1959, vol. 25, pp. 336–340.
23 I mention only G. Rosenbluth, *Canadian Anti-Combines Administration*, Toronto, University of Toronto Press, 1963. L. Skeoch, *Restrictive Trade Practices in Canada*, Toronto, McClelland and Stewart, 1966. Much more was produced by the Anti-Combines Investigation Branch of the Department of Corporate and Consumer Affairs and by the Economic Council of Canada.
24 R. A. Musgrave, *The Theory of Public Finance*, New York, McGraw-Hill, 1959.
25 Beginning in 1951 the Foundation produced an annual volume on some aspect of the tax system.
26 J. H. Perry, *Taxation in Canada*, Toronto, University of Toronto Press, 1951. *Taxes, Tariffs and Subsidies: A History of Canadian Fiscal Development*, Toronto, University of Toronto Press, 1955.
27 I. Brecher, 'Investment, Income and Output', *Canadian Journal of Economics and Political Science*, 1950, vol. 16, pp. 83 ff. pp. 94 ff.
28 Leslie Frost, Treasurer of Ontario, *Debates of the Legislative Assembly of Ontario*, April 2, 1948.
29 F. A. McGregor, *Canada and International Cartels*, Ottawa, 1945. J. D. Gibson, 'The Changing Influence of the United States on the Canadian Economy', *Canadian Journal of Economics and Political Science*, 1956, vol. 22, pp. 421–436. C. D. Blyth and E. B. Carty, 'Non-Resident Ownership of Canadian Industry', *Canadian Journal of Economics and Political Science*, 1956, vol. 22, pp. 449–460.
30 J. E. Coyne, 'Living Within Our Means', an address to the Canadian Club of Winnipeg, January 18, 1960. 'Foreign Debt and Unemployment', an address to The Canadian Club of Toronto, November 14, 1960. 'Strong Roots for New

252 *A history of Canadian economic thought*

Growth', an address to the Annual Meeting of the Newfoundland Board of Trade, St. John's, January 31, 1961. 'Balance of Payment Problems in North America', an address to the Economic Club of New York, March 7, 1961.
31 Canada. Task Force on the Structure of Canadian Industry *Report*, Privy Council Office, Ottawa, 1968.
32 The categorization is that of the scientific community in which Hymer found himself at the end of his career. In fact, he began in the Coase-Williamson tradition of the New Institutionalism, which was not the tradition of a conventional, anti-trust business economist.
33 'Multinational Corporations and the Law of Uneven Development' in *The Multinational Corporation: a Radical Approach*, R. Cohen, *et al.*, eds, Cambridge, Cambridge University Press, 1979, p. 66.
34 ibid., p. 73.
35 Canada. Task Force on the Structure of Canadian Industry, *Report*, Privy Council Office, Ottawa, 1968.
36 M. Watkins, 'A New National Policy' in T. Lloyd and J. McLeod (eds.) *Agenda 1970: proposals for a creative politics*, Toronto, University of Toronto Press, 1968, p. 169.
37 ibid., p. 175.
38 R. C. Mathews, 'What the Private Planning Association is Today', *Monetary Times*, October, 1968, pp. 43–45.
39 H. A. Innis, 'Minerva's Owl', *The Bias of Communication*, Toronto, University of Toronto Press, 1951, p. 3.
40 'A Twenty Year Perspective: Some Reflections on the Keynesian Revolution in Canada', T. Brewis, *et al.*, *Canadian Economic Policy Since the War*, Private Planning Association, Canadian Trade Committee, 1966, p. 38.
41 ibid., p. 40.
42 H. S. Gordon, *The Economists Versus the Bank of Canada*, Toronto, The Ryerson Press, 1961.
43 Melbourne, Melbourne Univerity Press, 1951.
44 Johnson's report was published as 'Alternative Guiding Principles for the Use of Monetary Policy in Canada' in *Essays in Monetary Economics*, London, Unwin University Books, 1967, pp. 195–236.
45 ibid., p. 205.
46 ibid., p. 206.
47 ibid., p. 209.
48 'Equilibrium Growth in an International Economy', *Canadian Journal of Economics and Political Science*, 1953, vol. 19, pp. 478–500.
49 'The Economic Theory of Customs Unions', *Money, Trade and Economic Growth*, London, Unwin University Books, 1962, pp. 46–74. Lipsey has pointed to his outstanding work on the theory of tariffs, particularly 'Optimum Tariffs and Retaliation', *Review of Economic Studies*, 1953, vol. 21, pp. 142–153.
50 'Exogenous Change in an Open Economy', in *General Equilibrium Analysis*, London, George Allen and Unwin, 1974, pp. 283–310.
51 R. G. Lipsey, 'Harry Johnson's Contributions to the Pure Theory of International Trade', *Canadian Journal of Economics*, 1978, vol. 11, pp. s34–s54, pp. s41–s43.
52 'Keynes's *General Theory*: Revolution or War of Independence?' in *The Shadow of Keynes*, by E. S. Johnson and H. G. Johnson, Oxford, Basil Blackwell, 1978, p. 234.

53 Chicago, Aldine Publishing Company, 1972.
54 London, Gray-Mills Publishing, 1973.
55 London, George Allen & Unwin, 1974.
56 'What Passes for Economics in the English Establishment' in *The Shadow of Keynes*, Oxford, Basil Blackwell, 1978, p. 224.
57 'The General Theory after Twenty-five Years' in *On Economics and Society*, Chicago, University of Chicago Press, 1975, p. 67.
58 ibid., p. 69.
59 'Keynesian Economics, Equilibrium and Time', *The Harry G. Johnson Symposium, Canadian Journal of Economics*, 1978, vol. 11, supplement, pp. S3–S10.
60 'The Theory of Economic Growth, M. B. Kraus and H. G. Johnson, *General Equilibrium Analysis*, London, George Allen & Unwin, 1974, p. 335.
61 'Towards a Generalized Capital Accumulation Approach to Economic Development', *The Canadian Quandary*, Toronto, McGraw Hill, 1963, pp. 227–235. See especially, 'Appendix; What makes for Economic Growth?', 'Planning and the Objectives of a Free Enterprise Economy', *The Canadian Quandary*, op. cit., pp. 33–45, pp. 43–45.
62 Canadian Institute of Public Affairs, *Economic Planning in a Democratic Society*, Toronto, University of Toronto Press, 1963, pp. 56–64.
63 ibid., p. 38.
64 See his 'On Demolishing Barriers to Trade' in *Rebuilding the Liberal Order*, London, Institute of Economic Affairs, 1969, pp. 11–19.
65 R. F. Neill, *A New Theory of Value*, Toronto, University of Toronto Press, 1972, p. 40.
66 See also *On Economics and Society*, Chicago, University of Chicago Press, 1975, pp. 129–196.
67 'On Demolishing Barriers to Trade', op. cit., p. 13.
68 H. G. Johnson, 'Keynes's *General Theory*: Revolution or War of Independence?' in *The Shadow of Keynes*, op. cit., p. 234.
69 'Scholars as Public Adversaries: The Case of Economics', *On Economics and Society*, Chicago, University of Chicago Press, 1975, p. 150.
70 Review, R. Dehem, 'L'éfficacité du système économique: criteriologie de la politique économique', *Canadian Journal of Economics and Political Science*, vol. 21, pp. 102–104.
71 C. L. Barber, 'Canadian Tariff Policy', *Canadian Journal of Economics and Political Science*, 1955, vol. 21, pp. 513–530. See also J. R. Melvin and B. W. Wilkinson, *Effective Protection in the Canadian Economy*, Toronto, University of Toronto Press, 1968.
72 H. E. English, *Industrial Structure in Canada's Competitive Position*, Montreal, Private Planning Association, 1964.
73 H. C. Eastman and S. Stykolt, *The Tariff and Competition in Canada*, Toronto, Macmillan, 1967. S. Stykolt, *Efficiency in the Open Economy*, Toronto, Oxford University Press, 1969.
74 For a bibliography see R. G. Harris and D. Cox, *Trade, Industrial Policy, and Canadian Manufacturing*, Toronto, Ontario Economic Council, 1984, pp. 157–165.
75 T. M. Brown, *Canadian Economic Growth*, Canada, Royal Commission on Health Services, Ottawa, 1964. N. H. Lithwick, *Economic Growth in Canada: A Quantitative Analysis*, Toronto, University of Toronto Press, 1967. D. Walters,

Canadian Income Levels and Growth: An International Perspective, Economic Council of Canada, Ottawa, 1968.

76 J. C. Weldon and A. Asimakopulos, 'A Synoptic View of Some Simple Models of Growth', *Canadian Journal of Economics and Political Science*, 1965, vol. 30, pp. 52–79. T. K. Rymes *On Concepts of Capital and Technical Change*, Cambridge, Cambridge University Press, Cambridge, 1971.

77 Toronto, McGraw-Hill, 1966.

78 For an extended list of most of the academically respectable works see A. E. Safarian, *Foreign Direct Investment: A Survey of Canadian Research*, Montreal, The Institute for Research on Public Policy, 1985.

79 W. D. Wood and R. S. Thoman (eds), Kingston, Industrial Relations Center, Queen's University, 1965.

80 Yves Dubé, Pierre Harvey and André Raynauld were active participants.

81 A. D. Scott, 'Policy for Declining Regions: a Theoretic Approach', op. cit., pp. 73–93.

82 T. N. Brewis, 'The Problem of Regional Disparities', op. cit., pp. 99–114. Yves Dubé managed to sit on the fence between these positions.

83 For an excellent account of the transformation of the information environment of federal-provincial transfers see J. S. Dupré, 'Tax Powers Versus Spending Responsibilities: An Historical Analysis of Federal-Provincial Finances', in University League for Social Reform, *The Prospect for Change*, Toronto, McGraw-Hill, 1965, pp. 83–101. If Gordon Goundry is right, the real politics of federal-provincial bargaining is a 'horse trade' or a 'poker game' in which each province tries to extract as much as it can from the others, without giving up anything.

84 Toronto, Macmillan, 1969.

85 See N. H. Lithwick and G. Paquet, *Urban Studies: A Canadian Perspective*, Toronto, Methuen, 1968. N. H. Lithwick, *Canada's Science Policy and the Economy*, Toronto, Methuen, 1969.

86 A. D. Scott, 'The Evaluation of Federal Grants', *Economica*, 1952, vol. 19, pp. 377–394.

87 A. Breton, 'A Theory of Government Grants', *Canadian Journal of Economics and Political Science*, 1965, vol. 31, pp. 173–187. J. C. Weldon, 'Public Goods (and Federalism), *Canadian Journal of Economics and Political Science*, 1966, vol. 32, 230–238. A. Breton, 'Public Goods (and Federalism): A Reply', *Canadian Journal of Economics and Political Science*, 1966, vol. 32, pp. 238–242. D. Winch, 'Breton's Theory of Government Grants', *Canadian Journal of Economics and Political Science*, 1967, vol. 33, 115–117.

88 Canada, Royal Commission on Taxation *Report*, Ottawa, 1966.

89 *Canadian Journal of Economics*, 1968, vol. 1, supplement.

90 op. cit., pp. 195–205.

91 'Problems of Canadian Nationalism', *International Journal*, 1961, vol. 16, pp. 238–250.

92 'Problems of Canadian Nationalism', *The Canadian Quandary*, Toronto, McGraw-Hill, 1963, p. 19.

93 A. Breton, 'The Economics of Nationalism', *Journal of Political Economy*, 1964, vol. 72, pp. 376–386.

94 M. Watkins, 'The Economics of Nationalism and the Nationality of Economics: a critique of neoclassical theorizing' in *The Harry Johnson Memorial Symposium, Canadian Journal of Economics*, 1978, vol. 11, supplement, pp. s87–s120,

p. s101. I have changed the tense of the verbs. The Johnson articles are: 'A Theoretical Model of Economic Nationalism in New and Developing States', *Political Science Quarterly*, 1965, vol. 80, pp. 169–185; 'Introduction', 'Economic Nationalism in Canadian Policy', and 'The Ideology of Economic Policy in the New States', H. G. Johnson, ed., *Economic Nationalism in Old and New States*, Chicago, University of Chicago Press, 1967, pp. v–xi, 85–97, 124–41.

95 A. Rotstein, 'The 20th Century Prospect: Nationalism in a Technological Society', The University League for Social Reform, *Nationalism in Canada*, Toronto, McGraw-Hill, 1966, pp. 341–363.

96 M. Watkins, 'Nationalism', *Canadian Journal of Economics and Political Science*, 1966, vol. 32, pp. 388–392. 'Technology and Nationalism', The University League for Social Reform, op. cit., pp. 284–302.

97 'The Economics of Nationalism and the Nationality of Economics ...', op. cit.

98 'Le nationalisme, l'unité nationale et la théorie économique de l' information', *Canadian Journal of Economics*, 1970, vol. 3, pp. 183–198.

99 J. Carr, G. F. Mathewson, and J. C. McManus, *Cents & Nonsense*, Toronto, Holt, Rinehart & Winston, 1972.

11 THE ECONOMICS OF THE WEST

1 V. C. Fowke, *Canadian Agricultural Policy: the Historical Pattern*, London, Oxford University Press, 1946; *The National Policy and the Wheat Economy*, Toronto, University of Toronto Press, 1957.

2 op. cit., *Canadian Agricultural Policy: the Historical Pattern*, p. 4.

3 op. cit., p. 3.

4 R. F. Neill, *A New Theory of Value*, Toronto, University of Toronto Press, 1972, p. 142.

5 D. C. North, 'Location Theory and Regional Economic Growth' *Journal of Political Economy*, 1955, vol. 63, pp. 243–258. Charles Tiebout, 'Exports and Regional Economic Growth', *Journal of Political Economy*, 1956, vol. 64, pp. 160–168.

6 P. Hartland, 'Factors in Economic Growth in Canada', *Journal of Economic History*, 1955, vol. 15, pp. 13–22.

7 O. J. Firestone, *Canada's Economic Development, 1867–1953*, London, Bowes & Bowes, 1958.

8 Kenneth Buckley, Review of O. J. Firestone, *Canada's Economic Development, 1867–1953, American Economic Review*, 1959, vol. 49, pp. 431–433.

9 Kenneth Buckley, 'The Role of Staple Industries in Canada's Economic Development', *Journal of Economic History*, 1958, vol. 18, pp. 439–50.

10 ibid., p. 444.

11 W. W. Rostow, *The Stages of Economic Growth*, Cambridge, 1960.

12 G. W. Bertram, 'Economic Growth in Canadian Industry, 1870–1915: The Staple Model and the Take-Off Hypothesis', *Canadian Journal of Economics and Political Science*, 1963, vol. 29, pp. 159–184.

13 G. W. Bertram, 'Historical Statistics on Growth and Structure of Manufacturing in Canada, 1870–1957', *Canadian Political Science Association Conference on Statistics, June, 1962*, Toronto, 1964, pp. 93–151. E. J. Chambers and G. W. Bertram, 'Urbanization and Manufacturing in Central Canada, 1870–1890',

256 A history of Canadian economic thought

   Canadian Political Science Association, Conference on Statistics, June, 1964, Toronto, 1966, pp. 225–258.
14 op. cit., 1967, p. 95.
15 ibid., p. 78.
16 ibid., pp. 96–98.
17 ibid., p. 84.
18 *The Canadian Economy: Prospect and Retrospect*, Cambridge, Harvard University Press, 1961, pp. 118–119.
19 op. cit., pp. 81, 100.
20 ibid., pp. 101–103.
21 M. H. Watkins, 'A Staple Theory of Economic Growth', *Canadian Journal of Economics and Political Science*, 1963, vol. 29, pp. 141–158. W. T. Easterbrook and M. H. Watkins, *Approaches to Canadian Economic History*, op. cit., pp. 49–73.
22 ibid., 1967, p. 48.
23 ibid., p. 68.
24 ibid., p. 69.
25 T. M. Brown, *Canadian Economic Growth*, Ottawa, 1965. H. N. Lithwick, *Economic Growth in Canada*, Toronto, 1967. D. Walters, *Canadian Income Levels and Growth*, Ottawa, 1968.
26 op. cit., 1967, p. 15.
27 E. J. Chambers and D. F. Gordon, 'Primary Products and Economic Growth: An Empirical Measurement', *Journal of Political Economy*, 1966, vol. 74, pp. 315–332, p. 317.
28 J. H. Dales, J. C. McManus, and M. H. Watkins, 'Primary Products and Economic Growth: A Comment', *Journal of Political Economy*, 1967, vol. 75, pp. 876–880.
29 F. Lewis, 'The Canadian Wheat Boom and Per Capita Income: New Estimates', *Journal of Political Economy*, 1975, vol, 83, pp. 1249–1258.
30 D. Grant, 'The Staple Theory and Its Measurement', *Journal of Political Economy*, 1974, vol. 82, pp. 1249–1253.
31 R. E. Caves, 'Export-led Growth and the New Economic History', in J. N. Bhagwati, R. W. Jones, R. A. Mundell and J. Banek, eds, *Trade, Balance of Payments and Growth*, Amsterdam, 1971, pp. 403–442. G. W. Bertram, 'The Relevance of the Wheat Boom in Canadian Economic Growth', *Canadian Journal of Economics*, 1973. vol. 6, pp. 545–566.
32 R. E. Caves, op. cit., p. 408.
33 ibid., pp. 411–418.
34 E. Vickery, 'Exports and North American Economic Growth: "Structuralist" and "Staple" Models', *Canadian Journal of Economics*, 1974, vol. 7, pp. 53–54.
35 op. cit., pp. 559–560.
36 C. Southey, 'The Staples Thesis, Common Property, and Homesteading', *Canadian Journal of Economics*, 1978, vol. 11, pp. 547–559.
37 J. H. Dales, *The Protective Tariff in Canada's Development*, Toronto, University of Toronto Press, 1966.
38 op. cit., p. 150.
39 H. A. Innis, 'Unused Capacity as a Factor in Canadian Economic History', in *Essays in Canadian Economic History*, Toronto, University of Toronto Press, 1956, p. 150.
40 K. H. Norrie, 'The National Policy and Prairie Economic Discrimination,

1870–1930' in D. H. Akenson, ed. *Canadian Papers in Rural History*, Gananoque, Langdale Press, 1978, pp. 13–32, pp. 22, 24.
41 P. J. George, 'Rates of Return and Government Subsidization of the CPR', *Canadian Journal of Economics*, 1968, vol. 1, pp. 740–762.
42 F. Lewis and M. MacKinnon, 'Government Loan Guarantees and the Failure of the Canadian Northern Railway', *Journal of Economic History*, 1987, vol. 47, pp. 175–196.
43 C. M. Studness, 'Economic Opportunity and Westward Migration of Canadians in the Late Nineteenth Century', *Canadian Journal of Economics and Political Science*, 1964, vol. 30, pp. 570–584.
44 K. H. Norrie, 'The Rate of Settlement of the Canadian Prairies, 1870–1911', *Journal of Economic History*, 1975, vol. 35, pp. 410–427.
45 W. Marr and M. Percy, 'Government and the Rate of Prairie Settlement', *Canadian Journal of Economics*, 1978, vol. 11, pp. 757–767.
46 F. D. Lewis, 'Farm Settlement on the Canadian Prairies, 1898–1911', *Journal of Economic History*, 1981, vol. 41, pp. 517–535.
47 W. L. Marr, *Canadian Journal of Economics*, 1981, vol. 14, pp. 136–145.
48 M. McInnis, 'The Changing Structure of Canadian Agriculture, 1867–1897', *Journal of Economic History*, 1982, vol. 42, pp. 191–198.
49 D. McCalla, 'The Wheat Staple and Upper Canadian Development', mimeo, 1978, pp. 1–22, p. 12.
50 'A Belated Review of Harold Adams Innis, The Fur Trade in Canada', *Canadian Historical Review*, 1979, vol. 50, pp. 419–441.
51 J. H. Dales, 'Comment'; M. C. Urquhart, 'New Estimates of Gross National Product, Canada, 1870–1926: Some implications for Canadian Development', S. L. Engerman and R. E. Gallman, eds, *Long-Term Factors in American Economic Growth*, National Bureau of Economic Research Conference on Income and Wealth, Chicago, University of Chicago Press, 1986, pp. 92–93.
52 R. E. Ankli and R. M. Litt, 'The Growth of Prairie Agriculture: Economic Considerations', in *Canadian Papers in Rural History*, D. H. Akenson, ed. Gananoque, Langdale Press, 1978, pp. 44–45.
53 M. Altman, 'A Revision of Canadian Economic Growth: 1870–1910 (a Challenge to the Gradualist Interpretation)', *Canadian Journal of Economics*, 1987, vol. 20, pp. 86–113, p. 107.

12 A NORTH AMERICAN DISCOURSE

1 'The Current and Prospective State of Economics in Canada', T. N. Guinsburg and G. I. Reuber, *Perspectives on the Social Sciences in Canada*, Toronto, University of Toronto Press, p. 104.
2 J. F. Graham, 'Chez Who?', *Canadian Journal of Economics*, 1971, vol. 4, p. 432.
3 Toronto, University of Toronto Press, 1977.
4 *Studies in Political Economy*, 1981, vol. 6.
5 Kingston, McGill-Queen's, 1989.
6 Roy Mathews, 'The Private Planning Association, What It Is Today', *Monetary Times*, Oct. 1968, pp. 43–45.
7 Economic Council of Canada, *Looking Outward*, Ottawa, 1975.
8 R. G. Lipsey and M. G. Smith, *Taking the Initiative: Canada's Trade Options*

258 *A history of Canadian economic thought*

    in a Turbulent World, Toronto, C. D. Howe Research Institute, 1985. R. J. Wonnacott with R. Hill, *Canadian and US Adjustment Policies in a Bilateral Trade Agreement*, Toronto, Canadian American Committee and the C. D. Howe Research Institute, 1987. R. G. Lipsey and R. C. York, *Evaluating the Free Trade Deal*, Toronto, C. D. Howe Research Institute, 1988.

9. G. K. Kardouche and F. Caramazza, *Wage and Price Controls for Canada? A commentary on the final Report of the Prices and Incomes Commission*, Montreal, C. D. Howe Research Institute, 1973.
10. Toronto, University of Toronto Press, 1965.
11. T. J. Courchene, *Money, Inflation and the Bank of Canada*, Montreal, C. D. Howe Research Institute, 1976. *The Strategy of Gradualism: An Analysis of Bank of Canada Policy from Mid-1975 to Mid-1977*, Montreal, C. D. Howe Research Institute, 1978.
12. C. E. Beigie and J. Maxwell, *Quebec's Vulnerability in Energy*, Montreal, C. D. Howe Research Institute, 1977. R. Dehem, *On The Meaning of 'Economic Association'*, Montreal, C. D. Howe Research Institute, 1978. Judith Maxwell and Caroline Pestieau, *Economic Realities of Contemporary Confederation*, Montreal, C. D. Howe Research Institute, 1980. Yvon Allaire and Roger Miller, *Canadian Business Response to the Legislation on Francization in the Workplace*, Montreal, C. D. Howe Research Insitute, 1980.
13. K. J. Rea, *Political Economy of Northern Development*, Ottawa, The Science Council of Canada, 1976.
14. N. H. Britton and J. M. Gilmour, *The Weakest Link*, Ottawa, The Science Council of Canada, 1978. G. P. F. Steed, *Threshold Firms: Backing Canada's Winners*, Ottawa, The Science Council of Canada, 1982. *Canada as a Conserver Society: Resource Uncertainties and the Need for New Technologies*, Ottawa, The Science Council of Canada, 1977. *Forging the Links*, Ottawa, The Science Council of Canada, 1979. *Hard Times, Hard Choices: A Statement*, Ottawa, The Science Council of Canada, 1981. *Canadian Industrial Development*, Ottawa, The Science Council of Canada, 1984. Michael Jenkin, *The Challenge of Diversity*, Ottawa, The Science Council of Canada, 1983.
15. *Hard Times...*, op. cit., p. 54.
16. ibid., p. 9.
17. *Canada as a Conserver Society*, op. cit., p. 66.
18. K. S. Palda, *The Science Council's Weakest Link*, Vancouver, The Fraser Institute, 1979. *Industrial Innovation: Its Place in the Public Policy Agenda*, Vancouver, The Fraser Institute, 1980. Y. Kotowitz, *Positive Industrial Policy: the Implications for R. & D.*, Toronto, Ontario Economic Council, 1985.
19. M. Walker, ed. *The Illusion of Wage and Price Controls*, Vancouver, The Fraser Institute, 1976.
20. *Free Market Zones: Deregulating Canadian Enterprise*, Vancouver, The Fraser Institute, 1983.
21. J. T. Addison and J. Buton, *Trade Unions and Society*, Vancouver, The Fraser Institute, 1984.
22. D. G. McFetridge and D. A. S. Smith, *The Economics of Vertical Disintegration*, Vancouver, The Fraser Institute, 1988.
23. D. J. Daly and S. Globerman, *Tariff and Science Policies: Application of a Model of Nationalism*, Toronto, Ontario Economic Council, 1976. E. G. West applied a quantitative test to the Baumol-Bowen hypothesis concerning frozen productivity levels in performing arts.

24 E. G. West, *Subsidizing the Performing Arts*, Toronto, Ontario Economic Council, 1985.
25 G. F. Mathewson and G. D. Quirin, *Fiscal Transfer Pricing in Multinational Corporations*, Toronto, University of Toronto Press, Ontario Economic Council, 1979.
26 S. H. Ingerman, *Economic Policy, Economic Theory, and the Democratic Left*, Ottawa, Canadian Center for Policy Alternatives, 1981.
27 W. W. Donner and D. D. Peters, *The Monetarist Counter-Revolution: A Critique of Canadian Monetary Policy, 1975-1979*, Ottawa, Canadian Institute for Economic Policy, 1979.
28 *Unemployment and Inflation*, Ottawa, Canadian Institute for Economic Policy, 1980, p. 34.
29 ibid., p.57.
30 ibid., p. 97.
31 D. Crane, *Beyond the Monetarists: Post-Keynesian Alternatives to Rapid Inflation, Low Growth and High Unemployment*, Ottawa, Canadian Institute for Economic Policy, 1981.
32 R. S. Ritchie, *An Institute for Research on Public Policy*, Ottawa, Information Canada, 1969.
33 *Canada's Competition Policy Revisited: Some New Thoughts on an Old Story*, Montreal, Institute for Research on Public Policy, 1981.
34 *The Design of Federations*, Montreal, Institute for Research on Public Policy, 1980.
35 Paul Phillips, *Unemployment Insurance: The Battle Ground in the Debate on the Economic Crisis*, Ottawa, Canadian Center for Policy Alternatives, 1986.
36 R. T. Naylor, *Monetarism and Canadian Policy Alternatives*, Ottawa, Canadian Center for Policy Alternatives, 1982.
37 W. L. Marr and D. G. Paterson, *Canada: An Economic History*, Toronto, Macmillan, 1980. Richard Pomfret, *The Economic Development of Canada*, Toronto, Methuen, 1981.
38 R. Comeau, *Economie québécoise*, Québec, Les Presses de l'Université du Québec, 1969. R. Tremblay, *L'économie québécoise: histoire, développement, politiques*, Montréal, Les Presses de l'Université du Québec, 1976. I. M. Drummond, *Progress without Planning: the Economic History of Ontario from Confederation to the Second World War*, Toronto, University of Toronto Press, 1987. K. J. Rea, *The Prosperous Years: The Economic History of Ontario, 1939-1975*, Toronto, University of Toronto Press, 1985.
39 Kari Levitt, *Silent Surrender*, Toronto, Macmillan, 1971. R. T. Naylor, *The History of Canadian Business: 1867-1914*, Toronto, James Lorimer, 1975. Duncan Cameron, ed., *Explorations in Canadian Economic History: Essays in Honour of Irene M. Spry*, Ottawa, University of Ottawa Press, 1985.
40 J. E. Stiglitz, 'Introduction', J. E. Stiglitz and G. F. Mathewson, eds, *New Developments in the Analysis of Market Structures*, Proceedings of a Conference held by the International Economics Asscociation, Ottawa, 1968. Cambridge, MIT Press, 1986.
41 ibid., p. xix.
42 ibid., p. xxii.
43 G. F. Mathewson, *Market Structure and Performance in the Pharmaceutical Industry*, Canada. Commission of Inquiry on the Pharmaceutical Industry, Ottawa, Supply and Services Canada, 1984. G. F. Mathewson, R. Winter and C.

T. Campbell, *Regulation of the Canadian Life Insurance Market: Some Issues Affecting Consumers*, Ottawa, Canada, Department of Corporate and Consumer Affairs, 1983. G. F. Mathewson, *Competition Policy and Vertical Exchange*, Ottawa, Canada. Royal Commission on the Economic Unity and Development Prospects for Canada, Supply and Services Canada, 1985. *Information, Entry, and Regulation in Markets for Life Insurance*, Toronto, Ontario Economic Council, 1982.

44 Jean Tirole, *The Theory of Industrial Organization*, Cambridge, MIT Press, 1988.

45 Irving Brecher, *Canada's Competition Policy Revisited: Some New Thoughts on an Old Story*, Montreal, The Institute for Research on Public Policy, 1981, p. xi *et passim*.

46 Economic Council of Canada, *Interim Report on Competition Policy*, Ottawa, 1969.

47 L. A. Skeoch with B. C. McDonald, Ottawa, Supply and Services Canada, 1976.

48 C. Green, Toronto, McGraw-Hill-Ryerson, 1976.

49 Ottawa, 1978.

50 J. R. S. Prichard, W. T. Stanbury and T. W. Wilson, eds, *Canadian Competition Policy: Essays in Law and Economics*, Toronto, Butterworths, 1979.

51 B. Dunlop, David McQueen and M. Treblicock, Toronto, Canada Law Book Inc., 1987.

52 Brecher, op. cit., p. 5.

53 'The Understanding and Control of Inflation: Is There a Crisis in Macro-Economics?' *Canadian Journal of Economics*, 1981, vol. 14, pp. 545–576.

54 Lipsey, op. cit., p. 456.

55 ibid., p. 554.

56 *The Demand for Money: Theory and Evidence*, 3rd edition, New York, Harper, 1985.

57 R. G. Lipsey, Review, *Macroeconomics*, First Canadian Edition, R. Dornbush, S. Fischer and G. R. Sparks, Toronto, McGraw-Hill-Ryerson, 1982. *Modern Macro Economics*, Michael Parkin, Scarborough, Prentice-Hall, 1982. *Macro Economics: Theory and Policy in Canada*, D. A. Wilton and D. M. Prescott, Don Mills, Addison Wesley, 1982, *Canadian Journal of Economics*, 1983, vol. 16, pp. 532 ff.

58 ibid., p. 528.

59 'The Keynesian Recovery', *Canadian Journal of Economics*, 1986, vol. 19, pp. 626–641.

60 'The Porter Commission Report in the Context of Earlier Canadian Monetary Documents', *Canadian Journal of Economics*, 1977, vol. 10, pp. 34–49. 'Proposals for the Revision of Banking Legislation', *Canadian Journal of Economics*, 1978, vol. 11. pp. 124–128. See also R. A. Shearer, J. F. Chant, and D. E. Bond, *Money, Banking and the Financial Institutions of Canada*, Scarborough, Prentice-Hall, 1984, pp. 351–382.

61 Shearer, op. cit., 1977, p. 41.

62 J. F. Chant and A. L. K. Acheson, 'Choice of Monetary Instruments and the Theory of Bureaucracy', Ottawa, Carleton Economic Papers, Carleton University, 1971; 'Mythology and Central Banking', Ottawa, Carleton Economic Papers, Carleton University, 1971; 'Bureaucratic Theory and the Choice of Central Bank Goals: the Case of the Bank of Canada' Ottawa, Carleton Economic Papers, Carleton University, 1972.

Notes 261

63 J. K. Galbraith and A. L. Guthrie, Review, *Efficiency and Regulation: A Study of Deposit Institutions*, Ottawa, Economic Council of Canada, 1976. Canada, Department of Finance White Paper, *Canadian Banking Legislation*, Ottawa, Supply and Services Canada, 1976, *Canadian Public Policy*, 1977, vol. 3, pp. 101–106.
64 Canada, (Estey) Royal Commission of Inquiry into the Collapse of the CCB and Northland Bank, *Report*, Ottawa, Supply and Services Canada, 1986.
65 D. A. Auld and F. C. Miller, *Principles of Public Finance: a Canadian Text*, 2nd edition, Toronto, Methuen, 1982. R. W. Boadway and D. E. Wildasin, *Public Sector Economics*, 2nd edition, Boston, Little, Brown and Co., 1984. R. A. Musgrave and R. M. Bird, *Public Finance in Theory and Practice*, First Canadian Edition, Toronto, McGraw-Hill, 1987.
66 *The Growth of Government Spending in Canada*, Toronto, Canadian Tax Foundation, 1970.
67 *Financing Canadian Government: a Quantitative Overview*, Toronto, Canadian Tax Foundation, 1979, p. 94.
68 R. M. Bird, ' Federalism and Regional Disparities: A Review Article', *Canadian Public Policy*, 1987, vol. 13, pp. 380–383.
69 W. I. Gillespie, 'Post War Canadian Fiscal Policy Revisited', *Canadian Taxation Journal*, 1979, vol. 1, pp. 156–176. 'The Mythology of Musgrave's Multiple Budget Approach', *Canadian Taxation Journal*, 1981, vol. 3, pp. 38–44. *The Redistribution of Income in Canada*, Ottawa, Gage, Institute of Canadian Studies, Carleton University, 1980.
70 W. I. Gillespie, 'The 1981 Federal Budget: Muddling Through or Purposeful Tax Reform', *Canadian Taxation Journal*, 1983, vol. 4, pp. 975–1002. W. P. Hettich and S. L. Winer, 'A Positive Model of Tax Structure', *Journal of Public Economics*, 1984, vol. 24, pp. 67–87. 'Vertical Imbalance in the Fiscal System of Federal States', *Canadian Journal of Economics*, 1986, vol. 19, pp. 745–765.
71 R. W. Boadway and J. M. Treddenick, 'General Equilibrium Effects of the Canadian Tariff Structure', *Canadian Journal of Economics*, 1978, vol. 11, pp. 424–446. R. W. Boadway, Neil Bruce and Jack Mintz, 'Corporate Taxation and the Cost of Holding Inventories', *Canadian Journal of Economics*, 1982, vol. 15, pp. 278–93.
72 A. E. Safarian, *Canadian Federalism and Economic Integration*, Ottawa, Privy Council Office, Government of Canada, 1974.
73 R. W. Boadway and F. Flatters, 'Efficiency and Equalization Payments in a Federal System of Government: A Synthesis and Extension of Recent Results', *Canadian Journal of Economics*, 1982, vol. 15, pp. 611–633.
74 *Financing Confederation*, Ottawa, Economic Council of Canada, 1982.
75 'Financing Confederation', *Canadian Public Policy*, 1982, vol. 8, pp. 183–310.
76 R. W. Boadway, F. Flatters and A. Leblanc, 'Revenue Sharing and the Equalization of Natural Resource Revenues', *Canadian Public Policy*, 1983, vol. 9, pp. 174–180.
77 R. W. Boadway and K. Norrie, 'Constitutional Reform Canadian Style: An Economic Perspective', *Canadian Public Policy*, 1980, vol. 6, pp. 492–505. J-. L. Migué, 'Le Marché Politique au Canada', *Canadian Public Policy*, 1976, vol. 2, pp. 78–90.
78 Albert Breton, *Discriminatory Government Policies in Federal Countries*, Montreal, Private Planning Association, 1967, *An Economic Theory of Representative Government*, Chicago, Aldine, 1974. Albert Breton and Anthony Scott,

The Economic Constitution of Federal States, Toronto, University of Toronto Press, 1978. Albert Breton and Ronald Wintrobe, *The Logic of Bureaucratic Conduct: an Economic Analysis of Competition, Exchange, and Efficiency in Private and Public Organizations*, Cambridge, Cambridge University Press, 1982.

79 W. I. Gillespie and J. A. Johnson, 'Sales Tax Reform: A Critique of the Federal Government's Proposals' *Canadian Public Policy*, 1976, vol. 2, pp. 638–644. J. A. Gray, R. A. McLarty, W. I. Gillespie and J. A. Johnson, 'Sales Tax Reform: A Comment on Gillespie and Johnson' and 'Reply', *Canadian Public Policy*, 1977, vol. 3, pp. 106–114. W. I. Gillespie, 'Tax Reform: the Battle Field, the Strategy, the Spoils', *Canadian Public Administration*, 1983, pp. 182–202. Wayne R. Thirsk, 'The Value-Added Tax in Canada: Saviour or Siren Song?', *Canadian Public Policy*, 1987, vol. 13, pp. 259–283.

80 D. J. Savoie, *Regional Economic Development: Canada's Search for Policies*, Toronto, University of Toronto Press, 1986.

81 Michael Bradfield, *Regional Economics: Analysis and Policies in Canada*, Toronto, McGraw-Hill-Ryerson, 1988, p. 254.

82 O. J. Firestone, ed. *Regional Economic Development*, Ottawa, University of Ottawa Press, 1974, pp. iv–x.

83 R. Parenteau, 'Vers une politique de développement régional dans le contexte fédéral canadien', O. J. Firestone, op. cit., pp. 133–153.

84 *Regional Economic Policy: the Canadian Experience*, Toronto, McGraw-Hill-Ryerson, 1978.

85 Barry Wellar, ed. *National and Regional Economic Development Strategies: Perspectives on Canada's Problems and Prospects*, Ottawa, University of Ottawa Press, 1981, pp. 69–85.

86 Benjamin Higgins and Donald J. Savoie, *Regional Economic Development: Essays in Honour of François Perroux*, Boston, Unwin Hyman, 1988.

87 *Regional Economic: Analysis and Policies in Canada*, Toronto, McGraw-Hill-Ryerson, 988.

88 ibid., pp. 254–255.

89 *Report*, Ottawa, Minister of Supply and Services Canada, 1985.

90 op. cit., vol. 1, pp. 263–275; vol. 2, pp. 410–413, pp. 529–534.

12 A NORTH AMERICAN DISCOURSE – APPENDIX

91 Montréal, Association canadienne-française pour l'avancement des sciences, 1989, pp. 309–328.

Bibliography

The following is a list of all the works cited in this book, with some minor exceptions. In some cases in which several pieces from one work were cited, and the work itself was cited on its own count, only the work appears in the bibliography. In one or two cases in which a large number of works were cited as examples of a genre, the examples have not been listed in the bibliography. In cases in which a seminal work was followed by a cluster of journal comments, the comments have not been listed in the bibliography.

Acheson, Thomas W. (with D. Frank and J. D. Frost) (1985) *Industrialization and Underdevelopment in the Maritimes, 1880–1930*, Toronto, Garamond Press.

Addison, John T. (and J. Buton) (1954) *Trade Unions and Society*, Vancouver, The Fraser Institute.

Aitken, Hugh G. J. (1960) 'The Present State of Economic History', *Canadian Journal of Economics and Political Science*, vol. 26, pp. 87–95.

Allaire, Yvan (and R. Miller) (1980) *Canadian Business Response to the Legislation on Francization in the Workplace*, Montreal, C. D. Howe Research Institute.

Altman, Morris (1987) 'A Revision of Canadian Economic Growth: 1870–1910 (A Challenge to the Gradualist Interpretation)', *Canadian Journal of Economics*, vol. 20, pp. 86–113.

Andreano, Ralph L. (1970) *The New Economic History*, New York, John Wiley & Sons.

Angers, François-Albert (1961) 'Naissance de la pensée économique au Canada français' *Revue de l'histoire de l'Amerique français*, vol. 15, pp.204–229.

—— (1979) 'Preface', in Esdras Minville, *L'économie du Québec et la science économique*, Montréal, Fides.

Ankli, Robert E. (1973) 'The Buckley GNP Estimates, 1900–1925', Presented to the Sixth Conference on the Application of Econometric Methods to Canadian Economic History, University of Saskatchewan, Saskatoon, October 13.

—— (1978) 'The Growth of Prairie Agriculture: Economic Considerations', in D. H. Akenson (ed.) *Canadian Papers in Rural History*, Gananoque, Langdale Press, pp. 35–64.

Anon (1786) *An Account of the Present State of Nova Scotia*, London.

Arès, Richard (1938) *Catechisme de l'organization corporative*, Montréal.

—— (1949) *La confédération, pacte ou loi?*, Montréal, Ed. de l'Action nationale.

—— (1962) *Le rôle de l'état dans un Québec fort*, Montréal, Bellarmin.
Armstrong, Robert (1984) *Structure and Change: An Economic and Social History of Quebec: 1760–1850*, Toronto, Gage.
Arnold, Walter (1861) *Money and Banking*, Toronto, Blackburn's City Steam.
Asselin, Olivar (1938) 'L'industrie dans l'économie du Canada français', appendix to *L'achat chez nous*, Montréal.
Atkinson, Christopher W. (1844) *A Historical and Statistical Account of New Brunswick, B. N. A., with Advice to Immigrants*, Edinburgh, Anderson.
Atlantic Canada Economics Association (1971–) *A. C. E. A. Papers*.
Atlantic Provinces Royal Commission on Maritime Union (1970) *Report*, Halifax, The Commission.
Atlantic Provinces Economic Council (1965) *A Development Program for the Atlantic Provinces*, Halifax.
Auld, Douglas A. (1982) (and F. C. Miller) *Principles of Public Finance: a Canadian Text*, (2nd edition) Toronto, Methuen.
Balcom, A. B. (1920) 'The Rise in Prices', *University Magazine*, vol. 19, pp. 16–23.
—— (1935-36) 'The Jones Report, an Interpretation', *Dalhousie Review*, vol. 15, pp. 1–13.
Ball, John A. (1934) *Canadian Anti-Trust Legislation*, Baltimore, Williams Co.
Barbeau, Victor (1936) *Mesure de notre taille*, Montréal, Le Devoir.
—— (1937) *Pour nous grandir*, Montréal, Le Devoir.
—— (1939) *L'avenir de notre bourgeoisie*, Montréal, Editions de la Jeunesse Indépendent Catholique.
Barber, Clarence L. (1955) 'Canadian Tariff Policy', *Canadian Journal of Economics and Political Science*, vol. 21, pp. 513–530.
—— (1980) (and J. McCallum) *Unemployment and Inflation*, Ottawa, Canadian Institute for Economic Policy.
Bates, Stewart (1937) 'Classificatory Note on the Theory of Public Finance', *Canadian Journal of Economics and Political Science*, vol. 3, pp. 163–180.
Beard, Charles (1935) *An Economic Interpretation of the Constitution of the United States*, New York, Macmillan.
Beaubien, Louis (1901) *Agriculture et colonisation*, Montréal.
Beausoleil, Cléopas (1871) *System protecteur ou de la necesssité d'un réform du tarif canadien*, Montréal, Nouveau-Monde.
—— (1891) *La reciprocité*, Québec, Conférence de C. Beausoleil, M. P., au Club National de Montréal, 6 fevrier, 1891.
—— (1891) *Vive la protection*, Montréal.
Bédard, L'Abbé (1984) 'Le Play et la réforme social', *La Revue Canadienne*, vol. 30, pp. 664–694.
Beigie, Carl E. (and J. Maxwell) (1977) *Quebec's Vulnerability in Energy*, Montreal, C. D. Howe Research Institute.
Bélanger, Gérard (1985) 'La lecture des économists, est-elle si pauvre?', *Recherches sociographiques*, vol. 26, pp. 361–364.
Berger, Carl (1969) *Imperialism and Nationalism, 1884–1914: a Conflict in Canadian Thought*, Toronto, University of Toronto Press.
—— (1970) *The Sense of Power: Studies in Canadian Imperialism*, Toronto, University of Toronto Press.
—— (1976) *The Writing of Canadian History*, Toronto, Oxford University Press.
Bertram, Gordon W. (1962) 'Historical Statistics on Growth and Structure of

Manufacturing in Canada, 1870–1957', *Canadian Political Association Conference on Statistics, June, 1962*, Toronto, University of Toronto Press (1964).
—— (1963) 'Economic Growth in Canadian Industry, 1870-1915: The Staple Model and the Take-Off Hypothesis', *Canadian Journal of Economics and Political Science*, vol. 29, pp. 159–184.
—— (1973) 'The Relevance of the Wheat Boom in Canadian Economic Growth', *Canadian Journal of Economics*, vol. 6, pp. 545–566.
Bhatia, K. (and M. Frankena) (1973) 'Canadian Contributions to Economic Journals, 1968-1972', *Canadian Journal of Economics*, vol. 6, pp. 121–124.
Bilodeau, Georges-Marie (1926) *Pour rester au pays*, Québec, L'action Sociale.
—— (1931) *Le vrai remède*, Québec, L'action Sociale.
Binhammer, Helmut H. (1988) *Money Banking and the Canadian Financial System*, (5th edition) Toronto, Methuen.
Bird, Richard (1970) *The Growth of Government Spending in Canada*, Toronto, Canadian Tax Foundation.
—— (1979) *Financing Canadian Government: a Quantitative Overview*, Toronto, Canadian Tax Foundation.
—— (1987) 'Federalism and Regional Disparities: a Review Article', *Canadian Public Policy*, vol. 13, pp. 380–383.
Bladen, Vincent W. (and A. F. W. Plumptre) (1927) 'Analysis of Price Indexes in Canada', *Canadian Historical Review*, vol. 8, p. 246.
—— (1927) 'Operating Combinations in Canadian Industry as Revealed by the Census of Manufacturing', *American Economic Review*, vol. 17, pp. 601–604.
—— (1928) 'the Size of Establishments in Canadian and American Industry', *Contributions to Canadian Economics*, vol. 1, pp. 56–61.
—— (1932) 'Combines and Public Policy', *Proceeding of the Canadian Political Science Association*, vol. 4, pp. 168–170.
—— (1935) 'The Economics of Federation', *Canadian Journal of Economics and Political Science*, vol. 1, pp. 348–351.
—— (1941 and 1956) *An Introduction to Political Economy*, Toronto, University of Toronto Press.
—— (1960) 'A Journal is Born', *Canadian Journal of Economics and Political Science*, vol. 26, pp. 1–6.
Blaug, Mark (1968) *Economic Theory in Retrospect*, Homewood, Richard D. Irwin.
—— (1980) *The Methodology of Economics*, Cambridge, Cambridge University Press.
Blythe, C. D. (and E. B. Carty) (1956) 'Non-Resident Ownership of Canadian Industry', *Canadian Journal of Economics and Political Science*, vol. 22, pp. 449–460.
Boadway, Robin W. (and J. M. Treddenick) (1978) 'General Equilibrium Effects of the Canadian Tariff Structure', *Canadian Journal of Economics*, vol. 11, pp. 424–446.
—— (and K. Norrie) (1980) 'Constitutional Reform Canadian Style: An Economic Perspective', *Canadian Public Policy*, vol. 6, pp. 492–505.
—— (and N. Bruce and J. Mintz) (1982) 'Corporate Taxation and the Cost of Holding Inventories', *Canadian Journal of Economics*, vol. 15, pp. 278–93.
—— (and F. Flatters) (1982) 'Efficiency and Equalization Payments in a Federal System of Government: A Synthesis and Extension of Recent Results', *Canadian Journal of Economics*, vol. 15, pp. 611–633.

—— (and F. Flatters and A. Leblanc) (1983) 'Revenue Sharing and the Equalization of Natural Resource Revenues', *Canadian Public Policy*, vol. 9, pp. 174-180.
—— (and D. E. Wildasin) (1984) *Public Sector Economics*, (2nd edition) Boston, Little, Brown and Co.
Boggs, Theodore (1915) 'Capital Investments and Trade Balances within the British Empire', *Quarterly Journal of Economics*, vol. xx, pp. 768-93.
—— (1922) *International Trade Balance in Theory and Practice*, New York, Macmillan.
Boland, Lawrence A. (1982) *The Foundations of Economic Method*, London, George Allen & Unwin.
Boreham, Gordon F. (and R. G. Bodkin) (1988) *Money and Banking: Analysis and Policy in a Canadian Context*, (3rd edition) Toronto, Holt.
Boucher, Pierre (1664) *Histoire véritable et naturelle des moeurs et productions de la Nouvelle France*, Paris. (Republished in 1964, Boucherville, Société historique de Boucherville).
Bouchette, Joseph (1832) *The British Dominions in North America*, London, Longman.
Bouchette, Robert E. (1901) *Emparons-nous de l'industrie*, Ottawa, L'Imprimerie générale.
—— (1905) *Etudes sociales et économiques sur le Canada*, Montréal, Wilson.
—— (1913) *L'indépendance économique du Canada français*, Montréal, Wilson et Lafleur.
Bourgault, Pierre L. (1972) *Innovation and the Structure of Canadian Industry*, Ottawa, The Science Council of Canada.
Boyle, George (1941) *Democracy's Second Chance: Land, Work and Co-operation*, New York, Sheed and Ward.
Bradfield, Michael (1988) *Regional Economics: Analysis and Policies in Canada*, Toronto, McGraw-Hill.
Brecher, Irving (1950) 'Investment Income and Output', *Canadian Journal of Economics and Political Science*, vol. 16, pp. 83 ff.
—— (1957) *Monetary and Fiscal Thought and Policy in Canada, 1919-1939*, Toronto, University of Toronto Press.
—— (1981) *Canada's Competition Policy Revisited: Some New Thoughts on an Old Story*, Montreal, Institute for Research on Public Policy.
Breckenridge, Roeliff M. (1894) *The Canadian Banking System, 1777-1890*, New York, Macmillan.
Breton, Albert (1965) 'A Theory of Government Grants', *Canadian Journal of Economics and Political Science*, vol. 31, pp. 173-187.
—— (1967) *Discriminatory Government Policies in Federal Countries*, Montreal, Private Planning Association.
—— (1974) *An Economic Theory of Representative Government*, Chicago, Aldine.
—— (1978) (with A. D. Scott) *The Economic Constitution of Federal States*, Toronto, University of Toronto Press.
—— (1980) (with A. Scott) *The Design of Federations*, Montreal, Institute for Research on Public Policy.
—— (with R. Wintrobe) (1980) *The Logic of Bureaucratic Conduct: an Economic Analysis of Competition, Exchange, and Efficiency in Private and Public Organizations*, Cambridge, Cambridge University Press.
Brewis, Thomas N. *et al.* (eds) (1966) *Canadian Economic Policy Since the War*, Montreal, Private Planning Association.

—— (1969) *Regional Economic Policy in Canada*, Toronto, Macmillan.
Britnell, George E. (1939) *The Wheat Economy*, Toronto, University of Toronto Press.
Britton, John N. N. (and J. M. Gilmour) (1978) *The Weakest Link*, Ottawa, The Science Council of Canada.
Brown, R. B. (1967) 'D'Arcy McGee and the Economic Aspects of the New Nationality', *Canadian Historical Association Annual Report*, pp. 95–104.
Brown, Robert C. (1964) *Canada's National Policy*, Princeton, Princeton University Press.
Brown, T. Merritt (1964) *Canadian Economic Growth*, Ottawa, The Queen's Printer.
Bryce, Robert B. (1986) *Maturing in Hard Times*, Kingston and Montreal, McGill-Queen's.
Buchanan, Isaac (1864) *The Relations of the Industry of Canada with the Mother Country and the United States*, Montreal, Lovell.
—— (1866) *A Government Specie-Paying Bank of Issue and other Subversive Legislation Proposed by the Minister of Finance*, Hamilton, Spectator.
Buckley, Kenneth (1958) 'The Role of Staple Industries in Canada's Economic Development', *Journal of Economic History*, vol. 18, pp. 439–452.
—— (1959) Review of O. J. Firestone, *Canada's Economic Development, 1867–1953, American Economic Review*, vol. 49, pp. 431–433.
—— (1970) *Capital Formation in Canada, 1896–1930*, Toronto, McClelland and Stewart.
Byles, Bernard (1872) *Sophisms of Free Trade and Popular Political Economy Examined*, Philadelphia, Henry Carey Baird.
Cameron, Duncan, ed. (1985) *Explorations in Canadian Economic History: Essays in Honour of Irene M. Spry*, Ottawa, University of Ottawa Press.
Canada (1926) *Report*, Royal Commission on Maritime Rights, Ottawa.
—— (1935) *Report*, Royal Commission on Financial Arrangements between the Dominion and the Provinces, Ottawa.
—— (1937) *Report*, Royal Commission on Price Spreads, Ottawa.
—— (1939) *Report*, Royal Commission on Dominion-Provincial Relations, Ottawa.
—— (1944) *Report*, Royal Commission on Provincial Development and Rehabilitation, Ottawa.
—— (1945) *Employment and Income*, Department of Reconstruction.
—— (1957–58) *Report*, Royal Commission on Canada's Economic Prospects, Ottawa.
—— (1964) *Report*, Royal Commission on Banking and Finance, Ottawa.
—— (1966) *Report*, Royal Commission on Taxation, Ottawa.
—— (1968) *Report*, Task Force on the Structure of Canadian Industry, Ottawa, Privy Council Office.
—— (1978) *Report*, Royal Commission on Corporate Concentration. Ottawa.
—— (1985) *Report*, Royal Commission on the Economic Union and Development Prospects for Canada, Ottawa.
—— (1986) *Report*, Royal Commission of Inquiry into the Collapse of the CCB and Northland Bank, Ottawa.
Canadian Institute of Public Affairs (1963) *Economic Planning in a Democratic Society*, Toronto, University of Toronto Press.
Carey, Henry C. (1858–59) *Principles of Social Science*, Philadelphia, J. B. Lippincott.
Carmichael-Smyth, R. (1849) *The Employment of the People and the Capital of Great Britain in Her Own Colonies*, London, W. P. Metchim.

Carr, Jack Leslie (1972) (with Mathewson, F. G. and McManus, J. C.) *Cents and Nonsense*, Toronto, Holt, Rinehart and Winston.

Carrier, Hervé (1960) *Le sociologue canadien, Léon Gérin: 1863–1951*, Montréal, Institut Social Populaire.

Carrothers, William A. (1935) 'Problems of the Canadian Confederation', *Canadian Journal of Economics and Political Science*, vol. 1, pp. 26–40.

—— (1941) *The British Columbia Fisheries*, Toronto, University of Toronto Press.

Carson, Richard (1973) *Comparative Economic Systems*, New York, Macmillan.

Cassidy, Harry M. (1943) *Social Security and Reconstruction in Canada*, Toronto, Ryerson.

Caves, Richard E. (and R. H. Holton) (1961) *The Canadian Economy: Prospect and Retrospect*, Cambridge, Harvard University Press.

—— (1965) '"Vent for Surplus" Models of Trade and Growth', in R. E. Baldwin *et al.*, *Trade Growth, and the Balance of Payments: Essays in Honor of Gottfried Haberler*, Chicago, Rand McNally and North Holland Publishing Co. pp. 95–115.

—— (1971) 'Export-led Growth and the New Economic History' in J. N. Bhagwati *et al.*, *Trade, Balance of Payments and Growth*, Amsterdam, North Holland. pp. 403–442.

Chambers, Edward J. (and Bertram, G. W.) (1966) 'Urbanization and Manufacturing in Canada, 1870–1890', *Canadian Political Science Association Conference on Statistics, June, 1964*, Toronto, pp. 225-258.

—— (and Gordon, D.) (1966) 'Primary Products and Economic Growth, an Empirical Measurement', *Journal of Political Economy*, vol. 74, pp. 315–32.

Chant, John F. (and A. L. K. Acheson) (1971) 'Choice of Monetary Instruments and the Theory of Bureaucracy', Ottawa, Carleton Economic Papers.

—— (and A. L. K. Acheson) (1971) 'Mythology and Central Banking', Ottawa, Carleton Economic Papers.

—— (and A. L. K. Acheson) (1972) 'Bureaucratic Theory and the Choice of Central Bank Goals: the Case of the Bank of Canada', Carleton Economic Papers.

Chapleau, Joseph A. (1881) *Discourse de l'Honourable M. Chapleau, prononcé a Ste. Thérès le 3 Novembre, 1881*, Montréal.

—— (1882) *Discourse en proposant la vente du Chemin de Fer Québec Montréal, Ottawa et Occidental, à l'assemblée legislative*, Québec, Coté.

Clark, W. C. (1917) 'Shall Maximum Prices Be Fixed', *Bulletin of the Departments of History and Political and Economic Science at Queen's University*, no. 27.

Clark-Jones, Melissa (1987) *A Staple State: Canadian Industrial Resources in Cold War*, Toronto, University of Toronto Press.

Clement, Wallace (and G. Williams) (1989) *The New Canadian Political Economy*, Kingston, McGill-Queen's.

Coady, Moses M. (1939) *Masters of their Own Destiny*, London, Harper.

Coase, Ronald H. (1937) 'The Nature of the Firm', *Economica*, vol. 14, pp. 386–405.

—— (1988) 'R. H. Coase Lectures', *Journal of Law, Economics and Organization*, vol. 4, pp. 3–64.

Coe, V. F. (1935) 'The Gains of Trade', *Canadian Journal of Economics and Political Science*, vol. 1, pp. 588–598.

Cohen, Robert, (1979) ed. *The Multinational Corporation: a Radical Approach*, Cambridge, Cambridge University Press.

Comeau, Robert (1969) *Economie québécoise*, Montréal, Presses de l'Université du Québec.

Cooney, R. (1832) *A Compendious History of the Northern Part of the Province of New Brunswick and of the District of Gaspé*, Halifax, Joseph Howe.

Cooper, J. I. (1937) 'Some Early French Canadian Advocacy of Protection', *Canadian Journal of Economics and Political Science*, vol. 3, pp. 530–540.

Copes, Parsival (1982) 'The Market as an Open Access Commons: A Neglected Aspect of Excess Capacity', *Discussion Paper 82-04-2*, Burnaby, Simon Fraser University.

Cornwall, John (and Wendy Maclean) (1984) *Economic Recovery for Canada*, Ottawa, Canadian Institute for Economic Policy.

Courchene, Thomas (1976) *Money, Inflation and the Bank of Canada*, Montreal, C. D. Howe Research Institute.

—— (1978) *The Strategy of Gradualism: An Analysis of Bank of Canada Policy from Mid-1975 to Mid-1977*, Montreal, C. D. Howe Research Institute.

Coyne, James (1959) *Money and Growth*, Remarks prepared for delivery at a meeting of the Canadian Club of Montreal, Nov. 16.

—— (1959) *Credit and Capital*, Remarks prepared for delivery at a meeting of the Investment Dealers Association of Canada (Ontario District) Toronto, Dec. 14.

—— (1960) *Living Within Our Means*, an address to the Canadian Club of Winnipeg, Jan. 8.

—— (1960) *Foreign Debt and Unemployment*, an address to the Canadian Club of Toronto, Nov. 14.

—— (1961) *Strong Roots for New Growth*, an address to the Annual Meeting of the Newfoundland Board of Trade, St. John's, Jan. 31.

—— (1961) *Balance of Payment Problems in North America*, an address to the Economic Club of New York, Mar. 7.

Crane, David (1981) *Beyond the Monetarists: Post-Keynesian Alternatives to Rapid Inflation, Slow Growth and High Unemployment*, Ottawa, Canadian Institute for Economic Policy.

Creighton, Donald C. (1937) *The Commercial Empire of the St. Lawrence*, Toronto, Ryerson.

Crosskill, John H. (1838) *A Comprehensive Outline of the Geography and History of Nova Scotia*, Halifax.

Cudmore, S. A. (1912) *Economics for Canadian Students*, Toronto.

Currie, Archibald W. (1942) *Canadian Economic Development*, Toronto, Nelson.

Dales, John H. (1960) 'A Comparison of Manufacturing Industry in Quebec and Ontario', in Mason Wade, ed., *La Dualité Canadienne*, Québec, Presses Universitaires Laval.

—— (1966) *The Protective Tariff in Canada's Development*, Toronto, University of Toronto Press.

—— (1968) 'Canadian Scholarship in Economics', in R. H. Hubbard and Watson Kirkconnel, eds, *Scholarship in Canada, 1967: Achievement and Outlook*, Toronto, University of Toronto Press, pp. 82–93.

—— (1986) 'Comment', in S. L. Engerman and R. E. Gallman, eds, *Long Term Factors in American Economic Growth*, Chicago, University of Chicago Press, pp. 92–93.

Daly, Donald J. (and S. Globerman) (1976) *Tariff and Science Policies: Application of a Model of Nationalism*, Toronto, Ontario Economic Council.

Davis, Robert (1867) *The Currency, What It Is and What It Should Be*, Ottawa, Hunter & Rose.

Dehem, Roger (1968) *Planification économique et fédéralisme*, Genève, Librarie Droz.
—— (1978) *Précis d'histoire de la théorie économique*, Québec, Les Presses de l'Université Laval.
—— (1978) *On the Meaning of Economic Association*, Montreal, C. D. Howe Research Institute.
—— (1982) *Précis d'économie internationale*, Paris, Dunod.
Denison, Merrill (1966) *Canada's First Bank*, Toronto, McClelland and Stewart.
Denys, Nicolas [L. A.] (1672) *The Description and Natural History of The Coasts of North America*, Paris.
Desjardins, Alphonse (1912) *Le Caisse Populaire*, Montréal, L'Ecole sociale populaire.
Dimand, Robert (1988) 'An Early Contribution to Mathematical Economics: J. B. Cherryman's review of Cournot', *Canadian Journal of Economics*, vol. 21, pp. 610–616.
Donald, William J. A. (1915) *The Canadian Iron and Steel Industry*, New York, Houghton Mifflin.
Donner, Arthur (and D. D. Peters) (1979) *The Monetarist Counter-Revolution: a Critique of Canadian Monetary Policy, 1975–1979*, Ottawa, Canadian Institute for Economic Policy.
Douglass, William A. (1884) 'Wages', *Proceedings of the Canadian Institute*, November 27.
—— (1885) 'Rent, a Criticism of Professor Walker's Work on that Subject', *Proceedings of the Canadian Institute*, December 12.
—— (1887) 'The Antagonism of Social Forces', *Proceedings of the Canadian Institute*, February, 19.
—— (1912) 'Canadian Problems and Politics', *Westminster Review*, vol. 177, pp. 399–404.
Drapeau, Stanislas (1863) *Etudes sur les développements de la colonisation du Bas-Canada depuis des ans: 1851–1861*, Québec, Brousseau.
—— (1864) *Coup d'oeil sur les resources productives*, Québec, Brousseau.
Drummond, Ian M. (1987) *Progress without Planning: The Economic History of Ontario from Confederation to the Second World War*, Toronto, University of Toronto Press.
Dubé, Yves (1965) 'Tax Power Versus Spending Responsibilities: An Historical Analysis of Federal-Provincial Finances', University in League for Social Reform *The Prospect for Change*, Toronto, University of Toronto Press.
Dumesnil, Clement (1849) *De l'abolition des droits fédaux et seigneriaux au Canada*, Montréal, Rédaction Québec.
Dunlop, J. Bruce (1987) (with D. McQueen and M. Treblicock) *Canadian Competition Policy*, Toronto, Canada Law Book Inc.
Durham, John George Lambton, The First Earl of (1839) *Report on the Affairs of British North America from the Earl of Durham*, Toronto, Examiner.
Easterbrook, W. Thomas (and H. G. J. Aitken) (1958) *Canadian Economic History*, Toronto, Macmillan.
—— (1959) 'Recent Contributions to Economic History in Canada', *Journal of Economic History*, vol. 19, pp. 76–102.
—— (1959) 'Trends in Canadian Economic Thought', *South Atlantic Quarterly*, vol. 58, pp. 91–107.

—— (1967) (with M. H. Watkins) *Approaches to Canadian Economic History*, Toronto, McClelland and Stewart.
Eastman, Harry C. (and S. Stykolt) (1967) *The Tariff and Competition in Canada*, Toronto, Macmillan.
Eccles, William J. (1972) *France in America*, New York, Harper.
—— (1979) 'A Belated Review of Harold Adams Innis, *The Fur Trade in Canada*', *Canadian Historical Review*, vol. 50, pp. 1-22.
Economic Council of Canada (1969) *Interim Report on Competition Policy*, Ottawa.
—— (1975) *Looking Outward*, Ottawa.
—— (1982) *Financing Confederation*, Ottawa.
Elliot, G. A. (1936) 'Transfer of Means of Payment and the Terms of Trade', *Canadian Journal of Economics and Political Science*, vol. 2, pp. 481–492.
Ely, Richard T. (1894) *Socialism and Social Reform*, New York, Thomas Y. Crowell.
English, H. Edward (1964) *Industrial Structure in Canada's Competitive Position*, Montreal, Private Planning Association.
Fabre, Hector (1871) *Confederation, indépendance, annexation*, address to the Canadian Institute at Quebec, March 15, 1871.
Falardeau, Jean-Charles (1944) 'Problems and First Experiments of Social Research in Quebec', *Canadian Journal of Economics and Political Science*, vol. 30, pp. 664–694.
—— (1953) *Essais sur le Québec contemporain*, Québec, Presses Université Laval.
Faucher, Albert (1949–51) 'L'enseignement des sciences sociales au Canada de langue français', *Royal Commission Studies*, Commission Royale d'inquête sur l'avancement des Arts, lettres et sciences au Canada, Ottawa, pp. 191–203.
—— (1962) L'histoire économique de la Province de Québec jusqu'à la fin du XIX siècle', in F. Dumont et Y. Martin, *Situation de la recherche sur le Canada français*, Québec, Les Presses Université Laval. pp. 45–53.
—— (1970) *Histoire économique et unité canadienne*, Montréal, Fides.
—— (1988) *Cinquant ans de sciences sociales à l'Université Laval: l'histoire de la Faculté des sciences sociales (1938–1988)*, Québec, Presses de l'Université Laval.
Fauteux, Joseph-Noêl (1927) *Essai sur l'industrie au Canada sous le régime français*, Québec, L-. A. Proulx.
Fay, Charles Ryle (1923) 'Mearns and the Miramichi: An Episode in Canadian Economic History', *Canadian Historical Review*, vol. 4, pp. 316–320.
—— (1924–25) 'The Problems of the Maritime Provinces', *Dalhousie Review*, vol. 4, pp. 438–451.
—— (1930) 'The Economic Development of the Maritime Provinces', *The Cambridge History of the British Empire*, Cambridge, U. P., vol. 4, ch. 24, pp. 657–671.
—— (1934–37) 'The Toronto School of Economics', *Economic History*, vol. 3, pp. 168–171.
—— (1956) *Life and Labour in Newfoundland*, Toronto, University of Toronto Press.
Firestone, Otto J. (1958) *Canadian Economic Development, 1867–1958*, London, Bowes & Bowes.
—— (1974) (ed.) *Regional Economic Development*, Ottawa, University of Ottawa Press.
Forbes, Ernest R. (1978) 'In Search of Post Confederation Maritime Historiography, 1900–1967', *Acadiensis*, vol. 8, pp. 23-31.
—— (1979) *The Maritimes Rights Movement, 1919–1927*, Kingston and Montreal, McGill–Queen's.

Fortin, Pierre (1984) 'La recherche économique dans les universités de Québec français: les sources de rupture avec le passé et les défis de l'avenir', G.- H. Levesque, *Continuité et rupture, les sciences sociales au Québec*, Montréal, PUM.

Fournier, Jules (1865) *Le Canada: son présent et son avenir politique et finances*, Montréal.

Fournier, Pierre (1978) 'Les nouveaux paramètres de la bourgeoisie québecoise', *Le capitalisme au Québec*, Montréal, Albert Saint-Martin.

Fowke, Vernon C. (1946) *Canadian Agricultural Policy: the Historical Pattern*, London, Oxford University Press.

—— (1952) 'The National Policy – Old and New', *Canadian Journal of Economics and Political Science*, vol. 18, pp. 271–286.

Freeman, Ralph Evans (1928) *Economics for Canadians*, Toronto.

Friedman, Milton (1953) *Essays in Positive Economics*, Chicago, University of Chicago Press.

—— (1962) *Capitalism and Freedom*, Chicago, University of Chicago Press.

—— (1968) 'The Role of Monetary Policy', *American Economic Review*, vol. 58, pp. 1-17.

Gagnon, Marcel-Aimé (1962) *La vie orageuse d'Olivar Asselin*, Montréal, Editions de l'homme.

Galbraith, John K. (and A. L. Guthrie) (1977) *Review, Efficiency and Regulation: A Study of Deposit Institutions*, Ottawa, Economic Council of Canada; *Canadian Banking Legislation*, Ottawa, Department of Finance White Paper, *Canadian Public Policy*, vol. 3, pp. 101–106.

Galbraith, Thomas (1863) *New Monetary Theory*, Montreal, J. Starke.

—— (1874) *Bensalem or the New Economy*, New York, Thomas Galbraith.

—— (1882) *A New Chapter Added to Political Economy Pointing Out a 100 Millions Dollar Capital*, Toronto, Hunter & Rose.

Galt, Alexander Tilloch (1860) *Canada, 1849–1859*, London, Hardwicke.

George, Peter (1968) 'Rates of Return in Railway Investment and Implications for Government Subsidization of the Canadian Pacific Railway', *Canadian Journal of Economics*, vol. 1, pp. 740–762.

—— (1989) 'Classical Writings in Canadian Economic History: Natural Resources in Canadian Economic Development', in Deborah C. Poff (ed.) *Research Tools in Canadian Studies*, Montreal, Association for Canadian Studies.

Gérin-Lajoie, Antoine (1874) *Jean Rivard le défricheur*, Montréal, Editions du Devoir (1925).

—— (1876) *Jean Rivard l'économiste*, Montréal, Editions du Devoir (1925).

Gesner, Abraham (1847) *New Brunswick, with Notes for Emigrants*, London, Simons and Ward.

—— (1849) *The Industrial Resources of Nova Scotia*, Halifax, A. & W. MacKinlay.

Gibbon, John M. (1935) *Steel of Empire*, Toronto, McClelland.

Gibson, J. D. (1956) 'The Changing Influence of the United States on the Canadian Economy', *Canadian Journal of Economics and Political Science*, vol. 22, pp. 421–36.

Gillespie, W. Irwin (1976) (with J. A. Johnson) 'Sales Tax Reform: A Critique of the Federal Government's Proposals', *Canadian Public Policy*, vol. 2, pp. 638–644.

—— (1979) 'Post War Canadian Fiscal Policy Revisited', *Canadian Taxation Journal*, vol. 1, pp. 156–176.

—— (1980) *The Redistribution of Income in Canada*, Agincourt, Gage.

—— (1981) 'The Mythology of Musgrave's Multiple Budget Approach', *Canadian Taxation Journal*, vol. 3, pp. 38–44.
—— (1983) 'Tax Reform, the Battle Field, the Strategy, the Spoils', *Canadian Public Administration*, vol. X, pp. 182–202.
—— (1983) 'The 1981 Federal Budget: Muddling Through or Purposeful Tax Reform', *Canadian Taxation Journal*, vol. 4, pp. 975–1002.
Girod, Amury (1834) *Conversations sur l'agriculture par un habitant de Varennes*, Québec, Frécette.
Goodhart, Charles (1985) *The Evolution of Central Banking*, London, London School of Economics.
Goodwin, Craufurd D. W. (1961) *Canadian Economic Thought*, London, Cambridge University Press.
—— (1969) 'A Forgotten Fore Runner of Social Credit, William Alexander Thompson', *Journal of Canadian Studies*, vol. 4, pp. 41–5.
Gordon, H. Scott (1954) 'The Economic Theory of a Common Property Resource: the Fishery', *Journal of Political Economy*, vol. 62, pp. 124–142.
—— (1961) *The Economists versus the Bank of Canada*, Toronto, Ryerson.
Goselin, Paul-Eugène (ed.) (1964) *Etienne Parent*, Montréal, Fides.
Goulding, Jay (1982) *Newfoundland in Crisis*, Ottawa, Sisyphus Press.
Gourlay, Robert (1822) *Statistical Account of Upper Canada*, London, Simpkin.
Graham, John (1963) *Fiscal Adjustment and Economic Development: a Case Study of Nova Scotia*, Toronto, University of Toronto Press.
—— (1971) 'Chez Who?', *Canadian Journal of Economics*, vol. 4, pp. 431–440.
Grant, D. (1974) 'The Staple Theory and Its Measurement', *Journal of Political Economy*, vol. 82, pp. 1249–1253.
Granatstein, Jack L. (1982) *The Ottawa men: the Civil Service Mandarins, 1935–1957*, Toronto, Oxford University Press.
Green, Allan (1986) 'Growth and Productivity Change in the Canadian Railway Sector, 1871–1926', in S. L. Engerman and R. E. Gallman, *Long Term Factors in American Economic Growth*, Chicago, University of Chicago Press.
Green, Christopher (1976) *Canadian Industrial Organization and Policy*, Toronto, McGraw-Hill.
Griffin, George D. (1883) *Important Information on Banking*, Hamilton, Griffin.
Grubel, Herbert (1983) *Free market Zones: Deregulating Canadian Enterprise*, Vancouver, The Fraser Institute.
Haliburton, Robert Grant (1868) *Inter-Colonial Trade our Only Safeguard against Disunion*, Ottawa, Desbarats.
—— (1872) *A Review of British Diplomacy and its Fruits*, London, Low.
Haliburton, Thomas C. (1829) *An Historical and Statistical Account of Nova Scotia*, Halifax, Joseph Howe.
—— (1832) *A General Description of Nova Scotia*, Halifax, Joseph Howe.
—— (1836) *The Clockmaker*, Halifax, Joseph Howe.
Hammond, Bray (1957) *Banks and Politics in America*, Princeton, Princeton University Press.
Hankin, Francis (and T. W. A. MacDermot) (1933) *Recovery by Control*, Toronto, J. M. Dent.
Harpell, James John (1911) *The Canadian National Economy*, Toronto, Macmillan.
Harris, Richard G. (and D. Cox) (1984) *Trade, Industrial Policy, and Canadian Manufacturing*, Toronto, Ontario Economic Council.

Hartland, Penelope (1955) 'Factors in Economic Growth in Canada', *Journal of Economic History*, vol. 15, pp. 13–22.
Hartle, Douglas G. (1979) *Public Policy, Decision Making, and Regulation*, Montreal, Institute for Research on Public Policy.
Harvey, D. C. (1933-34) 'The Intellectual Awakening of Nova Scotia', *Dalhousie Review*, vol. 13, pp. 1–22.
Hawtrey, Ralph G. (1928) *Trade and Credit*, London, Longmans Green.
Hettich, Walter P. (1984) (with S. L. Winer) 'A Positive Model of Tax Structure', *Journal of Public Economics*, vol. 24, pp. 67–87.
—— (1986) (with S. L. Winer) 'Vertical Imbalance in the Fiscal System of Federal States', *Canadian Journal of Economics*, vol. 19, pp. 745–765.
Higgins, Benjamin (1951) *What Do Economists Know?*, Melbourne, Melbourne University Press.
—— (1959) *Economic Development: Principles, Problems and Policy*, New York, Norton.
—— (1970) (with A. Martin, A. Raynauld) *Les orientations de développement économique regional dans la province du Québec*, Ottawa, Ministère de l'expansion économique régional.
—— (and D. J. Savoie) (1988) *Regional Economic Development: Essays in Honour of François Perroux*, Boston, Unwin Hyman.
Hincks, Francis (1884) *Reminiscences of His Public Life*, Montreal, Drysdale.
Hincks, William (1861) 'On the True Aims, Foundations and Claims to Attention of the Science of Political Economy', *The Canadian Journal*, vol. 6, pp. 20–28.
—— (1862) 'An Enquiry into the Natural Laws which Regulate the Interchange of commodities between Individuals and Nations and the Effects of Interference with Them', *The Canadian Journal*, vol. 7, pp. 180–190.
—— (1866–67) 'Notes on some Practically Interesting Questions in Economical Science Bearing on the Prosperity of Countries Situated Such as Ours', *The Canadian Journal*, vol. 11, pp. 96–113.
Hollander, Samuel (1979) *The Economics of David Ricardo*, Toronto, University of Toronto Press.
Hood, William (and A. Scott) (1955) *Output, Labour and Capital in the Canadian Economy*, Ottawa, Royal Commission on Canada's Economic Prospects.
Howe, Joseph (1909) *Speeches and Public Letters*, Halifax, Chronicle.
Howitt, Peter (1986) 'The Keynesian Recovery', *Canadian Journal of Economics*, vol. 19, pp. 626–641.
Hurlbert, Jesse Beaufort (1870) *Field and Factory Side by Side, or How to Establish and Develop Native Industries*, Montreal, Lovell.
—— (1882) *Protection and Free Trade with Special Reference to Canada and Newly Settled Countries: History of Tariffs and What They Teach*, Ottawa, A. S. Woodburn.
Husbandman, A. (1897) *Money and the Money Question*, Toronto, Hunter & Rose.
Hutchison, Terrence W. (1978) *On Revolutions and Progress in Economic Thought*, Cambridge, Cambridge University Press.
Ingerman, Sidney H. (1981) *Economic Policy, Economic Theory and the Democratic Left*, Ottawa, Center for Policy Alternatives.
Inman, Mark K. (1959) *Economics in a Canadian Setting*, Toronto, Copp Clark.
Innis, Harold A. (1923) *A History of the Canadian Pacific Railway*, London, P. S. King.

—— (1929) 'Notes and Comments', *Contributions to Canadian Economics*, vol. 2, pp. 5-7.
—— (1930) *The Fur Trade in Canada*, New Haven, Yale University Press.
—— (1931) 'Government Ownership in Canada', *Schriften des Vereins für Sozialpolitick*, vol. 176, pp. 241-279.
—— (1933) (*et al.*) *The Problems of Staple Production in Canada*, Toronto, Ryerson Press.
—— (1934) (*et al.*) *The Canadian Economy and its Problems*, Toronto, Canadian Institute of International Affairs.
—— (1935) 'The Role of Intelligence: Some Further Notes', *Canadian Journal of Economics and Political Science*, vol. 1, pp. 280-287.
—— (1936) *Settlement and the Mining Frontier*, Toronto, Macmillan.
—— (1936) 'The State of Economic Science in Canada', *Commerce Journal*, February.
—— (1938) (ed.) *Essays in Political Economy*, Toronto, University of Toronto Press.
—— (1940) *The Cod Fisheries*, New Haven, Yale University Press.
—— (1940) *The Diary of Alexander McPhail*, Toronto, University of Toronto Press.
—— (1941) 'Introduction', R. H. Fleming, *Minutes of Council, Northern Department of Rupert Land, 1821-1831*, Publications of the Champlain Society, pp. xi-lxxvii.
—— (1942) 'Imperfect Regional Competition and Political Institutions of the North Atlantic Seaboard', *Commerce Journal*, pp. 21-26.
—— (1951) *The Bias of Communication*, Toronto, University of Toronto Press.
—— (1954) *The Cod Fisheries*, Toronto, University of Toronto Press.
—— (1956) *Essays in Canadian Economic History*, Toronto, University of Toronto Press.
—— (1972) 'Snarkov Island', 'A Defence of the Tariff', R. F. Neill, *A New Theory of Value*, Toronto, University of Toronto Press, pp. 146-159.
Jackson, G. E. (1922) 'Wheat and the Trade Cycle', *Canadian Historical Review*, vol. 3, pp. 256-274.
—— (1928) 'Cycles of Employment in Canada', *Contributions to Canadian Economics*, vol. 1, pp. 40-53.
James, R. Warren (1965) *John Rae, Political Economist: an Account of His Life and a Compilation of His Main Writings*, Toronto, University of Toronto Press.
Jenkin, Michael (1983) *The Challenge of Diversity*, Ottawa, The Science Council of Canada.
Johnson, Harry G. (1944) *The Antigonish Movement*, Antigonish, Extension Department, St. Francis Xavier University.
—— (1953) 'Equilibrium Growth in an International Economy', *Canadian Journal of Economics and Political Science*, vol. 19, pp. 478-500.
—— (1955) Review of R. Dehem, *L'éfficacité du système économique: criteriologie de la politique économique*, *Canadian Journal of Economics and Political Science*, vol. 21, pp. 102-114.
—— (1961) 'Problems of Canadian Nationalism', *International Journal*, vol. 16, pp. 238-250.
—— (1962) *Money, Trade and Economic Growth*, London, Unwin University Books.
—— (1963) *The Canadian Quandary*, Toronto, McGraw-Hill.
—— (1965) 'A Theoretical Model of Nationalism in New and Developing States', *Political Science Quarterly*, vol. 80, pp. 169-185.
—— (1965) Review of M. C. Kemp, *The Pure Theory of International Trade*, *Canadian Journal of Economics and Political Science*, vol. 31, pp. 139-144.

—— (1967) *Economic Nationalism in Old and New States*, Chicago, University of Chicago Press.
—— (1967) *Essays in Monetary Economics*, London, Unwin University Books.
—— (1968) 'Canadian Contributions to the Discipline of Economics since 1945', *Canadian Journal of Economics*, vol. 1, pp. 129-146.
—— (1969) 'On Demolishing Barriers to Trade', *Rebuilding the Liberal Order*, London, Institute of Economic Affairs.
—— (1972) *Macroeconomics and Monetary Theory*, Chicago, Aldine Publishing Company.
—— (1973) *The Theory of Income Distribution*, London, Gray-Mills Publishing.
—— (1974) 'The Current and Prospective State of Economics in Canada', T. N. Guinsburg and G. I. Reuber, *Perspectives on the Social Sciences in Canada*, Toronto, University of Toronto Press.
—— (1974) *General Equilibrium Analysis*, London, George, Allen & Unwin.
—— (1975) *On Economics and Society*, Chicago, University of Chicago Press.
—— (1975) (with E. S. Johnson) *In The Shadow of Keynes*, Oxford, Basil Blackwell.
—— (1978) (Lipsey, R. G. et al., eds) *The Harry Johnson Memorial Symposium*, *Canadian Journal of Economics*, vol. 11, Supplement.
—— (1979) (E. J. Belton) *Bibliography of the Published Works of Dr. Harry G. Johnson*, Thunder Bay, Lakehead University.
Jones, Robert Leslie (1946) *History of Agriculture in Ontario, 1613-1880*, Toronto, University of Toronto Press.
Kardouche, George K. (and F. Caramazza) (1973) *Wage and Price Controls for Canada?*, Montreal, C. D. Howe Research Institute.
Kearney, John F. (1983) *Common Tragedies: a Study of Resource Access in the Bay of Fundy Herring Fisheries*, Halifax, Institute of Resource and Environmental Studies, Dalhousie University.
Keirstead, Burton S. (1942) *Essentials of Price Theory*, Toronto, University of Toronto Press.
—— (1944) *The Economic Effects of the War on the Maritime Provinces*, Halifax.
—— (1948) *Theory of Economic Change*, Toronto, University of Toronto Press.
—— (1953) *An Essay on the Theory of Profits and Income Distribution*, London, Oxford University Press.
—— (1959) *Capital, Interest and Profit*, London, Oxford University Press.
Kemp, H. R. (1931) 'Is a Revision of Taxing Powers Necessary', *Proceedings of the Canadian Political Science Association*, vol. 3, pp. 185-201.
Kemp, Murray C. (and Asimkopulos, A.) (1952) 'A Note on Social Welfare Functions and Cardinal Utility', *Canadian Journal of Economics and Political Science*, vol. 18, pp. 195-200.
—— (1954) 'Welfare Economics: A Stock Taking', *Economic Record*, vol. 30, pp. 245-251.
—— (1954) 'Arrow's General Possibility Theorem', *Review of Economic Studies*, vol. 21, pp. 240-243.
Keynes, John M. (1936) *The General Theory of Employment, Interest and Money*, London, Macmillan.
Kierzkowski, Alexandre-Edouard (1852) *La question de la tenure seigneurale de bas-Canada ramenée à une question de crédit fonçier*, Montréal, Lovell.
King, William Lyon Mackenzie (1935) *Industry and Humanity*, Toronto, Macmillan.
Kitch, E. W. (1983) 'The Fire of Truth', *Journal of Law and Economics*, vol. 26, pp. 163-234.

Knight, Frank H. (1934) 'Social Science and the Political Trend', *University of Toronto Quarterly*, vol. 3, pp. 280–287.
Knox, Frank A. (1934) 'Leviathan or Octopus', *Queen's Quarterly*, vol. 41, pp. 493–498.
Knox, John Jay (1903) *A History of Banking in the United States*, New York, Bradford Rhodes.
Kotowitz, Yehuda (1985) *Positive Industrial Policy: the Implications for R. & D*, Toronto, Ontario Economic Council.
Krehm, William (1975) *Price in a Mixed Economy: Our Record of Disaster*, Toronto, Thornwood Publications.
—— (1977) *The Dynamics of Economic Breakdown*, Toronto, Thornwood Publications.
Laidlaw, Alexander F. (1961) *The Campus and the Community: the Global Impact of the Antigonish Movement*, Montreal, Harvest House.
—— (1967) *The Antigonish Movement in Retrospect*, an address given at the University of Toronto, December 9.
Laidler, David (1985) *The Demand for Money*, (3rd edition) New York, Harper.
Lamontagne, Maurice (1954) *Le fédéralisme canadien*, Québec, Les Presses Universitaires Laval.
—— (1980) *The Double Deal*, Montreal, Optimum Publishing Company.
Lamson, Cynthia, and Hanson, A. J., eds (1984) *Atlantic Fisheries and Coastal Communities: Fisheries Decision-Making Case Studies*, Halifax, Dalhousie Ocean Studies Programme.
Langelier, John-Chrysostome (1867) *Biographie de François Vezina, Caissier de la Banque Nationale*, Québec, Darveau.
La Rue, François-Alexandre-Hubert (1870) *Etude sur les industries du Québec*, Québec, Brousseau.
—— (1870–71) *Mélanges historiques, litteraires, et économie politique*, Québec.
Laureys, Henry (1914) *Essai de géographie économique du Canada*, Brussels, Falk.
—— (1927) *La conquête des marchés extérieurs*, Montréal, Bibliothéque de l'Action Français.
—— (1935) *La technique de l'exportation*, Montréal, Lévesque.
Lazar, Fred (1981) *The New Protectionism: Non-Tariff Barriers and Their Effects on Canada*, Ottawa, Canadian Institute for Economic Policy.
Leacock, Stephen B. (1920) *The Unsolved Riddle of Social Justice*, Toronto.
—— (1935) 'What Is Left of Adam Smith?', *Canadian Journal of Economics and Political Science*, vol. 1, pp. 41–51.
League for Social Reconstruction (1935) *Social Planning for Canada*, Toronto, Thomas Nelson & Sons.
Leman, Beaudry (1920) *Les institutions de crédit*, Montréal, L'Action Français.
—— (1952) *Hier et demain*, Montréal, Banque Canadienne Nationale.
Lemelin, C. (1973) 'Canadian Contributions to Economic Journals, un commentaire', *Canadian Journal of Economics*, vol. 6, pp. 559–602.
Levitt, Kari (1970) *Silent Surrender*, Toronto, Macmillan.
Lewis, Frank D. (1975) 'The Canadian Wheat Boom and Per Capita Income: New Estimates', *Journal of Political Economy*, vol. 83, pp. 1249–1258.
—— (1981) 'Farm Settlement on the Canadian Prairies, 1898–1911', *Journal of Economic History*, vol. 41, pp. 517–535.
—— (and M. MacKinnon) (1987) 'Government Loan Guarantees and the Failure of

the Canadian Northern Railway', *Journal of Economic History*, vol. 47, pp. 175–196.

Lewis, William Arthur (1963) 'Economic Development with Unlimited Supplies of Labour', *The Economics of Underdevelopment*, New York, Oxford University Press.

Lipsey, Richard (1981) 'The Understanding and Control of Inflation: Is There a Crisis in Macro-Economics?', *Canadian Journal of Economics*, vol. 14, pp. 545–576.

—— (1983) Review of *Macroeconomics*, R. Dornbush, S. Fisher, and G. R. Sparks; *Modern Macro Economics* Michael Parkin; *Macro Economics: Theory and Policy in Canada*, D. A. Wilson and D. M. Prescott; *Canadian Journal of Economics*, vol. 16, pp. 532 ff.

—— (and M. G. Smith) (1985) *Taking the Initiative: Canada's Trade Options in a Turbulent World*, Toronto, C. D. Howe Research Institute.

—— (1985) *Economics*, New York, Harper.

—— (and R. C. York) (1988) *Evaluating the Free Trade Deal*, Toronto, C. D. Howe Research Institute.

Lithwick, N. Harvey (1967) *Economic Growth in Canada: a Quantitative Analysis*, Toronto, University of Toronto Press.

—— (and G. Paquet) (1968) *Urban Studies: A Canadian Perspective*, Toronto, Methuen.

—— (1969) *Canada's Science Policy and the Economy*, Toronto, Methuen.

—— (1978) *Regional Economic Policy: the Canadian Experience*, Toronto, McGraw-Hill-Ryerson.

Little, Ottis (1748) *The State of Trade in the Northern Colonies Considered with an Account of their Produce and a Particular Description of Nova Scotia*, London G. Woodfall.

Logan, Harold Amos (1928) *The History of Trade Union Organization in Canada*, Chicago, University of Chicago Press.

Lomas, Alton A. (1950) *The Industrial Development of Nova Scotia, 1830–1854*, M. A. Dissertation, Dalhousie University, Halifax, Nova Scotia.

Lower, Arthur R. M. (1938) *The North American Assault on the Canadian Forest*, Toronto, Ryerson.

—— (1943) 'The Development of Canadian Economic Ideas', J. F. Normano, *The Spirit of American Economics*, vol. 1, New York, Day, pp. 211–241.

Macaulay, George Henry (1863) *The System of Landed Credit*, Québec, Desbarats and Derbishire.

Macdonald, John A. (1876) *Debates of the House of Commons*, speech, March 7.

Macdonald, L. R. (1971) 'France and New France: the Internal Contradictions', *Canadian Historical Review*, vol. 71, pp. 122–143.

Macdonald, N. (1939) *Canada: 1769–1841, Immigration and Settlement*, Toronto.

MacIver, Robert M. (1919) *Labour in a Changing World*, New York, Dutton.

Mackintosh, William Archibald (1923) 'Economic Factors in Canadian History', *Canadian Historical Review*, vol. 4, pp. 12–25.

—— (1936) 'Some Aspects of a Pioneer Economy', *Canadian Journal of Economics and Political Science*, vol. 2, pp. 457–463.

—— (1937) 'An Economist Looks at Economics', *Canadian Journal of Economics and Political Science*, vol. 3, pp. 311–321.

—— (1939) *The Economic Background of Dominion-Provincial Relations*, Ottawa, J. O. Patenaude.

Bibliography 279

—— (1938) 'Adam Shortt', *Canadian Journal of Economics and Political Science*, vol. 4, pp. 164-176.
—— (1953) 'Innis on Canadian Economic Development', *Journal of Political Economy*, vol. 61, pp. 185-195.
—— (1964) *The Economic Background of Dominion-Provincial Relations*, Toronto, McClelland and Stewart.
MacLean, John (1867) *Protection and Free Trade*, Montreal, Lovell.
—— (1880) *The Complete Tariff Handbook*, Toronto, Hunter.
Macpherson, Crawford B. (1967) 'The Social Sciences in Contemporary Canada', J. Park, *The Culture of Contemporary Canada*, Toronto, Ryerson.
Marcotte, J-. H. (1936) *Osons! Notre émancipation économique et national l'exige*, Thérien Frères.
Marr, William L. (and M. Percy) (1978) 'Government and the Rate of Prairie Settlement', *Canadian Journal of Economics*, vol. 11, pp. 757-767.
—— (and D. G. Patterson) (1980) *Canada: an Economic History*, Toronto, Macmillan.
—— (1981) 'The Wheat Economy in Reverse: Ontario's Wheat Production, 1887-1917', *Canadian Journal of Economics*, vol. 14, pp. 136-145.
Marsh, Leonard C. (1943) Report on Social Security for Canada, Prepared for the Advisory Committee on Reconstruction, Canada, Parliament, House of Commons Special Committee.
Martin, Chester (1973) *'Dominion Lands' Policy*, Toronto, McClelland and Stewart.
Martin, Robert Montgomery (1837) *History of Nova Scotia*, London, Whittaker.
Masters, Donald C. (1937) *The Reciprocity Treaty of 1854*, Toronto, University of Toronto Press.
—— (1938) *The Rise of Toronto*, Toronto, University of Toronto Press.
—— (1941) 'Toronto vs. Montreal', *Canadian Historical Review*, vol. 22, pp. 133-146.
Mathews, Keith (1978) 'Historical Fence Building: a Critique of the Historiography of Newfoundland', *Newfoundland Quarterly*, vol. 99, pp. 21-30.
Mathews, Roy C. (1968) 'What the Private Planning Association is Today', *Monetary Times*, October, pp. 43-45.
Mathewson, G. Frank (and G. D. Quirin) (1979) *Fiscal Transfer Pricing in Multinational Corporations*, Toronto, Ontario Economic Council.
—— (1982) *Information, Entry, and Regulation in Markets for Life Insurance*, Toronto, Ontario Economic Council.
—— (with R. Winter and C. T. Campbell) (1983) *Regulation of the Canadian Life Insurance Market: Some Issues Affecting Consumers*, Ottawa, Department of Consumer and Corporate Affairs.
—— (1984) *Market Structure and Performance in the Pharmaceutical Industry*, Ottawa, Supply and Services.
—— (and R. A. Winter) (1985) *Competition Policy and Vertical Exchange*, Toronto, University of Toronto Press.
Mavor, James (1916) *Government Telephones: the Experience of Manitoba, Canada*, New York, Moffat.
—— (1923) *Applied Economics*, New York.
—— (1928) 'An Introduction to Canadian Economic History', *Contributions to Canadian Economics*, vol. 1, pp. 7-16.
—— (1925) *Niagara in Politics: a Critical Account of the Ontario Hydro Electric Power Commission*, New York.

280 *A history of Canadian economic thought*

Maxwell, J. A. (1931) 'Expenditure of Canadian Provincial Governments', *Contributions to Canadian Economics*, vol. 4, pp. 41–52.
—— (1936) 'Economic Theory and National Purpose', *Canadian Journal of Economics and Political Science*, vol. 2, pp. 119–127.
—— (1936) 'Aspects of Canadian Federalism', *Dalhousie Review*, vol. 16, pp. 275–284.
Maxwell, Judith, (and C. Pestieau) *Economic Realities of Contemporary Confederation*, Montreal, C. D. Howe Research Institute.
McCalla, Douglas (1969) 'Commercial Politics of the Toronto Board of Trade', *Canadian Historical Review*, vol. 50, pp. 51–67.
—— (1974) 'The Canadian Grain Trade in the 1840's', *Canadian Historical Association, Historical Papers*.
—— (1978) 'The Wheat Staple and Upper Canadian Development', *Canadian Historical Association, Historical Papers*, pp. 34–46.
—— (1986) (with Peter George) 'Measurement, Myth, and Reality: Reflections on the Economic History of Nineteenth Century Ontario', *Journal of Canadian Studies*, vol. 21, no. 3, pp. 71–86. Toronto, Copp Clark Pitman.
—— (1987) (ed.) *Perspectives on Canadian Economic History*
—— (1990) (ed.) *The Development of Canadian Capitalism*, Toronto, Copp Clark Pitman.
McCallum, John (1980) *Unequal Beginnings: Agriculture and Economic Development in Quebec and Ontario until 1870*, Toronto, University of Toronto Press.
McCormick, J. (1880) *The Conditions of Modern Labour and Modern Civilization*, Toronto.
McCulloch, Thomas (1960) *The Stepsure Letters*, Toronto, McClelland and Stewart.
McCurdy, Fleming Blanchard (1924) *Nova Scotia's Right to Live*, Halifax.
—— (1925) *A Statement of Nova Scotia's Position*, an Address to the Canadian Club of Toronto, Apr. 27.
McFetridge, Donald G. (1977) *Government Support of Scientific Research and Development*, Toronto, Ontario Economic Council.
—— (1985) 'Preface', G. F. Mathewson and R. A. Winter, *Competition Policy and Vertical Exchange*, Toronto, University of Toronto Press.
—— (and D. A. S. Smith) (1988) *The Economics of Vertical Disintegration*, Vancouver, The Fraser Institute.
McGibbon, J. (1936) 'Economics and the Social Order', *Canadian Journal of Economics and Political Science*, vol. 2, pp. 68–73.
McGoun, A. F. (1916–17) 'The Nature of Interest and the causes of its Fluctuation', *Quarterly Journal of Economics*, vol. 31, pp. 547–570.
—— (1923) 'Higher and Lower Desires', *Quarterly Journal of Economics*, vol. 37, pp. 291–301.
McGregor, F. A. (1945) *Canada and International Cartels*, Ottawa, Restrictive Trade Practices Commission.
McInnis, R. Marvin (1982) 'The Changing Structure of Canadian Agriculture, 1867–1897', *Journal of Economic History*, vol. 42, pp. 191–198.
—— (1986) 'Output and Productivity in Canadian Agriculture, 1870–71 to 1926–27', in S. L. Engerman and R. E. Gallman, *Long Term Factors in American Economic Growth*, Chicago, University of Chicago Press.
McIvor, Russell C. (1958) *Canada's Monetary, Banking and Fiscal Development*, Toronto, Macmillan.

McManus, John C. (1972) 'An Economic Analysis of Indian Behavior in the North American Fur Trade', *Journal of Economic History*, vol. 32, pp. 78–91.
McNally, D. (1981) 'Staple Theory as Commodity Fetishism: Marx, Innis and Canadian Political Economy', *Studies in Political Economy*, vol. 6, pp. 35–64.
McQueen, R. (1935) 'The Economics of Federalism', *Canadian Journal of Economics and Political Science*, vol. 1, pp. 351–367.
Melvin, James R. (and B. W. Wilkinson) (1968) *Effective Protection in the Canadian Economy*, Toronto, University of Toronto Press.
Migué, Jean-Luc (1970) 'Le nationalisme, l'unité national et la théorie économique de l'information', *Canadian Journal of Economics*, vol. 3, pp. 183–198.
—— (et Bélanger, G.) (1972) *Le prix de la santé*, Montréal, Hurtubise.
—— (1976) 'Le marché politique au Canada', *Canadian Public Policy*, vol. 2, pp. 78–90.
—— (1979) *L'économiste et la chose publique*, Québec, Les Presses de l'Université de Québec.
—— (1979) *Nationalistic Policies in Canada: an Economic Approach*, Montreal, C. D. Howe Research Institute.
Milani, Lois D. (1971) *Robert Gourlay, Gadfly, Forerunner of the Rebellion in Upper Canada*, Thornhill, Ampersand Press.
Mill, John S. (1921) *Principles of Political Economy*, London, Longmans Green.
Minville, Esdras (1933) *La politique qu'il nous faut*, Montréal, L'Association Catholique de la Jeunesse Canadienne.
—— (1939) 'La bourgeoisie et l'économie', in *L'Avenir de notre bourgeoisie*, Montréal, Valiquette.
—— (1948) *Invitation à l'étude*, Montréal, Fides.
—— (1942–45) *Notre milieu*, Montréal.
—— (1979) *L'économique du Québec et la science économique*, Montréal, Fides.
Montigny, Benjamin-Antoine-Testard de
—— (1895) *La colonisation, le nord de Montréal à la région Labelle*, Montréal, Beauchemin.
—— (1896) *Manuel d'économie domestique*, Montréal, Librairie St-. Joseph.
—— (1901) *Etoffe du Pays*, Montréal, Beauchemin.
Montpetit, Edouard (1939) 'Pour une économie canadienne-française', *Proceedings and Transactions of the Royal Society of Canada*, ser. 3, sec. 1, vol. 33, pp. 193–217.
—— (1939–42) *La conquête économique*, Montréal, Valiquette.
Mousseau, Joseph-Alfred (1876) *Le tarif, protection et libre-échange*, Montréal, La Minerve.
Munro, G. R. (1982) 'Fisheries, Extended Jurisdiction and the Economics of Common Property Resources', *Canadian Journal of Economics*, vol. 15, pp. 405–425.
Musgrave, Richard A. (1959) *The Theory of Public Finance*, New York, McGraw-Hill.
—— (and Harberger, A. C.) (1968) *The Carter Tax Commission, Canadian Journal of Economics*, vol. 1, Supplement.
—— (and R. M. Bird) (1987) *Public Finance in Theory and Practice*, (First Canadian edition) Toronto, McGraw-Hill.
Myers, Gustavus (1914) *History of Canadian Wealth*, Chicago, Kerr.
Myint, Hla (1958) 'The "Classical Theory" of International Trade and the Underdeveloped Countries', *Economic Journal*, vol. 68, pp. 317–337.

282 A history of Canadian economic thought

Naylor, R. Thomas (1975) *The History of Canadian Business, 1867-1914*, Toronto, James Lorimer.

—— (1982) *Monetarism and Canadian Policy Alternatives*, Ottawa, Canadian Center for Policy Alternatives.

Neill, Robin F. (1967) 'Adam Shortt: a Bibliographical Comment', *Journal of Canadian Studies*, vol. 2, pp. 53–61.

—— (1972) *A New Theory of Value*, Toronto, University of Toronto Press.

—— (1974) 'National Policy and Regional Development: a Footnote to the Deutsch Report on Maritime Union', *Journal of Canadian Studies*, vol. 9, pp. 12–19.

—— (1968) 'Social Credit and National Policy', *Journal of Canadian Studies*, vol. 3, pp. 3–13.

—— (1982) 'The Old Economics and the New National Policy', *A. C. E. A. Papers*, vol. 11, pp. 147–154.

—— (1987–88) 'Rationality and the Informational Environment: a Reassessment of the Work of Harold Adams Innis', *Journal of Canadian Studies*, vol. 22, pp. 36–53.

Neufeld, Edward P. (1955) *Bank of Canada Operations, 1935-54*, Toronto, University of Toronto Press.

—— (1972) *The Financial System of Canada*, Toronto, Macmillan.

Newbigin, Marion (1926) *The Great River, the Lands and the Men*, London, Christophers.

Niosi, Jorge (1978) *Le contrôl financier du capitalisme canadien*, Montréal, PUQ.

—— (1980) *La bourgeoisie canadienne*, Montréal, Boreal Express.

—— (1988) *The Decline of the American Economy*, Montreal, Black Rose Books.

Norrie, Kenneth H. (1975) 'The Rate of Settlement of the Canadian Prairies, 1870-1911', *Journal of Economic History*, vol. 35, pp. 410–427.

—— (1978) 'The National Policy and Prairie Economic Discrimination, 1870-1930', in D. H. Akenson, (ed.) *Canadian Papers in Rural History*, Gananoque, Langdale Press.

North, D. C. (1955) 'Location theory and regional Economic Growth', *Journal of Political Economy*, vol. 63, pp. 243–258.

Nova Scotia (1934) *Report*, Royal Commission of Economic Enquiry, Halifax.

Ouellet, Fernand (1980) *Economic and Social History of Quebec: 1760-1850*, Toronto, Macmillan.

Palda, Kristan S. (1979) *The Science Council's Weakest Link*, Vancouver, The Fraser Institute.

—— (1980) *Industrial Innovation: Its Place in the Public Policy Agenda*, Vancouver, The Fraser Institute.

Palgrave (John Eatwell *et al.* eds) (1987) *The New Palgrave: a dictionary of economics*, New York, Stockton.

Panitch, Leo (1977) *The Canadian State: Political Economy and Political Power*, Toronto, University of Toronto Press.

—— (1981) *(et al.)* Rethinking Political Economy, *Studies in Political Economy*, vol. 6.

Paquet, Gilles (and J. P. Wallot) (1969) 'Canada 1760-1850: Anamorphoses et Prospective', Extrait de *Economie Québecoise*, Cahiers de l'Université du Quebec, 1-2, Montréal, Les Presses de l'Université du Québec.

—— (and J. P. Wallot) (1973) *Patronage et pouvoir dans le Bas-Canada (1774-1812)*, Montréal, Les Presses de l'Université du Québec.

—— (1983) 'Albert Faucher, économiste-historien', 'Bio-bibliographie d'Albert Faucher', *Actualité Economique*, vol. 59, pp. 395–400.

—— (1985) 'La fruit dont l'ombre est la saveur: réflections aventureuse sur la pensée économique au Québec', *Recherches sociographiques*, vol. 26, pp. 356-398.
—— (and Souque, J-. P., Trent, J., eds) (1985) *Social Science Research in Canada. Stagnation or Regeneration?* Ottawa, Science Council of Canada.
—— (1987) *La pensée économique au Québec français*, Montréal, Association canadienne-française pour l'avancement des sciences.
Parent, Etienne (1846) *Importance de l'étude de l'économie politique*, Montréal, Revue Canadienne.
—— (1852) *De l'importance des devoirs du commerce*.
—— (1852) *Considérations sur le sort des classes ouvrières*, Québec, Fréchette.
—— (1852) *De l'intelligence dans ses rapports avec la société*.
Parizeau, Jacques (1968) 'La recherche en sciences économiques', L. Beaudoin, ed., *La recherche au Canada français*, Montréal, PUM.
Park, Soo-Bin (1982) 'Some Sampling Properties of Minimum Expected Loss (Melo) Estimates of Structural Coefficients', *Journal of Econometrics*, vol. 18, pp. 295-311.
Partridge, Edward A. (1925) *A War on Poverty*, Winnipeg, Wallingford.
Pearson, Lester B. (1972) *Mike: The Memoirs of the Right Honourable Lester B. Pearson*, Toronto, University of Toronto Press.
Penlington, Norman (1965) *Canada and Imperialism*, Toronto, University of Toronto Press.
Penner, Norman (1977) *The Canadian Left, a Critical Analysis*, Scarborough, Prentice Hall.
Pentland, H. Clare (1960) *Labour and the Development of Industrial Capitalism in Canada*, Toronto, University of Toronto Press.
Perry, J. Harvey (1951) *Taxation in Canada*, Toronto, University of Toronto Press.
—— (1955) *Taxes, Tariffs and Subsidies: a History of Canadian Fiscal Development*, Toronto, University of Toronto Press.
Phillips, Paul (1986) *Unemployment Insurance: The Battle Ground in the Debate on the Economic Crisis*, Ottawa, Canadian Center for Policy Alternatives.
Plumptre, A. F. Wynne (and A. E. Gilroy) (1934) 'Review of Economic Textbooks for Use in Canadian High Schools', *Contributions to Canadian Economics*, vol. 7, pp. 123-124.
—— (1936) 'The Nature of Political and Economic Development in the British Dominions', *Canadian Journal of Economics and Political Science*, vol. 3, pp. 488-507.
—— (1940) *Central Banking in the British Dominions*, Toronto, University of Toronto Press.
Poetschke, Leonard (1970) *Problem and Policies*, a paper delivered at the Joint Canadian Economics Association, Canadian Council on Rural Development Conference, Winnipeg, Nov. 14.
Pomfret, Richard (1981) *The Economic Development of Canada*, Toronto, Methuen.
Porritt, Edward (1911) *The Revolt in Canada Against the New Feudalism*, London, Cassell and Company.
—— (1913) *Sixty Years of Protection in Canada, 1846-1912*, Winnipeg, Grain Growers' Guide.
—— (1920) *The Evolution of Canada*, New York.
Porter, G. (1973) 'Recent Trends in Canadian Business and Economic History, *Business History Review*, vol. 67, pp. 141-157.

284 A history of Canadian economic thought

Prichard, J. Robert S. (1979) (with W. T. Stanbury and T. W. Wilson) *Canadian Competition Policy: Essays in Law and Economics*, Toronto, Butterworths.

Provencher, J. A. N. (1864) 'Crédit fonçier', *La Révue Canadienne*, vol. 1, pp. 7–20.

Québec (Province) (1956) *Report*, Royal Commission of Inquiry on Constitutional Problems, Québec, Gouvernement du Québec.

—— (1973) *Le cadre et les moyens d'une politique québecoise concernant les investissements étrangers*, Québec.

—— (1979) *Bâtir le Québec: énonce de politique économique*, Québec, Editeur officiel du Québec.

Queen's University, Departments of Economics and Political Science (1933) 'The Proposal for a Central Bank', *Queen's Quarterly*, vol. 40, pp. 424–440.

—— (1933) 'Financial Manipulation', *Queen's Quarterly*, vol. 40, pp. 264–283.

—— (1933) 'Financial Problems of our Federal System', *Queen's Quarterly*, vol. 40, pp. 580–598.

—— (1934) 'Canadian Trade Policy in a World of Economic Nationalism', *Queen's Quarterly*, vol. 42, pp. 81–98.

Rae, John (1832) *Statement of Some New Principles on the Subject of Political Economy*, in R. Warren James, *John Rae, Political Economist*, Toronto, University of Toronto Press, (1965) vol. 2.

Raynauld, André (1961) *Croissance et structures économiques de la Province de Québec*, Québec, Ministère de l'Industrie et du Commerce, Province de Québec.

—— (1962) 'Recherches économiques récentes sur la Province de Québec', in Yves Dumont et Fernand Martin, eds, *Situation de la recherche sur le Canada français*, Québec, Presses de l'Université Laval.

—— (1971) 'La propriété et la performance des entreprises établis au Québec', *Etudes internationales*, vol. 2, pp. 81–109.

Rea, Kenneth J. (1976) *Political Economy of Northern Development*, Ottawa, The Science Council of Canada.

—— (1985) *The Prosperous Years: The Economic History of Ontario, 1939–1975*, Toronto, University of Toronto Press.

Reeves, John (1793) *History of the Government of the Island of Newfoundland*, London, J. Sewell.

Renaud, Paul-Emile (1923) *Du travail en Nouvelle France*, Montréal.

—— (1928) *Les origines économiques du Canada*, Mamers, G. Enault.

Reynolds, Lloyd G. (1940) *The Control of Competition in Canada*, Cambridge, Cambridge University Press.

Rist, Charles (1940) *History of Monetary and Credit Theory*, London, George Allen & Unwin.

Ritchie, Ronald S. (1969) *An Institute for Research on Public Policy*, Ottawa, Information Canada.

Robbins, Lionel (1932) *Essay on the Significance of Economic Science*, London, Macmillan.

Robitaille, Lucie (1962) *Présence de Victor Barbeau*, Montréal.

Rogers, Norman McL. (1931) 'The Compact Theory of Confederation', *Proceedings of the Canadian Political Science Association*, vol. 3, pp. 205–230.

Rose, John (1969) *Speech of the Honourable John Rose, Minister of Finance, Canada, on Introducing the Resolutions on Banking and Currency*, Ottawa, Hunter and Rose.

Rosenbluth, Gideon (1954) 'Industrial Concentration in Canada and the United

States', *Canadian Journal of Economic and Political Science*, vol. 20, pp. 332-346.
—— (1957) *Concentration in Canadian Manufacturing*, Princeton, Princeton University Press.
—— (1963) *Canadian Anti-Combines Administration*, Toronto, University of Toronto Press.
Ross, Victor (1920-34) *A History of the Canadian Bank of Commerce*, 3 vols. Toronto, Oxford University Press.
Rostow, Walter W. (1960) *The Stages of Economic Growth*, Cambridge, Cambridge University Press.
Rotstein, Abraham (1966) 'The 20th Century Prospect: Nationalism in a Technological Society', in The University League for Social Reform, *Nationalism in Canada*, Toronto, McGraw-Hill.
Rymes, Thomas K. (1971) *On concepts of Capital and Technical Change*, Cambridge, Cambridge University Press.
Safarian, A. Edward (1966) *Foreign Ownership of Canadian Industry*, Toronto, University of Toronto Press.
—— (1985) *Foreign Direct Investment: A Survey of Canadian Research*, Montreal, Institute for Research on Public Policy.
Sager, Eric W. (1981-83) 'Newfoundland's Historical Revival and the Legacy of David Alexander', *Acadiensis*, vol. 11-12, pp. 104-114.
Saint-Germaine, Maurice (1973) *Une économie à libérer*, Montréal, PUM.
Saint-Pierre, Arthur (1909) *L'avenir du Canada français*, Montréal, Imprimerie du Messager.
—— (1914) *Questions et oeuvres sociales de chez nous*, Montréal, L'Ecole sociale populaire.
—— (1954) 'Léon Gérin, un disciple canadien de Frédéric Le Play', *Proceedings and Transactions of the Royal Society of Canada*, ser. 1, sec. 1, vol. 48, pp. 91-103.
Sales, André (1985) La construction social de l'économie québécoise', *Recherches sociographiques*, vol. 26, pp. 319-360.
Samuelson, Paul A. (1966) (and A. D. Scott) *Economics: an Introductory Analysis*, Toronto, McGraw-Hill.
Saunders, Stanley A. (1932) *The Economic Welfare of the Maritime Provinces*, Wolfville, Acadia University.
—— (1936) 'The Maritime Provinces and the National Policy', *Dalhousie Review*, vol. 16, pp. 87-89.
—— (1939) *The Economic History of the Maritime Provinces*, Ottawa, Royal Commission on Dominion-Provincial Relations.
Savoie, Donald J. (1986) *Regional Economic Development: Canada's Search for Policies*, Toronto, University of Toronto Press.
Schumpeter, Joseph A. (1954) *History of Economic Analysis*, New York, Oxford University Press.
Science Council of Canada (1977) *Canada as a Conserver Society*, Ottawa.
—— (1979) *Forging the Links*, Ottawa.
—— (1981) *Hard Times Hard Choices*, Ottawa.
—— (1984) *Canadian Industrial Development*, Ottawa.
Scott, Anthony D. (1952) 'The Evaluation of Federal Grants', *Economica*, vol. 19, pp. 377-394.
—— (1954) 'Conservation Policy and Capital Theory', *Canadian Journal of Economics and Political Science*, vol. 20, pp. 504-513.

―― (1955) *The Economics of Natural Resources*, Toronto, University of Toronto Press.
―― (1979) 'Development of Economic Theory on Fisheries Regulation', *Journal of the Fisheries Research Board of Canada*, vol. 36, pp. 725-741.
Scott, Frank R. (1935) 'The Efficiency of Socialism', *Queen's Quarterly*, vol. 42, pp. 215-225.
Shearer, Ronald A. (1977) 'The Porter Commission Report in the Context of Earlier Canadian Monetary Documents', *Canadian Journal of Economics*, vol. 10, pp. 34-49.
―― (1978) 'Proposals for the Revision of Banking Legislation', *Canadian Journal of Economics*, vol. 11, pp. 124-128.
―― (with J. F. Chant and D. E. Bond) (1985) *Money, Banking and the Financial Institutions of Canada*, Scarborough, Prentice-Hall.
Shepherd, J. J. (1979) *Out of Joint with the Times*, Ottawa, Canadian Institute for Public Policy.
―― (1980) *The Transition to Reality*, Ottawa, Canadian Institute for Public Policy.
Shortt, Adam (1987) *Adam Shortt's History of Canadian Currency and Banking: 1600-1880*, Toronto, Canadian Bankers' Association.
―― (1914) 'Railroad Construction and National Prosperity: an Historic Parallel', *Proceedings and Transactions of the Royal Society of Canada*, ser. 3, sec. II, vol. 8, pp. 295-308.
Skelton, Oscar D. (1911) *Socialism: a Critical Analysis*, New York, Houghton Mifflin.
―― (1913) *General Economic History of The Dominion*, Toronto, Publishers Assoc.
―― (1914, 1917) 'Federal Finance', *Bulletin of the Departments of History and Political and Economic Science of Queen's University*, no. 16, no. 29.
―― (1916) *The Railway Builders*, Toronto, Glasgow Brook.
―― (1920) *The Life and Times of Sir Alexander Tilloch Galt*, Toronto, Oxford University Press.
―― (1925) Review of D. A. McGibbon, *Introduction to Economics for Canadians*, *Canadian Historical Review*, vol. 6, p. 87.
―― (1932) 'Fifty Years of Political and Economic Science in Canada', *Fifty Years in Retrospect: Canada, 1882-1932*, Toronto, The Royal Society of Canada.
Skeoch, Lawrence (1966) *Restrictive Trade Practices in Canada*, Toronto, McClelland and Stewart.
―― (with B. C. McDonald) (1976) *Dynamic Change and Accountability in a Canadian Market Economy*, Ottawa, Supply and Services.
Slater, David W. (1967) 'Economic Policy and Economic Research in Canada since 1950', *Queen's Quarterly*, vol. 74, pp. 1-20.
Smith, Adam (1933) *The Wealth of Nations*, London, J. J. Dent and Sons.
Smith, Goldwin (1971 reprint) *Canada and the Canadian Question*, Toronto, University of Toronto Press.
Smith, Vera (1936) *The Rationale of Central Banking*, London, P. S. King.
Southey, Clive (1978) 'The Staples Thesis, Common Property, and Homesteading', *Canadian Journal of Economics*, vol. 11, pp. 547-59.
Speitoff, Arthur (1952) 'The Historical Character of Economic Theories', *Journal of Economic History*, vol. 12, pp. 131-139.
―― (1953) 'Pure Theory and Economic Gestalt Theory: Ideal Types and Real Types', in F. C. Lane and J. C. Riemersma, eds, *Enterprise and Secular Change*, Homewood, Richard D. Irwin, pp. 431-463.

—— (1970) 'Arthur Speitoff on Economic Styles', *Journal of Economic History*, vol. 30, pp. 644–652.
Spengler, Joseph J., ed. (1960) *Essays in Economic Thought: Aristotle to Marshall*, Chicago, Rand McNally.
Steed, G. P. F. (1982) *Threshold Firms: Backing Canada's Winners*, Ottawa, The Science Council of Canada.
Stewart, Bryce M. (1926) *Canadian Labour Laws and the Treaty*, New York, Columbia University Press.
Stewart, John (1806) *An Account of Prince Edward Island in the Gulf of St. Lawrence*, London, Winchester and Son.
Stiglitz, Joseph E. (and G. F. Mathewson) (1986) *New Developments in the Analysis of Market Structures*, Cambridge, MIT Press.
Studness, C. M. (1964) 'Economic Opportunity and Westward Migration of Canadians in the Late Nineteenth Century', *Canadian Journal of Economics and Political Science*, vol. 30, pp. 570–584.
Stykolt, Stefen (1969) *Efficiency in the Open Economy*, Toronto, Oxford University Press.
Tanghe, Raymond (1935) *Le crédit au Canada*, Montréal.
—— (1947) *Géographie économique du Canada*, Montréal, Fides.
—— (1948–49) *Théories économiques et réalisations sociales du XIXe siècle*,
Tassé, Joseph (1873) *La Vallée de l'Outaouais*, Montréal, E. Senécal.
—— (1891) *Philemon Wright ou colonisation et commerce de bois*. Montréal, La Minerve.
Taylor, Henry (1839) *Considerations on the Past, Present and Future of the Canadas*, Montreal, Lovell.
Taylor, Kenneth W. (1960) 'Economic Scholarship in Canada', *Canadian Journal of Economics and Political Science*, vol. 26, pp. 6–18.
Teeple, Gary (ed.) (1972) *Capitalism and the National Question in Canada*, Toronto, University of Toronto Press.
Thomas, Arron (1968) *The Newfoundland Journal of Arron Thomas 1794*, J. M. Murray, ed. Don Mills, Longmans.
Thomas, H. M. (1935) 'The Corporate State', *Queen's Quarterly*, vol. 42, pp. 242–252.
Thompson, T. Phillips (1887) *The Politics of Labour*, New York, Belford Clark.
Thirsk, Wayne R. (1987) 'The Value-Added Tax in Canada: Saviour or Siren Song?', *Canadian Public Policy*, vol. 13, pp. 259–283.
Timlin, Mabel F. (1942) *Keynesian Economics*, Toronto, University of Toronto Press.
—— (1945) 'The Economics of Control', *Canadian Journal of Economics and Political Science*, vol. 11, pp. 258–293.
—— (1946) 'Price Flexibility and Employment', *Canadian Journal of Economics and Political Science*, vol. 12, pp. 204 ff.
—— (1946) 'General Equilibrium Analysis and Public Policy', *Canadian Journal of Economics and Political Science*, vol. 12, pp. 483 ff.
Tirole, Jean (1988) *The Theory of Industrial Organization*, Cambridge, MIT Press.
Tremblay, Raymond (1976) *L'économie québecoise: histoire, développement, politiques*, Montréal, Les Presses de l'Université du Québec.
Trotter, Reginald G. (1927) 'Canadian History in the Universities of the United States', *Canadian Historical Review*, vol. 8, pp. 190-207.
Tucker, Gilbert N. (1936) *The Canadian Commercial Revolution*, New Haven, Yale University Press.

Tupper, Charles (1914) *Political Reminiscences*, London, Constable.
Underhill, Frank H. (1935) 'The Conception of a National Interest', *Canadian Journal of Economics and Political Science*, vol. 1, pp. 396–408.
Upper Canada (1835) *Report*, House of Assembly, Select Committee appointed to inquire into the state of the trade and commerce of the Province of Canada.
Urquhart, M. C. (1986) 'New Estimates of Gross National Product, Canada, 1870–1926: Some Implications for Canadian Development', S. L. Engerman and R. E. Gallman, *Long Term Factors in American Economic Growth*, Chicago, University of Chicago Press.
Urwick, Edward J. (1935) 'The Role of Intelligence in the Social Process', *Canadian Journal of Economics and Political Science*, vol. 1, pp. 64–76.
—— (1937) 'The Ethics of Competition', *Canadian Journal of Economics and Political Science*, vol. 3, pp. 250–263.
Vezina, Roger (1941) *La monnaie et le crédit*, Montréal, Valiquette.
Vickery, E. (1974) 'Exports and North American Economic Growth: "Structuralist" and "Staple" Models', *Canadian Journal of Economics*, vol. 7, pp. 32–58.
Viner, Jacob (1924) *Canada's Balance of International Indebtedness: 1900–1913*, Cambridge, Mass., Harvard University Press.
Wains, W. J. (with J. A. Maxwell and J. S. M. Allely) (1937) 'Federal Public Finance: Canada, Australia, South Africa', *Canadian Journal of Economics and Political Science*, vol. 3, pp. 181–209.
Wakefield, Edward G. (1833) *England and America*, 2 vols., London, Bentley.
Walinsky, Louis Joseph (1967) *Evaluation of Economic Research Relating to the Atlantic Region*, Fredericton, Atlantic Provinces Research Board.
Walker, Michael (1976) *The Illusion of Wage and Price Controls*, Vancouver, The Fraser Institute.
Walters, Dorothy (1968) *Canadian Income Levels and Growth*, Ottawa, Economic Council of Canada.
Watkins, Melville H. (1963) 'A Staple Theory of Economic Growth', *Canadian Journal of Economics and Political Science*, vol. 29, pp. 141–158.
—— (1966) 'Nationalism', *Canadian Journal of Economics and Political Science*, vol. 32, pp. 388–392.
—— (1966) 'Technology and Nationalism', in University League for Social Reconstruction, *Nationalism in Canada*, Toronto, McGraw-Hill. pp. 388–392.
—— (1970) 'A New National Policy', T. Lloyd and J. McLeod, eds, *Agenda 1970: proposal for a creative politics*, Toronto, University of Toronto Press, pp. 284–302.
—— (1970) 'The Dismal State of Economics in Canada', in I. Lumsden, *Close the 49th Parallel*, Toronto, University of Toronto Press, pp. 197–208.
—— (1977) 'The Staple Theory Revisited', *Journal of Canadian Studies*, vol. 12, pp. 83–96.
Weldon, Jack C. (with Assimakopulos, A.) (1965) 'A Synoptic view of Some Simple Models of Growth', *Canadian Journal of Economics and Political Science*. vol. 30, pp. 52–79.
—— (1980?) *Pension Policy: Practice and Positive Theory*, Ottawa, Canadian Center for Policy Alternatives.
Weller, Barry (1981) *National and Regional Economic Development Strategies; Perspectives on Canada's Problems and Prospects*, Ottawa, University of Ottawa Press.
West, Edwin G. (1985) *Subsidizing the Performing Arts*, Toronto, Ontario Economic Council.

Wickett,. M. (1897) 'The Study of Political Economy at Canadian Universities', *Appendix to the Report of the Ontario Bureau of Industries*.

Williams, Glen (1983) *Not for Export*, Toronto, McClelland and Stewart.

Williams, J. H. (1929) 'The Theory of International Trade Reconsidered', *Economic Journal*, vol. 39, pp. 195–209.

Willson, Hugh Bowlby (1870) *A Plea for Uncle Sam's Money, or, Greenbacks versus bank notes*, New York, *New York Herald*.

Wilson, F. A. (1850) (and A. B. Richards) *Britain Redeemed and Canada Preserved*, London, Longman.

Wonnacott, Paul (1965) *The Canadian dollar, 1948–1962*, Toronto, University of Toronto Press.

Wonnacott, Ronald J. (and R. Hill) (1987) *Canadian and U. S. Adjustment Policies in a Bilateral Trade Agreement*, Toronto, C. D. Howe Research Institute.

Wood, W. D. (and R. S. Thoman eds) (1965) *Areas of Economic Stress in Canada*, Kingston, Industrial Relations Center, Queen's University.

Young, A. (1928) 'Increasing Returns and Economic Progress', *Economic Journal*, vol. 38, pp. 527–542.

Young, John (1922) *The Letters of Agricola*, Halifax, Minister of Public Works.

Index

Aberhart, William 100
Acheson, Keith 215
Action Social Catholique 152
Aitken, Hugh G. J. 173, 194, 211
Alchian, A. 222
Altman, Morris 203
Angers, François-Albert ix, x, 22, 40, 41, 42, 51, 53, 55, 149, 153, 154, 155, 157, 160, 163, 168, 188, 227
Ankli, Robert E. 203
Antigonish Movement 33
Apostle, Richard 38
Archambault, P. 152
Arès, Richard 157
Arnold, Walter 1–3, 104–5
Arrow, Kenneth 59
Ashley, W. J. 111–12
Asimakoplis, A 184
Asselin, Olivar 152–3
Association for the Promotion of Canadian Industry 78
Atlantic Canada Economics Association 37
Atlantic Development Board 34
Atlantic Provinces: (Deutsch) Royal Commission on Maritime Union 34, 35, 36
Atlantic Provinces Research Board 34
Attwood, Thomas 102–3, 106

Bacon, Francis 68, 75, 83, 227
Balcom, A. B. 124
Baldwin, R. E. 196
Barbeau, Victor 156–7
Barber, Clarence L. 186, 210
Barrett, Gene 38

Barzel, Yoram 222
Bates, Stewart 144
Beaubien, Louis 156
Beausoleil, Cleopas 48, 49
Beavington, George 100, 140
Bélanger, Gèrard 168, 170
Bentham, Jeremy 14
Bernard, J. T. 171
Bertram, Gordon W. 162, 194–5, 196, 197, 200, 203
better terms 30, 31
Bilodeau, Georges-Marie 52
Bird, Richard 216, 217
Birmingham School 20
Bladen, Vincent W. 124, 132, 159
Blaug, Mark 22
Boadway, Robin W. 217
Boggs, Theodore 125
Bohm-Bawerk, Eugen von 57, 59, 60
Boland, Lawrence A. ix
Bonin, Bernard 225
Boucher, Pierre 2–3, 6, 10, 14
Bouchette, Joseph 12–13, 16
Bouchette, Robert E. 52–3, 149, 150–1, 153, 154, 156, 161
Bourrasa, Henri 153
Boyer, M. 171
Bradfield, Michael 218
Brecher, Irving x, 140–2, 211, 212, 214
Brecher, Richard x
Breckenridge, Roeliff M. 93
Breton, Albert 188, 189, 209, 211, 218
Brewis, Thomas N. 34, 187
Britnell, George E. 135
Brown, George 117
Brown, William 107

Index

Bryce, Robert B. 141
Buchanan, Isaac 21, 48, 54, 76, 78–82, 83, 96, 97, 98, 99, 101–4
Buchanan, J. M. 170
Buckley, Kenneth 95, 114, 158, 191, 193–7, 202
Byles, Bernard 101–2, 104

Canada: (Carter) Royal Commission on Taxation 188; (Dawson) Royal Commission on Provincial Development and Rehabilitation 33; (Gordon) Royal Commission on Canada's Economic Prospects 177, 196, 206, 215; (Macdonald) Royal Commission on the Economic Union and Development Prospects for Canada 206, 219; (Macmillan) Royal Commission on Banking and Currency 145; (Porter) Royal Commission on Banking and Finance 174, 181, 214, 215; (Rowell-Sirois) Royal Commission on Dominion–Provincial Relations 33, 114, 145, 146, 163, 206; Royal Commission on Corporate Concentration 206, 213; (Stevens) Royal Commission on Price Spreads 138, 145; White Paper on Employment and Income 174; Task Force on the Structure of Canadian Industry 179
Canada Land Company 8
Canada Tax Foundation 176
Canadian Bankers Association 98
Canadian Economics and Political Science Association 134
Canadian Institute for Economic Policy 209–10
Canadian Institute for Policy Alternatives 211
Canadian Political Science Association 121
capital theory 6, 14–15, 59–61, 64–5, 69, 75
Carey, Henry C. 21, 22, 48, 79, 81, 83, 101–2
Carmichael-Smyth, R. 30
Carrothers, William A. 135, 138, 143
Carson, Richard ix

Cartier, Etienne 114
Cartwright, Richard 118
Casey, G. E. 107
Caves, Richard E. 2, 71, 196, 199, 200
Centre d'Etudes et de Recherches en Economique Philanthropique 211
Centre de Recherche et Développement en Economique 211
Chamberlin, E. H. 139, 164
Chambers, Edward J. 71, 96, 191, 196, 198–9, 200, 202, 203
Chant, John F. 215
Cherryman, J. B. 125
Child, Joshua 65
Clark, A. B. 143
Clark, J. B. 59
Clark, J. M. 122
Clark, Robert 176
Clark, W. C. 140, 141, 145
Clement, Wallace 206
Coase, Ronald H. 111, 134, 170, 212, 222
Coats, R. H. 125
Cobbet, William 9
Cochon, Joseph 4
colonization 52
Collins, Enos 93
Committee for an Independent Canada 209
Courchene, Thomas 207, 216, 217, 218, 219
Cournot, A. A. 125
Coyne, James 177, 180
Creighton, Donald C. 135
crise d'agriculture 16, 46
Cudmore, S. A. 122
Currie, Archibald W. 148
Curtis, C. A. 140, 141, 142

Dagnais, M. 171
Dales, John H. 95, 163, 201, 203
Daly, Donald J. 209
Dansereau, Arthur 49
Davenport, H. J. 122
Davis, Anthony 38
Dehem, Roger 159, 160, 162
Denison, E. F. 186
Denys, Nicolas 3–5
Department of Industry Trade and Commerce 35–6

292 Index

Department of Regional Economic Expansion 35–6, 38, 187
Desjardins, Alphonse 55
Deutsch, John 222
Dimand, Robert 125
Dionne, G. 171
division of labour, principle of 3, 9, 10, 61–2, 76
Donald, William J. A. 119, 121
Douglas, Major 106
Douglass, William A. 118
Drapeau, Stanislas 50
Due, John 176
Dufour, J-. M. 171
Dumesnil, Clement 46
Duncan, Jonathan 101–2
Dunlop, J. Bruce 213
Durham, John George Lambton, The First Earl of 41
Durham Report 13, 15, 96

Easterbrook, W. Thomas 76, 173, 194, 211
Eccles, William J. 203
Ecole des Hautes Etudes 26, 153–5
Ecole Social Populaire 152
Economic Council of Canada 185, 207, 211, 215
economics: Austrian 22, 74, 75; Banking School of monetary ix, 98–9, 100, 101, 105, 107, 108, 123, 140, 142; Birmingham School of monetary 98–9, 101–4, 105, 106, 107, 108, 113, 119, 123, 142, 226; classical 1, 76, 109, 110, 111, 117; Cleometrics 37; Currency School of monetary 93, 96, 97, 89–9, 100, 101, 107, 108; German Historical School of 21, 28, 29, 31, 77, 110, 111–12, 133, 146, 163, 185, 227; Historical see German Historical School of; Institutional 111, 133–4, 135, 227; in the context of action 22, 39; Keynesian ix, 123, 129, 130, 141, 143, 147, 148, 156, 158, 159, 160, 161, 163, 164, 167, 170, 172, 173, 174, 176, 178, 179–85, 205; laissez-faire 10, 28, 40, 41, 43, 65, 74, 75, 76, 103, 112; liberal 9, 40, 44, 75, 97, 116–19, 164; marginalist 79, 110; Marxian 5, 35, 112, 192; mercantilist 9; Monetarist 103, 104, 172, 205, 207, 210, 214, 222; monetary 92–108; Nationalist School of 58, 72–91, 113; neoclassical 1, 35, 38, 39, 109–11, 112, 120, 122, 129, 132, 133, 147, 159, 165–7, 168, 170, 172, 174, 185, 187, 197, 205, 210, 215, 218, 221, 222; neo-conservative 180; neo-Keynesian 1, 36, 123, 140, 147, 159, 172, 173, 174, 175, 176, 179–85, 205, 214; neo-Marxist see Western Marxist; Populist 106; New Classical 172, 205, 214, 222; New Industrial 5, 38, 212–13, 222; New Institutional 38, 111, 112, 133–4, 135, 170, 190, 205; of land settlement in Canada 12; of nationalism 189–90; of natural resources 175; Physiocratic 25, 26, 51, 52, 75, 192; positivist ix, 23, 149, 155, 158–63, 165, 167, 172, 180, 185, 191, 210, 215, 227; profession of 119–21, 125–8, 143; protectionist 21–2, 29, 30, 47–9, 77–91; post-Keynsian 184; regional 169, 176–7, 187–8, 218–19; Toronto School of historical 31, 161; Upper Canadian 74–7; Western Marxist 35, 134, 147, 173, 174, 177–9, 212, 218, 219
Edgeworth, F. Y. 144
Elliot, G. A. 143
Ely, Richard T. 112
English, H. Edward 186, 213

Falardeau, Jean-C. 160, 161
Faucher, Albert 155, 159, 161, 163, 171
Fauteux, Joseph-Noël 155, 171
Fay, Charles Ryle 32, 131–2, 133, 146
Feyerabend, Paul 166
Financial Reform League see National Currency League
Firestone, Otto J. 193–4, 200
Fisher, Irving 57, 59, 60, 105
Flatters, Frank 217
Fleming, Sanford 113
Fluet, C. D. 171
Flux, A. W. 120

foreign ownership of industry 169, 177–9, 207
Fortin, Pierre 225
Fowke, Vernon C. 58, 159, 160, 191, 202, 203
Frank, A. G. 165
Fraser Institute 208–9
free banking 97, 99, 101, 102
Freeman, Ralph Evans 122
Friedman, Milton 103, 104, 161, 184, 205, 208

Gagnon, Marcel-Aimé 153
Galbraith, J. K. 196, 208, 210
Galbraith, Thomas 107
Galt, Alexander Tilloch 54, 75, 84, 85, 88, 97, 103
Galt, John 8
Gaulle, Charles de 168
George, Henry 117
George, Peter 202
Gérin-Lajoie, Antoine 51–2, 150
Gérin Léon 51, 149, 150, 153, 156, 157
Gesner, Abraham 21–2, 28
Gide, Charles 155
Gillespie, W. Irwin 216
Girod, Amury 46
gold standard 78, 96, 98, 100, 103, 125
Goodhart, Charles 99
Goodwin, Craufurd D. W. x, 72, 77, 78, 92, 100, 125
Gordon, D. 198–9
Gordon, H. Scott 175, 180
Gordon, Walter 177, 188, 209
Gorsebrook Research Institute, St. Mary's University 38
Gourlay, Robert 9–12, 13, 14, 18, 46, 76, 100
Graham, John 205
Granatstein, Jack L. 140
Gras, N. S. B. 135
Greeley, Horace 78, 79
Griffin, George D. 103
growth poles, theory of 35, 210
Grubel, Herbert 208

Haberler, Gottfried von 145, 164
Haliburton, Thomas C. 26
Hamilton, Alexander 73
Hammond, Bray 106

Hankin, Francis 137–8
Harberger, A. C. 188
Harpell, James John 119
Harrod, R. F. 145, 161, 162, 174, 182, 183, 186
Hartland Penelope 114, 193
Hawtrey, Ralph G. 102–3, 105, 134, 164
Hettich, Walter P. 216
Higgins, Benjamin 162, 180
Hinks, Francis 96, 100–1, 107
Hinks, William 117
Hirschman, A. O. 35, 176, 196
Hollander, Samuel ix
Holton, R. H. 196, 200
Hood, William 162, 215
Howe, Joseph 29–30, 93
Howe Research Institute 206–7
Howitt, Peter 214
Hume, David 9, 75, 227
Hurlbert, Jesse Beaufort 82–4, 125
Hymer, Steven 178–9

imperfect competition 111
incomes policy 208, 210
industrial strategy 26, 207, 208
Ingerman, Sidney H. 209
Ingram, J. K. 111
Inman, Mark K. 159
Innis, Harold A. ix, 5, 22, 58, 74, 77, 92, 95, 111, 112, 119, 121, 123, 124, 131, 134, 135, 146, 148, 155, 158, 161, 173, 183, 185, 191, 192, 194, 201, 203, 225, 227
Institute for Public Policy 211
Institute for Research on Public Policy 210
Interprovincial Conference, 1887 47
Irvine, William 106, 140

Jackson, G. E. 124, 146
James, R. Warren x, 57, 70
Jenkin, Michael 219
Johnson, Harry G. 71, 162, 173, 174, 180–6, 187, 189, 204–5, 209
Johnson, J. Keith 65

Kahn, R. F. 144
Kaldor, Nicolas 139
Kalecki, M. 211

Keirstead, Burton S. 33
Kemp, Murray C. 162
Keynes, John M. 40, 111, 140, 144, 147, 173, 174, 181, 185, 211
Kierzkowski, Alexandre-Edouard 46
Kindleberger, C. P. 196
King, E. H. 97
King, William Lyon Mackenzie 125
Klein, Lawrence 185
Knight, Frank H. 122, 134, 135
Knox, Frank A. 140, 141, 142
Kuhn, T. S. 185
Kuznets, Simon S. 162

Laidler, David 214
Lakatos, Imre 166
Lamontagne, Maurice 159, 160, 161, 163
Lancaster, K. J. 182
Lanctôt, Gustave 155
land settlement, Gourlay's theory of 10, 15
Lange, Oscar 174
Langelier, John-Chrysostome 54
Laport, Pierre 168
La Rue, François-Alexandre-Hubert 50–1
Lasage, Jean 167
Lauderdale, J. M. 117
Laureys, Henry 153
Laurier, Wilfrid 48, 49, 152
Leacock, Stephen B. 112, 123
League for Social Reconstruction 138
Legitimization Crisis Theory 130, 165, 205
Leman, Beaudry 158
Lemelin, Charles 155
Leontief, Wasily 161, 162, 164
LePlay, P. G. F. 51, 150
Lerner, A. P. 174
Leslie, Cliff 111
Lévesque, G-. H. 159
Lévesque, René 149, 168
Levitt, Kari 95
Lewis, Frank D. 202
Lewis, William Arthur 163, 196
Lipsey, Richard 182, 186, 213–14
List, Frederic 21, 22, 40, 48
Lithwick, N. Harvey 197, 218
Little, Ottis 23–4

Lower, Arthur R. M. 131, 135, 161

Macaulay, George Henry 53
McDermot, T. W. L. 137–8
Macdonald, John A. 65, 73, 78, 84, 85–91
MacGregor, Donald 124, 143, 144
MacIver, Robert M. 136
Mackay, R. A. 144
Mackenzie, W. L. 93
Mackintosh, William Archibald 114, 122, 123, 124, 129–30, 135, 140, 141, 146, 147
MacLean, John 82–4
Madison, James 73
Malthus, Thomas R. 9, 11, 117
Manigault, G. 107
Marcottte, J-. H. 156–7
Maritimes Rights Movement 31
Maritime union 35, 36
Marr, William L. 202
Marshall, Alfred 79, 144
Marshall, L. C. 122
Martin, Chester 18–19
Marx, Karl 44, 59, 136–7, 166, 192
Masters, Donald C. 135
Mathewson, G. Fran 209, 212
Mavor, James 112, 119, 121, 125, 136, 146
Maxwell, J. A. 143
McCallum, John 210
McCulloch, John R. 14, 79, 80, 83, 117
McCulloch, Thomas, 25
McGee, D'Arcy 84–5
McGibbon, D. A. 122, 123
McInnis, R. Marvin 191
McIvor, Russell C. 92
McManus, John C. 133
McQueen, R. 213
Meade, J. E. 183
Melvin, James R. 219
Merritt, W. H. 101
Metcalfe, Governor General Sir Charles 13
Michell, Humphrey 124
Migué, Jean-Luc 44, 170, 190
Miliband, Ralph 165, 212
Mill, James 14
Mill, John S. 57, 58, 71, 83, 86–8, 165

Ministry of State for Regional Economic Development 36
Minville, Esdras 40, 41–2, 51, 55, 149, 154–5, 161, 163
Mitchell, W. C. 124
Montigny, Benjamin-Antoine-Testard de 52
Montpetit, Edouard 52, 141, 149, 150, 155–6, 158, 161
Moore, Milton 176, 188
Morgan, H. J. 78, 104
Mousseau, Joseph-Alfred 48
Munro, G. R.,
Musgrave, Richard A. 188
Myers, Gustavus 118, 136
Myint, Hla 71
Myrdal, Gunnar 35, 176

National Currency League 78, 95 98, 103, 106, 107
National Policy 30, 31, 42, 48, 51, 58, 65, 72, 73, 85–91, 95, 98, 114, 115, 116, 159, 187, 193, 201
Naylor, R. Thomas 95, 108
neoconservative 205–6
Neufeld, Edward P. 92, 95
Nevers, Edmond de 153
Newbigin, Marion 135
New Canadian Political Economy 35, 37, 112, 134, 165–7, 178, 190, 205, 206
New Economic History 198–9
New Energy Policy 206
Newton, Isaac 75
Niosi, Jorge 170
Norrie, Kenneth H. 191, 201, 202
North, DC 192–3, 195
North–South Institute 211
Nova Scotia: (Jones) Royal Commission of Provincial Economic Enquiry 33, 143–4, 145
Nova Scotia Voluntary Planning Board 34

O'Connell, Joseph 37
Ohlin, B. 145, 164
Ontario Economic Council 209
Owen, Robert 10

Pacific Group for Policy Alternatives 211
Palgrave 178
Panitch, Leo 206
Papineau, Louis-Joseph 47, 93
Paquet, Gilles x, 160, 168, 170, 171, 225
Parent, Etienne 41, 43–5, 49, 51, 56, 149, 150, 156, 161
Parenteau, Roland 218
Pareto, Vilfredo 144
Parizeau, Jacques 149, 184
Park, Soo-Bin ix
Parkin, Michael 214
Parkinson, J. F. 141
Partridge, Edward A. 119
Patinkin, Don 174
Pearson, Lester B. 138
Peel, Robert 96, 100, 103
Percy, M. B. 202
Perroux, François 149, 162, 164, 176, 219
Perry, J. Harvey 176
Pigou, A. C. 144, 164
Plumptre, A. F. Wynne 124, 129, 131, 135, 140, 141, 142, 147–8
Porritt, Edward 118
Private Planning Association 179, 196, 206

quantity of money theory of prices 9, 99, 102, 140, 164, 183–4
Québec (Province): (Tremblay) Royal Commission of Inquiry on Constitutional Problems 163
Quesnay, François 9

Rae, John ix, 22, 57–71, 76, 78, 81–2, 83, 87, 96, 100, 107, 185, 226
Rasminsky, Louis 140
Raynauld, André 160, 161, 162–3, 169, 171, 218, 219
Reciprocity Treaty, 1854 42, 53, 78–9
Reeves, John 5
Renaud, Paul-Emile 155
Reuber, Grant 187
Reynolds, Lloyd G. 139
Ricardo, David 6, 10, 14, 67, 81, 83
Riel, Louis 48
Rist, Charles 158, 164

Ritchie, S. J. 117
Robertson, D. H. 164
Robbins, Lionel 61, 110, 134
Robinson, Joan 111, 134, 184, 211
Rodbertus, J. K. 151
Rogers, Norman McL. 143, 144
Rose, John 97, 101
Rosenbluth, Gideon 162, 175, 222
Rostow, Walter W. 95, 194–5, 196
Rotstein, Abraham 189–90, 209

Safarian, A. Edward 186
Saint-Pierre, Arthur 152
Sales, André 168, 170, 171
Samuelson, Paul A. 159, 161, 174
Saunders, Stanley A. 135
Savoie, Donald J. 218
Say, J. B. 80, 117
Schumpeter, Joseph A. 1, 171, 213
Science Council of Canada 207–8, 219
Scott, Anthony D. 159, 162, 175, 188, 211, 222
Scottish Enlightenment 10, 61, 75, 76, 187, 227
seigneurial system 2, 3, 4, 8, 45–7, 52, 53
Semaines Sociales du Canada 152
Senior, Nassau 44
Shearer, Ronald A. 214
Shortt, Adam 76–7, 92, 93, 96, 100, 105, 106, 107, 111, 119, 122, 123, 124, 142, 146, 155, 174, 180, 215, 226
Shoup, Carl 165, 218
Simon, Henry 165, 188
Sinclair, John 9
Skelton, Oscar D. 112–13, 122, 123–4, 131, 136–7, 140, 141, 145, 146
Skeoch, Lawrence 213
Smith, Adam 6, 9, 14, 25, 40, 44, 59, 61, 65, 66, 70, 71, 75, 80, 81, 83, 85, 86, 111, 117, 123, 146, 151, 185
Smith, David 222
Smith, E. Peshine 79
Smith, Goldwin 49, 117
Smith, Vera 99
Society for the Encouragement of Agriculture, Home Manufactures and Commerce 29

Sociologie Economique 51, 149, 160, 165–7, 168, 169, 227
Southey, Clive 17–18, 200–1
Studness, C. M. 202
Stykolt, Stephen 175
Swanson, W. W. 141, 143
Sydenham, Governor General, Lord 10, 18, 96, 99, 100, 101, 142, 146

Tanghe, Raymond 153–4, 158
Tassé, Joseph 51
Taussig, F. W. 121, 122, 145
Taylor, Henry 16–17
Thomas, Arron 5
Thompson, G. P. *see* Sydenham
Thompson, W. A. 107
theory of exchange 69
Thurow, Lester 210
Tiebout, Charles 192–3
Tilley, Samuel Leonard 114
Timlin, Mabel F. 158, 174
Tories 74
Towers, Graham 145
Tucker, Gilbert N. 135
Tulloch, G. 170
Tupper, Charles 30, 84
Turner, F. J. 146

Underhill, Frank H. 1, 143
Urquhart, M. C. 71, 96, 162, 181, 203, 222
Urwick, Edward J. 135

Van Horn, William 113
Veblen, Thorstein B. 57, 111, 112, 122, 123
vent for surplus theory 2, 16, 71
Vezina, François 54–5
Vezina, Roger 158
Vickery, E. 199–200
Viner, Jacob 122, 125, 145

Wakefield, Edward G. 3, 10, 13–15, 18, 30
Walinsky, Louis Joseph 34
Wallace, William 98, 106
Walras, M. E. Leon 144
Watkins, Melville H. 95, 129–30, 148, 178, 179, 190, 191, 196, 197
Weintraub, Sydney 210

Weldon, Jack C. 162
Wheat Boom 31, 115, 125
Whigs: Country 74, 76; Court 74, 75, 76, 84, 85, 113, 187
Wicksteed, Philip H. 22
Williams, Glen 206
Williamson, O. E. 170, 212
Willson, Hugh Bowlby 107
Winer, Stanley 216
Wonnacott, Paul 207

Woodsworth, J. S. 140
Wright, C. W. 121, 122
Wrong, G. M. 123
Wyman, Erastus 117

Yntema, T. O. 145
Young, Allyn 122
Young, John (Halifax) 25
Young, John (Montreal) 29, 119